Technological innovation is said to be breaking down borders. The Internet, the explosion of globalised financial markets, increased foreign direct investment by transnational corporations – all are portrayed as evidence of a global market in which the nation-state is little more than an anachronism. Yet some economies have proved more innovative and dynamic than others, and there seems no reason to believe that these differences in national economic performance will become a thing of the past. On the contrary, as many of the chapters in this book argue, with a global market, any competitive advantage is likely to bring larger rewards, and government action aimed at enhancing the competitive advantage of firms becomes more, rather than less, important. It is within this context that technological globalisation is analysed in this book.

NOTES ON CONTRIBUTORS

Paul Alexander is a well-known writer in the field of anthropological studies, especially on the problems of the fishing communities of Southeast Asia. He has a professorial appointment in the Department of Anthropology at the University of Sydney, New South Wales.

Raoul Andersen is a cultural-social anthropologist who specializes in the problems of the small coastal community. He is director of the Marine Man Program and Chairman of the Department of Anthropology at Memorial University, St. John's, Newfoundland.

Lee G. Anderson is a marine economist who holds appointments with the College of Marine Studies and the Department of Economics at the University of Delaware, Newark, Delaware. His textbook on the economics of marine resource management is to be published in 1976.

Robert Boardman is a member of the Centre for Foreign Policy Studies and of the Department of Political Science at Dalhousie University, Halifax, Nova Scotia. Most of his writing is in the field of Western European politics and on the theory of international relations.

Alastair D. Couper is head of the Department of Maritime Studies at the University of Wales Institute of Science and Technology, Cardiff, Wales. A master mariner as well as geographer by training, he is actively engaged as consultant to governments and international agencies on technical aspects of shipping and port management.

Edgar Gold is a member of the Faculty of Law and co-director of the Ocean Law '80 Project at Dalhousie University, Halifax, Nova Scotia. Both a master mariner and a lawyer, he specializes in admiralty law, the law of the sea, and the marine policy problems of the developing world.

Ronald Hope is director of the Seafarers Education Service and College of the Sea in London, England. An economist, he writes frequently on shipping and related matters.

Douglas M. Johnston is a prolific writer on the law of the sea, marine policy, coastal zone management, and other subjects. He is Chairman of Graduate Studies in the Faculty of Law, co-ordinator of the Marine and Environmental Law Programme, and co-director of the Ocean Law '80 Project at Dalhousie University, Halifax, Nova Scotia, and has been a government adviser and consultant on marine-related matters.

Roger Mesznik is a recent graduate of the Graduate School of Business at Columbia University and holds a teaching appointment in the Department of Economics and Finance at Baruch College, City University of New York.

Edward Miles is a well-known writer on international politics, international organization, and the law of the sea. Formerly associated with several international agencies, he now holds a professorial appointment with the Institute for Marine Studies at the University of Washington, Seattle, Washington.

Choon-ho Park is a leading analyst of marine policy and related problems in East Asia and the North Pacific. At present he holds a research appointment with the Harvard Law School, Cambridge, Massachusetts, and teaching appointments with the Fletcher School of Law and Diplomacy and the University of Hawaii.

Donald A. Pepper is an official engaged in policy planning for the Marine and Fisheries Service of the federal Department of the Environment in Ottawa, Canada. An economist, he has recently completed research in the Department of Maritime Studies at UWIST, Cardiff, Wales.

Giulio Pontecorvo is a senior economic specialist and consultant in the field of ocean studies. He has a professorship in the Graduate School of Business at Columbia University, New York.

Geoffrey Stiles is a member of the Department of Anthropology and the Marine Man Program at Memorial University, St. John's, Newfoundland. In recent years he has been closely associated with research on the problems of the coastal communities of Newfoundland.

Technology, globalisation and economic performance

Technology, globalisation and economic performance

Edited by

DANIELE ARCHIBUGI

*Institute for Studies on
Scientific Research and Documentation,
Italian National Research Council*

and

JONATHAN MICHIE

The Judge Institute of Management Studies, University of Cambridge

CAMBRIDGE
UNIVERSITY PRESS

Published by the Press Syndicate of the University of Cambridge
The Pitt Building, Trumpington Street, Cambridge CB2 1RP
40 West 20th Street, New York, NY 10011–4211, USA
10 Stamford Road, Oakleigh, Melbourne 3166, Australia

First published 1997

Printed in Great Britain at the University Press, Cambridge

A catalogue record for this book is available from the British Library

Library of Congress cataloguing in publication data

Technology, globalisation and economic performance / edited by
    Daniele Archibugi and Jonathan Michie.
        p.   cm.
    Includes index.
    ISBN 0 521 55392 X (hbk) – ISBN 0 521 55642 2 (pbk)
    1. Technological innovations – Economic aspects.   2. Technology and
state.   3. Competition, International.   4. National state.
    I. Archibugi, Daniele.   II. Michie, Jonathan.
    HC79.T4T4312   1997
    338'.064–dc20   96-26908   CIP

ISBN 0 521 55392 X hardback
ISBN 0 521 55642 2 paperback

SE

Contents

viii   **Contents**

Figures

Tables

Contributors

DANIELE ARCHIBUGI	Institute for Studies on Scientific Research and Documentation, Italian National Research Council, Rome
MARTIN BELL	Science Policy Research Unit, University of Sussex
JOHN CANTWELL	Department of Economics, University of Reading
MARTIN FRANSMAN	Institute for Japanese–European Technology Studies, University of Edinburgh
CHRISTOPHER FREEMAN	Science Policy Research Unit, University of Sussex
FRANCO MALERBA	Department of Political Economy, Bocconi University, Milan
STAN METCALFE	PREST, University of Manchester
JONATHAN MICHIE	The Judge Institute of Management Studies, University of Cambridge
DAVID C. MOWERY	Haas School of Business, University of California at Berkeley
LUIGI ORSENIGO	Department of Political Economy, Bocconi University, Milan
JOANNE OXLEY	Haas School of Business, University of California at Berkeley
PARI PATEL	Science Policy Research Unit, University of Sussex
KEITH PAVITT	Science Policy Research Unit, University of Sussex

Foreword

This book is essentially about the question: 'Where do technological capabilities reside?' There are several different points of view on this matter.

Economists and science and technology policy-makers, often have been drawn to the view that technological capabilities reside in the nation-state. Recently, this perspective has been articulated in a body of writings about 'national innovation systems'. Under this theory, firms, who are key actors in the implementation and development of new technology, are seen as embedded in a larger national institutional and cultural system that includes universities, financial institutions and labour markets, bodies of law that mould and constrain what firms can do, government policies that support technological advance and assist national business firms, and other features that draw a divide between what is inside, and what is outside, a particular nation-state. Sophisticated versions of this theory recognise that, within a nation-state, firms often differ considerably, and also that there are many transnational connections and institutions. However, the nation-state is presumed to be the most meaningful unit for the study of technological capabilities and their development.

In contrast, business school scholars and business historians see business firms themselves as the locus of technological capabilities. The focus is not so much on the legal proprietary aspects of much of technology, as on the intertwining of technology with organisation and management, on the tacit nature of many important capabilities, and on organisational learning and history as the key factors determining what a firm can do at any time. Sophisticated advocates of this theory do not deny that the national environments within which firms reside strongly influence their capabilities. However, the focus is on the firms themselves.

Still other theories focus on entities larger than the firm, but smaller than the nation-state. Thus Marshall's industrial district idea has been resuscitated by a number of writers. Under this theory, it is Silicon Valley, as contrasted with the United States more broadly, or particular firms that happen to reside in Silicon Valley, that possesses the relevant capabilities. Still other theories focus on networks that link individuals, firms and other institutions, but which may be geographically dispersed. An important example is the recent writing on inter-firm agreements for co-operative R&D and technological sharing.

The chapters in this book can be regarded as an extended debate about whether the nation-state is any more a meaningful repository of technological capabilities. A few of the authors seem to doubt that it ever was. However, most who posit the current meaningfulness of borders point to developments that have occurred over the past quarter-century, which, they argue, have eroded the relevance of the nation-state so far as technology is concerned.

Several of the authors who take this view clearly espouse a 'firm'-oriented theory of technological capabilities, and point to the growing internationalisation of firms. Others take a 'network' view of capabilities, and argue that networks increasingly are transnational. On the other hand, several authors argue that the evidence is weak that there has been much evening out of technological competencies among firms with their home bases in different countries, except among firms based in the trilateral countries. Some of these authors argue that national innovation systems continue to matter, strongly.

The purpose of a foreword is to whet the reader's appetite for the real stuff of a book, not to pre-empt it. This is a fascinating book, rich with information and different points of view regarding inter-firm and inter-country differences in technological capabilities. I urge the reader to move on to the real stuff.

Richard Nelson
Columbia University

Preface and acknowledgements

This book developed from a special issue of the *Cambridge Journal of Economics* on Technology and Innovation which we edited and which was published in February 1995. We selected the papers which focused particularly on the apparent contrast between the idea of the importance of national systems of innovation, on the one hand, and the claim that the globalisation of technology is making national policy an anachronism, on the other. We also added a couple of pieces which we considered key to the development of research in this area.

We are therefore grateful to the Editors of the *Cambridge Journal of Economics* for having supported this project, and in particular to the Managing Editor Ann Newton for the additional burden of work it put on her. Geoff Harcourt, Alan Hughes and Jochen Runde provided helpful comments on the draft of our Introduction to that Special Issue for which we are grateful and on which we have drawn in our introductory chapter to this book. For comments on the draft version of that chapter we are grateful to Rinaldo Evangelista, Mario Pianta and Giorgio Sirilli.

Daniele Archibugi is grateful to Cambridge University's Department of Applied Economics, the Judge Institute of Management Studies and Robinson College, all of which provided hospitality during his two-year stay while working on this project. We are also grateful to the European Commission for a 'Euroconference' grant awarded to us along with Jeremy Howells for 1995–6 which allowed us to draw on a range of expertise during three conferences at which the issues covered in this book were discussed in detail.

We are grateful to the authors for having delivered their chapters not only promptly but also on compatible and virus-free disks. And we are grateful to Richard Nelson for having contributed the Foreword.

Patrick McCartan of Cambridge University Press did an excellent job throughout the whole process from producing the original proposals for this book, along with a companion volume on *Technology, Trade and*

xviii   **Preface and acknowledgements**

Growth which we have also edited, right through to publication. Carol Jones has constantly helped during the preparation of the manuscript. We are also grateful to Patrizia Principessa and Cinzia Spaziani for their assistance.

Finally we are grateful, for having put up with weekend editing, respectively to Paola, seven-year-old Clara and one-year-old Orlando; and to Carolyn, seven-year-old Alex and one-year-old Duncan.

Daniele Archibugi
Jonathan Michie

1 Technological globalisation and national systems of innovation: an introduction

DANIELE ARCHIBUGI AND JONATHAN MICHIE

Knowledge and technological innovation play a crucial role in economic activities. While this has long been recognised by managers, scientists and engineers, it is only really over the past decade or so that economists have devoted much effort to studying the way in which knowledge actually leads to the generation and diffusion of technological innovation. This attention has, however, produced a vast literature which has begun to shine some light into the 'black box' of the relationship between technology and the productive process (see, in particular, Rosenberg, 1982, 1994). The initial hypotheses in a handful of pioneering works during the 1950s and 1960s on the economic determinants and impact of innovation have since been corroborated by a substantial amount of theoretical and empirical research.[1]

The most fruitful lesson provided by recent research is that technological change should be explored within the social fabric in which the innovative activities are actually developed and used. Innovation is far more than just a series of isolated events shaped by enlightened inventors, forward-looking entrepreneurs or dynamic corporations. Certainly, individuals and firms play a crucial role in the development of specific innovations, but the process which nurtures and disseminates technological change involves a complex web of interactions among a range of different subjects and institutions (David and Foray, 1995; Smith, 1995).

To map these interactions, however, is not easy. Innovation-related information flows are of a multifarious nature:

- They take place through both market and non-market transactions. A substantial amount of technology and knowledge transfer takes place regardless of any economic incentives. Individuals imitate and learn; and know-how is often exchanged informally and voluntarily (von Hippel, 1987; Carter, 1989; Schrader, 1991; Pasinetti, 1993; Lundvall and Johnson, 1994).
- Such flows can take the form of either tangible or intangible assets. Firms

1

use a variety of sources to innovate: a piece of machinery and a scientific paper may both be important sources of innovation (Pavitt, 1984; von Hippel, 1988; Archibugi *et al.*, 1991; Evangelista, 1995).

- They involve not only businesses but also public institutions. Universities, research centres and other government agencies play a crucial role in fostering technological advance, as do profit-seeking business firms (Nelson, 1987; Dasgupta and David, 1994; Stephan, 1996; Metcalfe, this volume, chapter 10).

These various aspects of the process are unlikely to be 'captured' in their entirety by looking at standard economic variables such as prices and quantities alone. To understand technological change it is crucial to identify the economic, social, political and geographical context in which innovation is generated and disseminated. This space may be local, national or global. Or, more likely, it will involve a complex and evolving integration, at different levels, of local, national and global factors.

The purpose of the present book is to explore the role played by national and global forces in shaping technological advance. While several of the individual chapters are devoted to analyses of either the national or the global dimension of innovative activities, all of them do so in the context of the strong and growing interactions between these national and global factors. The aim of this introductory essay is to draw out the main issues raised in the individual chapters of the book and to locate them within the current academic and policy debates taking place within the field of the economics of technological change.

The relative importance of national and global forces has been the subject of a vast literature. Some authors have claimed that the current process of globalisation is eroding the significance of nations as meaningful subjects of technological change (Chesnais, 1994). Others, on the contrary, have argued that the significance of globalisation has been overemphasised since the bulk of firms' innovative activities are still carried out in their home countries (Patel and Pavitt, 1991).

The contributions published in this book suggest, however, that the thesis which might be dubbed 'techno-nationalism' is not necessarily contradicted by what might at first sight appear to be the alternative thesis, 'techno-globalism'. The two concepts describe, rather, two strictly interrelated aspects of contemporary technological change. Certainly, a globalised economy is transforming the landscape for the generation and diffusion of innovation, but this does not appear to decrease the importance of national characteristics nor, even less, of national institutions and their policies. On the contrary, by magnifying the potential costs and benefits which will result from any one country's competitive advantage or disadvantage – as a growing proportion of the home market risks being lost to imports, while a growing proportion of domestic output may be dependent on winning export orders – globalisation will increase the impact which national policy will have on domestic living standards.

Before taking this discussion further, however, some consideration is required of the two key concepts which inform the book – namely, national systems of innovation on the one hand, and the globalisation of technology on the other – and also of the main actors – broadly, private firms and public institutions – through which these systems and trends evolve.

Concepts and actors

National systems of innovation

The importance of nation-specific factors in developing technological innovation has been boldly affirmed since the mid-1980s. Chris Freeman (1987) introduced the concept of 'national systems of innovation' (NSI) to describe and interpret the performance of the economically most successful country of the post-war period, Japan. Over the subsequent years this concept has experienced a remarkable diffusion and has been applied to several countries and to different areas.[2] As Nelson and Rosenberg noted (1993, p.3):

There clearly is a new spirit of what might be called 'technonationalism' in the air, combining a strong belief that the technological capabilities of a nation's firms are a key source of their competitive prowess, with a belief that these capabilities are in a sense national, and can be built by national action.

Studies in this field were pioneered by two research teams. The first team, led by Bengt-Åke Lundvall (1992) at the Aalborg University Centre, investigated the analytical content of the notion of national systems of innovation by looking at the roles played by users, the public sector and financial institutions. The second team, co-ordinated by Richard Nelson (1993), assembled a number of case-studies to describe the main features of the innovative systems of high, medium and low income countries. More recently, the OECD has taken up the idea of national systems of innovation and is making an attempt to operationalise it through the collection and analysis of indicators. In particular, their analysis is focused on the financial dimension, the interconnections among the various institutions and the distribution of knowledge across national agents.

Although the concept of national systems of innovation is defined and applied differently,[3] the various authors share the view that nation-specific factors play a crucial role in shaping technological change. Some of these factors are institutional, such as education, public support to industrial innovation, and defence-related technology schemes. Others are rooted in history, and concern the culture, size, language and vocation of a nation. Crucial to the definition of a national system is how the different parts, such as universities, research centres, business firms and so on, interact with each other.

The globalisation of technology

New technologies have always played a crucial role in the processes of economic and social globalisation. Aeroplanes, computers and satellite-based communications make possible an ever-expanding degree of information exchange, commodity trade and individual contact across the globe. Indeed, it is often argued that the current globalisation would be impossible without such technologies (see, for example, Giddens, 1991). Communication and transport technologies, however, might be better described not so much as reflecting the globalisation of technology as representing *the technologies of globalisation* since they service the increasingly global operation of cultural, social and economic life.

The concept of the globalisation of technology is rather different in that it seeks to describe and explain how the process of economic and social globalisation is not only affected by but is also itself affecting the production, distribution and transfer of technology (see, for example, Bartlett and Ghoshal, 1990; Dunning, 1992; Granstrand *et al.*, 1992; Howells and Wood, 1993). The strategies developed by both government and business institutions to generate technology are no longer based on a single country. Firms have to compete with a larger number of international rivals and this often compels them to upgrade their products and processes. Inward and outward technology spillovers have also increased as a consequence of the enlarged market dimension.

The actors

The descriptions provided above indicate that these concepts of 'techno-nationalism' and 'techno-globalism' are of relevance for both public and business institutions, but also that these differing institutions will relate in their own ways to the processes under discussion. Public institutions typically operate at the scale of their own territorial state, yet are influenced heavily by the process of globalisation since the activities which take place within their own territory have effects beyond their borders and may in turn be challenged by decisions taken in other states.

National institutions at times compete to achieve leadership in science and technology (S&T), as was the case in the mid-1980s with the US

Strategic Defense Initiative and the European Eureka programme (see Pianta, 1988b). In other cases, governments opt for co-operative strategies, as indicated by the large number of inter-governmental organisations in charge of specific international regimes. International property rights, international scientific exchanges, joint R&D programmes funded by international organisations such as the European Commission, and so on, all illustrate S&T governmental policies that are no longer simply national in scope.

The international orientation of firms is of course nothing new. One of the obvious ways for firms to grow has long been to export to overseas markets. In the post-war period, however, a more demanding form of internationalisation has gained importance, namely foreign direct investment (FDI), which implies the deployment of permanent facilities in host countries, which in turn obliges firms to become familiar with more than one national institutional system. Business companies have also developed other, more sophisticated forms of cross-border operation, such as joint-ventures, non-equity collaborations and so on. The extent to which firms are still 'loyal' to their own home country is a matter of debate. Some argue that multinational corporations have lost their national identity and pursue only their global strategies. Others point out that the competitive advantage of large companies is still linked to their home country (for a review of the different positions, see Porter, 1990; Reich, 1991; Dunning, 1992, 1993; Chesnais, 1994).

While governments cannot be seen as exclusively national agents, neither can firms be considered as stateless. And in spite of the increasing similarities of public and business actors as players in the domestic and foreign space, some basic differences persist: public institutions are by and large supposed to be accountable to their nation-based citizens, while business firms are allowed to be, and to some extent may be, accountable to stateless shareholders. This creates at various levels a complex web of interactions between inter-firm rivalry, on the one hand, and relations between nation-states on the other. In order to expand their activites overseas, firms often seek the protection of foreign governments, although this in turn might jeopardise the relationship the firm has with its own home government – and such a process might also lead to a clash between the governments concerned. On the other hand, governments have to consider the pros and cons associated with inward investment into their country: foreign direct investment might upgrade their productive capacity but might also increase their dependency on foreign capital.

These issues are explored in a growing literature on international political economy and international relations (Strange, 1988; Porter, 1990; Stopford and Strange, 1991). The chapters of this volume tackle these issues from the perspective of technological change, a privileged viewpoint from which to understand public and business strategies *vis-à-vis* the globalisation process. Governments and firms should select the capabilities to be developed in the home country and those to be acquired in the international markets when they deal with a strategic asset such as technological capabilities.

The origin of the concept of national systems: Friedrich List

Is there a place in economics for the study of how nation-specific factors affect the structure of production, consumption and growth? Consider the tables of contents from Adam Smith's *The Wealth of Nations* to Samuelson's *Economics*: we find 'the division of labour', 'the commodity', 'wages', 'profits', 'the laws of supply and demand', 'the supply of money' and so on. This reflects the way that economics has developed as an analytical rather than as a historical discipline. History has been allowed to enter only when extraordinary events such as the Great Crash or the postwar recovery needed to be interpreted.

In 1841 Friedrich List published his book on *The National System of Political Economy*, which even from the table of contents looked substantially different from the main Anglo-Saxon textbooks of his age. The first part was devoted to a discussion of the history of various peoples: the Italians, the Hanseatic League, the Flemish and the Dutch, the English, the Spanish and the Portuguese, the French, the Germans, the Russians, the North Americans. Economic theory proper was discussed *after* history, in the second part of the treatise. It is no coincidence that List was German. At the beginning of the nineteenth century, German cultural life was dominated by the philosophy of history, which had as its main concern the explanation and prediction of the rise and fall of nations.

Influenced by the rise of American society, in which he lived for several years, List tried to provide an *economic* explanation for the changing positions of nations in history. He was convinced that economic life played a crucial role in it, and therefore he was highly critical of those German philosophers who ignored the material aspects of civilisation. However, he also insisted that economic growth depended heavily on the social and cultural resources accumulated by a nation. Friedrich List can therefore be considered both a late exponent of the German philosophy of history and an early member of the German historical school in economics.

Today, economists remember List as a fierce opponent of the theory of free trade as advocated by Adam Smith and his followers. It is certainly true that he was one of the few explicit supporters of trade protection – a doctrine that has received bitter criticism from economists, although less so from policy-makers and others. But in List's native town of Reutlingen, he is remembered as the pioneer of railways; he spent a large part of his life urging the princes who ruled 'the Germany of the one hundred homelands' to develop transportation. He understood that infrastructure, which in his day meant, above all, the railways, was a fundamental component of any strategy for economic growth since it allowed commodities, individuals and information to circulate.

To get a balanced view of List's ideas it is perhaps necessary to combine the reminiscences of economists with those of the inhabitants of Reutlingen. List was not in favour of protection for its own sake; rather, he understood that economic growth required the creation of endogenous capabilities based on what he called 'intellectual capital' and learning (see Freeman's chapter in this volume).

List's main concern could be formulated in a simple question: which strategies should a backward nation adopt to catch up with leading countries? The free circulation of commodities was hardly the right answer. The law of comparative advantage predicts that both the leader and the follower would gain from trade. List argued, however, that in the long run the former would be likely to have preserved its advantage and the latter its underdevelopment. From a dynamic perspective, free trade would most likely preserve and expand inequality among nations.[4]

Relatively underdeveloped countries should accept free-trade policies only if the knowledge and expertise relating to the traded goods were equally freely traded. But this of course was not the practice followed by the then technological leader, the British Empire. In spite of the free-trade ideology espoused by the major British economists, the British government was keen to preserve its own technological leadership by hampering any transfer of knowledge to competing countries. Likewise, the trade of strategic machinery to other countries was heavily controlled by government policies (see Landes, 1969; Bruland, 1989). A large part of List's life was devoted to the denunciation of this covert but tenacious British protectionism.

But List was also aware that the problems involved in the circulation and assimilation of know-how go beyond the attempts of the technological leaders to defend that lead. He also pointed out the objective asymmetry, that to transfer and assimilate knowledge is much more difficult and complex than to trade in commodities. Even if the leading nations were prepared to share their know-how with catching-up countries, the latter would still have to devote substantial energies to the attempt to assimilate it, including the development of their own endogenous scientific and technological capabilities.

List also understood that the development of endogenous capabilities had to be considered within the context of what was already in his day seen as the growing globalisation of economic activities. This offered an opportunity for latecomer nations to acquire best-practice techniques, although there was no guarantee that all nations would benefit to the same extent. On the question of how a latecomer could attempt to upgrade in the context of an increasingly global economy, he suggested four policy options:

- Investing in education to promote an adequately trained work-force.
- Creating a network of infrastructures to allow the dissemination of the most important economic resource, know-how.
- Creating economic ties among countries, such as customs unions. To strengthen their effectiveness, he also advocated the development of institutional systems of states.
- And then last and, actually, least – protecting infant industries to allow them to develop the expertise needed to face international competition.

National systems today

A century and a half after List, the concept of national systems of innovation is once again on the academic and policy-making agenda. The country case-studies published in Nelson (1993) and the thematic issues discussed in Lundvall (1992) are reminiscent of, respectively, parts one and two of List's main work. Quite rightly, Freeman, in this volume, starts his own historical journey on the nature of NSIs from List's insights. Taken together, the resulting body of literature today on NSIs identifies the following crucial aspects in defining the structure and explaining the behaviour of nations:

- *Education and training.* Education and training are vital components of economic development. In spite of the international diffusion of education and of the increasing, although still limited, number of students enrolled in foreign universities, education is still largely national in scope. Substantial differences can be found between countries in the proportion of the relevant age group actually participating in education, whether primary, secondary or higher. Moreover, the distribution of students by disciplines also varies markedly among countries, as shown with reference to the East Asian countries by Mowery and Oxley (this volume, table 5.7).
- *Science and technology capabilities.* The level of resources devoted by each nation to formal R&D and other innovation-related activities (such as design, engineering, tooling-up, and so on) represents a basic characteristic of NSIs. The bulk of the world's R&D activities are carried out in industrially advanced countries, while developing coun-

tries report a very small fraction of world R&D activities. Even within the relatively homogeneous group of OECD nations, there are significant differences in R&D intensity: a small club of countries, including the United States, Japan, Germany, Switzerland and Sweden, devote around 3 per cent of their GDP to formal R&D activities. Other countries report a much smaller R&D intensity, although they might be less disadvantaged in terms of other innovative inputs. Another difference relates to how R&D expenditure splits between the public and the business sectors; big government programmes in space, defence and nuclear technologies often shape the entire structure of the S&T system of a nation.

- *Industrial structure.* Firms are the principal agents of technological innovation. The industrial structure of a nation heavily conditions the nature of its innovative activities. Large firms are more likely to undertake basic research programmes and are also more likely to be able to afford long-term investment in innovative activities whose payback may not only be spread years into the future but may also be extremely uncertain. The level of competition faced by companies in their domestic market also plays a crucial role in the R&D investment outcome.

- *S&T strengths and weaknesses.* Each country has its own strengths and weaknesses in different S&T fields. Some nations have specialisations in leading-edge technologies, while others have strengths in areas which are likely to provide only diminishing returns in the future. Moreover, some countries tend to be highly specialised in a few niches of excellence, while others have their S&T resources distributed more uniformly across all fields (Archibugi and Pianta, 1992). There are several determinants of national S&T specialisation, including the size of a country, R&D intensity, market structure and the international division of labour. The resulting S&T specialisation may influence a nation's future economic performance since countries with technological strengths in rising areas are likely to benefit from increasing returns which in turn will allow them to expand their technological and production capabilities.

- *Interactions within the innovation system.* The propensity of the different institutions to co-ordinate their activities and to interact with other actors differs widely between countries. Governments do interact heavily with large domestic firms (the so-called 'national champions'). Fransman, in this volume, describes the working of the Japanese Ministry for International Trade and Industry (MITI), one of the most cited successful institutions for the promotion of innovation in industry. In other countries, small firms have been keen to share their

expertise and co-operate in developing a common competitive strategy, as demonstrated by the Italian industrial districts. Such interactions are often able to multiply the effects of innovation undertaken at
the country level and increase its diffusion. Its absence can hamper
substantially the economic effectiveness of resources devoted to S&T.

• *Absorption from abroad.* The operation of these various aspects of
national systems of innovation need to be considered within the
context of increasing international integration. In the post-war period,
several countries have benefited from an international regime which
has deliberately encouraged the international transmission of knowledge (Nelson and Wright, 1992). Some countries, especially in the
Third World, have benefited from bilateral technology transfer. A
general lesson drawn from recent research, however, confirms List's
original insight that no technology transfer can be effective without an
endogenous effort to acquire that knowledge; see the chapters in this
volume by Freeman (chapter 2), Bell and Pavitt (chapter 4) and
Mowery and Oxley (chapter 5).

The list sketched above is far from being complete. Several other aspects
would need to be added to provide a complete description of a national
system. But the factors singled out above do indicate that the explanatory
power of the NSI notion is of a *comparative* nature. The description of a
specific national system is useful when it is compared with that of other
countries. These comparisons can be either qualitative or quantitative. The
qualitative approach was followed by, among others, Nelson (1993),
Freeman (1987) and Porter (1990). Others have measured cross-country
differences using indicators such as the level of resources devoted to R&D,
the relative importance of the public and the business sectors, the level of
international integration, and the distribution of the innovations produced
across sectors (see Archibugi and Pianta, 1992; Amendola, Guerrieri and
Padoan, 1992; Patel and Pavitt, 1994). However, we are still far from having
achieved a coherent conceptual and empirical framework within which to
explain the variation among countries in their success in innovating (for a
preliminary attempt, see Smith, 1995).

Implications of the national systems of innovation literature

The growing literature briefly discussed above makes clear that nations
differ in the methods used to promote innovation and also in the quantity
and significance of the innovations which have resulted from this effort.
What are the implications of this for understanding the process of technological change, and what are the public policy implications?

First, while some of the key characteristics of innovative systems can be transferred from one country to another, others cannot be so easily transplanted, especially in the short term. Freeman, in his contribution to this volume, describes the way in which the decision by a few companies based in Germany and in the United States to establish internal R&D laboratories diffused gradually across several nations. Yet more than a century later, the significance of industrial R&D is very far from being uniform across countries (see Archibugi and Pianta, 1994). Only in a few advanced countries is industrial R&D at the core of the innovation system. Thus the dissemination of basic institutional innovations (such as the development of a business R&D network, or state-promoted education, or the creation of major government-led technology-intensive programmes) often requires a substantial effort as well as considerable time to be replicated successfully in other countries. But not even time and effort can eliminate the continued existence of significant cross-country differences. The route which leads each nation to build its technological competence is highly path-dependent; this would not be surprising to philosophers of history nor to technology historians (see David, 1975; Arthur, 1989; Mokyr, 1990).

Second, there is no single model which alone is able to deliver successful economic performance. In the post-war period, Japan and Germany achieved high growth rates in part because of their massive investment in industrial R&D and technology. But other countries, such as Italy, managed to achieve the same goal while devoting a much lower effort to technology. There is more than one technological avenue leading to the wealth of nations (Denison, 1967; Abramovitz, 1989; Mowery and Rosenberg, 1989; Maddison, 1991; Fagerberg, 1994).

Third, nations which fail to exploit innovation can find themselves in an underdevelopment trap. In this context Freeman, in this volume, discusses why it was that the Soviet Union and Eastern European countries, in spite of their very high investment in R&D, failed to sustain their economic development. He also compares Latin America to the countries of East Asia, pointing to a number of factors behind the industrial development of the East Asian economies which have been lacking in Latin America.

Fourth, historically a country's innovation system has often played an important part in securing and consolidating competitive advantage and can become the driving force for economic hegemony (Freeman, 1987). The change this century from British to American economic and political leadership was associated in part with the Americans' ability to pioneer the systematic exploitation of knowledge in the productive system. The growth of East Asian countries has also been associated with their catching-up in a number of important technologies and to their acquired leadership in sectors of growing importance. The more innovative economies have also tended to be quick to adapt and imitate innovations produced elsewhere.

These implications drawn from the concept of national systems of innovation are, of course, based upon historical experience. Is there any reason to believe that the same patterns will continue in the future? There are two interrelated factors which might be thought to lower the importance of nation-specific factors in the future. The first is the existence of strong technology systems which tend to be similar across countries in spite of their differences. The second is the dissemination and transfer of know-how across borders which, in principle, would allow all nations to benefit from best-practice methods and techniques.

Technology systems versus national systems?

Rosenberg (1976), Nelson and Winter (1977), Dosi (1982) and Freeman *et al.* (1982) all suggest that significant technological change is generally brought about as a result of specific regimes designed to serve specific purposes. A large number of technology and industry case-studies have confirmed this to be so.[5]

From a historical perspective, it is possible to identify technology systems which, even in the same periods, worked separately and independently. A thousand years ago basic agricultural techniques in China were quite different from those in Europe which in turn were different from those in the Middle East. According to Gille (1978) this was due to the lack of circulation of information as well as to institutional rigidity. This is a far cry from the modern world system which has grown on the basis of the generation, circulation and diffusion of production techniques. The technical features of the majority of artifacts are similar across countries.

The similarities across technology systems are much broader than the narrow engineering characteristics of products (see Edquist, 1992). Technology systems are also defined by industrial concentration, barriers to entry, industrial R&D intensity, and the methods used to secure returns from innovation. Malerba and Orsenigo, in this volume, show that the characteristics of technological areas in terms of concentration, industrial turbulence and innovative dynamism across the four main European countries are rather similar; thus, in spite of the institutional differences of Germany, France, Great Britain and Italy,[6] some technology-specific elements tend to be surprisingly similar.

Does this consideration reduce the significance of nation-specific factors? According to Nelson (1993, p.518):

if one focuses narrowly on what we have defined as 'innovation systems' these tend to be sectorally specific. But if one broadens the focus the factors that make for commonality within a country come strongly into view, and these largely define the factors that make for commonality across sectors within a country.

This view is confirmed by Costello (1993), who compared the productivity growth of five major industries in six countries. Her results demonstrate stronger correlations across industries within a country than across countries within the same industry. Thus, rather than seeing the concepts of technology systems on the one hand and national systems of innovation on the other as being alternatives, only one of which at most can be applicable, it appears to be the case, rather, that both technology-specific and nation-specific factors shape the innovative process. The organisation of industry tends to be technology-specific, while the impact of innovation is heavily influenced by the overall national economic environment. The challenge for both theory and policy is to establish these interrelations, and if possible to intervene to create positive feedbacks within this interrelationship.

What differentiates countries is not their methods of production in certain industries, but their relative strengths and weaknesses in different industries. For example, the US innovation system is defined by strong government intervention in defence-related areas, and this is reflected in its sectoral strengths in aircraft and nuclear technology. Japan, on the other hand, has negligible industrial activity in the aircraft sector. In spite of these differences, the industrial and technological features of the aircraft sector tend to be the same in both the United States and Japan. However, it would be wrong to predict the sectoral specialisation of a nation on the grounds of institutional features alone: Italy, a country with medium R&D intensity and low industrial concentration is very active in automobiles, one of the industries generally associated with both high R&D and industrial concentration.

Is the globalisation of technology making the nation-state redundant?

The second factor which might be thought to diminish the importance of nation-specific factors is the increasing globalisation of technological and other industrial and economic processes. Several writers have stressed that we are experiencing a dramatic increase in the extent of economic globalisation. International trade and capital flows, foreign direct investment, migration – all have increased substantially over the last twenty years (Holland, 1987; Dunning, 1992, 1993; Chesnais, 1994). A corresponding globalisation is said to have occurred in social, cultural and political life, impacting on local communities, including nation-states, and lowering ties of national identity, citizenship, and political sovereignty (Held, 1991; Robertson, 1992). On the other hand, globalisation is certainly not a new phenomenon (Wallerstein, 1974, 1979, 1980).[7]

Several chapters in this book are therefore devoted to understanding and measuring to what extent economic and social globalisation has actually affected the generation and diffusion of technological innovation. Later in this volume we make a distinction between three separate processes which are often subsumed within the catch-all general term technological globalisation:

- International *exploitation* of national technological capabilities: firms try to exploit their innovations on global markets either by exporting products which embody them or by licensing the know-how.
- *Collaboration* across borders among both public and business institutions to exchange and develop know-how. Firms are expanding their non-equity agreements to share the costs and risks of industrial research (see Hagedoorn and Schakenraad, 1990, 1993). Metcalfe, in this volume, points out that the scientific community has always been international in scope, although public research centres and academia have recently increased their proportion of cross-border linkages substantially.[8]
- The *generation* of innovations across more than one country, which refers particularly to the activities of multinational corporations. This aspect is discussed in the chapters by Cantwell and Patel in this volume.

On the first two of these dimensions to the globalisation of technology, it is hardly controversial that they have increased in importance. Trade and patent flows, international technical agreements and scientific co-authorships have all shown a dramatic increase over the past two decades or so. But it is intellectually sloppy to assume that this implies that nation-states have become less important in some way without specifying the mechanisms by which this latter conclusion follows. If, for example, increased globalisation means that any loss of relative competitiveness translates into a far greater loss of markets – abroad and at home – with a concomitantly greater loss of jobs and threat to living standards than would have been the case in the days when the world economy was less 'global', then this would imply that the benefits from national action to enhance competitiveness would be that much greater. And conversely any inaction would risk far greater losses.

Certainly in this case, while globalisation may result in national action having greater payoffs, and national inaction greater costs, it could still be the case that although globalisation makes national action more rather than less important, at the same time it makes it more difficult, or less feasible. But again it is important not to jump to fashionable and easy conclusions unthinkingly. If national action has become more important yet more difficult, then this increased difficulty may itself call for more serious and far-reaching intervention from national governments to overcome such difficulties.

So while for the first two of our globalisation categories above the key controversy is over how to respond to trends which are reasonably well established (albeit exaggerated by some), in the third category, of the extent to which multinational corporations have increased their technological operations in host countries, the evidence itself is less well established. Patel, in this volume, taking into account the patented inventions of more than 500 of the world's largest enterprises, shows that the vast majority of inventions are developed in the firms' home nation. According to him, multinational corporations – the companies which by definition are globally oriented – tend to be loyal to their home-base country when they have to locate a strategic asset such as technology. However, the results presented by Patel appear at odds with those of Cantwell, also in this volume.[9] From a historical perspective, Cantwell shows that the share of innovations generated by firms in host countries has increased considerably.

Patented inventions, however, capture only the most formalised part of technological knowledge. Multinational corporations might be keener to decentralise forms of knowledge which do not belong to the core of their business strategy. Companies might be more willing to locate abroad facilities which are less critical to their strategy, such as software, engineering, design and so on. Less developed countries offer an adequately trained workforce but at salaries which are much lower than in the developed countries, while information technologies make the geographical location of high-tech jobs less relevant. This justifies the widespread concern that industrial countries could lose skill-intensive jobs to the benefit of the South.[10]

On what might induce companies to centralise or decentralise their technological activities, Howells and Wood (1993) suggest that the advantages of centralisation include: the benefits of economies of scale and scope which are associated with larger R&D operations; the minimum efficient size which is associated with indivisibilities of certain scientific instruments and facilities; the increased security over in-house research, which amongst other things reduces the risk of competitors copying or leap-frogging in key research fields; and the ability to create a well-established dense local innovation network with higher education institutes, contract research companies and other support agencies. The main advantages they see associated with decentralisation are: a more effective and applicable R&D effort focused on the actual needs of the business and operational units; improved communications or coupling between R&D and other key corporate functions; fewer problems in 'programme dislocation' when a project is transferred from R&D to production; and better responsiveness to various local market needs. To this list might be added: to keep a window open on the technological developments of other countries; and to take advantage of the fields of excellence of the host country.

An extensive survey of companies' headquarters and host facilities has identified the type of work undertaken in overseas R&D laboratories (Pearce and Singh, 1992). The most frequent activities carried out in host countries are to derive new production technology and to adapt existing products to the local markets to make them accepted by local communities. Even the taste of Coca-Cola, the most typical standardised product of the global economy, is not quite the same in the USA, Japan and Italy (see Ohmae, 1990).

Multinational corporations apply a variety of strategies to capitalise on their technological advantages. Bartlett and Ghoshal (1990) have provided a useful categorisation of three different, although not mutually exclusive, strategic approaches:

- *Centre-for-global*. This is the traditional 'octopus' view of the multinational corporation: a single 'brain' located within the company's headquarters concentrates the strategic resources: top management, planning, and technological expertise. The brain distributes impulses to the tentacles (that is, the subsidiaries) scattered across host countries. Even when some overseas R&D is reported, this is basically concerned with adapting products to local users' needs.
- *Local-for-local*. Each subsidiary of the firm develops its own technological know-how to serve local needs. The interactions among subsidiaries is, at least from the viewpoint of developing technological innovations, rather low. On the contrary, subsidiaries are integrated into the local fabric. This may occur with conglomerate firms or companies which are not characterised by strong global products.
- *Local-for-global*. This is the case of multinational corporations which, rather than concentrating their technological activities in a home country, distribute R&D and technological expertise in a variety of host countries. This allows the company to develop each part of the innovative process in the most suitable environment: semiconductors in Silicon Valley, automobile components in Turin, software in India. The effectiveness of such a strategy relies on the intensity of intra-firm information flows.

Techno-nationalism versus techno-globalism?

Much of the debate about techno-nationalism and techno-globalism has direct policy implications (in this book they are explicitly addressed in the chapters by Fransman and Metcalfe). What is the point of government policies to promote innovation in industry if the benefits can be transferred to other countries? Is there any guarantee that firms will use these benefits to the advantage of the nation which provides support? For example, Reich

(1991, p.3) argues that it is not in the interests of a nation to support national champions. He advocates instead policies to foster the infrastructure of a nation:

Rather than increase the profitability of corporations flying its flag, or enlarge the worldwide holdings of its citizens, a nation's economic role is to improve its citizens' standard of living by enhancing the value of what they contribute to the world economy. The concern over national 'competitiveness' is often misplaced. It is not what we own that counts; it is what we do.

In the United States in particular, there has been widespread concern that government policies could be benefiting foreign firms just as much as domestic ones. For example, much of the US government funded defence and space R&D in semiconductors was exploited by Japanese companies to develop high-tech competitive products (see the debate in Lee and Reid, 1991; Caldwell Harris and Moore, 1992; Tyson, 1992; Scherer, 1992; and Nelson and Wright, 1992). The USA and other industrial countries have therefore called for a more tightly regulated international regime of intellectual and industrial property rights. In other words, the focus has shifted from the generation of technology to devices to guarantee sufficient returns from it on international markets.[11]

This has implications for industrial and technology policy. Metcalfe (this volume) differentiates between two broad categories of government action, namely direct financial incentives to companies for their innovative programmes, and public supply of infrastructures to make a country attractive for the deployment of S&T activities. Globalisation may be thought to have reduced the usefulness of the first kind of government policy, especially when the benefits are received by companies with subsidiaries in several countries. But policies of the second kind, which include education, effective industry–university partnerships, communications, and so on, have certainly increased in importance (see Tassey, 1991). In the global economy, nations have to upgrade their infrastructure to attract technology-intensive activities. Fransman, in this volume, after describing the activities of the Japanese MITI, asks: how could MITI have so much power with such a small amount of financial resources? The question itself indicates that policies aimed at creating an innovative and industrially dynamic environment can be much more important than simply handing cash to companies.

An essential factor in the post-war 'golden age of capitalism' was the existence of an international regime favourable to the diffusion of S&T (see Pianta, 1988a; Nelson and Wright, 1992). But today any such regime appears to be under constant threat from the operation of large corporations (see Holland, 1987; Barnet and Cavanagh, 1994; Michie and Grieve Smith, 1995). From this perspective, the real opposition to *techno-nationalism* is not, as is so often suggested, *techno-globalism* but rather *techno-liberalism*. It is therefore no surprise that the literature on national systems (Porter, 1990; Lundvall, 1992; Nelson, 1993), including the relevant chapters in this book (by Freeman, Fransman, Mowery and Oxley and Metcalfe), advocates a stronger role for government to foster innovation.

Notes

1 Reviews of the recent economic literature on technological change can be found in Dosi (1988) and Freeman (1994).
2 See, for example, the chapters by Freeman, Lundvall and Nelson in Dosi *et al.* (1988).
3 For an attempt to highlight these differences, see McKelvey (1991) and Humbert (1994).
4 See Kitson and Michie (1995) for a discussion of the political economy of trade and trade policy. There this distinction is made between, on the one hand, mainstream theory – where it is asserted that all will benefit, with those lagging dragged along – and, on the other, the more likely scenario, where those stuck in a vicious cycle of decline may well see their disadvantage intensified.
5 See, for example, the studies on semiconductors (Dosi, 1984; Malerba, 1985) and biotechnology (Orsenigo, 1989).
6 Highlighted by, for example, the country case-studies of Keck, Chesnais, Walker and Malerba in Nelson (1993); and by Cohendet *et al.* (1992).
7 And for a sceptical view of the above claims regarding globalisation see Michie (1995, 1996).
8 On which, see also Malerba *et al.* (1991).
9 See also Casson (1991) and Cantwell (1994).
10 See *Business Week* (1994). On the argument that jobs in the North are being lost to the South, see Wood (1994), and for a more sceptical view see Eatwell (1995) and Singh and Zammit (1995); for a related argument to Wood's, see Galbraith (1996), commented on by Michie (1996).
11 David and Foray (1995) argue that, given the nature of contemporary technological expertise, the institutional international context should today favour the diffusion and imitation of innovation rather than the protection of intellectual property rights.

References

Abramovitz, M. 1989. *Thinking about Growth*, Cambridge, Cambridge University Press.
Amendola, G., Guerrieri, P. and Padoan, P.C. 1992. International patterns of technological accumulation and trade, *Journal of International and Comparative Economics*, 1: 173–97.
Archibugi, D., Cesaratto, S. and Sirilli, G. 1991. Sources of innovative activities and industrial organization in Italy, *Research Policy*, 20: 299–313.

Archibugi, D. and Pianta, M. 1992. *The Technological Specialization of Advanced Countries. A Report to the EC on Science and Technology Activities*, Boston, Kluwer.

1994. Aggregate convergence and sectoral specialisation in innovation, *Journal of Evolutionary Economics*, 4 (4): 17–33.

Arthur, B. 1989. Competing technologies, increasing returns, and lock-in by historical events, *Economic Journal*, 99: 116–31.

Barnet, R.J. and Cavanagh, J. 1994. *Global Dreams. Imperial Corporations and the New World Order*, New York, Simon & Schuster.

Bartlett, C.A. and Ghoshal, S. 1990. Managing innovation in transnational corporations, in C.A. Bartlett, Y. Doz and G. Hedlund (eds.), *Managing the Global Firm*, London, Routledge.

Bruland, K. 1989. *British Technology and European Industrialization*, Cambridge, Cambridge University Press.

Business Week. 1994. High-tech jobs all over the map, 19 December, pp. 42–7.

Caldwell Harris, M. and Moore, G.E. (eds.) 1992. *Linking Trade and Technology Policies*, Washington, D.C., National Academy Press.

Cantwell, J.A. (ed.) 1994. *Transnational Corporations and Innovatory Activities*, London, Routledge.

Carter, A. 1989. Know-how trading as economic exchange, *Research Policy*, 18: 155–63.

Casson, M. (ed.) 1991. *Global Research Strategy and International Competitiveness*, Oxford, Basil Blackwell.

Chesnais, F. 1994. *La mondialisation du capital*, Paris, Syros.

Cohendet, P., Llerena, P. and Sorge, A. 1992. Technological diversity and coherence in Europe: an analytical overview, *Revue d'Economie Industrielle*, 59: 9–26.

Costello, D. 1993. A cross-country, cross-industry comparison of productivity growth, *Journal of Political Economy*, 101: 207–22.

Dasgupta, P. and David, P. 1994. Toward a new economics of science, *Research Policy*, 23: 487–521.

David, P. 1975. *Innovation, Technical Choice, and Growth*, Cambridge, Cambridge University Press.

David, P. and Foray, D. 1995. Accessing and expanding the science and technology knowledge base, *Science Technology Industry Review*, no. 16, pp. 13–68.

Denison, E.F. 1967. *Why Growth Rates Differ*, Washington, D.C., Brookings Institution.

Dosi, G. 1982. Technological paradigms and technological trajectories, *Research Policy*, 11: 147–61.

1984. *Technical Change and Industrial Transformation. The Theory and Application to the Semiconductor Industry*, London, Macmillan.

1988. Source, procedures and microeconomic effects of innovation, *Journal of Economic Literature*, 36: 1126–71.

Dosi, G., Freeman, C., Nelson, R., Silverberg, G. and Soete, L. (eds.) 1988. *Technical Change and Economic Theory*, London, Pinter.

Dunning, J. 1992. *The Globalization of Business*, London, Routledge.

1993. *Multinational Enterprises and the Global Economy*, Wokingham, Addison-Wesley.

Edquist, C. 1992. Systems of innovation. Conceptual and theoretical remarks, paper presented at a Workshop on Systems of Innovation, Bologna, October.

Eatwell, J. 1995. The international origins of unemployment, in Michie and Grieve Smith (eds.).

Evangelista, R. 1995. Embodied and disembodied innovative activities: evidence from the Italian innovation survey, in OECD.

Fagerberg, J. 1994. Technology and international differences in growth rates, *Journal of Economic Literature*, 42: 1147–75.

Foray, D. and Freeman, C. (eds.) 1993. *Technology and the Wealth of Nations: The Dynamics of Constructed Advantage*, London, Pinter.

Freeman, C. 1987. *Technology Policy and Economic Performance*, London, Pinter. 1994. The economics of technical change, *Cambridge Journal of Economics*, 18: 463–514.

Freeman, C., Clark, J.A. and Soete, L. 1982. *Unemployment and Technological Innovation*, London, Pinter.

Freeman, C. and Soete, L. 1993. Conclusions, in Foray and Freeman (eds.).

Freeman, C. and Soete, L. (eds.) 1990. *New Explorations in the Economics of Technical Change*, London, Pinter.

Galbraith, J. 1996. Uneven development and the destabilization of the North: a Keynesian view, *International Review of Applied Economics*, 10: 107–20.

Giddens, A. 1991. *Consequences of Modernity*, Cambridge, Polity Press.

Gille, B. 1978. *Histoire des Techniques*, Paris, Editions Gallimard.

Granstrand, O., Håkanson, L. and Sjölander, S. (eds.) 1992. *Technology Management and International Business: Internationalization of R&D and Technology*, Chichester, Wiley.

Hagedoorn, J. and Schakenraad, J. 1990. Inter-firm partnerships and cooperative strategies in core technologies, in Freeman and Soete (eds.). 1993. Strategic technology partnering and international corporate strategies, in Hughes (ed.).

Held, D. 1991. Democracy, the nation-state and the global system, *Economy and Society*, 20: 138–72.

Hodgson, G. and Screpanti, E. (eds.) 1991. *Rethinking Economics: Markets, Technology and Economic Evolution*, Aldershot, Edward Elgar.

Holland, S. 1987. *The Global Economy*, London, Weidenfeld & Nicolson.

Howells, J. and Wood, M. 1993. *The Globalisation of Production and Technology*, London, Belhaven Press.

Hughes, K. (ed.) 1993. *European Competitiveness*, Cambridge, Cambridge University Press.

Humbert, M. 1994. The globalisation of technology as a challenge for a national innovation system, EAEPE Conference, Copenhagen, 28–30 September.

Kitson, M. and Michie, J. 1995. Conflict and cooperation: the political economy of trade and trade policy, *Review of International Political Economy*, 2: 632–57.

Landes, D. 1969. *The Unbound Prometheus: Technological and Industrial*

Development in Western Europe from 1750 to the Present, Cambridge, Cambridge University Press.

Lee, T.H. and Reid, P.P. (eds.) 1991. *National Interests in the Age of Global Technology*, Washington, D.C., National Academy Press.

List, F. 1841. *The National System of Political Economy*, English translation, London, Longman & Co., 1885.

Lundvall, B.-Å. (ed.) 1992. *National Systems of Innovation*, London, Pinter.

Lundvall, B.-Å. and Johnson, B. 1994. The learning economy, *Journal of Industry Studies*, 1(2): 23–42.

Maddison, A. 1991. *Dynamic Forces in Capitalist Development. A Long-Run Comparative View*, Oxford, Oxford University Press.

Malerba, F. 1985. *The Semiconductor Business: The Economics of Rapid Growth and Decline*, London, Pinter.

Malerba, F., Morawets, A. and Pasqui, G. 1991. *The Nascent Globalization of Universities and Public and Quasi-Public Research Organizations*, Brussels, European Commission, FAST.

McKelvey, M. 1991. How do national systems of innovation differ? A critical analysis of Porter, Freeman, Lundvall and Nelson, in Hodgson, and Screpanti (eds.).

Michie, J. 1995. Introduction, in Michie and Grieve Smith (eds.).

1996. Creative destruction or regressive stagnation?, *International Review of Applied Economics*, 10: 121–6.

Michie, J. and Grieve Smith, J. (eds.) 1995. *Managing the Global Economy*, Oxford, Oxford University Press.

Mokyr, J. 1990. *The Lever of Riches: Technological Creativity and Economic Progress*, Oxford, Oxford University Press.

Mowery, D. and Rosenberg, N. 1989. *Technology and the Pursuit of Economic Growth*, Cambridge, Cambridge University Press.

Nelson, R. 1987. *Understanding Technical Change as an Evolutionary Process*, Amsterdam, North-Holland.

Nelson, R. (ed.) 1993. *National Innovation Systems*, New York, Oxford University Press.

Nelson, R. and Rosenberg, N. 1993. Technical innovation and national systems, in Nelson (ed.).

Nelson, R. and Winter, S. 1977. In search of a useful theory of innovation, *Research Policy*, 6: 36–113.

Nelson, R. and Wright, G. 1992. The rise and fall of American technological leadership: the postwar era in historical perspective, *Journal of Economic Literature*, 30: 1931–60.

OECD. 1995. *Innovation, Patents and Technological Strategies*, Paris, OECD.

Ohmae, K. 1990. *The Borderless World: Management Lessons in the New Logic of the Global Market Place*, London, Collins.

Orsenigo, L. 1989. *The Emergence of Bio-Technologies*, London, Pinter.

Pasinetti, L. 1993. *Structural Economic Dynamics: A Theory of the Economic Consequences of Human Learning*, Cambridge, Cambridge University Press.

Patel, P. and Pavitt, K. 1991. Large firms in the production of the world's technology: an important case of 'non-globalisation', *Journal of International Business Studies*, 22: 1–21.
   1994. National innovation systems: why they are important and how they might be measured and compared, *Economics of Innovation and New Technology*, vol. 3: 77–95.
Pavitt, K. 1984. Sectoral patterns of technical change: towards a taxonomy and a theory, *Research Policy*, 13: 343–73.
Pearce, R.D. and Singh, S. 1992. *Globalising Research and Development*, London Macmillan.
Pianta, M. 1988a. *New Technologies Across the Atlantic*, Hemel Hempstead, Harvester Wheatsheaf.
   1988b. High technology programmes: for the military or for the economy?, *Bulletin of Peace Proposals*, no. 1, pp. 53–79.
Porter, M. 1990. *The Competitive Advantage of Nations*, London, Macmillan.
Reich, R. 1991. *The Work of Nations*, London, Simon & Schuster.
Robertson, R. 1992. *Globalization. Social Theory and Global Culture*, London, Sage.
Rosenberg, N. 1976. *Perspectives on Technology*, Cambridge, Cambridge University Press.
   1982. *Inside the Black Box: Technology and Economics*, Cambridge, Cambridge University Press.
   1994. *Exploring the Black Box*, Cambridge, Cambridge University Press.
Scherer, F.M. 1992. *International High-technology Competition*, Cambridge, Mass., Harvard University Press.
Schrader, S. 1991. Informal technology transfer between firms: cooperation through information trading, *Research Policy*, 20: 153–70.
Singh, A. and Zammit, A. 1995. Employment and unemployment: North and South, in Michie and Grieve Smith (eds.).
Smith, K. 1995. Interactions in knowledge systems: foundations, policy implications and empirical methods, *Science Technology Industry Review*, no. 16, pp. 69–102.
Stephan, P.E. 1996. An essay on the economics of science, *Journal of Economic Literature*, forthcoming.
Stopford, J. and Strange, S. 1991. *Rival States, Rival Firms: Competition for World Market Shares*, Cambridge, Cambridge University Press.
Strange, S. 1988. *States and Markets*, London, Pinter.
Tassey, G. 1991. The functions of technology infrastructure in a competitive economy, *Research Policy*, 20: 345–61.
Tyson, L.D. 1992. *Who's Bashing Whom? Trade Conflicts in High-Technology Industries*, Washington, D.C., Institute for International Economics.
von Hippel, E. 1987. Cooperation between rivals: informal knowhow trading, *Research Policy*, 16: 291–302.
   1988. *The Sources of Innovation*, Oxford, Oxford University Press.
Wallerstein, I. 1974. *The Modern World System*, New York, Academic Press.

1979. *The Capitalist World Economy*, Cambridge, Cambridge University Press.
1980. *The Modern World System II: Mercantilism and the Consolidation of the European World Economy*, Cambridge, Cambridge University Press.
Wood, A. 1994. *North–South Trade, Employment and Inequality: Changing Fortunes in a Skill-Driven World*, Oxford, Oxford University Press.

2 The 'national system of innovation' in historical perspective

CHRISTOPHER FREEMAN

Introduction: The National System of Friedrich List

According to this author's recollection the first person to use the expression 'national system of innovation' was Bengt-Åke Lundvall and he is also the editor of a highly original and thought-provoking book (1992) on this subject. However, as he and his colleagues would be the first to agree (and as Lundvall himself points out) the idea actually goes back at least to Friedrich List's conception of 'The National System of Political Economy' (1841), which might just as well have been called 'The National System of Innovation'.

The main concern of List was with the problem of Germany overtaking England and, for underdeveloped countries (as Germany then was in relation to England), he advocated not only protection of infant industries but a broad range of policies designed to accelerate, or to make possible, industrialisation and economic growth. Most of these policies were concerned with learning about new technology and applying it. The racialist and colonialist overtones of the book were in strong contrast to the internationalist cosmopolitan approach of the classical free-trade economists, and List's belief that Holland and Denmark should join the German 'Bund' and acquire German nationality because of their 'descent and whole character' reads somewhat strangely in the European Union of today. Nevertheless, despite these unattractive features of his outlook, he clearly anticipated many contemporary theories.

After reviewing the changing ideas of economists about development in the years since the Second World War, the World Bank (1991, pp. 33–5) concluded that it is intangible investment in knowledge accumulation which is decisive rather than physical capital investment, as was at one time believed. This report cites the 'New Growth Theory' (Romer, 1986; Grossman and Helpman, 1991) in support of this view but the so-called 'New' Growth Theory has in fact only belatedly incorporated into neoclassical models the realistic assumptions which have become commonplace among economic historians and neo-Schumpeterian economists. Indeed, it could just as well have cited Friedrich List (1841), who, in criticising a passage from Adam Smith, said:

in opposition to this reasoning, Adam Smith has merely taken the word *capital* in that sense in which it is necessarily taken by rentiers or merchants in their book-keeping and their balance sheets . . . He has forgotten that he himself includes (in his definition of capital) the intellectual and bodily abilities of the producers under this term. He wrongly maintains that the revenues of the nation are dependent only on the sum of its material capital. (p. 183)

and further:

The present state of the nations is the result of the accumulation of all discoveries, inventions, improvements, perfections and exertions of all generations which have lived before us: they form the intellectual[1] capital of the present human race, and every separate nation is productive only in the proportion in which it has known how to appropriate those attainments of former generations and to increase them by its own acquirements. (p. 113)

List's clear recognition of the interdependence of tangible and intangible investment has a decidedly modern ring. He saw too that industry should be linked to the formal institutions of science and of education:

There scarcely exists a manufacturing business which has not relation to physics, mechanics, chemistry, mathematics or to the art of design, etc. No progress, no new discoveries and inventions can be made in these sciences by which a hundred industries and processes could not be improved or altered. In the manufacturing State, therefore, sciences and arts must necessarily become popular. (p. 162)

It was thanks to the advocacy of List and like-minded economists as well as the long-established Prussian system, that Germany developed one of the best technical education and training systems in the world. This system not only was, according to many historians (e.g. Hobsbawm, 1968; Landes, 1969; Barnett, 1988), one of the main factors in Germany overtaking Britain in the latter half of the nineteenth century, but to this day is the foundation for the superior skills and higher productivity of the German labour force (Prais, 1981) in many industries. Many British policies for education and training for over a century can be realistically viewed as spasmodic, belated and never wholly successful attempts to catch up with German technological education and training systems.

Not only did List anticipate these essential features of current work on national systems of innovation, he also recognised the interdependence of the import of foreign technology and domestic technical development. Nations should not only acquire the achievements of other more advanced nations, but they should also increase them by their own efforts. Again, there was already a good model for this approach to technological learning in Prussia: the acquisition of machine tool technology. It was British engineers (especially Maudslay) and mechanics who were responsible for the key innovations in machine tool technology in the first quarter of the nineteenth century. This technology was described by Paulinyi (1982) as the 'Alpha and Omega of modern machine-building' because it enabled the design and construction of metal-working precision machinery for all other industries. Those involved attempted to maintain a considerable degree of secrecy, but its importance was recognised by the Prussian government, which took decisive steps to acquire the technology despite the fact that the British government was attempting to ban the export of machine tools (with the imposition of heavy fines for contravention).

The Prussian government, which had set up Technical Training Institutes (*Gewerbe-Institute*), made sure that they received imported British machine tools for reverse engineering and for training German craftsmen, who then disseminated the technology in German industry (Paulinyi, 1982). British craftsmen were also attracted to Prussia as much of the technology depended on tacit knowledge. (Three out of four of the leading machine tool entrepreneurs in Britain at that time had themselves spent years with Maudslay in his workshop.) The transfer of technology, promoted and coordinated by the Prussian state, was highly successful: the German machine tool industry and machine-building proved capable of designing and manufacturing the machinery necessary to make steam locomotives in the 1840s and 1850s. This set Prussia (later Imperial Germany) well on the road to overtaking Britain. Although he did not cite this particular example, List therefore was not talking in a purely abstract way about industrialisation and technology transfer but about a process which was unfolding before his eyes. It was summed up by Landes (1969, p. 151):

Only the government could afford to send officials on costly tours of inspection as far away as the United States; provide the necessary buildings and equipment; feed, clothe, house, and in some cases pay students for a period of years. Moreover, these pedagogical institutions were only part – though the most important part – of a larger educational system designed to introduce the new techniques and diffuse them through the economy; there were also non-teaching academies, museums, and, most important perhaps, expositions.
   . . . Finally, the government provided technical advice and assistance, awarded subventions to inventors and immigrant entrepreneurs, bestowed gifts of machinery, allowed rebates and exemptions of duties on imports of industrial equipment. Some of this was simply a continuation of the past – a heritage of the strong tradition of direct state interest in economic development. Much of it, in Germany particularly, was symptomatic of a passionate desire to organize and hasten the process of catching up.
   In so far as this promotional effort stressed the establishment of rational stan-

dards of research and industrial performance, it was of the greatest significance for the future.

Not only did List analyse many features of the national system of innovation which are at the heart of contemporary studies (education and training institutions, science, technical institutes, user–producer interactive learning, knowledge accumulation, adapting imported technology, promotion of strategic industries, etc.), he also put great emphasis on the role of the state in co-ordinating and carrying through long-term policies for industry and the economy. Here, as often, he took issue with Jean-Baptiste Say, his favourite target in his polemics with the classical school, who had argued that governments did not make much difference, except in a negative way.

The United States was of course even more successful than Germany in overtaking Britain in the second half of the nineteenth century and List had learnt a great deal from his residence in the United States and especially from Hamilton's (1791) *Report on Manufactures*. The widespread promotion of education (though not of industrial training) was even more remarkable in the United States than in Germany. However, the abundance of cheap, accessible materials, energy and land, together with successive waves of immigration, imparted to the United States national system some specific characteristics without parallel in Europe. The pro-active role of the state was greater in Germany whilst foreign investment played a greater role in the United States.

Although List anticipated many features of the contemporary debate about national systems of innovation (even though his terminology was different), it would of course be absurd to imagine that he could have foreseen all the changes in the world economy and national economies over the next century and a half. In particular, he did not foresee the rise of in-house professionalised research and development in industry, still less the rise of multinational (or transnational) corporations (TNCs), operating production establishments in many different countries and increasingly also setting up R&D outside their original base. These are major new developments which deeply affect the whole concept of national systems. This chapter will discuss the rise of R&D in the next section and, subsequently, types of comparison of national systems to which this has led. It will then discuss the role of TNCs and the ways in which they may affect the performance of national economies in different continents.

The rise of specialised research and development

Bjørn Johnson (1992), in an excellent chapter in the Lundvall book on *National Systems of Innovation* emphasises the important point that institutions are often thought of simply as a source of 'institutional drag' (i.e. of inertia in the system), whereas of course institutional innovations may also give new impetus to technical and economic change.

Appropriately enough it was in Germany that the major institutional innovation of the in-house industrial R&D department was introduced in 1870. Product and process innovation by firms took place of course for more than a century before that but it was the German dyestuffs industry (Beer, 1959) which first realised that it could be profitable to put the business of research for new products and development of new chemical processes on a regular, systematic and professional basis. Hoechst, Bayer and BASF have continued and strengthened this tradition down to the present day when their R&D laboratories now employ many thousands of scientists and engineers. Undoubtedly such discoveries and innovations as synthetic indigo, many other synthetic dyestuffs and pharmaceuticals and the Haber-Bosch process for fertilisers were the main factors in establishing the German chemical industry's leading position before and after the First World War. When the three companies merged in 1926 to form the giant IG Farben Trust they further reinforced their R&D (Freeman, 1974) and made many of the key innovations in synthetic materials, fibres and rubbers (PVC, polystyrene, urea-formaldehyde, Buna, etc.).

The enormous success of the German chemical industry led to imitation of the social innovation of the R&D department in the chemical firms of other countries (e.g. CIBA in Switzerland). The in-house R&D lab also emerged in other industries which had the same need to access the results of basic research from universities and other research institutions and to develop their own new products. In the US and German electrical industries, in-house R&D labs appeared in the 1880s, but contract labs, such as Edison's institute, played a bigger part in the US system (Hughes, 1989).

From their origins in the chemical and electrical industries specialised R&D labs gradually became, during the latter part of the nineteenth century and the first half of the twentieth century, characteristic features of most large firms in manufacturing industry (although not of the vast majority of small firms or of service industries) (Mowery, 1980, 1983; Hughes, 1989; Hounshell, 1992). This change in industrial behaviour and the growth of government laboratories, independent contract research institutes and university research impressed many observers and led to the comment by a leading physicist that the greatest invention of the nineteenth century was the method of invention itself. A great many inventions had of course been made for centuries or indeed for millennia before 1870 but the new professional R&D labs seemed like a giant step forward. This perception was powerfully reinforced in the Second World War. Science was already important in the First World War – more important than most

Table 2.1. *Estimated gross expenditure on research and development as a percentage of GNP, 1934–83*

	1934	1967	1983	1983 Civil R&D only
USA	0.6	3.1	2.7	2.0
EC[a]	0.2	1.2	2.1	1.8
Japan	0.1	1.0	2.7	2.7
USSR	0.3	3.2	3.6	1.0

Note:
[a] Estimated weighted average of twelve EC countries.
Source: Author's estimates based on Bernal (1939) adapted to 'Frascati' definitions (OECD, 1963a), OECD statistics, and adjustments to Soviet statistics based on Freeman and Young (1965).

people realised at the time – but it was the Manhattan Project and its outcome at Hiroshima which impressed on people throughout the world the power of science and especially, as it seemed, Big Science. Many other developments on both sides, such as radar, computers, rockets and explosives, resulted from large R&D projects, mobilising government, industrial and academic engineers and scientists.

It was therefore hardly surprising that in the climate which existed after the Second World War, the prestige of organised, professional R&D was very high. The proposals made by a visionary physicist (Bernal, 1939) to increase British R&D by an order of magnitude seemed absurdly Utopian at the time but this was in fact achieved in the new political climate after the Second World War. A similar rapid expansion occurred in all industrial countries in the 1950s and 1960s (table 2.1) and even in Third World countries there was a trend to establish research councils, national R&D labs and other scientific institutions, to do nuclear physics and in some cases to try and make nuclear weapons (e.g. Argentina, India, Brazil, Israel, Yugoslavia). It was hardly surprising either that a simplistic linear model of science and technology 'push' was often dominant in the new science councils that advised governments. It seemed so obvious that the atom bomb (and it was hoped nuclear power for electricity) was the outcome of a chain reaction: basic physics → large-scale development in big labs → applications and innovations (whether military or civil). The linear model was specifically endorsed in the influential report of Vannevar Bush, 'Science, the endless frontier' (see Stokes, 1993).

This meant that the R&D system was seen as *the* source of innovations

– an impression that was reinforced by the system of measurement which was adopted, first by the National Science Foundation in the United States and later, during the 1950s and 1960s, by all the other OECD countries. This was standardised by the so-called Frascati Manual (OECD, 1963a) and, despite the fact that the authors pointed out that technical change did not depend just on R&D but on many other related activities, such as education, training, production engineering, design, quality control, etc., R&D measures were very frequently used as a surrogate for all these activities which helped to promote new and improved products and processes. Furthermore, the importance of all the feedback loops from the market and from production into the R&D system was often overlooked or forgotten. The simple fact that the R&D measures were the only ones that were available reinforced these tendencies.

Their effect could be seen in many national reports as well as in the 'Science Policy Reviews' conducted by the OECD in its member countries in the 1960s and 1970s. The admirable aim of these reviews, like the reviews of member countries' economic policies (which still continue and on which they were modelled), was to produce a friendly but independent and critical assessment of each country's performance against an international comparative yardstick. In practice they concentrated mainly on the formal R&D system and technical education. This was of course still quite a useful thing to do but it meant that the 'national system' was usually defined in rather narrow terms. Academic research on invention and innovation had amply demonstrated that many factors were important for innovative success other than R&D. However, the practical difficulties of incorporating these factors in international comparisons were very great. 'League Table' comparisons of R&D were much easier and more influential.

Gradually, during the 1950s and 1960s, the evidence accumulated that the rate of technical change and of economic growth depended more on efficient diffusion than on being first in the world with radical innovations and as much on social innovations as on technical innovations. This was reflected in the change of emphasis in various OECD reports (OECD, 1963b, 1971, 1980, 1988, 1991, 1992) and in the introduction of Country Reports on 'Innovation'. Basic science was of course still recognised as being very important but much more was said about technology and diffusion than hitherto.

Although various OECD reports are a convenient record of changing ideas and policies for science and technology, they rarely originated these changes. The OECD documents summed up and reflected recent experience and changes in the member countries and disseminated what were thought to be the lessons of this experience. The OECD was also, however, more ready than most international organisations to involve independent researchers, so that its reports also embody some input from academic research on technical change as well as from industrial R&D management sources. The next section will very briefly summarise the relevant results of some of this work (more fully surveyed in Freeman, 1994) and especially the results of international comparisons. Comparisons with Japan were especially influential after Japan joined the OECD in the 1970s.

Some contrasting features of national systems of innovation in the 1970s and 1980s

As empirical evidence and analysis began to accumulate about industrial R&D and about innovation, both in Japan and in the United States and Europe, it became increasingly evident that the success of innovations, their rate of diffusion and the associated productivity gains depended on a wide variety of other influences as well as formal R&D. In particular, *incremental* innovations came from production engineers, from technicians and from the shop-floor. They were strongly related to different forms of work organisation (see especially Hollander, 1965).

Furthermore, many improvements to *products* and to services came from interaction with the market and with related firms, such as sub-contractors, suppliers of materials and services (see especially von Hippel, 1976, 1988; Lundvall, 1985, 1988, 1993; Sako, 1992). Formal R&D was usually decisive in its contribution to *radical* innovations but it was no longer possible to ignore the many other contributions to, and influences upon, the process of technical change at the level of firms and industries (Carter and Williams, 1957; Jewkes *et al.*, 1958; Nelson, 1962; Mansfield, 1968, 1971).

Not only were inter-firm relationships shown to be of critical importance, but the external *linkages* within the narrower professional science-technology system were also shown to be decisive for success with radical innovations (National Science Foundation, 1973; Gibbons and Johnston, 1974). Finally, research on diffusion revealed more and more that the *systemic* aspects of innovation were increasingly influential in determining both the rate of diffusion and the productivity gains associated with any particular diffusion process (see especially Carlsson and Jacobsson, 1993). The success of any specific technical innovation, such as robots or CNC depended on other related changes in *systems* of production. As three major new 'generic' technologies (information technology, biotechnology and new materials technology) diffused through the world economy in the 1970s and 1980s, systemic aspects of innovation assumed greater and greater importance.

At the *international* level two contrasting experiences made a very powerful impression in the 1980s both on policy-makers and on researchers: on the one hand the extraordinary success of first Japan and then South Korea in technological and economic catch-up; and on the other hand the collapse of the socialist economies of Eastern Europe.

At first, in the 1950s and 1960s, the Japanese success was often simply attributed to copying, imitating and importing foreign technology and the statistics of the so-called 'technological balance of payments' were often cited to support this view. They showed a huge deficit in Japanese transactions for licensing and know-how imports and exports and a correspondingly large surplus for the United States. It soon became evident, however, as Japanese products and processes began to outperform American and European products and processes in more and more industries, that this explanation was no longer adequate even though the import of technology continued to be important. Japanese industrial R&D expenditures as a proportion of civil industrial net output surpassed those of the United States in the 1970s and total civil R&D as a fraction of GNP surpassed the USA in the 1980s (table 2.1). The Japanese performance could now be explained more in terms of R&D intensity, especially as Japanese R&D was highly concentrated in the fastest growing civil industries, such as electronics. Patent statistics showed that the leading Japanese electronic firms outstripped American and European firms in these industries, not just in domestic patenting but in patents taken out in the United States (Freeman, 1987; Patel and Pavitt, 1991, 1992).

However, although these rough measures of research and inventive activity certainly did indicate the huge increase in Japanese scientific and technical activities, they did not in themselves explain how these activities led to higher quality of new products and processes (Grupp and Hofmeyer, 1986; Womack et al., 1990); to shorter lead times (Mansfield, 1988; Graves, 1991) and to more rapid diffusion of such technologies as robotics (Fleck and White, 1987; Mansfield, 1989). Moreover, the contrasting example of the (then) Soviet Union and other Eastern European countries showed that simply to commit greater resources to R&D did not in itself guarantee successul innovation, diffusion and productivity gains. It was obvious that *qualitative* factors affecting the national systems had to be taken into account as well as the purely *quantitative* indicators.

Some major differences between the two national systems of Japan and the Soviet Union as they were functioning in the 1970s are summarised in table 2.2. The most striking contrast of course was the huge commitment of Soviet R&D to military and space applications with little direct or indirect spin-off to the civil economy. It has now been shown that the desire to keep pace with the USA in the superpower arms race led to about three-quarters of the massive Soviet R&D resources going into defence and space research. This amounted to nearly 3 per cent of GNP, so that only about 1

Table 2.2. *Contrasting national systems of innovation, 1970s*

Japan	USSR
High GERD/GNP^a (2.5 per cent)	Very high GERD/GNP^a (c. 4 per cent)
Very low proportion of military/space R&D(<2 per cent of R&D)	Extremely high proportion of military/space R&D (>70 per cent of R&D)
High proportion of total R&D at enterprise level and company-financed (approx. 67 per cent)	Low proportion of total R&D at enterprise level and company-financed (<10 per cent)
Strong integration of R&D, production and import of technology at enterprise level	Separation of R&D, production and import of technology and weak institutional linkages
Strong user–producer and sub-contractor network linkages	Weak or non-existent linkages between marketing, production and procurement
Strong incentives to innovate at enterprise level involving both management and work-force	Some incentives to innovate made increasingly strong in 1960s and 1970s but offset by disincentives affecting both management and work-force
Intensive experience of competition in international markets	Relatively weak exposure to international competition except in arms race

Note:
^{a} Gross expenditure on R&D/Gross National Product.

per cent remained for civil R&D. This *civil* R&D/GNP ratio was less than half of most Western European countries and much smaller than the Japanese ratio (table 2.1).

Nevertheless, it could have been far more productive if the social, technical and economic linkages in the system and the incentives to efficient performance had been stronger. The Soviet system grew up on the basis of separate research institutes – within the academy system (for fundamental research), for each industry sector (for applied research and development) and for the design of plant and import of technology (the Project Design organisations) (Barker and Davies, 1965; Amann *et al.*, 1979). The links between all these different institutions and enterprise-level R&D remained rather weak despite successive attempts to reform and improve the system in the 1960s and 1970s.

Moreover, there were quite strong disincentives in the Soviet system

Table 2.3. *Divergence in national systems of innovation in the 1980s*

East Asia	Latin America
Expanding universal education system with high participation in tertiary education and with high proportion of engineering graduates	Deteriorating education system with proportionately lower output of engineers
Import of technology typically combined with local initiatives in technical change and at later stages rapidly rising levels of R&D	Much transfer of technology, especially from the United States, but weak enterprise-level R&D and little integration with technology transfer
Industrial R&D rises typically to >50 per cent of all R&D	Industrial R&D typically remains at <25 per cent of all R&D
Development of strong science–technology infrastructure and at later stages good linkages with industrial R&D	Weakening of science–technology infrastructure and poor linkages with industry
High levels of investment and major inflow of Japanese investment and technology with strong yen in 1980s. Strong influence of Japanese models of management and networking organisation	Decline in (mainly US) foreign invest-ment and generally lower levels of investment. Low level of international networking in technology
Heavy investment in advanced telecommunications infrastructure	Slow development of modern telecommunications
Strong and fast-growing electronic industries with high exports and extensive user feedback from international marketing	Weak electronic industries with low exports and little learning by international marketing

retarding innovation at enterprise level (Gomulka, 1990), such as the need to meet quantitative planned production targets. Thus, whereas the inte-gration of R&D, production, and technology imports at firm level was the strongest feature of the Japanese system (Baba, 1985; Takeuchi and Nonaka, 1986; Freeman, 1987), it was very weak in the Soviet Union except in the aircraft industry and other defence sectors. Finally, the user–pro-ducer linkages which were so important in most other industrial countries were very weak or almost non-existent in some areas in the Soviet Union.

There were some features of their national systems in which the two countries resembled each other, and both did of course enjoy high economic growth rates in the 1950s and 1960s. Both had (and still have) good education systems, with a high proportion of young people participating in tertiary education and strong emphasis on science and technology. Both also had methods of generating long-term goals and perspectives for the science–technology system, but whereas in Japan the long-term 'visions' were generated by an interactive process involving not only MITI and other government organisations but also industry and universities (Irvine and Martin, 1984), in the USSR the process was more restricted and dominated to a greater extent by military/space requirements.

A similar sharp contrast can be made between the national systems of innovation typically present in Latin American countries in the 1980s and those in the 'Four Dragons' of East Asia (table 2.3) and especially between two 'newly industrialising countries' (NICs) in the 1980s: Brazil and South Korea (table 2.4). The Asian countries started from a *lower* level of industrialisation in the 1950s but, whereas in the 1960s and 1970s the Latin American and East Asian countries were often grouped together as very fast growing NICs, in the 1980s a sharp contrast began to emerge: the East Asian countries' GNP grew at an average annual rate of about 8 per cent, but in most Latin American countries, including Brazil, this fell to less than 2 per cent, which meant in many cases a falling per capita income. There are of course many explanations for this stark contrast. Some of the Asian countries introduced more radical social changes, such as land reform and universal education, than most Latin American countries and clearly a structural and technical transformation of this magnitude in this time was facilitated by these social changes. In the case of Brazil and South Korea it is possible to give some more detailed quantitative indicators of some of these contrasting features. As table 2.4 shows, the contrast in educational systems was very marked as well as those in enterprise-level R&D, telecommunications infrastructure and the diffusion of new technologies (see Nelson, 1993 for more detailed comparisons and Villaschi, 1993 for a detailed study of the Brazilian national system).

'Globalisation' and national systems

It has been argued in the previous section that a variety of *national* institutions have powerfully affected the relative rates of technical change and hence of economic growth in various countries. The variations in national systems which have been described are of course extreme contrasting cases. Nevertheless, they have certainly been important features of world development in the second half of the twentieth century and they point to *uneven* development of the world economy and *divergence* in growth rates.

Table 2.4. *National systems of innovation, 1980s: some quantitative indicators*

Various indicators of technical capability and national institutions	Brazil	South Korea
Percentage of age group in third-level of (higher) education	11 (1985)	32 (1985)
Engineering students as percentage of population	0.13 (1985)	0.54 (1985)
R&D as percentage GNP	0.7 (1987)	2.1 (1989)
Industry R&D as percentage of total	30 (1988)	65 (1987)
Robots per million in employment	52 (1987)	1060 (1987)
CAD per million in employment	422 (1986)	1437 (1986)
NCMT per million in employment	2298 (1987)	5176 (1985)
Growth rate of electronics (per cent)	8 (1983–7)	21 (1985–90)
Telephone lines per 100	6 (1989)	25 (1989)
Per capita sales of telecommunication equipment	$10 (1989)	$77 (1989)
Patents (US)	36 (1989)	159 (1989)

Moreover, differences in national systems are also very important between Japan, the United States and the EU and between European countries themselves, as a major comparative study between more than a dozen national systems of innovation illustrates (Nelson, 1993). The comparative study of Ireland and other small countries by Mjøset (1992) also demonstrates this point and the comparison between Denmark and Sweden by Edquist and Lundvall (1993) shows that big differences exist between neighbouring countries which superficially appear very similar in many ways. Moreover, Archibugi and Pianta (1992) have demonstrated the growing pattern of specialisation in technology and trade and Fagerberg

(1992) has shown the continuing importance of the home market for comparative technological advantage.

However, the whole concept of *national* differences in innovative capabilities determining national performance has been recently challenged on the grounds that transnational corporations (TNCs) are changing the face of the world economy in the direction of globalisation. For example, Ohmae (1990) in his book *The Borderless World* argues that national frontiers are 'melting away' in what he calls the ILE (inter-linked economy) – the Triad of USA, EU and Japan, now being joined by NICs. This ILE is becoming 'so powerful that it has swallowed most consumers and corporations, made traditional national borders almost disappear, and pushed bureaucrats, politicians and the military towards the status of declining industries' (p. xii).

As against this, Michael Porter (1990, p. 19) has argued that:

Competitive advantage is created and sustained through a highly localised process. Differences in national economic structures, values, cultures, institutions and histories contribute profoundly to competitive success. The role of the home nation seems to be as strong or stronger than ever. While globalisation of competition might appear to make the nation less important, instead it seems to make it more so. With fewer impediments to trade to shelter uncompetitive domestic firms and industries, the home nation takes on growing significance because it is the source of the skills and technology that underpin competitive advantage.

In addition to Porter's argument, Lundvall (1993) points out that if uncertainty, localised learning and bounded rationality are introduced as basic and more realistic assumptions about microeconomic behaviour, rather than the traditional assumptions of perfect information and hyper-rationality, then it must follow that local and national variations in circumstances may often lead to different paths of development and to increasing diversity rather than to standardisation and convergence.

At first sight, the activities of multinational corporations might appear to offer a powerful countervailing force to this local variety and diversity. The largest corporations in the world, whether their original domestic base was in Europe, the United States, Japan or elsewhere, have often been investing in many different new locations. This investment, even though initially it may have been in distribution and service networks, or in production facilities, has more recently also included R&D. Whilst the greater part of the 1980s' investment has been within the OECD area itself and in oil-producing countries and could be more accurately described therefore as 'Triadisation' rather than 'globalisation', it has also flowed, even though very unevenly, to other countries of the Third World and there is now a small trickle to the former socialist group of countries.

As Harry Johnson (1975) long ago pointed out, in this sense the multi-nationals do indeed unite the human race. Since the basic laws of physics, chemistry, biology and other sciences apply everywhere there is an underlying unified technology which can in principle be applied anywhere with identical or very similar results. Insofar as large 'global' TNCs are able to sell their products and services worldwide and to produce them in many different locations, they can and do act as very powerful agencies tending towards the worldwide standardisation of technology and output. As the model developed by Callon (1993) indicates, the diffusion process can tend to enhance similarities between adopters.

Even in the case of consumer goods where it might be reasonable to suppose that there would continue to be wide variations in consumer tastes, we are all sufficiently familiar with such products as Coca-Cola and such services as those provided by McDonald's to recognise the reality of such global production and distribution networks, offering standardised products and services worldwide. Is it not realistic to suppose that an ever-larger proportion of world production and trade will take this form? Supporting such a view are not only the obvious examples of hotel chains, soft drinks, canned beer, tourist agencies and credit cards but theoretical economic arguments based on static and dynamic economies of scale in production, advertising, marketing, design and finance, as well as the ability of large multinationals to take advantage of surviving differences between nations in costs of capital, labour, energy and other inputs.

However, it would be unwise to assume that these tendencies are the only or even necessarily the strongest tendencies within the world economy. Nor are they so unequivocally desirable that they should be promoted by both national and international economic policies. In fact, the arguments for preserving and even encouraging diversity may sometimes outweigh the shorter-term advantages of the scale economies derived from standardisation and their propagation through transnational companies, free trade and free flows of investment. In fact, the two processes (global standardisation in some areas but increasing diversity in others) co-exist.

Whilst there are certainly some products and services, such as those already mentioned, where there is indeed a demand which is 'global' in nature and where local variations in taste, regulation, climate and other circumstances can be largely or wholly ignored, there are far more products and services where such variations certainly cannot be ignored without dire consequences. Innumerable examples leap to mind where climatic conditions affect the performance of machines, instruments, vehicles and materials and even more examples are obvious in relation to variations in national standards, specifications and regulations. Whilst it is true that international standardisation is a countervailing force through the activities of the International Standards Organisation (ISO) and many other bodies attempting to achieve harmonisation of technical standards, it is also true that the experience of the European Union over the past twenty years demonstrates the extreme difficulties attending this process in many areas (as well as the feasibility in others). And all this still does not take into account the cultural aspects of the problem which deeply affect such areas as food, clothing and personal services.

So far we have been discussing mainly the case of established products and pointing to some factors which limit global standardisation even in the simplest cases. Advocates of a strong globalisation hypothesis would of course accept most of these points, although they might argue that some of them will tend constantly to diminish as the media, travel, education and international organisations all exert their long-term influences. Rothwell (1992) has pointed to the 'electronification' of design as an important factor facilitating the internationalisation of design and R&D. It can be argued further that local variations can easily be dealt with inside the framework of the global strategies of the multinational corporations. Indeed, globalisation of R&D has already led to local adaptation and modification of products to meet national variations, as a normal and almost routine activity of TNCs. Companies such as Honda go one step further and claim to have a strategy of diversity in worldwide design which goes beyond the simple modification of a standard product to the idea of local variation at the design stage in several different parts of the world. However, the vast majority of Japanese-based TNCs remain essentially Japanese companies with international operations rather than truly international companies and the same is true of US and most other MNCs in relation to their home environment (Hu, 1992). Most R&D activities of MNCs are still overwhelmingly conducted in the domestic base of the company and are heavily influenced by the local national system of innovation. Moreover, ownership and control still remain overwhelmingly based on the domestic platform.

The statistics are rather poor but analysis of all the available data and cross-checking with the patent statistics (Patel and Pavitt, 1991; Patel, this volume) suggests that the R&D activities of US companies outside the USA amount to less than 10 per cent of the total, whilst those of Japanese companies are much lower – less than 2 per cent – though rising. The picture in Europe is more complex both because of the development of the European Community and the Single European Market, and because of the existence of several technically advanced small countries where the domestic base is too small for the strong MNCs which are based there (Netherlands, Sweden, Belgium, Switzerland). A larger part of national R&D activities in these countries and most other parts of Europe is undertaken by foreign multinationals and their 'own' TNCs perform much more

R&D abroad than is the case with the USA or Japan. Only a small part of total world R&D is conducted outside the leading industrial countries and only a very small part of this is financed by TNCs.

Qualitative analysis of the transnational activities of corporations shows that most of it is *either* local design modification to meet national specifications and regulations *or* research to facilitate monitoring of local science and technology. The more original research, development and design work is still overwhelmingly concentrated in the domestic base, although there are important exceptions in the drug industry and electronics industry where specialised pools of scientific ability play an important role.

As long as we are dealing with a static array of products and discussing only minor variations to adjust to local consumer tastes and environments, then the standardisation arguments, the globalisation arguments and even some of the simplifying neoclassical assumptions about perfect information are at the borderlines of credibility and usefulness. But once we leave this world and enter the dynamic world of radical innovations, both technical and organisational, and of extremely uneven and unequal access to new developments in science and technology, then the whole picture is transformed. More realistic assumptions and a more realistic vision are essential if economic theory is to be of any help in policy-making.

Lundvall (1993) points out that, even in the case of continuous *incremental* innovation in open economies, the drive towards standardisation is limited. Geographical and cultural proximity to advanced users and a network of institutionalised (even if often informal) user–producer relationships are an important source of diversity and of comparative advantage, as is the local supply of managerial and technical skills and accumulated tacit knowledge. He gives several examples of such localised learning generating strong positions in the world market. Whilst he accepts that TNCs might locate in such 'national strongholds' in order to gain access to the fruits of this interactive learning process, he points out that it is not always simple to enter such markets because of the strength of the non-economic relationships involved. Competing standards for the global market may be important weapons in such situations as well as other forms of product differentiation and quality improvement.

When it comes to *radical* innovations the importance of institutional variety and localised learning is even greater. Posner's (1961) theory of technology gaps and imitation lags is of fundamental importance here. It may be many years before imitators are capable of assembling the mix of skills, the work organisation and other institutional changes necessary to launch into the production and marketing of entirely new products.

It is of course true that in the global diffusion of radical innovations, TNCs may have an extremely important role. They *are* in a position to transfer specialised equipment and skills to new locations if they so wish and to stimulate and organise the necessary learning processes. They are also in a position to make technology exchange agreements with rivals and to organise joint ventures in any part of the world. It is for this reason that many governments in Europe as well as in the Third World and the ex-socialist countries have been anxious to offer incentives to attract a flow of inward investment and associated technology transfer from firms based in Japan and the United States.

However, such efforts will meet with only limited success unless accompanied by a variety of institutional changes designed to strengthen autonomous technological capability within the importing countries. This is especially true of those generic technologies which have been at the centre of the worldwide diffusion process over the past two decades. Here it is essential to emphasise the interdependencies between innovations and between technical innovations and organisational innovations. A theory of technical change which ignores these interdependencies is no more helpful than a theory of economics which ignores the interdependencies of prices and quantities in the world economy.

Perez (1983) has pointed out that the social and institutional framework which is hospitable to one set of technologies will not be so suitable for a radically new technology. Whereas incremental innovations can be easily accommodated, this may not be the case with radical innovations which by definition involve an element of creative destruction. When we are talking about large clusters of radical innovations combined with rapid processes of incremental innovation, then the problems of structural and social adjustment can be very great. This is quite obvious when we consider such aspects as the change in management techniques and skill-mix which are called for, but it also applies to many other types of institutional change in standards, patents, new services, new infrastructure, government policies and public organisations.

It is in this context that the concept of national systems of innovation assumes such great importance and in the light of this approach it is not surprising that the recognition of the scope and depth of the computer revolution, which was accelerated by the microprocessor in the 1970s, has been followed by a growing recognition of the importance of organisational and managerial change ('multi-skilling', 'lean production systems', 'downsizing', 'just-in-time' stock control, worker participation in technical change, quality circles, continuous learning, etc., etc.).

The diffusion of a new techno-economic paradigm is a trial-and-error process involving great institutional variety. There are evolutionary advantages in this variety and considerable dangers in being locked in too early to a standardised technology. A technological monoculture may be more dangerous than an ecological monoculture. Even when a technology matures and shows clear-cut advantages and scale economies it is important to retain flexibility and to nourish alternative sources of radically new technology and work organisation.

National and international policies thus confront the need for a sophisticated dual approach to a complex set of problems. Policies for diffusion of standard generic technologies are certainly important and these may sometimes entail the encouragement of inward investment and technology transfer by MNCs. But also important are policies to encourage local originality and diversity.

Conclusions

This chapter has attempted to show that historically there have been major differences between countries in the ways in which they have organised and sustained the development, introduction, improvement and diffusion of new products and processes within their national economies. These differences can perhaps be most easily demonstrated in the case of Britain in the late eighteenth and early nineteenth centuries when she achieved leadership in world technology and world trade and could temporarily claim to be 'the workshop of the world'.

Historians (Mathias, 1969; von Tunzelmann, 1994) are generally agreed that no single factor can explain this British success; rather, it can be attributed to a unique combination of interacting social, economic and technical changes within the national economic space. It was certainly not just a succession of remarkable inventions in the textile and iron industries, important though these were. Among the more important changes were the transition from a domestic 'putting out' system to a factory system of production; new ways of managing and financing companies (partnership and later joint stock companies); interactive learning between new companies and industries using new materials and other inputs as well as new machinery; the removal of many older restrictions on trade and industry and the growth of new markets and systems of retail and wholesale trade; a new transport infrastructure; a hospitable cultural environment for new scientific theories and inventions, and, certainly not least important, the dissemination and widespread acceptance of economic theories and policies which facilitated all these changes. It was the British Prime Minister who said to Adam Smith: 'We are all your pupils now'. The benefits from foreign trade and in some cases piracy and plunder also played their part, especially in the process of capital accumulation, but it was the mode of investment of this capital within the national economy, rather than the simple acquisition of treasure or luxury expenditure which was a decisive impulse to economic growth.

Of course, many of these changes also took place within other European countries but there were distinct and measurable differences in the rate and direction of institutional and technical change, the rate of economic growth, of foreign trade and of standards of living, which were fairly obvious at the time as well as to historians since. This can be seen not only from the writings of economists but from those of novelists and travellers. It was therefore hardly surprising that Friedrich List and other economists on the continent of Europe were concerned to develop theories and policies which would help them to understand the reasons for British commercial supremacy and enable Germany (and other countries) to catch up. The introductory section attempted to show that in this endeavour, List antici-pated many contemporary ideas about national systems of innovation including the crucial importance of technological accumulation through a combination of technology imports with local activities and pro-active interventionist policies to foster strategic 'infant' industries.

In the second half of the nineteenth century, new developments in the natural sciences and in electrical engineering led to progressive entrepre-neurs and reformers realising that in the new and fastest-growing indus-tries, learning by doing, using and interacting in the old British ways had to be accompanied or replaced by more professional and systematic processes of innovation and learning. The organisational innovation of the in-house R&D department put the introduction of new products and processes on a firmer foundation whilst new institutions and departments of higher and secondary education provided the new more highly qualified scientists, engineers and technicians. The second section of the chapter argued that it was in Germany and the United States that these institu-tional innovations began and made the greatest impact on national systems in the second half of the nineteenth century and the early twentieth century.

The rapidly widening gap between a small group of industrialised coun-tries and the rest of the 'under-developed' world (Durlauf and Johnson, 1992; Dosi *et al.*, 1992) as well as the 'forging ahead', 'catching up' and 'falling behind' (Abramovitz, 1986) among the leaders clearly called for some explanation of why growth rates differed so much. The brave simpli-fying assumptions of neoclassical economics might lead people to expect convergence rather than divergence in growth rates (perfect information and costless, instant transfer of technology). Nor did formal growth theory and models provide much help since most of the interesting phenomena were confined to a 'residual' which could not be satisfactorily disaggregated and because of the interdependencies involved.

Many economic historians and proponents of what have now become known as national systems of innovation would claim that the differences were due to varying types of institutional and technical change which may be the subject of qualitative description, even though difficult to quantify. The second and third sections of the chapter argued that the oversimplification of quantitative R&D comparisons was an inadequate method in itself. The third section attempted to show by the examples of Japan and the former Soviet Union, and of the East Asian and Latin American 'NICs' that institutional differences in the mode of importing, improving, developing and diffusing new technologies, products and processes played a major role in their sharply contrasting growth rates in the 1980s.

Finally, the chapter discussed the controversial issue of 'globalisation' and its bearing on national systems of innovation. It is ironical that just as the importance of technology policies and industrial policies has been increasingly recognised alike in OECD and in developing countries, the limitations of *national* policies are increasingly emphasised and the relevance of *national* systems increasingly questioned (see, for example, Humbert, 1993).

The global reach of transnational corporations, the drastic cost reductions and quality improvements in global telecommunications networking and other rapid and related changes in the world economy must certainly be taken into account in any satisfactory analysis of national systems (Chesnais, 1992).

It is tempting at first sight to follow Ohmae (1990) and to discard national economies and nation-states as rapidly obsolescent categories. The speed of change and the difficulties of focusing analysis may be illustrated by the confusion in terminology. Ohmae maintains that nation-states are losing their power and their influence both 'upwards' and 'downwards', on the one hand to supranational institutions (the EU, NAFTA, UN organisations, etc., as well as transnational companies) and on the other hand to sub-national (or 'infranational') provincial, urban or local authorities and organisations (the disintegration of federal and centralised states, the growing importance in some areas of local government agencies and even of various forms of tariff-free zones, and of 'Silicon Valleys'). Unhappily, at least in the English language, the same word 'regions' has to be used to describe both processes – the very large 'regional' trading blocs such as NAFTA, or the emerging East Asian 'region', and the much smaller sub-national 'regions'. Some terminological innovation is needed here and for the purposes of this chapter, the expressions 'upper regions' and 'nether regions' will be used. It is undoubtedly important to keep track of both and of their interaction with national systems.

The work of geographers as well as economists (e.g. Storper and Harrison, 1991; Saxenian, 1991; Scott, 1991, Lundvall, 1992; Antonelli, 1994) has convincingly demonstrated the importance of nether regions for network developments and new technology systems. They have argued that local infrastructure, externalities, especially in skills and local labour markets, specialised services and not least, mutual trust and personal relationships have contributed greatly to flourishing nether regions. It should not be forgotten, however, that 'nether-regional systems of innovation' and 'economies of agglomeration' have always underpinned national systems from the beginnings of the industrial revolution (Arcangeli, 1993). Much earlier, Marshall (1890) had stressed the importance of what were then known as 'industrial districts' where 'the secrets of industry were in the air' (Foray, 1991). Piore and Sabel (1984) have especially underlined the importance of these nether regions in many parts of Europe both in the nineteenth century and again today.

Moreover, the vulnerability of national economies to external shocks is also by no means a new phenomenon of the last decade or two, even though the liberalisation of capital markets and international flows of trade and investment combined with computerisation and new telecommunications networks may have increased this vulnerability. Small and distant nations were already affected by shocks from the City of London under the Gold Standard and the Popular Front government in France suffered just as severely from the flight of capital in the 1930s as the Socialist government of France in the 1980s.

This chapter has argued that nation-states, national economies and national systems of innovation are still essential domains of economic and political analysis, despite some shifts to upper and nether regions. Indeed, Michael Porter (1990) may well be right in his contention that the intensification of global competition has made the role of the home nation more important, not less. Particularly from the standpoint of developing countries, national policies for catching up in technology remain of fundamental importance. Nevertheless, the interaction of national systems both with 'nether-region systems of innovation' and with transnational corporations will be increasingly important, as will be the role of international co-operation in sustaining a global regime favourable to catching up and development.

Note

1   I have used the expression 'intellectual capital' rather than 'mental capital' used in the early English edition.

References

Abramovitz, M. 1986. Catching up, forging ahead, and falling behind, *Journal of Economic History*, 46(2): 385–406.

Amann, R., Berry, M. and Davies, R.W. 1979. *Industrial Innovation in the Soviet Union*, New Haven, Yale University Press.

Antonelli, C. 1994. Technological districts, localized spillovers and productivity growth, *International Review of Applied Economics*, 8: 18–30.

Arcangeli, F. 1993. Local and global features of the learning process, in Humbert (ed.).

Archibugi, D. and Pianta, M. 1992. *The Technological Specialization of Advanced Countries. A Report to the EC on Science and Technology Activities*, Boston, Kluwer.

Baba, Y. 1985. Japanese colour TV firms. Decision-making from the 1950s to the 1980s, D.Phil. dissertation, University of Sussex, Brighton.

Barker, G.R. and Davies, R.W. 1965. The research and development effort of the Soviet Union, in Freeman and Young (eds.).

Barnett, C. 1988. *The Audit of War*, Cambridge, Cambridge University Press.

Beer, J.J. 1959. *The Emergence of the German Dye Industry*, Chicago, University of Illinois Press.

Bernal, J. D. 1939. *The Social Function of Science*, London, Routledge & Kegan Paul.

Callon, M. 1993. Variety and irreversibility in networks of technique conception and adoption, in Foray and Freeman (eds.).

Carlsson, B. and Jacobsson, S. 1993. Technological systems and economic performance: the diffusion of factory automation in Sweden, in Foray and Freeman (eds.).

Carter, C. F. and Williams, B. R. 1957. *Industry and Technical Progress*, Oxford, Oxford University Press.

Chesnais, F. 1992. National systems of innovation, foreign direct investment and the operations of multinational enterprises, in Lundvall (ed.).

Dosi, G., Freeman, C., Fabiani, S. and Aversi, R. 1992. The diversity of development patterns: on the processes of catching up, forging ahead and falling behind, paper to the International Economics Association, Varenna, Italy, October.

Durlauf, S. and Johnson, P.A. 1992. Local versus global convergence across national economies, mimeo, Stanford University.

Edquist, C. and Lundvall, B.-Å. 1993. Denmark and Sweden, in Nelson (ed.).

Fagerberg, J. 1992. The home market hypothesis re-examined: the impact of domestic-user–producer interaction in exports, in Lundvall (ed.).

Fleck, J. and White, B. 1987. National policies and patterns of robot diffusion: UK, Japan, Sweden and United States, *Robotics*, 3: 7–23.

Foray, D. 1991. The secrets of industry are in the air: industrial cooperation and the organisational dynamics of the innovative firm, *Research Policy*, 20: 393–407.

Foray, D. and Freeman, C. (eds.) 1993. *Technology and the Wealth of Nations*, London, Pinter.

Freeman, C. 1974. *The Economics of Industrial Innovation*, 1st edn, Harmondsworth, Penguin; 2nd edn, London, Pinter 1982.

1987. *Technology Policy and Economic Performance: Lessons from Japan*, London, Pinter.

1994. The economics of technical change: a critical survey article, *Cambridge Journal of Economics*, 18: 463–514.

Freeman, C. and Hagedoorn, J. 1992. Convergence and divergence in the internationalisation of technology', paper to MERIT Conference, University of Limburg, December.

Freeman, C. and Young, A. (eds.) 1965. *The Research and Development Effort in Western Europe, North America and the Soviet Union*, Paris, OECD.

Gibbons, M. and Johnston, R. D. 1974. The roles of science in technological innovation, *Research Policy*, 3: 220–42.

Gomulka, S. 1990. *The Theory of Technological Change and Economic Growth*, London, Routledge.

Graves, A. 1991. International competitiveness and technological development in the world automobile industry, D.Phil. dissertation, University of Sussex, Brighton.

Grossman, I. and Helpman, E. 1991. *Innovation and Growth in the Global Economy*, Cambridge, Mass., MIT Press.

Grupp, H. and Hofmeyer, O. 1986. A technometric model for the assessment of technological standards and their application to selected technology comparisons, *Technological Forecasting and Social Change*, 30: 123–37.

Hamilton, A. 1791. *Report on the Subject of Manufactures.* Reprinted US Government Printing Office, Washington, D.C., 1913.

Hobsbawm, E. 1968. *Industry and Empire*, London, Weidenfeld & Nicolson.

Hollander, S. 1965. *The Sources of Increased Efficiency: A Study of DuPont Rayon Plants*, Cambridge, Mass., MIT Press.

Hounshell, D. A. (1992) Continuity and change in the management of industrial research: the DuPont Company 1902–1980, in G. Dosi, R. Giannetti, and P. A. Toninelli, (eds.), *Technology and Enterprise in a Historical Perspective*, Oxford, Oxford University Press.

Hu, Y.S. 1992. Global or transnational corporations are national firms with international operations, *Californian Management Review*, 34: 107–26.

Hughes, T. P. 1989. *American Genesis*, New York, Viking.

Humbert, M. (ed.) 1993. *The Impact of Globalisation on Europe's Firms and Industries*, London, Pinter.

Irvine, J. and Martin, B. R. 1984. *Foresight in Science: Picking the Winners*, London, Pinter.

Jewkes, J., Sawers, D. and Stillerman, R. 1958. *The Sources of Invention*, London, Macmillan.

Johnson, B. 1992. Institutional learning, in Lundvall (ed.).

Johnson, H.G. 1975. *Technology and Economic Interdependence*, London, Macmillan.

Landes, M. 1969. *The Unbound Prometheus: Technological and Industrial Development in Western Europe from 1750 to the Present*, Cambridge, Cambridge University Press.

List, F. 1841. *The National System of Political Economy*, English edition, London, Longman, 1904.

Lundvall, B.-Å. 1985. *Product Innovation and User–Producer Interaction*, Industrial Development Research Series no. 31, Aalborg, Aalborg University Press.

1988. Innovation as an interactive process: from user–producer interaction to the national system of innovation, in G. Dosi *et al.* (eds.), *Technical Change and Economic Theory*, London, Pinter.

1993. User–producer relationships, national systems of innovation and internationalisation, in Foray and Freeman (eds.).

Lundvall, B.-Å. (ed.) 1992. *National Systems of Innovation*, London, Pinter.

Mansfield, E. 1968. *The Economics of Technical Change*, New York, W. W. Norton.

1971. *Research and Innovation in the Modern Corporation*, New York, W.W. Norton.

1988. Industrial innovation in Japan and in the United States, *Science*, 241: 1760–4.

1989. The diffusion of industrial robots in Japan and in the United States, *Research Policy*, 18: 183–92.

Marshall, A. 1890. *Principles of Economics*, London, Macmillan.

Mathias, P. 1969. *The First Industrial Nation*, London, Methuen.

Miyazaki, K. 1993. Dynamic competence building in Japanese and European firms: the case of opto-electronics, D.Phil. dissertation, University of Sussex, Brighton.

Mjøset, L. 1992. *The Irish Economy in a Comparative Institutional Perspective*, Dublin, National Economic and Social Council.

Mowery, D. C. 1980. The emergence and growth of industrial research in American manufacturing 1899–1946, Ph.D. dissertation, Stanford University

1983. The relationship between intrafirm and contractual forms of industrial research in American manufacturing 1900–1940, *Explorations in Economic History*, 20: 351–74.

National Science Foundation NSF 1973. *Interactions of Science and Technology in the Innovative Process*, NSF-667, Washington, D.C.

Nelson, R. R. (ed.) 1962. *The Rate and Direction of Innovative Activity*, Princeton, Princeton University Press/NBER.

(ed.) 1993. *National Innovation Systems*, New York, Oxford University Press.

OECD 1963a. *The Measurement of Scientific and Technical Activities* (Frascati Manual), Paris, OECD.

1963b. *Science, Economic Growth and Government Policy*, Paris, OECD.

1971. *Science, Growth and Society* (Brooks Report), Paris, OECD.

1980. *Technical Change and Economic Policy*, Paris, OECD.

1988. *New Technologies in the 1990s: A Socio-economic Strategy* (Sundqvist Report) Paris, OECD.

1991. *Technology and Productivity: The Challenges for Economic Policy*, Paris, OECD.

1992. *Technology and the Economy: The Key Relationships*, Paris, OECD.

Ohmae, K. 1990. *The Borderless World*, New York, Harper.

Patel, P. and Pavitt, K. 1991. Large firms in the production of the world's technology: an important case of 'non-globalisation', *Journal of International Business Studies*, 22(1): 1–21.

1992. The innovative performance of the world's largest firms: some new evidence, *Economics of Innovation and New Technology*, 2: 91–102.

Paulinyi, A. 1982. Der technologietransfer für die Metallbearbeitung und die preussische Gewerbeförderung 1820–1850, in F. Blaich (ed.), *Die Rolle des Staates für die wirtschaftliche Entwicklung*, Berlin, Blaich.

Perez, C. 1983. Structural change and the assimilation of new technologies in the economic and social system', *Futures*, 15: 357–75.

Piore, M. and Sabel, C. 1984. *The Second Industrial Divide: Possibilities for Prosperity*, New York, Basic Books.

Porter, M. 1990. *The Competitive Advantage of Nations*, New York, Free Press/Macmillan.

Posner, M. 1961. International trade and technical change, *Oxford Economic Papers*, 13: 323–41.

Prais, S. J. 1981. Vocational qualifications of the labour force in Britain and Germany, *National Institute Economic Review*, 98: 47–59.

Romer, P. 1986. Increasing returns and long-run growth, *Journal of Political Economy*, 94: 1002–37.

Rothwell, R. 1992. Successful industrial innovation: critical factors for the 1990s, SPRU 25th Anniversary, University of Sussex, Brighton. Reprinted in *R&D Management*, 22: 221–39.

Sako, M. 1992. *Contracts, Prices and Trust: How the Japanese and British Manage Their Sub-contracting Relationships*, Oxford, Oxford University Press.

Saxenian, A. 1991. The origins and dynamics of production networks in Silicon Valley, *Research Policy*, 20: 423–39.

Scott, A.J. 1991. The aerospace-electronics industrial complex of Southern California. The formative years 1940–1960, *Research Policy*, 20: 439–57.

Stokes, D.E. 1993. Pasteur's Quadrant: a study in policy science ideas, mimeo, Princeton University.

Storper, M. and Harrison, B. 1991. Flexibility, hierarchy and regional development: the changing structure of industrial production systems and their forms of governance in the 1990s, *Research Policy*, 20: 407–23.

Takeuchi, H. and Nonaka, I. 1986. The new product development game, *Harvard Business Review*, January/February: 285–305.

Villaschi, A. F. 1993. The Brazilian national system of innovation: opportunities and constraints for transforming technological dependency, D.Phil. dissertation, University of London.

von Hippel, E. 1976. The dominant role of users in the scientific instrument innovation process, *Research Policy*, 5: 212–39.

   1988. *The Sources of Innovation*, Oxford, Oxford University Press.

von Tunzelmann, N. 1994. Technology in the early nineteenth century, in R.C. Floud, and D.N. McCloskey (eds.), *The Economic History of Great Britain*, 2nd edn, vol. I, chapter 11, Cambridge, Cambridge University Press.

Womack, J., Jones, D. and Roos, D. 1990. *The Machine that Changed the World*, New York, Rawson Associates/Macmillan.

World Bank 1991. *World Development Report*, New York, Oxford University Press.

3 Is national technology policy obsolete in a globalised world? The Japanese response

MARTIN FRANSMAN

Introduction

It is increasingly being argued, particularly in Europe but also in the United States, that national technology policy, designed to give national firms a competitive edge based on superior technology, has become obsolete in a globalised world. The reason, the argument goes, is that in a world where trade, business and finance, and science and technology cross national borders, attempts by national governments and firms to appropriate the fruits of national technology programmes are doomed to fail.

This chapter examines this argument critically with reference to the Japanese response to globalisation in the area of technology policy. Why is the Japanese experience relevant in this context? The reason is that in Japan technology policy has been a central component of industrial policy. But the Japanese economy, like that of the major Western countries, has also become significantly more globalised over the last two decades. This is seen, for example, in indicators such as increased outward and inward direct foreign investment, the increase in foreign R&D laboratories in Japan, the growing number of international strategic technology alliances involving Japanese and Western firms, increased (temporary) outflow and inflow of researchers and engineers, and greater international co-authoring of science and technology research papers.

However, Japanese policy-makers, as will be shown in detail in this chapter, have responded, not by abandoning national technology policy, but by internationalising it while retaining its national objectives. Does this mean that the Japanese are following obsolete policies that are doomed to fail, as the above argument implies, or is there an acceptable justification for current Japanese technology policy? If the latter is true, is the Japanese case special, or is it at least to some extent valid for other, large Western countries? These two questions lie at the heart of the present chapter.

The convergence hypothesis

In a number of important recent articles several authors have put forward the argument that there has been a convergence in the economies of the major industrialised countries in the post-Second World War period (see, for example, Abramovitz, 1986; Baumol, 1986; Baumol *et al.*, 1989; Nelson, 1990; and Nelson and Wright, 1992). According to one strand of this argument, convergence has resulted from the increasing internationalisation of trade, business and technology. In Nelson and Wright's (1992, p.1961) words, 'the convergence model looks more and more plausible. In our view, it is the internationalization of trade, business and generic technology and the growing commonality of the economic environments of firms in different nations that have made it so.'

The convergence hypothesis itself, however, is not the concern of the present chapter. Of interest, rather, is a corollary that has been derived from this hypothesis, namely that convergence also implies that national technology policy has become obsolete.

The corollary: national technology policy has become obsolete

Why has it been argued that national technology policy has become obsolete? According to Nelson and Wright (1992, p.1961), 'national borders mean much less than they used to regarding the flow of technology, at least among the nations that have made the new needed social investments in education and research facilities'. Governments, however, have been slow to comprehend these important changes: 'National governments have been slow to recognize these new facts of life. Indeed, the last decade has seen a sharp increase in what has been called "techno-nationalism", policies launched by governments with the objective of giving their national firms a particular edge in an area of technology'.

'Techno-nationalist' policies, however, are unlikely to succeed in a globalised world:

Our argument is that these policies do not work very well any more. It is increasingly difficult to create new technology that will stay contained within national borders for very long in a world where technological sophistication is widespread and firms of many nationalities are ready to make the investment needed to exploit new generic technology (p.1961).

In other words, while national governments may assist national firms to create new technologies, these firms are unlikely to be able to appropriate the benefits of the technologies through increased competitiveness. The reason is that their counterparts elsewhere in the global economy, having made the necessary investments in training and research and development and therefore having accumulated the required 'social capabilities' (in Abramovitz's (1986) words), will also have access sooner rather than later to these technologies.

The leaks in the Japanese system

Japan is a late globaliser, but a globaliser none the less. As a globaliser Japan confronts the same 'leaks' in its national science and technology system as do the other industrialised countries. Although a greater proportion of advanced research is done in Japan in the corporate sector rather than the public sector (universities, public research institutes, etc.), where it is subject to normal corporate control, there is little evidence that this control has resulted in a significant 'knowledge lead' for Japanese companies. Even in those sectors where Japanese companies have enjoyed an overwhelming international dominance, such as consumer electronics, memory semiconductors and cameras, their competitiveness has been based more on quality and in some cases characteristic advantages than on superior underlying knowledge. The dramatic rise of Korean companies such as Samsung and Gold Star in international markets for memory semiconductors and the resurgence in these same markets of American companies like Motorola and Texas Instruments, bear testimony to the absence of a significant technology lead on the part of the Japanese companies.

These cases of comparative Japanese success, therefore, do not constitute a refutation of the convergence hypothesis, which allows for competitive divergences between firms and nations and even a process of 'falling behind'. To quote Nelson and Wright (1992, p.1961) once more,

While we argue that the principal factor driving convergence over the last quarter of a century has been internationalization, we do not dismiss the possibility that the United States may be in the process of slipping into second, third, or fifth rank in productivity and per capita income, and in terms of mastering the application of several important technologies. Although the forces that now bind together nations with sufficient 'social capabilities' are far stronger than they were in the past, there is certainly room for variance within that group.

International imitation

A major source of leakage from the Japanese system which has contributed to convergence is the competitive process of imitation as other companies, on the basis of the capabilities which they have accumulated, have emulated Japanese success. The case of semiconductors just referred to, and the closely related case of semiconductor process equipment, the production of which has been encouraged by the Sematech programme in the United States, provide striking examples of the imitation process.

Table 3.1. *International strategic technology alliances in semiconductors involving Japanese companies*

Companies	Area
Toshiba–Siemens–IBM	265M DRAM
NEC–AT&T	Semiconductor manufacturing
Fujitsu–AMD	Flash memories
Intel–Sharp	Flash memories
Hitachi–Texas Instruments	DRAM
Mitsubishi Electric–SGS–Thomson	Flash memories

At the same time, however, the case of automobiles provides a more cautionary tale of the difficulties and costs that may arise in the attempt to imitate. The latter case is of particular interest because, despite a good understanding of the reasons for Japanese superiority in productivity and quality in the automobile industry aided by several excellent studies, and despite the possession of similar underlying knowledge, Western competitors have nevertheless found it extremely difficult to close the gap (see, for example, Womack *et al.*, 1990; Clark and Fujimoto, 1991). The reason for the difficulty in the automobile case is that the problem stems not from lack of knowledge on the part of Western companies, but from the difficulty of *implementing* both intra- and inter-firm organisational innovations such as the just-in-time and sub-contracting systems. This case illustrates, therefore, the competitive divergences that may continue to exist between converging firms that have similar 'social capabilities' in Abramovitz's sense.

International strategic technology alliances

A more direct channel for the leakage of knowledge from the Japanese system has been the spate of international strategic technology alliances that have been concluded between Japanese companies and Western competitors. Again, the case of semiconductors provides a useful illustration of the phenomenon, as is shown in table 3.1. This shows some of the recent alliances that have been established between Japanese companies and Western competitors. The main motivation behind these alliances has been the growing R&D costs in developing next generation semiconductor products and processes. These costs are now so high that few companies can afford to pay them alone. Table 3.1 also shows that the general pattern has been for Japanese companies, threatened more by competition from their Japanese rivals than from Western companies, to form alliances with the latter. These alliances, however, imply a further leakage from the Japanese

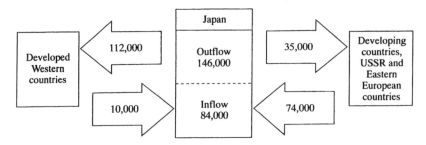

Figure 3.1. Researcher/engineer exchanges between Japan and other countries, 1989. (*Source:* Japan, Ministry of Justice, *Annual Report of Statistics on Legal Migrants for 1989.*)

system as Japanese companies pass on knowledge, acquired from their internal R&D as well as from Japanese government programmes in which they have participated, to their Western partners.

More generally, data from the Japanese Ministry of International Trade and Industry (MITI) show a cumulative total of 135 international research joint ventures involving Japanese companies between the years 1982 and 1987 (Mowery and Teece, 1992, p.125). Of these, thirty-two were in electrical machinery (including computing and telecommunications), twenty-four in chemicals, and ten in transport machinery.

International movement of researchers and engineers

While the leakage of knowledge from Western countries to Japan as Japanese companies have learned from their Western counterparts has been well documented, a reverse flow of knowledge has begun to increase in significance. One channel for this reverse flow is the (usually temporary) migration of foreign engineers and researchers to Japan where they are employed in government and company laboratories and factories. This migration is shown in figure 3.1. Although the flow of engineers and researchers into Japan is increasing, and although this constitutes an increasingly important source of leakage from the Japanese system, figure 3.1 also shows that there is still a significant 'deficit' in Japan's 'trade' in this area. While in 1989 112,000 engineers and researchers departed for Western industrialised countries, 10,000 entered Japan, an out–in ratio of 11. Japan's relationship with developing countries is to some extent the mirror image of this, with 74,000 engineers and researchers entering Japan and 35,000 departing, an out–in ratio of 0.5.

Further details are provided in figure 3.2 on the source and destination

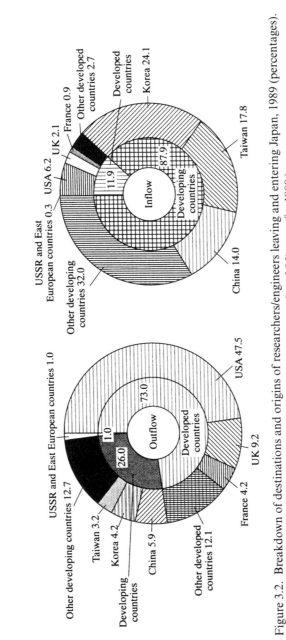

Figure 3.2. Breakdown of destinations and origins of researchers/engineers leaving and entering Japan, 1989 (percentages). (*Source*: Japan, Ministry of Justice, *Annual Report of Statistics on Legal Migrants for 1989*.)

of the engineers and researchers who come to and go from Japan. Of all those who entered Japan, 12% came from the industrialised Western countries, 6.2% coming from the United States, 2.1% from the UK and 0.9% from France. Korea sent the largest proportion of engineers and researchers to Japan, 24% of the total, followed by Taiwan and China, with 18% and 14% respectively.

Direct foreign investment

Increasing direct foreign investment in Japan is also a growing source of leakage from the Japanese system, as foreign companies based in Japan 'tap into' Japanese science and technology. Here too, however, there remains a substantial imbalance, with outflows greatly exceeding inflows. The overall picture is shown in figure 3.3. This reveals that in 1989 direct investment from Japan to the United States totalled $17.3 billion, while that in the opposite direction was $1.2 billion, an out–in ratio of 14. In the same year, direct investment from Japan to the EC was $9.8 billion, while the figure for flows from the EC to Japan was $327 million, an out–in ratio of 33. Between 1985 and 1989, Japanese direct investment to the United States increased 5.1 times while US direct investment to Japan increased 2.5 times. (For comparative purposes it is worth noting that the out–in ratio for direct investment from the EC to the United States in 1989 was 3.)

Foreign research laboratories in Japan

A further source of leakage of knowledge from the Japanese system comes from the activities of the R&D laboratories of foreign companies located in Japan.

How extensive are these laboratories? Data from MITI indicate that in 1990 there were 137 foreign R&D laboratories in Japan (Mowery and Teece, 1992, p.115). Interestingly, the bulk of these laboratories were in areas where Japanese industry is weakest in international comparative terms rather than where it is strongest, namely in chemicals and pharmaceuticals rather than electrical machinery. In chemicals there were fifty-nine laboratories, in pharmaceuticals twenty-five, and in electrical machinery eleven. However, it is unclear from these data how extensive were the research activities undertaken by these laboratories or what kind of development work was being done.

Data from the Japanese Science and Technology Agency (STA), however, suggest that most foreign laboratories in Japan had located in the country primarily to adapt their products to local conditions rather than to

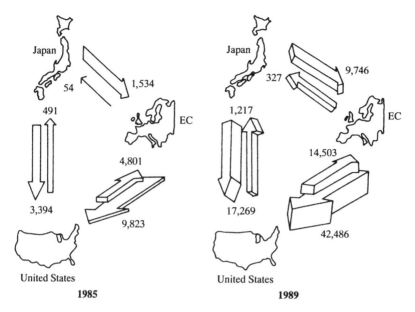

Figure 3.3. Flows of direct investment between Japan, the United States and the EC, 1985 and 1989 (million dollars). The figures for the EC are the sum of ten countries for 1985 and twelve for 1989. (*Sources:* Compiled by the Japan Science and Technology Agency from (i) United States, Department of Commerce, *Survey of Current Business* (USA–Japan and USA–EC), and (ii) Japan, Ministry of Finance, *Monthly Statistics of Finance.*)

'tap' into the Japanese science and technology system. An STA survey concluded that just over 90% of the foreign laboratories located their operations in Japan 'To plan and localize new products meeting host country needs'. Only about 30% located because 'Japan [was] seen as leader in R&D in my field'; just under 30% 'To monitor technological developments and activities [in Japan]'; just under 20% because 'Japan [was] seen as leader in production technology in my field'; and just over 10% because of the 'Existence of outstanding research personnel [in Japan]' (Science and Technology Agency, 1991).

Technology trade

A further direct leakage occurs when Japanese companies sell their technology abroad. This leakage is picked up in figures for technology trade which take account of items such as the sale abroad of patents and other

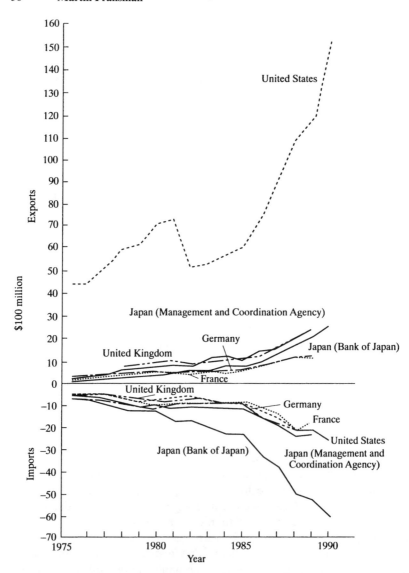

Figure 3.4. Trends in technology trade of selected countries – the status of science and technology in Japan and other nations.

know-how. Figure 3.4 shows that Japan's exports of technology increased significantly between 1975 and 1990, although so have its imports.

Figure 3.4 also shows the ratio of exports to imports of technology for some of the other major industrialised countries. As can be seen, the United

Table 3.2. *Japan's technology trade, 1970–90 (100 million yen)*

Year	Exports (A)	Imports (B)	Ratio A/B
1970	197	1479	0.13
1971	213	1638	0.13
1972	212	1655	0.13
1973	231	1850	0.12
1974	324	2153	0.15
1975	421	2069	0.20
1976	519	2373	0.22
1977	548	2647	0.21
1978	594	2460	0.24
1979	703	2791	0.25
1980	803	3011	0.27
1981	1063	3775	0.28
1982	1392	4369	0.32
1983	1351	4707	0.29
1984	1651	5401	0.31
1985	1724	5631	0.31
1986	1527	5454	0.22
1987	1870	5515	0.34
1988	2098	6429	0.33
1989	2782	7347	0.38
1990	3589	8744	0.41

Note: Figures are values in each calendar year.
Source: Bank of Japan, *Balance of Payments Monthly.*

States is the only country with a surplus in its balance on technology trade, a significant surplus. Japan, on the other hand, remained in deficit throughout this period and the deficit has increased. According to Bank of Japan figures (table 3.2), the Japanese ratio of exports to imports increased from 0.13 in 1970 to 0.41 in 1990.

Further information is provided in figure 3.5 on the ratio of exports to imports of technology by Japanese sector. Here it can be seen that it is only construction and iron and steel that have enjoyed clear surpluses. The three most important sectors, namely electrical machinery, transport equipment and chemicals, have been in deficit over the period from 1975 to 1989, although for all three the deficit narrowed sharply towards the end of the period, and for transport equipment and chemicals had almost disappeared by 1989.

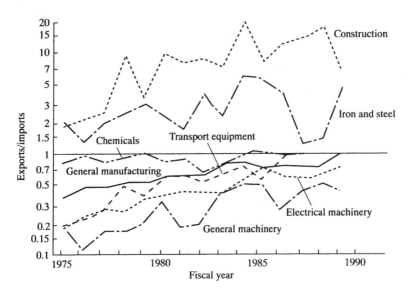

Figure 3.5. Trends in technology trade balance in major industry sectors.
(*Source:* Japan, Management and Coordination Agency, Statistics Bureau, *Report on the Survey of Research and Development.*)

Internationally co-authored papers

Leakages also take place from the Japanese system as Japanese researchers exchange information and knowledge with their counterparts abroad. One indicator of this exchange is internationally co-authored papers. Figure 3.6 provides data on the growing proportion of Japanese papers (included in the Science and Engineering Literature Database) which are internationally co-authored. This shows that the proportion of Japanese papers included in this database which were internationally co-authored increased from around 5% in 1981 to 7.5% in 1986. This latter figure compared with about 10% in the United States. The European countries, smaller and in closer geographical proximity, had higher proportions. In the UK the proportion was 17% while in France and Germany, where there has been a greater internationalisation of the science and technology system, the proportion was 21%.

Conclusion

From the above data it can be seen that although Japan still lags behind in many respects in terms of the globalisation of its science and technology system, the degree of internationalisation has increased significantly over

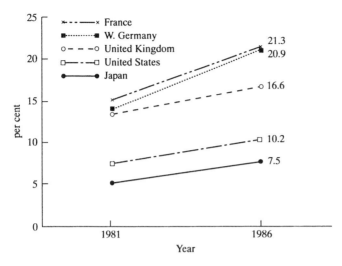

Figure 3.6. Trends in internationally co-authored papers by country. (*Source:* Compiled by the Japan Science and Technology Agency from Computer Horizons Inc., *Science and Engineering Literature Database 1989.*)

the last decade. This implies that the 'self-containedness' of the system has decreased in line with the convergence hypothesis outlined above. Does this mean, however, that the corollary of this hypothesis, that national technology policy has become increasingly obsolete, also applies in the Japanese case? This question will now be examined.

The role of the Japanese government in the science and technology system

Some general considerations

To begin with, it is worth stressing that the Japanese government since the Meiji Restoration of 1868 has *always* taken the position that it has an important necessary role to play in strengthening the science and technology base for Japanese companies. The role that the government has played, however, has changed as Japan has moved through the 'early catch-up', 'late catch-up', and 'frontier-sharing' stages of its economic development. (For a detailed study of this role in the case of computer and semiconductor industries, see Fransman 1993.)

In the current frontier-sharing stage, the Japanese government, specifically the Ministry of International Trade and Industry (MITI), believes that it must continue to play a pro-active role by encouraging the development of those areas of science and technology that are important for the future global competitiveness of Japanese companies. This and the following points regarding MITI's involvement in the science and technology system are based on detailed interviews with senior MITI officials closely involved in the policy-making process in the area of science and technology held from July to December 1992.

Market failure

MITI officials stress that the criterion of 'market failure', which has long been used in the Ministry, is of overriding importance in deciding on where and when to act in the area of science and technology. In other words, where private companies either do or can take care of necessary scientific and technological development, MITI will steer clear of these areas.

MITI identifies two areas where market failure is possible. The first is where there is significant 'risk' and where companies as a result do not undertake sufficient R&D. Several further points must be made here. MITI does not argue that wherever there is significant risk there is insufficient corporate R&D. The Ministry accepts that in some cases where there is substantial risk there may be sufficient or even excessive R&D. One reason for this may be that the expected payoff from R&D is sufficient to compensate the company for the risk that it is taking. Accordingly, MITI will only consider acting where it judges (a) that the degree of risk results in insufficient R&D and (b) that more R&D is necessary to increase the competitiveness of Japanese companies. (It is worth noting that in economists' jargon MITI is actually referring to *uncertainty*. For economists, risk is probabilistically predictable, and therefore insurable, while uncertainty is not.)

The second reason why private companies might fail to develop the needed area of R&D follows from the size of investment that is required. Once again MITI accepts that even extremely large investments might be justified by a private company (or by companies acting in co-operation) without government involvement, as a result of the satisfactory payoff expected, and that in these cases government action may be unnecessary. A case in point may be the international strategic technology alliances in the field of semiconductors, referred to earlier, where governments have not been involved. Clearly, although these two reasons for market failure might be distinct, they may interact. Thus, an expensive area of R&D may also be highly uncertain in terms of payback. On the other hand, there may be little uncertainty, but the investment required may still be too large for private companies to contemplate in the light of the expected payoff.

Basic research

A further priority has become important since the mid- to late-1980s for MITI and the other organs of the Japanese government involved in science and technology, such as the Science and Technology Agency and the Ministry of Education, Science and Culture. This is the area of basic research, which the Japanese government believes it must play an increasingly important role in fostering. Although the government acknowledges that Japan has managed to perform extremely well globally in a number of industries without a particularly strong basic research base in Japan, and although in this sense the linear model of technology development which emphasises the sequential movement from basic through applied research to development and commercialisation is rejected, it nevertheless feels that it is increasingly important for Japan to strengthen its capabilities in basic research.

Why is basic research being given high priority in Japan? This question poses something of a puzzle since, as just mentioned, the Japanese authorities acknowledge that they have done extremely well so far with little basic research. Furthermore, although basic research is not a global free good and there can be substantial costs involved in exploiting basic research, it remains true that basic research is more 'open' and therefore less appropriable than more applied research. Why, then, have the Japanese attached increasing priority to basic research?

There are several answers to this question. The first is that, having gradually moved 'upstream' from efficient production and commercialisation through development to applied research, the link to basic research is the last one to make. While many Western companies, as documented in numerous case-studies, have failed to commercialise adequately the fruits of their significant basic research, the Japanese hope that with the 'downstream' portion of the value chain working effectively, a productive interface can now be forged with basic research. It is this hope that lies behind the establishment of basic research laboratories such as Hitachi's Advanced Research Laboratory and NEC's Princeton, New Jersey, and Tsukuba laboratories. Companies like NEC nevertheless emphasise that their 'basic' research is in effect 'oriented basic research'. The orientation of the research is partly determined by its ultimate commercial objectives, and partly by its corporate context which emphasises the 'downstream' part of the value chain.

While many large Japanese companies have felt the expected return from oriented basic research to be sufficiently attractive to allocate a portion of their R&D funds to this research without government involvement, both companies and government in Japan are in agreement that the latter has an important role to play in encouraging this kind of research. To begin with, it is felt that although, generally speaking, Japanese universities have not been as good as many of their Western counterparts in *frontier* research, these universities have nevertheless been a far more important source of external knowledge for Japanese companies than is usually acknowledged in academic analysis and policy-oriented discussion of Japan. The reason, simply, is that in most cases companies are not interested in frontier research but rather in more pragmatically oriented research which is more easily and rapidly commercialisable. This kind of research tends to be *intra-frontier* research and, furthermore, many Japanese universities are good at this kind of research. Supporting this view, a study based on publication citation has concluded that the scientific research of Japanese companies 'draws most heavily on Japanese, not foreign sources', universities being the most important Japanese source (Hicks *et al.*, 1992, p.1).

One role for government, therefore, is to help upgrade both the quantity and quality of basic research undertaken in Japanese universities and also government and semi-government research institutes. Not only do Japanese companies plug in directly to research in Japanese universities, they also recruit their researchers and developers from these universities. Strengthening basic research in the universities will therefore help companies in at least two ways. (While the Japanese Management and Coordination Agency estimates that about 6.4 per cent of the R&D of Japanese companies is basic research, the figure for national research institutions is 27.1 per cent, and that for universities and colleges 53.2 per cent (Science and Technology Agency, 1991, p.126). 'Basic research' was defined as 'research undertaken primarily for the advancement of scientific knowledge, where a specific practical application may be indirectly sought' (p.124).)

A second reason for the high priority now being given to basic research is that, having reached the international frontier in many areas of research, many Japanese companies no longer have the option of following their Western counterparts as they did before. They therefore have no choice but to play a greater role in charting the future scientific and technological directions that they will follow through basic or oriented basic research.

Thirdly, Japan's government, and to a lesser extent companies, now acknowledge that they are under an increasing international obligation to make a significantly larger contribution to the global stock of knowledge from which in the past they have so usefully drawn. This consideration has been an important force further motivating the prioritising of basic research. However, in the absence of the first and second reasons for the greater emphasis on basic research, it is unlikely that the third reason alone would have resulted in as great a commitment in Japan to basic research.

The Japanese government's contribution to science and technology expenditure

The Japanese government's share of total R&D expenditure is far lower than that of the other large Western countries, as is shown in figure 3.7. The

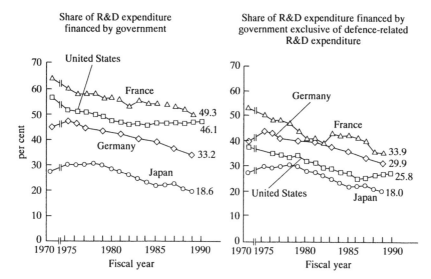

Figure 3.7. Trends in government-financed share of R&D expenditures in selected countries.

Notes:

[a] For comparison, statistics for all countries include research in social sciences and humanities.

[b] Government percentages exclusive of defence-related research expenditures are calculated by the following equation.

$$\frac{(\text{Government-financed R\&D expenditures}) - (\text{Defence-related R\&D expenditures})}{(\text{R\&D expenditures}) - (\text{Defence-related R\&D expenditures})} \times 100 (\%)$$

[c] The 1989 data for the USA are provisional and the 1990 data are an estimate.
[d] The defence-related R&D expenditures for Germany in 1989 are provisional.
[e] Germany: the years for which data are not available are indicated on a straight line.
[f] The 1989 and 1990 data for France are provisional.
Source: Science and Technology Agency (1991), p.115.

contribution of the government is 18.6% compared to 33.2% for Germany, 46.1% for the United States, and 49.3% for France. If defence-related R&D expenditures are excluded, the Japanese figure becomes 18.0% compared to 25.8% for the USA, 29.9% for Germany, and 33.9% for France. It should be noted, however, that although these figures are frequently quoted, it is the declared intention of the Japanese government to increase its share of national R&D expenditure to a proportion more commensurate with that of these other Western countries. It is not yet clear how long it will take to achieve this, because of the other priorities that are taking precedence in the current fiscal attempts to stimulate the recession-bound Japanese economy.

While Japanese companies undertake a slightly smaller proportion of total R&D than companies in the United States and Germany, as will shortly be shown, they receive a significantly smaller proportion of their R&D expenditures from their government than do companies in the USA, Germany, France and the UK. This is seen in table 3.3 which shows the flow of R&D funding between government, industry and universities.

A number of points emerge from this table. First, in Japan industry receives only 1.2% of its R&D expenditure from government. This compares with 33.0% in the United States, 22.4% in France, 16.5% in the UK, and 11.5% in Germany. The reason for the high US figure is the large amount of defence R&D undertaken by industry, but funded by government. In the largest Japanese industrial electronics companies approximately 5% of total R&D is funded by the Japanese government (see Fransman, 1993).

Second, 2.2% of the research undertaken in Japanese universities is funded from industry. This compares with 7.5% in Germany, 5.9% in the UK, and 5.5% in the USA. The fact that the Japanese government finances a smaller proportion of total R&D than its Western counterparts, however, does not mean that a greater proportion of R&D in Japan is undertaken in industry compared to Western countries. Figure 3.8 shows that while 69.7% of total R&D is performed by industry in Japan, the corresponding figure for Germany is 73.5%, for the USA 72.1%, for the UK 66.4%, and for France 59.5%. However, table 3.3 shows that Japanese industry finances a substantially greater proportion of the R&D that it undertakes compared to the large Western countries. This implies that a far greater proportion of the R&D of Japanese industry is targeted at the objectives of industry, rather than the objectives of non-industrial funders of R&D, notably, in the case of the USA, France and the UK, government funders of defence-related R&D. While in Japan 98.6% of R&D undertaken is financed by industry, in the USA the figure is 67.0%, in the UK 71.4%, in France 73.0%, and in Germany 86.8%.

The role of MITI in the Japanese science and technology system

MITI's share of total expenditure on science and technology by the Japanese government

While the Ministry of International Trade and Industry is usually held up as the major government influence on science and technology in Japan, the

Table 3.3. *Flows of R&D funds between industry, universities and colleges and government in selected countries*

Financing sector	Performing sector	Japan (1989) Amount (100m yen)	Japan (1989) Share %	United States (1990) Amount (100m yen)	United States (1990) Share %	Germany (1989) Amount (100m yen)	Germany (1989) Share %	France (1983) Amount (100m yen)	France (1983) Share %	UK (1988) Amount (100m yen)	UK (1988) Share %
Government→	Government	8,837	92.6	33,400	100.0	6,590	92.7	7,227	95.6	4,278	84.2
	Government	707	7.4	0	0.0	393	5.5	52	0.7	472	9.3
	Industry	1,028	1.2	71,300	33.0	4,526	11.5	3,646	22.4	3,888	16.5
Industry→	Industry	81,161	98.6	145,000	67.0	34,771	86.8	11,867	73.0	16,799	71.4
	Universities and colleges	10,921	51.3	28,860	68.6	7,115	92.5	4,424	97.6	4,222	77.9
	Universities and colleges	458	2.2	2,300	5.5	575	7.5	58	1.3	322	5.9

Notes:

[a] For comparison, statistics for all countries include research in social sciences and humanities.

[b] Percentages show the share of the R&D expenditure of financing by sector against the total R&D expenditure of performance by sector.

[c] The amounts are converted based on OECD purchase power parity.

[d] The US data are estimated.

Source: Science and Technology Agency (1991).

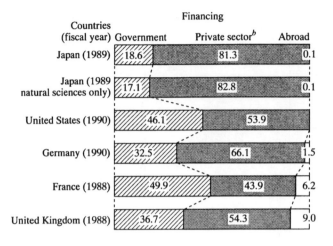

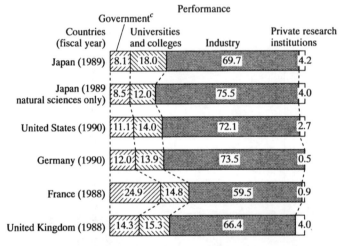

Figure 3.8 Shares of R&D expenditures in financing and performance sectors in selected countries.

Notes:

[a] For comparison, statistics for all countries include research in social sciences and humanities. The figures for Japan show also the amount for natural sciences only.

[b] In the financing column, the private sector includes any sector other than the government and abroad.

[c] Government in the performance column means government research institutions as defined by the OECD.

Source: Science and Technology Agency (1991), p.114.

Table 3.4. *Japan's science and technology budget breakdown by ministries and agencies (million yen)*[a]

Ministry or agency	Fiscal year	
	1990[c]	1991[c]
Diet	533	533
Science Council of Japan	951	1,051
National Police Agency	1,055	1,143
Hokkaido Development Agency	149	148
Defence Agency	104,268	115,045
Economic Planning Agency	809	850
Science and Technology Agency[d]	494,775	522,561
Environment Agency	9,217	10,900
Ministry of Justice	939	1,006
Ministry of Foreign Affairs	7,095	8,160
Ministry of Finance[d]	1,087	1,193
Ministry of Education[d]	894,301	936,324
Ministry of Health and Welfare	51,242	56,144
Ministry of Agriculture, Forestry and Fisheries[d]	70,108	73,557
Ministry of International Trade and Industry[d]	251,548	255,913
Ministry of Transport[d]	17,402	20,514
Ministry of Posts and Telecommunications[d]	30,657	33,904
Ministry of Labour[d]	4,190	5,046
Ministry of Construction	5,979	6,624
Ministry of Home Affairs	565	616
Total[b]	1,920,871	2,022,631

Notes:
[a] All amounts represent initial budgets or appropriations for the respective fiscal year.
[b] Since amounts have been rounded off, the sum of the amounts for each column, and the totals shown above do not necessarily agree.
[c] Some amounts include appropriations for humanities.
[d] Includes the Science and Technology Budget appropriations from Special Accounts.

Ministry accounts only for a relatively small proportion of expenditure on science and technology by the Japanese government. This is shown in table 3.4 which shows that in 1991 the Ministry of Education was the largest spender on science and technology, accounting for almost half of total government expenditure in this area. The Science and Technology Agency came

Table 3.5. *MITI's industrial technology R&D expenditures, 1987*

	Expenditure (100m yen)	Percentage of total R&D
Energy R&D	1145.7	52
Non-energy R&D of which:	1068.4	48
Large Scale (A)	(139.3) ⎫	
Future Tech. (A)	(60.4) ⎪	(23)
Key Tech. Centre (A)	(250.0) ⎬	
Information Tech. (M)	(57.9) ⎭	
MITI's total R&D	2214.1	100

Key: (A) = AIST/NEDO; (M) = Machinery and Information Industries Bureau.
Source: Watanabe (1992).

next with just under half of the Ministry of Education's budget. MITI came third with just under half of the Science and Technology Agency's budget. Fourth came the Defence Agency with just under half of MITI's budget.

These figures raise a puzzle: how can MITI be as influential in Japanese science and technology as is usually claimed by analysts if it only accounts for a relatively small proportion of the expenditure by the Japanese government in this area? This puzzle will be examined in more detail later.

MITI's expenditure on science and technology

A breakdown of MITI's expenditure on science and technology is given in table 3.5. A number of important points emerge from this table. The first is that energy R&D accounts for 52 per cent of MITI's science and technology expenditure. This means that non-energy industrial R&D – which includes the so-called hi-tech industries such as computers, semiconductors, biotechnology and new materials, which MITI has been credited with (and sometimes blamed for) fostering – accounts for only 48 per cent of MITI's science and technology budget.

Second, MITI-initiated co-operative R&D programmes involving the co-operation of competing Japanese companies, which many in the West have seen as the most important way in which MITI has fostered the generation and diffusion of new advanced technologies, account for a relatively small proportion of MITI's total science and technology budget.

Most of MITI's funding for non-energy 'high-technology' co-operative R&D projects comes from four programmes. The first of these is the Large-

Scale R&D Programme which began in 1966 and which is now under the control of MITI's Agency of Industrial Science and Technology (AIST) and MITI's New Energy and Industrial Technology Development Organisation (NEDO). The second programme is the R&D Programme on Basic Technologies for Future Industries. This programme began in 1981 and is also under the control of AIST and NEDO.

The third programme is that undertaken by the Japan Key Technology Centre (Kiban Gijutsu Kenkyu Sokushin Senta). This centre was established in October 1985 at the time that NTT, the largest domestic telecommunications carrier, was privatised. In fact the Key Technology Centre represented part of the politically negotiated compromise which emerged from the fierce battles between the Ministry of Posts and Telecommunications (MPT) and MITI in the early 1980s over regulatory control of the converging areas of computers and communications.

The Key Technology Centre is funded largely from dividends from government-owned shares in NTT and Japan Tobacco Inc. This brings the important advantage of funding for research which is relatively independent of the financial strictures of the Ministry of Finance. Although formally under the joint control of MITI and MPT, there is a *de facto* split down the middle of the Centre, with the two ministries each taking sole charge of the areas under their own jurisdiction. Typically, research projects are set up for a fixed period of time with research participation from companies, universities and government. Usually 70 per cent of the funding comes from the Centre with the remaining 30 per cent provided by the companies. Intellectual property rights usually remain with the participants in the project. In MITI the Key Technology Centre falls under the responsibility of AIST and NEDO. (For analysis of the Protein Engineering Research Institute, a biotechnology project funded by MITI's part of the Key Technology Centre, see Fransman and Tanaka, 1995.)

The fourth programme in MITI that funds co-operative R&D is that run by the Ministry's Machinery and Information Industries Bureau. Projects funded by this bureau in the area of information technology include the Fifth Generation Computer Project and, currently, the Real World Computing Project.

From table 3.5 it can be seen that these four programmes, which together represent most of MITI's non-energy co-operative R&D funding, account for only about 23 per cent of this Ministry's total spending on R&D. Assuming that the proportions remained the same in 1991, this would mean that these four programmes, which many have seen as having an important impact on the international competitiveness of Japanese companies, accounted for a mere 2.9 per cent of the total spending of the Japanese government on science and technology.

MITI's response to globalisation

MITI's response to the globalisation of the Japanese science and technology system can be characterised in three ways. First, MITI has retained its use of co-operative R&D projects as an important policy tool aimed at strengthening the international competitiveness of Japanese companies. This national objective is reflected in MITI's use of the term 'national R&D programmes'. (It should be noted, however, that MITI's international competitiveness objective is to some extent counter-balanced by another important MITI objective, namely achieving harmonious international trade relations.)

Second, MITI has acknowledged the importance of globalisation, not by attempting to insulate its national R&D programmes from global influence, but by internationalising them. This has been done by not simply allowing foreign companies to join 'national' R&D programmes, but by positively encouraging them to do so. This was facilitated by a new law which MITI drafted in 1988, the 'Law For Consolidating Research & Development Systems Relating to Industrial Technology'. This law had two major aims: to internationalise Japan's industrial technology, and to increase Japanese competencies in the areas of basic and scientific R&D. At the same time NEDO, established in 1980, was reorganised and an industrial technology department was set up within NEDO in order to help achieve these two aims. From 1989 foreign companies were allowed to join national R&D programmes.

It is important to emphasise, however, that while foreign companies were both allowed and encouraged to join MITI's national R&D programmes from 1989, these programmes continue to be set with national objectives in mind. The objectives include strengthening the competitiveness of *Japanese* companies and increasing basic and scientific research capabilities in Japan. In other words, while foreign companies are encouraged to join these programmes, they are not allowed to influence the choice of programme in the first place nor the objectives of the programme. In this way it may accurately be said that MITI has internationalised its national R&D programmes.

The third strand in MITI's response to globalisation has been to establish *purely internationalised* co-operative R&D programmes. While the original broad area of research has been chosen by MITI through its consultation procedures, these programmes have been opened to international negotiation in order to establish precise objectives and *modi operandi*. Examples of these internationalised programmes include the Human Frontier Science Programme, the Space Station Programme and the Intelligent Manufacturing System Programme.

In general it is true to say that MITI's approach to its internationalised co-operative R&D programmes is still evolving. A significant amount of suspicion on the part of Western policy-makers greeted MITI's launching of both its Human Frontier and its Intelligent Manufacturing System programmes. Many originally argued that these programmes represented attempts by MITI to strengthen further the competitiveness of Japanese companies by tapping more effectively into advanced Western research. The result was that strong pressure was put on MITI, on the whole rather successfully, to give a greater role to Western policy-makers in shaping both the objectives and the *modi operandi* of these programmes.

As MITI acceded to these pressures and opened the programmes to international consultation, so much of the suspicion changed into somewhat greater enthusiasm for the programmes and optimism regarding the benefits that will be received by all the participating countries. The main lesson that MITI has probably derived from its experience in launching these programmes is that it will have to begin consulting with Western policy-makers at a far earlier stage in the programme definition process but that significant progress in co-operative international research can be achieved with this international consultative process in place.

To summarise, MITI has responded to the globalisation of science and technology by retaining its objectives of strengthening both the competitiveness of Japanese companies and Japanese competencies in basic research and science; by internationalising its national co-operative R&D programmes through allowing and encouraging the participation of foreign companies; and by taking the initiative in establishing fully internationalised co-operative research programmes whose objectives and *modi operandi* are negotiated with the other participating countries.

MITI's national objectives and the globalisation of the Japanese science and technology system

From the above it is clear that MITI is attempting to internationalise its national R&D programmes while retaining their national objectives, and to establish purely internationalised programmes partly with the aim of furthering national objectives. But this contradicts the corollary of the convergence hypothesis discussed above. To quote Nelson and Wright (1992, p.1961) once more:

policies launched by governments with the objective of giving their national firms a particular edge in an area of technology . . . do not work very well any more. It is increasingly difficult to create new technology that will stay contained within national borders for very long in a world where technological sophistication is widespread and firms of many nationalities are ready to make the investment needed to exploit new generic technology.

So is MITI attempting to do the impossible? The present author's reply is that MITI's nationally oriented policies in a globalising world not only are consistent but are sensible. This is so for the following reasons.

The corollary of the convergence hypothesis *assumes* that 'new technology will not stay contained within national borders for very long' and then *deduces* from this that 'policies launched by governments with the objective of giving their national firms a particular edge in an area of technology . . . do not work very well any more'. The problem with this argument, as is suggested by MITI's current policies, is that while the assumption of the corollary may be true, this deduction does not necessarily follow.

More specifically, MITI's policies suggest that it is possible to formulate and implement programmes that give Japanese companies a competitive edge in particular technologies, even though some of the new generic technologies created under the programme 'leak' to non-Japanese competing countries. How can this be? Are there reasons for believing that MITI's policies are appropriate, or are they simply misguided?

The following are the reasons for believing that MITI's policies are indeed appropriate. First, not all the technology acquired by the participants in the national R&D project will leak to non-participating competing companies, even those that have the necessary 'social capabilities'. The reason is that technology created under these projects is not a public good which is freely available. A good deal of this technology will remain tacit and untransferable. Accordingly, a significant amount of the technology will remain with the participants who have undertaken the research and development. Polanyi (1967) defined tacit knowledge as existing when someone knows more than they can tell. In the case of the national R&D projects under discussion here – such as those referred to below – while the *results* of the projects are usually publicised at internationally open conferences, the *ways in which these results are obtained* are usually not disclosed in detail. (Typically, there is a significant degree of tacitness, in Polanyi's sense, regarding these ways.)

MITI's national R&D projects are all oriented to the research and development of practical implementable technological systems, rather than to the production of pure ideas or theories. They therefore have a high degree of tacitness. To substantiate this important point, further details are provided in *The Market and Beyond* (Fransman, 1993) of several of MITI's national R&D projects which illustrate the substantial degree of tacitness involved in these projects. The projects analysed include the High-Speed Computing System for Scientific and Technological Uses, the Optical Measurement and Control System and the Pattern Information Processing System, which are part of MITI's national Large-Scale R&D Programme; and the Superlattice Devices, and Three-Dimensional ICs projects that are part of MITI's R&D Programme on Basic Technologies for Future Industries. Three other projects under the latter programme in the area of biotechnology, the Bioreactor, Large-Scale Cell Cultivation, and the Utilisation of Recombinant DNA projects are analysed in detail in Fransman and Tanaka (1995).

An additional point regarding the implications of tacitness was made in *The Market and Beyond* to explain why the *dominant* Japanese companies in a particular technology area were willing to send some of their researchers to a MITI-initiated co-operative R&D project even though this would mean the leakage of some of their knowledge to weaker Japanese companies. The willingness of the dominant companies, it was shown, was partly attributable to the existence of a significant degree of tacitness *within* the co-operative R&D project. The fact that the dominant companies generally assigned a greater number of researchers to the project in the areas where they were dominant ensured, given the tacitness that existed, that they were able to derive a greater degree of benefit from the project than the weaker companies.

The implication of this point for MITI's national projects where non-Japanese companies participate is that the participation of these companies does not imply that they receive as much knowledge from the project as the Japanese companies (taken collectively and in some cases individually). Accordingly, while there may be some leakage abroad from the national R&D project, the amount of knowledge which actually leaks is significantly constrained by the tacitness involved.

The second reason for the appropriateness of MITI's policies is that even if *all* the knowledge created in national R&D projects and internationalised projects were to leak, that is *even if there were no tacitness*, it would still take *time* for the knowledge to leak. This implies that the creator of the knowledge would enjoy a *lead* in that knowledge for as long as it takes the knowledge to diffuse to competitors with the necessary social capabilities to acquire that knowledge. Furthermore, in a world where 'underlying' core knowledge is widely diffused and where social capabilities are evenly distributed amongst competitors, competitiveness may be driven primarily by the lead that a company has, even if the lead is short-lived. For example, even a short lead of a few months in processing power and price for a PC producer such as Compaq or Dell may mean a great deal in terms of competitiveness. This implies that to the extent that MITI's national R&D projects are able to provide Japanese companies with even a short-term lead, they may be able to help achieve the national objective of increasing the competitiveness of these companies.

Third, as is widely acknowledged, the competitiveness of Japanese firms is often determined by relatively strong competencies in the *downstream* parts of the value chain. In some cases it may be possible for Japanese firms to increase their competitiveness by linking the upstream technology that is derived from their participation in a national R&D project (e.g. technology which is the outcome of oriented-basic and applied research) with their existing downstream competencies. Accordingly, in those cases, where Japanese firms are able to acquire new technologies through national R&D projects, *even where there is no tacitness or lag in the diffusion of these upstream technologies to competitors* (a highly unrealistic assumption), they may still derive from these projects a competitive advantage over their competitors with weaker downstream competencies.

Fourth, although there may be leakages of technology from the national R&D project, these may be adequately compensated for by inflows of technology (leakages to Japan from other national science and technology systems) that occur as a result of the activities of the project. For example, the participation of foreign companies in a Japanese national R&D project may constitute a leakage, but this leakage may none the less be compensated for by the knowledge that the foreign companies bring into the project. Furthermore, the goodwill that both the project and possibly the Japanese system more generally may earn from opening to foreign participation may result in compensating inflows elsewhere in the system.

Fifth, Nelson and Wright (1992, p.1961) refer to 'policies launched by governments with the objective of giving their national firms a particular [competitive] edge in an area of technology'. However, the criterion that should be used in deciding whether technology policies with national objectives are viable or not is less demanding. The appropriate criterion is not whether participating national firms derive a competitive edge, *but whether they are better off with the project than without it and whether this benefit exceeds the cost of the project.* Under this criterion, some national R&D projects may be viable under internationalised conditions even if they do not give participating national companies a competitive edge.

The area of protein engineering, one of the core generic technologies in biotechnology, provides an example. In a report on biotechnology in Japan published in 1985 by the US-sponsored Japanese Technology Evaluation Programme it was concluded that 'Japan currently ranks fourth to the United States, United Kingdom and Western Europe in protein engineering. There is not much activity at the present time [in Japan] at either the universities or industries.' To remedy this situation, MITI established the Protein Engineering Research Institute (PERI) in April 1986 under the auspices of the Japan Key Technology Centre. Companies and universities sent researchers to PERI where generic protein engineering technologies were generated in areas such as protein structural analysis and computer graphics. The commercialisation of these technologies was undertaken outside the project in the individual participating companies under normal conditions of commercial secrecy. Many of the major Japanese companies in the biotechnology field and in related fields joined. In addition, two foreign companies joined, Nihon Roche, the Japanese subsidiary of the large Swiss pharmaceutical company, and Digital Equipment. (This was one of the earliest examples of foreign companies joining a Japanese national R&D project.)

By 1989 there was strong evidence that the research at PERI was of international frontier standards (for details, see Fransman and Tanaka, 1995). From the Japanese national point of view it seems clear that this project was viable (and in Japan it is acknowledged as being one of the most successful undertaken by the Key Technology Centre). This is so even though it is unlikely that the Japanese companies participating were able to derive a 'competitive edge' from the project in terms of better protein engineering technology than their Western competitors.

For these five reasons it may be concluded that MITI's co-operative R&D projects oriented to national objectives are viable in the internationalised world of the 1980s and 1990s. But if this argument is true for Japan, does it also hold for other large Western countries?

What are the implications of the Japanese case for other large Western countries?

With the exception of the fourth argument in the last section (which is based on the assumption of the comparative strength of Japanese companies in the downstream parts of the value chain), all the arguments given apply also to large Western countries. Let us take, for example, the fifth argument, that the benefits of the project may exceed its costs and make the national participating companies better off than they would have been. The case of protein engineering that was given in support of this argument may indeed be paralleled by the US case of Sematech. The Sematech project was ultimately oriented largely to the development of semiconductor equipment competencies at a time when Japanese companies such as Nikon had begun to establish an international competitiveness in this field. Current reports indicate that the Sematech co-operative R&D project has succeeded insofar as it has allowed many US semiconductor manufacturers to buy competitive US-produced semiconductor equipment where before the project Japanese equipment was likely to have been the only viable alternative.

Since four of the five arguments may also apply to large Western countries then, to the extent that these arguments are valid, it must be concluded that R&D projects oriented to the achievement of national objectives may be viable in an internationalised world. It is important, however, to note the assumptions on which these arguments are based, such as the assumption of tacitness, since these assumptions constrain the instances when such nationally oriented projects will be viable. It is certainly not being argued in the present chapter that there is necessarily very wide scope for nationally oriented R&D projects.

The MITI paradox

While the Ministry of Education controlled 46 per cent of the Japanese government's science and technology budget in 1991, and the Science and Technology Agency 26 per cent, MITI's proportion was only 13 per cent. How then can MITI be the most powerful ministry in the technology area as many argue? The author's answer to this intriguing question is that MITI is indeed the most powerful ministry in this area but that its power and influence come, not from its budget, but from two critical related sources: the companies which fall under its jurisdiction, and the highly effective global information network that it controls. These two sources require some elaboration.

Although MITI is not responsible for the whole of the manufacturing sector, the most dynamic parts of this sector fall under the ministry's jurisdiction. More specifically, the transportation, electronics (which includes semiconductors, computers and telecommunications) and chemical sectors, which account for the bulk of Japan's manufacturing value added and exports, are under MITI's jurisdiction, as are other less important or dynamic sectors such as textiles.

Until the late 1960s, MITI's direct control over foreign exchange allocations meant that manufacturing companies wanting to import needed inputs, including technology, had to get permission from this ministry. Furthermore, MITI also had a significant degree of control over capital allocations through its influence over the loans extended by the Japan Development Bank, which in turn influenced the extension of credit by the city banks. By selecting particular industries for promotion, MITI had an important impact on the fortunes of the companies included in those industries. In addition, MITI's laboratories and co-operative R&D projects provided an important boost to companies that were only just beginning to catch up with their Western counterparts. In this way MITI was able to wield a significant degree of influence over its companies in the manufacturing sector.

Two decades later, MITI's influence had changed substantially. Japanese companies – far larger, with much stronger technological capabilities, with access to international capital markets and often with high credit ratings –

needed MITI far less than they had previously. Having lost many of its direct controls, including control over foreign exchange allocations, MITI came to rely on 'administrative guidance' in order to pursue its industrial, technology and trade policies.

Japanese companies, however, continued to rely on MITI to do those things which they could not do adequately for themselves. These included the following. First, in the area of science and technology, MITI began increasingly to look to the longer-term future as Japanese companies successfully closed the technology gap with their foreign competitors. Japanese companies, while possibly 'longer-term oriented' than many of their Western counterparts, were nevertheless still significantly constrained by their need to generate profits and by the factors which bounded their corporate visions. These constraints meant that they were frequently unwilling to venture into new technology areas where future returns were highly uncertain. Understanding these constraints, MITI, as was shown earlier in this chapter, began increasingly to emphasise its role in helping to generate, and later diffuse, new technologies which were not receiving the attention that they possibly deserved from Japanese companies. In this way MITI has been able to ensure its continued relevance in the area of technology for many Japanese companies.

Secondly, with the growing importance of international trade conflict, MITI has come to play an indispensable role in mediating Japan's international economic relations with its trading partners. This is an area where by definition Japanese companies, driven by profit and market considerations, are unable individually or collectively to resolve the problems that arise. In the field of international trade, therefore, MITI's role has been crucial.

Thirdly, MITI has also in the last few decades come to play an important role in the fields of energy and environment. In the case of energy, the oil shocks of the 1970s revealed dramatically how important energy was to the Japanese economy. Once again, MITI, with its watchguard brief for the whole of the manufacturing sector, stepped in to develop a set of energy-related policies. The legacy of MITI's role in the field of energy is evident in the fact, referred to earlier, that over half of its expenditure in R&D currently relates to energy. In the area of the environment it is also acknowledged that for-profit companies are unable to deliver the activities that are necessary for the environmental protection and enhancement that is needed. Here too MITI has come to play an important role.

For these reasons, although MITI's power over Japanese companies has undoubtedly diminished, the ministry continues to play an indispensable role. This has ensured that MITI continues to have political 'clout', including the science and technology area where its influence far exceeds its share of the Japanese government's budget. However, MITI's influence comes not only from the important role that it continues to play in Japanese industry and trade, but also from the substantial global information network that it controls. The 'nodes' in this network extend out from MITI to include the formal and informal advisory and consultative committees that the ministry has established; the industry associations that have been formed, often under MITI's guidance, in the sectors over which MITI has jurisdiction which, as noted, are the most dynamic in the Japanese economy; the links that MITI has forged with other ministries and agencies, often through the secondment of MITI staff; and the activities of the Japan External Trade Recovery Organisation which provides detailed information on industry, technology and markets abroad.

MITI's global information network has given the ministry unparalleled high-quality information regarding both Japan and the rest of the global economy. This information, crossing countries, technologies, companies, industrial sectors and markets, has given MITI's decision-makers an enormously broad 'vision' on the basis of which to identify the strengths, weaknesses and opportunities facing the Japanese manufacturing sector. While this information network has not necessarily been particularly expensive to run, it has put MITI's bureaucrats in a strong position to identify what needs to be done and how (although MITI officials do not always 'get it right' – see Fransman, 1995b).

Conclusions

This chapter has been primarily concerned with two closely related issues. The first is the question of whether national technology policy, oriented to increasing the strength of national companies, is now obsolete in a world of global business, trade, and science and technology. The second issue has been the role of the Japanese government, and in particular its Ministry of International Trade and Industry, in the area of trade and technology.

Regarding the first issue, this chapter has shown that MITI has responded to the fact of the globalisation of the Japanese science and technology system (a globalisation that has been documented in detail) in two ways. The first has been by internationalising its national co-operative R&D programmes while retaining their national objectives, while the second has involved establishing new fully internationalised programmes that are also oriented towards national objectives. It has been shown, furthermore, that although there are over time significant leakages of knowledge from the Japanese science and technology system, MITI's policies aimed at strengthening Japanese companies through these programmes are none the less appropriate. Furthermore, it has been argued that most of the reasoning justifying MITI's policies is also relevant for large Western countries.

With regard to the role of the Japanese government in science and technology it has been shown that, although its proportion of total national R&D expenditure is significantly smaller than in similar Western countries, the government continues to play a crucial role in strengthening the science and technology base for Japanese companies which are the main 'engine' of the Japanese economy. The chapter has also dealt with the 'MITI paradox' which asks how MITI can have as much influence in the field of Japanese science and technology as is alleged if it only controls 13 per cent of the Japanese government's budget in this area. This paradox was resolved with reference to MITI's continuing important role *vis-à-vis* companies in the most dynamic sectors of the Japanese economy and its role as controller of a vast information network that criss-crosses not only Japan but also the other major economies of the world.

References

Abramovitz, M. 1986. Catching up, forging ahead, and falling behind, *Journal of Economic History*, 46: 386–406.

Baumol, W.J. 1986. Productivity growth, convergence, and welfare: what the long-run data show, *American Economic Review*, 76: 1072–85.

Baumol, W.J., Blackman, S.A.B. and Wolff, E.N. 1989. *Productivity and American Leadership*, Cambridge, Mass., MIT Press.

Clark, K.B. and Fujimoto, T. 1991. *Product Development Performance: Strategy, Organization and Management in the World Auto Industry*, Boston, Harvard Business School Press.

Fransman, M.J. 1993. *The Market and Beyond. Information Technology in Japan*, Cambridge, Cambridge University Press.

  1995a. *Japan's Resurgent Computer and Communications Industry: The Evolution of Industrial Giants and Global Competitiveness*, Oxford, Oxford University Press.

  1995b. *Visions of the Firm and Japan*, Oxford, Oxford University Press.

Fransman, M.J. and Tanaka, S. 1995. The strengths and weaknesses of the Japanese innovation system in biotechnology, in M.J. Fransman, G. Junne, and A. Roobeek (eds.), *The Biotechnology Revolution?*, Oxford, Blackwell.

Hicks, D., Ishizuka, T., Keen, P. and Sweet, S. 1992. Japanese corporations, scientific research and globalisation, DRC Discussion Paper no. 91. Science Policy Research Unit, University of Sussex, Brighton.

Mowery, D.C. and Teece, D.J. 1992. The changing place of Japan in the global scientific and technological enterprise, in T.S. Arrison *et al.* (eds.), *Japan's Growing Technological Capability: Implications for the US Economy*. Washington, D.C., National Academy Press.

Nelson, R.R. 1990. The US technology lead: where did it come from and where did it go?, *Research Policy*, 19: 117–32.

Nelson, R.R. and Wright, G. 1992. The rise and fall of American technological leadership: the postwar era in historical perspective, *Journal of Economic Literature*, 30: 1931–64.

Polanyi, M. 1967. *The Tacit Dimension*. Garden City, N.Y., Doubleday Anchor.

Science and Technology Agency, 1991. White Paper on Science and Technology. Tokyo, Japan Information Centre of Sciences and Technology.

Watanabe, C. 1992. Leading the way to comprehensive transitional R&D cooperation – NEDO's initiative, paper presented to the 1992 AAAS National Meeting, Chicago.

Womack, J.P., Jones, D.J. and Roos, D. 1990. *The Machine that Changed the World*. New York, Maxwell Macmillan International.

4 Technological accumulation and industrial growth: contrasts between developed and developing countries

MARTIN BELL AND KEITH PAVITT

Introduction

Several areas of economic analysis have given renewed attention during the 1980s to the long-run importance of technological learning and technical change. These issues have become a central feature in the new trade and growth theories (for example, Krugman, 1986; Lucas, 1988, Grossman and Helpman, 1990; and Romer, 1986, 1990). They have emerged as one of the major factors explaining differences among the developed countries in growth and trade performance (Fagerberg, 1987, 1988; Cantwell, 1989); and they underlie analyses of the extent to which, as a result of differing growth paths, economies with different initial income levels have been converging or diverging over time (for example, Abramovitz, 1986; Baumol, 1986; De Long, 1988; and Dowrick and Gemmel, 1991).

This chapter contributes to these areas of debate. It draws heavily on understanding of technological accumulation in the industrialised world in order to illuminate the situation in contemporary developing countries. And, since the basic processes of technological accumulation and technical change differ fundamentally between the agricultural and industrial sectors in low-income economies, it focuses on the industrial sector. This is the sector in which, at least relative to earlier expectations, disappointment at the realised extent of 'catching up' over the last four or five decades is perhaps greatest.

Even at the beginning of that period, it was widely recognised that there were difficulties in transferring agricultural technologies from developed to developing countries. However, because industrial technology is less location-specific than agricultural technology, it was assumed that developing countries had much greater scope in industry than in agriculture for benefiting from the international diffusion of high-productivity technologies which were already available in the advanced industrial economies. The models underlying such arguments drew a clear distinction between innovation and diffusion; and developing countries, it was argued, could benefit from the diffusion of industrial technologies without incurring the costs of techno-logical innovation. Consequently, the expectation was that, given a reason-ably rapid rate of investment in the physical capital in which the technologies were embodied (and 'learning' of the basic skills to operate them efficiently), developing countries would achieve high rates of growth of labour produc-tivity in industry, and probably also of total factor productivity.

We shall argue that these early and optimistic expectations about the dif-fusion of industrial technology to developing countries were profoundly misplaced, and they have become increasingly misleading as the nature of industrial technology has changed. In economies that are so-called 'bor-rowers' of ready-made technology from more technologically advanced economies, technological accumulation is misrepresented as a process of accumulating technology that is largely embodied in physical capital. Also, the process of technical change in dynamic industries in developing coun-tries bears little resemblance to the technology adoption process repre-sented in conventional innovation-diffusion models. As a consequence, we shall argue that policies which continue to rest on these perceptions of the processes of technological accumulation and technical change are likely to hinder rather than hasten industrial 'catching up'.

In discussing the reality of these processes, we focus primarily on micro-level and empirical issues. The theoretical debate in this area is being pursued elsewhere. In particular, the characteristics of technical change in market economies that we shall describe later in this chapter have led some analysts to develop evolutionary theories of technical change – emphasis-ing the central importance of dynamic competition through continuous innovation and imitation, together with disequilibria, uncertainty, learn-ing, and inter-firm and inter-country differences in competencies and behaviour (see, for example, Freeman, 1982; Nelson and Winter, 1982; Dosi, 1988; Dosi et al., 1988, 1990). Our purpose in this chapter is to draw on a wide range of empirical evidence from the developed, developing and centrally planned economies in order to summarise what seem to be key common and contrasting features of the nature and determinants of tech-nological accumulation and technical change.

In the first main section of the chapter we set out the framework for our analysis. In particular, we reject the clear-cut distinction between 'innova-tion' and 'diffusion', with its implication that 'adopters' play no role in developing or changing the technologies they choose and use. In contrast we emphasise the importance of active involvement in technical change even by firms, industries and economies which acquire technology devel-oped elsewhere. We therefore distinguish between two stocks of resources: (i) the skills, knowledge and institutions that make up a country's capacity to generate and manage change in the industrial technology it uses (i.e. its technological capabilities), and (ii) the capital goods, knowledge and labour skills required to produce industrial goods with 'given' technology (i.e. a country's industrial production capacity). By 'technological accumulation' we mean the accumulation of the first of these stocks of resources.

In the subsequent section we focus on the experience of the advanced industrial countries. We identify key characteristics of technological accumulation that seem to have been common across different industrial sectors. Next we distinguish between five categories of firm, each with different sources of, and opportunities for, technological accumulation and technical change. We argue that, in the experience of these countries, the longer-term development of new bases of competitive advantage has depended on both evolution *between* these different categories and particular patterns of technological accumulation *within* them.

In the following section we turn to contemporary developing countries where technological accumulation has been extremely uneven. In a few, it has been rapid – with significant positive implications for the technological and economic dynamism of industry. But in many others it has been extremely slow, with negative implications for the dynamics of industrialisation. While many factors account for these disparities, we suggest that two issues have been particularly important. First, for the later industrialising countries, technological accumulation has become less and less a by-product of the growth of industrial production capacity. Second, in only a few of them has policy facilitated that increasingly distinct accumulation process within the overall path of industrialisation – while hindering it in many. These policy differences are partly about trade policy – the issue that has dominated policy debate about industrial development. A range of other policy measures, with both positive and negative implications for the technological dynamism of industry, help to explain the inter-country differences. We therefore conclude in the final section by emphasising the importance of policies which focus explicitly on technological accumulation within the process of industrialisation, and we highlight the value of generating the new understanding that is needed about technology and the longer-term dynamics of industrial growth in both developed and developing countries.

The framework for analysis

The misleading distinction between 'innovation' and 'diffusion'

Technical change in industry has conventionally been seen as involving two main activities: first, the development and initial commercialisation of significant innovations; second, the progressively wider application of these innovations in a process that economists and others have described as 'diffusion'. The first of these activities is assumed to be heavily concentrated in the developed countries, becoming significant in developing economies only as they approach the international technological frontier – a pattern which is becoming evident in the recent data on international patenting by firms in the more industrialised developing countries such as Korea and Taiwan. Before that stage, developing countries are assumed to be involved in the international diffusion of technology; and, since this is seen simply as involving the choice and adoption/acquisition of established technologies, creative innovation is assumed to be irrelevant. From this perspective, 'technological accumulation' in industrialising countries is seen as involving technology that is embodied in the stock of capital goods, together with the associated operating know-how and product specifications required to produce given products with given techniques at the relevant production efficiency frontier.

In fact, diffusion involves more than the acquisition of machinery or product designs, and the assimilation of related operating know-how. It also involves continuing, often incremental, technical change by which the original innovations are (i) moulded to fit particular conditions of use in a widening range of specific situations, and (ii) further improved to attain higher performance standards beyond those originally achieved. The fact that innovation continues during the diffusion process has long been emphasised by more perceptive observers of the process – for example, more than twenty years ago by Rosenberg (1972, 1976) and more recently by Metcalfe (1988). Less emphasis has been given to the fact that, in technologically dynamic situations, this continuing process of technical change typically involves two stages in each successive application of the diffusing technology.

First, the basic features of the technology being incorporated in new production facilities may be improved upon, or adapted for application in specific situations. This typically entails a complex and creative process which is obscured by simple terms like 'technology adoption' or 'technology choice'. Its importance has been emphasised, for example, by Voss (1988) with reference to the 'adoption' of advanced manufacturing technology in industrialised countries, and Amsalem (1983) has shown the complexity and creativity of activities involved in the 'choice' of technology during investment in new textile and paper plants in developing countries.

Second, even after initial investment in new production capacity that incorporates the diffusing technology, technical change may continue through the subsequent operational lifetimes of the production facilities in each adopting firm. This post-adoption phase of technical change incorporates a stream of incremental developments and modifications which further improve the technology in use and/or mould it to continuing change in competitive input and product markets. The analysis of 'learning curves' in industrial production has commonly shown the significance of the economic gains from this continuing improvement in apparently 'given' technologies, but it has typically obscured the underlying processes (Bell and Scott-Kemmis, 1997). In fact, these 'learning curves' are generated by continuing paths of creative technical change (incremental innovation), as has been illustrated in the classic analysis of continuing cost reduction in Du Pont rayon plants after initial acquisition of the technology from Europe (Hollander, 1965); or in more general analyses of the role of 'continuous improvement' in contributing to the competitive success of Japanese firms (e.g. Imai, 1986). The significance of this incremental technological dynamism has also been highlighted in a handful of studies of firms in developing countries – for example in the steel industry in Brazil (Dahlman and Fonseca, 1987) and the petrochemical industry in Korea (Enos and Park, 1988); and more recent studies have emphasised the importance of continuing change in the organisational dimension of production technology (e.g. Hoffman, 1989; Meyer-Stamer et al., 1991; and Mody et al., 1992).

It is important to emphasise that the so-called adopters and users of technology may play significantly creative roles in both these stages of continuing technical change. That is obvious enough in the case of the second stage: the incorporation of technical change into existing production systems will often draw on inputs from external suppliers, but the technology-using firm itself must also play a significant role – both independently and in interaction with external suppliers. This technologically creative role is also important at the first of the two stages outlined above: investment in new production facilities obviously draws on a range of suppliers for capital goods, engineering services, project management services, and so forth; but technologically dynamic firms rarely play a purely passive role in the technological aspects of investment in the production facilities they will subsequently use. They may generate a significant part of the technology themselves, perhaps also incorporating it in the designs of capital goods to be used; they may interact with their suppliers in developing designs and specifications; and, at the very least, they are likely to control key decisions about the technology.

In the industrialised economies, the adopters and users of diffusing technology will typically already possess (albeit in varying degrees) the particular kinds of knowledge and skill needed to play these types of technologically creative role. In developing countries, however, these capabilities will usually have to be accumulated before the full, dynamic benefits from technology diffusion can be realised. This involves more than the accumulation of skills and know-how for operating new processes at their expected performance standards, or for producing products to existing specifications. Firms must accumulate the deeper forms of knowledge, skill and experience required to generate continuing paths of incremental change, which both improve on the original performance standards of the technology in use, and modify its inputs, outputs and processes in response to changing input and product markets. They may also strengthen their capabilities for seeking out and acquiring technology from other firms and economies. And they may then build on these capabilities to introduce more substantial technical changes: for example incorporating significant improvements into processes already used or into process technology acquired from elsewhere for new projects, modifying the existing types of product, producing substitutes for those already produced, diversifying into the production of input materials or equipment, or creating improved process or materials technologies for use by supplier industries. This phase may then blur into a fourth, in which firms produce the kinds of technical change which are usually thought of as 'innovations'.

Thus, while developing countries do depend heavily on the international diffusion of technology originally developed in the more industrialised countries, there is considerable scope for variation in the gains they can derive from adopting and using that technology. In particular, the intensity with which they accumulate their own capacities to generate and manage technical change in association with their acquisition and use of imported technology is likely to influence a range of important performance variables. These will include variables that differ widely between developing countries: the efficiency of investment in new production capacity (both the economic efficiency of input combinations 'chosen' in the light of local prices, and the level of technical efficiency initially attained); the subsequent rate of total factor productivity growth in existing firms and industries; and the competitiveness of their product specifications and designs. Over longer periods, the intensity with which these change-related resources are accumulated and applied in the process of technical change will influence other variables, such as the strength of backward and forward linkages to suppliers and customers; the ease of structural change towards more technology-intensive lines of production; and, as the international technology frontier is approached, the ability even to enter new product markets successfully.

The important distinction between 'production capacity' and 'technological capabilities'

As might be expected in the light of this discussion, the conventional concepts and terminology of 'innovation' followed by 'diffusion' have been

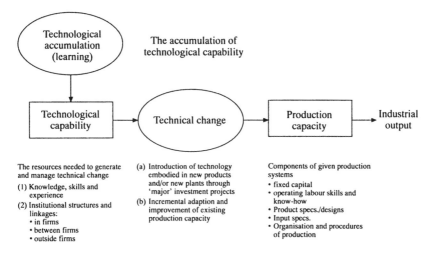

Figure 4.1. Technological accumulation: basic concepts and terms.

unhelpful in dealing with the technological dimension of industrialisation in developing countries. A range of alternatives have been suggested, generating a new technology-related vocabulary: 'technological mastery', 'technological capabilities', 'technological capacity', 'technological effort', 'technological learning', and so forth (see, for example, Teitel, 1982; Katz, 1984; Bell *et al.*, 1984; Dahlman *et al.*, 1987; Enos, 1991; and Zahlan, 1991); and more elaborate taxonomies of 'technological capabilities' have been developed (for example, by Lall, 1987, 1990).

Our own approach is summarised in figure 4.1. We draw a distinction between two stocks of resources: production capacity and technological capabilities. The former incorporates the resources used to produce industrial goods at *given* levels of efficiency and *given* input combinations: equipment (capital-embodied technology), labour skills (operating and managerial know-how and experience), product and input specifications, and the organisational methods and systems used. Technological capabilities consist of the resources needed to generate and manage technical change, including skills, knowledge and experience, and institutional structures and linkages. We emphasise the distinction between the two because we are primarily interested in the dynamics of industrialisation, and hence in the resources necessary to generate and manage that dynamism.

We also identify two processes: technical change and technological learning (or technological accumulation). The former encompasses any way in which new technology is incorporated into the production capacity of firms and economies. Technological accumulation (or technological learning) refers to any process by which the resources for generating and managing technical change (technological capabilities) are increased or strengthened. These processes of technological accumulation are the central focus of this chapter.

It is also useful to distinguish two types of technical change which correspond to the two 'stages' discussed above. One involves the incorporation of new technology in relatively large 'lumps' through investment in new, or substantially expanded, production facilities. The technology involved ('new' for the firm or economy) may be radically or only incrementally innovative relative to preceding vintages, and may be largely acquired from other firms or developed by the user firm – or some combination of both. The second form involves the incorporation of continuing 'trickles' of new technology into existing production facilities – through the types of incremental technical change discussed above.

There are two reasons for concentrating analytical and policy attention on technological capabilities. First, the 'intangible' resources required to generate and manage technical change can no longer be considered as a marginal adjunct to the resources constituting industry's production capacity. They are becoming quantitatively much more significant, reflecting the rising knowledge-intensity and change-intensity of industrial production. In the developed countries, leading companies' expenditures on R&D (i.e. their investment in creating new knowledge, and in assimilating it from elsewhere) are now often larger than their investment in fixed capital (for Japan, see Kodama, 1991). At the same time, in order to generate competitive rates of technical change, firms have greatly increased expenditures on raising the skills and knowledge of their human resources, and combined this with the development of novel institutional mechanisms for doing so – see, for example, Wiggenhorn (1990) for details of the striking case of Motorola (which has raised training and education expenditures from $7 million to $60 million per year and developed its own corporate university), or the more general review of 'corporate classrooms' in Eurich and Boyer (1985).

Second, alongside this quantitative trend is a less clearly definable qualitative shift towards increased differentiation and specialisation in the knowledge resources used by industrial firms. A growing distinction has emerged between the kinds of knowledge and skill required to *operate* given production systems, and the kinds of knowledge required to *change* them. The widening gap between these technology-using and technology-changing skills has reduced the possibilities of acquiring the latter largely by experience in the former. As a consequence, explicit investment in acquiring and accumulating knowledge and skill has become a necessary basis for building the human resource component of industry's change-generating capabilities. However, while investment in at least a basic level of operating skill and know-how is a necessary condition for entering any line of production, investment in associated change-generating skills and knowledge is a discretionary expenditure; and, as we shall emphasise later, there is good reason to expect firms to underinvest in these technological capabilities. This highlights the importance of policy intervention in this area, but we shall suggest that the most appropriate forms of intervention need to be very different from those which have dominated both debate and practice in recent decades.

Technological accumulation in the currently industrialised countries

In this section, we first define the main characteristics of technology accumulation and of the 'national systems of innovation' (see Nelson, 1993) in which it is embedded. Since it is more accurate to talk of *technologies* rather than *technology*, we then describe five typical forms of technological accumulation that can be observed in business firms. Finally, we describe how industrialised countries' patterns of technological accumulation relate to these different technological forms, and help to create the basis for dynamic changes in competitive advantage.

Key characteristics

The resource inputs

The resources involved in effective technological accumulation are much more diverse and pervasive than usually suggested by simple models of the innovation process. Formal research is almost never the core activity in accumulating the knowledge-base for technical change. This is because the central feature of technical artifacts is their *complexity*, reflected in a large number of performance parameters and constraints, that cannot be accurately represented or predicted in a simple theory or model, or fully specified in a series of blueprints or operating instructions. Trial, error and experience are therefore central to the improvement of technology. Thus, even research-intensive innovations require the design, construction and testing of prototype products and pilot process plants, and expenditure on these development activities usually far outweighs expenditure on research. Then, beyond research or development, the implementation of technical change involves (usually greater) expenditure on various kinds of product and process design and engineering, which are themselves important locations for accumulating new knowledge, and key channels for transforming such knowledge into the concrete realities of implemented technical change. Further, as Western companies have slowly been learning from Japanese experience, even more pervasive sets of knowledge and skill can be harnessed to drive forward intensive processes of 'continuous improvement' in production which play a major part in attaining and sustaining competitiveness in a dynamic world (Imai, 1986).

Tacit and specific knowledge

Much technological accumulation involves knowledge that is tacit: in other words, uncodifiable and person- (or institution-) embodied. This is because coping with complexity cannot be reduced to a simply derived and easily applicable 'best practice', but involves 'rules of thumb' that can be acquired and improved only with experience. The transfer of tacit knowledge, even the kind of knowledge needed for efficient operation of 'given' techniques, is therefore neither costless nor quick, since it requires the acquisition of this experience. Beyond that, the tacit components of the kinds of knowledge and skill needed for changing products and processes are also substantial (Senker, 1992), and their transfer may be yet slower and more expensive than the transfer of operating know-how (Scott-Kemmis and Bell, 1988). It is not surprising, therefore, that economic historians – amongst others – have emphasised the importance of the movement of people as a key mechanism for the international transfer of technology during, for example, the late industrialisation of North America (Jeremy, 1981), France and Germany (Henderson, 1965; Landes, 1969) and Norway (Bruland, 1989).

Whether tacit or codified and explicit, knowledge and skills are highly specific to particular categories of industrial products and processes. In terms that are blindingly obvious, a firm making cheap textiles would find it virtually impossible to diversify into making personal computers (although some of the Korean *chaebol* have made diversification jumps almost as great as this). It is less obvious – but equally true – that the computer firm could not make textiles efficiently, even assuming it had the incentive to do so. As industrial technologies have become increasingly complex, these kinds of specificity have become evident at much more detailed levels. In the Japanese steel industry, for example, small technologically dynamic firms seeking to diversify across quite narrow differences in products and processes (e.g. from construction bars to structural beams) have found it necessary in the 1990s to enter joint-ventures in order to gain access to the different expertise required.

The central importance of business firms

Given the specific, cumulative and partly tacit nature of technology, the most important components of technological accumulation are localised in firms, since they are associated with learning from specific experiences in developing and operating production systems. The nature of firm-centred technological accumulation varies greatly across product groups, firm size and levels of development; and, as suggested earlier, measured R&D activities are only the tip of the iceberg, since they are a form of accumulation typical of large firms in science-based technologies. In smaller firms, technological activities are sometimes part-time, and sometimes given other names like 'design' and 'production engineering'. Historical studies show that these R&D, design and production engineering capabilities often emerge as specialised functions within firms from prior activities in quality control and production organisation (Mowery and Rosenberg, 1989).

There has been a vigorous and productive tradition of applied management research to identify the conditions for the successful management of technical change in firms which have already accumulated substantial technological capabilities (see, for example, Rothwell, 1977; Harris and Mowery, 1990). It emerges that successful implementation at the project level depends on the effective integration of specialisms (discipline, function, division) within the firm, and on effective outside linkages with sources of expertise, and with the needs of eventual customers. However, understanding of the factors affecting firms' prior strategic choices about technological accumulation and diversification is much thinner.

Failure to recognise the largely firm-specific and localised nature of technological accumulation has been one of the major shortcomings of technological policy in the USSR and other centrally planned countries, where the R&D and design functions were separated (geographically and organisationally) from production units (Hanson and Pavitt, 1987). As we shall emphasise in a later section, similar policies have been followed in many developing countries, where government-funded R&D laboratories were established in the mistaken expectation that – without matching technological capabilities in firms themselves – they would produce practically useful results.

Inter-firm linkages and networks

While emphasising the central role of firms, one must not assume that individual enterprises are isolated actors in the process of technological accumulation. Technical change is generated out of complex interactions between firms. Some of these involve suppliers and customers in the input–output chain ('user–producer' technological relationships). Many others, however, involve a wide range of technology collaboration arrangements between competing as well as complementary firms (Chesnais, 1988; Cainarca et al., 1992; Hagedoorn and Schakenraad, 1992). Yet others involve linkages with public sector research activities (Senker and Faulkner, 1992).

The importance of technology-centred, user–producer relationships can be seen when they have been present in dynamic industries (for example, Lundvall, 1988, 1992). It can also be seen in situations where those links have been weak or absent – for example, the centrally planned countries positively discouraged the emergence of structures of interacting, specialised supplier and user firms, with harmful effects on the diffusion of technology and the efficiency of the capital stock (Hanson and Pavitt, 1987). Thus, an important part of the process of accumulating industrial technological capabilities involves building various kinds of institutional structure within which firms can interact in creating and improving the technology they use.

Cumulativeness

Technological learning by firms, even when reinforced by collaborative interaction with other firms, tends to be cumulative. Given the importance of specific and tacit knowledge, individuals and firms are not capable of learning simultaneously across a wide diversity of technological and organisational dimensions. Nor do they easily make frequent 'step-jumps' into totally new areas of technology. Instead, they tend to move along particular trajectories in which past learning (by doing and by other mechanisms) contributes to particular directions of technical change, and in which the experience derived from those paths of change reinforces the existing stock of knowledge and expertise.

This cumulative nature of firm-centred technological learning has three implications. First, differences in technical efficiency between countries arise not only from different factor endowments, or from barriers to entry, but also from differences in accumulated technological competence. These are reflected in the empirical tests of technology gap models of international trade and growth (Soete, 1981; Fagerberg, 1987, 1988).

Second, national technological competencies cannot be changed rapidly. Thus, we can observe that the sectoral patterns of technological accumulation in developed countries are relatively stable over a period of fifteen to twenty years (Pavitt, 1988).

Third, the rate and composition of a country's technological accumulation not only has a major influence on competitive efficiency in the shorter term, but also on the evolution of new bases of comparative advantage in production in the longer term.

Discontinuities in technical change

The cumulative nature of technological learning does not mean that technical change is always incremental. While a very large contribution to the totality of technical change is made by continuing paths of incremental advance, there have obviously been significant discontinuities. Whether these involve radical changes in the core technologies of products and processes (Tushman and Anderson, 1986) or radical changes in the configuration ('architecture') of only incrementally changing product and process elements (Henderson and Clark, 1990), they require substantial new knowledge-bases for competitive performance. However, firms' cumulative learning processes frequently enable them to cross such apparent discontinuities: they may have already accumulated a diverse knowledge-base (perhaps in anticipation of discontinuity) from which it is possible to move into the new areas; or they may be able to use linkages and networks to draw on new bodies of knowledge which complement their existing areas of technological competence. Nevertheless, existing firms are sometimes unable to create or exploit adequately rapidly the new bases of knowledge needed for competitive survival, and the trajectory of technical change may then be led by new entrant firms. However, even in these cases, the new entrants are rarely making massive 'jumps' in the composition of their knowledge-bases. More commonly, they are moving along their own cumulative learning paths in the new areas of knowledge – paths that often seem to have their roots in highly localised institutions and previously accumulated bodies of knowledge.

Industrial firms as creators of human capital

Some perspectives on the role of human capital in economic growth have given primary emphasis to formal education and training in institutions operating outside the structure of industrial firms. Sometimes with only passing reference to 'on-the-job training', firms themselves have been seen essentially as users, not creators, of the human capital they require. Such perspectives understate the central importance of firms as human capital creators in the process of technological learning – especially, but not only, in the experience of countries like Japan and Germany which have been particularly effective in exploiting the dynamic gains of technological accumulation.

Other perspectives have emphasised 'learning by doing' as an important mechanism for such human capital creation; and the significance of tacit knowledge (with the consequent importance of experience) certainly highlights the importance of 'doing' as a means of learning. However, two caveats should be noted about the role of learning by doing.

First, doing one kind of activity is seldom an adequate basis for learning about another. This obvious but often neglected point has become increasingly important as the knowledge-base for routine production activities has become increasingly differentiated from the kinds of knowledge, skill and experience that are required to generate and manage technical change (with the latter organised in increasingly specialised R&D laboratories, design offices, project management teams, production engineering departments, etc.). As the gap between these two kinds of technological competence has widened, the doing of routine production has contributed less of the kind of learning that can contribute to technical change; and specifically change-related doing has become an increasingly important basis for change-related learning (Bell *et al.*, 1982; Bell, 1984).

Second, while various forms of 'doing' are central to technological accumulation, learning should not be seen simply as a doing-based process that yields additional knowledge essentially as a by-product of activities undertaken with other objectives. It may need to be undertaken as a costly, explicit activity in its own right: various forms of technological training and deliberately managed experience accumulation. Such intra-firm efforts, undertaken as complements to education and training outside industry, have been especially significant in Japanese and German firms.

In these ways, the contributions made by firms to an economy's overall pool of technological capabilities are little different from the contributions of other institutions more explicitly concerned with education and training. However, the two types of institution are not just substitutable alternatives: particular kinds of skill and knowledge can be acquired only in firms and through their investments in learning – by doing or by training. But, because of the non-appropriability of the full returns to these investments, there is likely to be significant underinvestment from a social, and possibly also private, perspective. The role of government policy and other factors in influencing these patterns of intra-firm learning is poorly understood.

*The complementarity of technology imports and local
technological accumulation*

Technology acquired from other countries has been essential in the industrial growth of the developed countries. It was obviously important when economies were catching up from behind the technological frontier, but it remains important for those that are operating close to the frontier: a very large proportion of total international trade in technology (either as disembodied knowledge or as technology embodied in capital goods and engineering services) takes place between the advanced industrial countries themselves, rather than between them and the industrialising countries of the developing world. A significant proportion of the 'innovations' developed by firms in industrialised countries involve large elements of imitation of technology already developed in other countries (De Melto *et al.*, 1980; Smith and Vidvei 1992; Deiaco 1992), and a large amount of R&D in the developed countries is also 'imitative': that is, it is performed to monitor, assimilate and modify the technological developments of competitor firms that are often located in other countries (Levin *et al.*, 1987; Cohen and Levinthal, 1989).

This highlights two issues. First, there is often no clear-cut distinction between the kinds of activities and resources required for 'innovation' and so-called 'imitation'. Second, the argument that importing foreign technology and creating it locally are alternative (substitutable) means for generating technical change does not reflect the experience of the developed countries, where technology imports and local technological accumulation have in fact been complementary. This has taken several forms.

First, imported technology can contribute directly to technical change without there being any significant involvement of local technological capabilities. More often, only some elements of the necessary total combination of technology are imported and are combined with elements generated locally. The experience of European countries in the development of the North Sea oil industry illustrates both these patterns. In the early years of the 'infant industry', projects drew directly and almost totally on American technology, but this was followed by a rapid transition to more indirect patterns in which imported and locally developed elements were combined (Bell and Oldham, 1988).

Second, even when technical change depends heavily and directly on technology imports, these may be complemented by intensive efforts to accumulate locally the technological capabilities needed subsequently for improving what was acquired initially, for generating elements of technology to be combined with imported elements in later projects, or for building a more independent position in the long-term development of the technology. This, for example, was the pattern followed by the US Du Pont Corporation when it entered the rayon industry in the 1920s on the basis of imported technology (Hollander, 1965). It was also very evident in the early industrialisation experience of Japan, as Tanaka (1976) has shown for the development of the chemical industry between the 1870s and 1920s. The licensing of designs and the acquisition of foreign expertise and know-how for direct use in shipbuilding in the early part of this century was complemented by large investments in skill and know-how for developing and improving what was initially acquired from overseas, not just for using it (Fukasaku, 1986). Similarly, the early development of the automobile, electrical and railway rolling-stock industries was built on a combination of imported equipment and indigenous capability in metals and machinery; tie-ups with foreign firms (involving know-how licensing and direct foreign investment) were necessary, but localised reverse engineering was also a major channel for accumulation of product design and development capabilities once local firms had mastered production and component technologies (Nakaoka, 1987; Odagiri and Goto, 1992). In the post-war period, the high level of expenditure on imported technology by Japanese firms was more than matched by their complementary expenditure on engineering and R&D to ensure the dynamic assimilation of what had been imported (Ozawa, 1974, 1985; Tanaka, 1992).

Third, the process of importing technology may also be preceded, not just followed, by local investment in related technological capabilities. This can provide not only the knowledge-base needed by an informed buyer of foreign technology, but also for the dynamic assimilation of what is subsequently imported. The experience of Japan again provides examples: for instance, in the 1950s, entry into synthetic fibre production with licensed technology was preceded by substantial investment in R&D and related engineering activities (Ozawa, 1980).

Finally, imported technology also contributes to local accumulation itself, and not just to technical change. This is fairly obvious when technology imports are acquired through educational and informal channels – as with the training of design engineers or research scientists in foreign universities and research centres. It is often less visible in commercial technology transactions between firms – for instance, when the licensing of process specifications is accompanied by access to underlying design data, training in design routines, and opportunities to acquire experience in design projects. Such international learning arrangements blur into international forms of the types of technological collaboration discussed above. The primary objectives of such linkages and networks are usually less concerned with relocating existing knowledge and expertise from one firm to another and more with pooling intangible assets to develop new elements of technology. Nevertheless, these arrangements may then be important mechanisms for transferring internationally the resulting new technology.

Markets, governments and institutions

Market structure and competitive pressures
Conventional cross-sector studies of the influence of market structure on technological performance in developed countries are not very revealing. This is because recent research has shown that industrial structure is endogenous, being determined by conditions of technological opportunity and appropriability (Levin *et al.*, 1985; Pavitt *et al.*, 1987): when both are high, concentration tends to be high and innovating firms big (e.g. chemicals, electrical and electronics); when opportunity is high and appropriability is low, innovating firms tend to be small (e.g. capital goods).

However, the importance of competitive pressures and rivalry as an incentive for technological accumulation emerges from studies of the origins of competitiveness (for example, Porter, 1990), and from statistical studies of the technological activities of the world's large firms (Patel and Pavitt, 1992). Conversely an almost complete lack of competitive pressures was one reason why production units in centrally planned economies had no incentive to develop or adopt more efficient techniques.

Nevertheless, during the late industrialisation of currently developed countries, governments typically took measures to protect their infant industries from the competition of established producers in more industrialised countries. The extent and duration of that protection varied widely, but the historical relationship between protection and technological learning remains poorly understood (e.g. David, 1975; Bell *et al.*, 1984). In some cases, protection was provided only for relatively short periods – as in the case of the Japanese synthetic fibre industry in the 1950s (Ozawa, 1980). In others it persisted for long periods – sometimes with questionable justification in terms of local learning (as suggested, for example, by Paul David in the case of the US textile industry in the nineteenth century). But at other times the persistence of protection seems to have been an apparent necessity for developing effective mastery of the technology involved (e.g. in the case of the Japanese motor industry).

Governments and market failures: education, training and research

Nearly all governments in market economies have a similar core of policies that are designed explicitly to influence the rate and direction of technical change, and that are justified because they correct market failure. These include the adoption of common technical standards for interfaces and networks, and penalties or restrictions on technological change that damages health, safety and the environment. Other areas of government policy have focused on the creation of new knowledge through research, and on the diffusion of existing knowledge through education and training. There are significant externalities in these activities, in the sense that the full benefits are not necessarily appropriable by the firms investing in them. Major initiatives to stimulate them have therefore been taken by governments. With respect to research and new knowledge creation, therefore, governments in all developed market economies have established similar systems for the protection of intellectual property rights to reinforce the potential temporary monopoly rents afforded to would-be innovators by the natural time-lags and costs of imitation; and, in widely varying degrees and structures, they have provided more direct forms of financial support for research and innovation.

The contribution of government has been particularly large in the area of investment in education and training. However, significant differences in achievement have been identified among the developed countries, and differences have become apparent in the levels of education and skills of the two-thirds of the working population who do not receive a qualification in higher education. In particular, workers in Germany and Japan have higher qualifications and skills than those in the Anglo-Saxon countries, and this has measurable effects on productivity and product quality (see, for example, Prais, 1981).

These general themes related to public intervention in research, education and training are well recognised. However, two points about technological accumulation in the advanced industrial countries should be stressed: first, the nature of the economic significance of academic research; and second, the importance of public intervention in assisting the accumulation process through technological discontinuities.

The economic significance of academic research

The heavy hand of conventional theories has painted a blind spot into most analyses of the contribution of academic research to technological development. First, many economists, usually working with simple linear models of the innovation process, have assumed that the benefits from academic or 'basic' research have come in the form of published information that is subsequently drawn upon in more 'applied' stages of developing industrial technologies. Second, sociologists and others working with bibliometric indicators of scientific output and productivity have also focused on published information as the primary (or only) output from academic research.

Both these perspectives are wrong. They overlook the results of studies showing that the main economic benefits from basic research are not published information, but a supply of scientists and engineers with problem-solving skills, comprising background knowledge, familiarity with research methodologies and instrumentation, and membership of informal and often international networks of professional peers (Gibbons and Johnston, 1974; Nelson and Levin, 1986; Pavitt, 1991; Rosenberg and Nelson, 1992; Senker and Faulkner, 1992). Policies to develop academic research capacities – closely coupled to postgraduate training – have made important contributions to technological accumulation, even if they have not resulted in directly traceable inputs of knowledge and information for 'innovations'.

Policy intervention and technological discontinuities

The costs and risks of technical change and technological learning vary with the 'distance' of the jumps being attempted from existing techniques and bodies of technological competence. This has sometimes led governments in the advanced countries to support risky large jumps at the technological frontier – frequently with unhappy consequences (for example, supersonic airliners or fast-breeder nuclear reactors: see Eads and

Nelson, 1971). Despite the predominance of imitative innovation in their industrial growth, late industrialising countries also face risks when they take relatively large technological jumps behind the international frontier. These risks may be technical – as when the complexity of a British spinning mule imported by a group of Philadelphians in 1783 totally defeated their efforts even to assemble the components (Jeremy, 1981); or they may be more about market performance, particularly when facing competition from established producers in the advanced countries. Drawing on the industrialisation experience of Japan, Nakaoka (1987) points out that the degree of technical risk is closely correlated with the expected degree of learning: modest technical objectives are safe but allow little learning; ambitious technical objectives are risky but can lead to great strides forward in the accumulation of technological capabilities. According to Nakaoka, Japanese government policies assisted firms making relatively large 'jumps' during early learning phases by providing finance to cover risk, funds for training in the appropriate skills, and a market for the products developed during the learning processes. Ozawa (1980) illustrates similar forms of intervention in the case of the entry of Japanese firms to the synthetic fibre industry in the early post-war years: the government created conditions which not only reduced market risks but also stimulated firms to intensify investment in their technological capabilities alongside their investment in new production capacity.

The complementarity between infrastructural institutions and firms
    In addition to their institutional infrastructure for creating human capital, for helping to diffuse existing knowledge and for supporting the regulatory role of government, all the industrialised countries have developed institutions outside firms for generating new industrial knowledge and information. These may be public or quasi-public institutions (universities, government research laboratories, subsidised co-operative R&D centres, etc.), or they may be private commercial institutions (contract research organisations, industry-funded co-operative R&D centres, and so forth). In a trivial sense, these institutions are complements to industrial firms: their outputs of knowledge are inputs to firms. More significant is the complementarity of *innovative activity* in the two sets of institutions.
    Very rarely do these kinds of infrastructural institution act as substitutes for the innovative activities of firms themselves by generating complete innovations that are immediately implementable (or 'adoptable'). Much more commonly, they generate only some elements of the overall knowledge-sets that firms need to generate technical change. Thus, although these kinds of linkage are still poorly understood, several studies have found that the firms that make most use of the research or development activities of these kinds

of institution are not seeking to compensate for the absence of their own technological capabilities. Instead, they are firms that have significant in-house R&D, and they are seeking specific knowledge inputs to complement those in-house innovative activities (Mowery, 1983; Bell and Oldham, 1988; Arora and Gambardella, 1990; Kleinknecht and Reijnen, 1992).

Financial institutions and management

There have been persistent differences between the developed countries in their rates of technological accumulation. For some analysts, the differences can be attributed in part to differences in macroeconomic conditions, reflected in rates of inflation, interest and growth. For others, they reflect deep-seated differences among countries in the properties of institutions concerned with industrial finance and management.

Thus, there is now a body of opinion arguing that the German and Japanese systems for financing business activities, with their strong emphasis on 'insider' methods of corporate control, are more effective than the Anglo-Saxon systems in ensuring commitment to long-term corporate goals, including technological accumulation (Corbett and Mayer, 1991). There have also been strong criticisms of systems of corporate management that emphasise hierarchical organisational forms and short-term financial targets, to the neglect of functional skills in R&D, production and marketing, and effective linkages among them (Abernathy and Hayes, 1980; Chandler, 1989).

At the heart of this debate is a concern about how to devise a system of supporting institutions to ensure that market processes fully evaluate and encourage cumulative learning – or technological accumulation (Pavitt and Patel, 1988). In addition to the consequences of non-appropriability already discussed, the very processes of specialisation and professionalisation to which we have already alluded are likely to result in under-investment in learning for two further reasons. First, the potential benefits of learning are no longer always immediate and obvious (e.g. a cost-reducing incremental improvement in a process), but in the future and uncertain (e.g. from the laser in the 1960s to the compact disc in the 1980s). Second (and using the same examples), the knowledge required to evaluate accurately the potential value of learning has become increasingly complex, and beyond the comprehension of anyone not continuously active in the field.

In this context, the conventional project appraisal techniques used by managers and public policy-makers are inadequate, since they completely neglect the 'option value' of path-dependent technological learning (Myers, 1984). One possible solution is to treat potential technological investments explicitly as an option value (Mitchell and Hamilton, 1988). Another is to ensure that corporate and financial institutions have enough engineers to counteract the dangers of myopic (and incompetent) analysis by accountants and business school graduates. It has long been argued that this has been the case in Japan and Germany (Lawrence, 1980; Prais, 1981); the president of Sony recently asserted that it ought to become the case in the UK (Morita, 1992); and Amsden (1989) asserts that this is the case in South Korea.

Inter-sectoral differences and trajectories in the industrialised countries

Our discussion so far has described aspects of the experience of the advanced industrial countries that relate to technological accumulation in the industrial sector in general. However, patterns and paths of technology accumulation tend to differ between firms and industries. These differences raise two issues that we discuss below. First, we identify five sectoral categories that capture many of the differences between those paths of technological accumulation; second, these categories are associated with differing modes of maintaining existing bases of international competitiveness and with processes of inter-sectoral evolution that alter the basis of competitiveness over time.

Cross-sectional contrasts

Table 4.1 distinguishes between a number of broad firm-based categories of technical change and technological accumulation. The evidence supporting these generalisations relates to firms in the industrialised economies, being derived from detailed firm-level studies of innovation and from aggregated analysis of trends in patenting by major companies over recent decades (for more detail see Pavitt, 1984; and, for a recently developed alternative, see Malerba, 1992). Each of the categories is reflected in a model of technical change found in economic analysis. It is worth describing them in a little more detail since each has its distinctive method of technological accumulation, and its particular implications for policy.

In *supplier-dominated* firms, technical change comes almost exclusively from suppliers of machinery and other production inputs. This is typically the case in textiles, where most new techniques originate in firms in the machinery and chemicals industries. Technical choices reflect relative factor costs, and the opportunities for technological accumulation are focused mainly on improvements and modifications in production methods and associated inputs, and occasionally on product design. Most technology is transferred internationally embodied in capital goods and other inputs. As such, supplier-dominated firms bear some resemblance to those found in the conventional production function.

Table 4.1. *A technology-based classification of business firms*

Characteristic	Category of firm				
	Supplier-dominated	Scale-intensive	Information-intensive	Science-based	Specialised supplier
Typical core sector	Agriculture Housing Private services Traditional manufacturing	Bulk materials (steel, glass) Consumer durables Cars Civil engineering	Finance Retailing Publishing Travel	Electrical–electronics Chemicals	Capital goods Instruments Software
Size of firm	Small	Large	Large	Large	Small
Type of user	Price-sensitive	Mixed	Mixed	Mixed	Performance sensitive
Main focus of technological activities	Cost reduction	Mixed	Mixed	Mixed	Product improvement
Main sources of technological accumulation	*Suppliers* Production learning Advisory services Design	*Production engineering* Production learning Suppliers	*Corporate software and systems eng.* Equipment and software suppliers Engineering Design	*Corporate R&D* Basic research Production	*Design and development* Advanced users

	Process technology and related equipment (*Upstream*)	Process technology and related equipment (*Upstream*)	Process technology and related software (*Mixed*)	Technology-related products (*Concentric*)	Product improvement (*Concentric*)
Main direction of technological accumulation					
Main channels of imitation and technological transfer	Purchase of equipment and related services	Purchase of equipment Know-how licensing and related training Reverse engineering	Purchase of equipment and software Reverse engineering	Reverse engineering R&D Hiring experienced engineers and scientists	Reverse engineering Learning from advanced users
Main methods of protection against imitation	Non-technical (marketing, trade-marks)	Process secrecy Design and operating know-how	Copyright Design and operating know-how	R&D know-how Patents Design and operating know-how	Design know-how Patents Knowledge of users' needs
Main strategic management tasks	Use technology generated elsewhere to reinforce other competitive advantages	Incremental integration of new technology in complex systems Improvement and diffusion of best practice Exploit process technology advantages	Design and operation of complex information processing systems Development of related products	Develop related products Exploit basic science Obtain complementary assets Reconfigure divisional responsibilities	Monitor advanced users' needs Integrate new technology in products

Source: Based on Pavitt (1984).

In *scale-intensive* firms, technological accumulation is generated by the design, building and operation of complex production systems and/or products. Typical core sectors include the extraction and processing of bulk materials, cars, and certain consumer durables. Given the potential economic advantages of increased scale, combined with the complexity of products and/or production systems, the risks of failure associated with radical change are potentially very costly.

Process and product technologies therefore develop incrementally on the basis of earlier operating experience, and improvements in components, machinery and sub-systems. The main sources of technology are design and production engineering, operating experience, and suppliers of equipment and components. Technology accumulates as the capacity to design and build components, machinery and sub-systems; and eventually as the capacity to design and build large-scale, complex systems. International technology transfer requires the licensing of production and design know-how and related training, in addition to trade in machinery and other inputs. This style of technical change is best reflected in Schmookler's (1966) analysis of investment-induced technical change.

In *information-intensive* firms, we see the emergence of a major new form of technological accumulation, resulting from the revolutionary improvements over the past forty years in the capacity to store, process and transfer information. Although it is still too early to define precisely its nature and extent, technological accumulation in information-intensive firms comprises the design, building operation and improvement of complex systems for the storage and processing of information. Improvements tend to be experience-based and incremental, and their main sources are operating experience, so-called 'systems departments' in large user firms, and suppliers of systems and applications software (Barras, 1990). Although comprehensive data are scarce, surveys suggest that large firms in the service industries (e.g. banking and retailing) have become major centres in the accumulation of information technology.

In *science-based* firms, technological accumulation emerges mainly from corporate R&D laboratories, and is heavily dependent on knowledge, skills and techniques emerging from academic research. Typical core sectors are chemicals and electronics: fundamental discoveries (electromagnetism, radio waves, transistor effect, synthetic chemicals, molecular biology) open major new product markets over a wide range of potential applications. The major directions of technological accumulation in the firm are horizontal search for new and technologically related product markets. International technology transfer requires more than the purchase of production inputs and the licensing of production know-how. It also requires a strong capacity for reverse engineering (i.e. analysing and copying competitors' products), which itself requires a capacity for R&D and design activities. It also requires trained research scientists and engineers with foreign contacts. This style of technical change is best exemplified by the large innovating firm, described and analysed in the later writings of Schumpeter (1943).

Specialised supplier firms provide high-performance inputs into complex systems of production in the form of machinery, components, instruments or software. Technological accumulation takes place through the design, building and operational use of these production inputs. Specialised supplier firms benefit from the operating experience of advanced users, in the form of information, skills and the identification of possible modifications and improvements. Supplier firms accumulate the skills to match advances in machine design with user requirements, which – given the complexity and interdependence of production processes – put a premium on reliability and performance, rather than on price. International technology transfer takes place through the international purchasing activities of advanced user firms. This type of technical change is best typified by the writings of Stigler (1956) and Rosenberg (1976) on 'vertical disintegration' and 'technological convergence'.

The above categories hold reasonably well in developed countries, where some firms are active in more than one category (e.g. IBM in science-based and scale-intensive). As a consequence of the differentiated nature of technological accumulation, we can observe that developed countries differ markedly in their paths of technological specialisation (Pavitt, 1988). These patterns of technological accumulation also help explain the mechanisms through which the bases of countries' competitiveness change over time.

The dynamics of competitive advantage and structural change

These sectoral patterns of technological change begin to help us explain the links between processes of technological accumulation and two important features associated with national patterns of industrial development: first, the changing bases of competitive advantage in world markets; and second, the changing composition of output (or 'structural change').

In export markets we can identify two economic extremes. At one, in supplier-dominated sectors like textiles, the Heckscher–Ohlin assumptions about comparative advantage hold reasonably well: technology – in the form of tradable capital goods and other production inputs – is universally available, and (with some departures from rationality) technical choices are made largely on the basis of factor endowments. Low-wage countries can exploit their comparative advantage in such supplier-dominated sectors, provided their firms are effective in acquiring technology. At the other extreme, comparative advantage in the high-wage countries is dominated by technological leads and lags in science-based, scale-intensive and specialised supplier sectors (Soete, 1981; Guerriri, 1991). In between are the industrialising countries, who are progressively shifting (with varying degrees of success: see the next section) from one basis of competitive advantage to the other. Associated with these shifts are changes in the sectoral composition of output and exports, generally involving relative movements out of sectors associated with abundant endowments of the conventional factors of production (e.g. textiles, mining, food processing), towards machinery, transportation and chemicals.

At the same time, the historical experience of today's developed countries shows that paths of national technological development were cumulative and strongly influenced by prior experience (see David, 1975; and, in a different tradition, Porter, 1990). In general terms, technological accumulation involved the progressive acquisition of (largely country-specific and internationally immobile) 'intangible capital', in the form of personal, organisational and institutional skills that enabled countries to adopt and develop process and product technologies of increasing complexity. Changing bases of international competitiveness evolved along with, and increasingly as a result of, these technological trajectories.

Thus, each type of sector in table 4.1 implies a different locus of technological learning (and of specialised learning activities):
- production operations (quality control, production planning) in supplier-dominated firms;
- process and product improvements (production engineering, design) in scale-intensive firms;
- equipment and component development (design) in specialised supplier firms;
- exploitation of basic research for product and associated process developments (R&D) in science-based firms.

Over time, these learning processes within given sectors have laid the basis for local production in other sectors – for example by the vertical disintegration of production activities initially developed in one category of firm, by the transfer of accumulated knowledge and expertise to enhance the competitiveness of other types of firm (e.g. specialised suppliers), by the migration of skilled people from firms in one category to firms in another, or more generally by stimulating the awareness and development of new areas of knowledge and skill among local firms and technological institutions.

In some cases these learning-based changes in the structure of production have involved change in the characteristics of given industries. For example, technological accumulation within the motor industry transformed it from a small-scale, supplier-dominated sector to a high-volume scale-sensitive industry. More generally, learning-based structural change has involved the emergence of different, more technologically complex sectors on the basis of prior technological accumulation in less complex industries – such as:

- the emergence of the US textile machinery industry as a 'specialised supplier' sector in the nineteenth century on the basis of technological accumulation in textile firms (which then became 'supplier dominated');
- the emergence of specialised suppliers of production equipment on the basis of prior accumulation in scale-intensive sectors (e.g. consumer durables, cars and process industries);
- the emergence of science-based industries from prior accumulation in other categories (e.g. electronics industries on the basis of specialised supplier sectors, or science-based chemicals on the basis of less complex process industries).

Such trajectories have not been pre-ordained, in either their rate or their direction. None the less, in most cases three mechanisms seem to have been particularly influential: (i) factor endowments; (ii) directions of persistent investment, especially those with strong inter-sectoral linkages; (iii) the cumulative mastery of core technologies and their underlying knowledge-bases. The relative significance of these mechanisms has changed during the process of industrialisation. In the early stages, the directions of technical change in a country or region were strongly influenced by local market inducement mechanisms related to scarce (or abundant) factors of production and local investment opportunities. At higher levels of development, the local accumulation of specific technological skills itself became a focusing device for technical change.

Factor endowments.

The most obvious of the local inducement mechanisms has been the search to alleviate a relative factor scarcity. Its historical importance in the development of labour-saving techniques in the United States (and elsewhere in the developed world) is well documented, as is its importance in generating technical responses to differing natural resource endowments: see, for example, the effects of different fuel prices on the development paths of automobile and related mechanical technologies in the United States, on the one hand, and in Europe and East Asia, on the other. Space-saving technological search is said to have been important in the development of early post-war improvements in Japanese methods of mass production. Environment-saving inducement mechanisms may become more important in future.

Investment-led inducements and inter-sectoral linkages

A second set of inducement mechanisms are reflected in another analytical tradition that stresses the importance of the investment-induced nature of technical change (Schmookler, 1966), and of technical linkages and imbalances among firms and sectors (see Carlsson and Henriksson, 1991; Justman and Teubal, 1991). The exploitation of abundant natural resources is one variant, creating opportunities for local technical change, technological accumulation and competitiveness in upstream extraction and downstream processing. Witness the effects of abundant natural resources in Canada, the United States and Scandinavia, where (for example) the development of wood-using technologies in wood-abundant economies has contributed to the competitiveness of wood-processing machinery; and more generally, the development of natural resource-based sectors has contributed to competitiveness in the capital goods used in these sectors (Patel and Pavitt, 1991b). Other important linkages have included those from investment in mass-produced cars (and some other consumer durables) to technological accumulation in associated capital-goods-producing sectors; and those related to government investment programmes – see, for example, their effects on shipbuilding, and railways and communications equipment in the early modernisation of Japan (Nakaoka, 1987).

Mastery of core technologies

Cost and investment-led inducement mechanisms cannot explain the emergence of all areas of technology-based competitiveness. For example, Swiss competitiveness in marine diesels has little obvious link with any national endowment in maritime resources, but has a more obvious connection with the engineering competence developed initially in the production of textile machinery. At the higher levels of technological accumulation in today's developed countries, the central inducement mechanism sometimes has become the cumulative mastery and exploitation on world markets of core technologies with multiple potential applications. When the core technologies are science-based, and the linkage horizontal rather than vertical, trajectories are not traced through inducements from users to producers of capital goods, but through diversification into new product markets from an R&D base. Thus, Swiss strength in pharmaceuticals began in dyestuffs, just as Germany has retained its strength through the successive waves of major innovations in chemicals. The Swedish pattern is more complex, having begun in mining technology and ended up in (among other things) robots – the common core being machinery and metals.

Two features are common to countries that have followed such technology-based trajectories. First, they tend to make technological choices not simply on the basis of expected financial rewards, but also on the expected value of learning for the exploitation of future technological opportunities (Pavitt and Patel, 1988). Second, in science-based and scale-intensive sectors, country-specific inducement mechanisms and technological advantage are reflected in the technological activities a number of domestically based large firms (Patel and Pavitt, 1991a).

Technological accumulation in developing countries

Over the past forty years developing countries have rapidly accumulated and diversified their industrial production capacity. Their share of world manufacturing output and exports has increased, and has spread from products where firms are largely supplier-dominated with technology largely embedded in imported capital goods (e.g. traditional textiles) into products where scale-intensive, specialised supplier firms predominate (e.g. metals and metal products, capital goods, bulk chemicals, consumer durables), and even into science-based sectors (e.g. semiconductors and telecommunications equipment).

However, while differing widely between countries, these patterns of expansion and diversification have also been associated with considerable inter-country differences in two other areas: (i) the dynamic efficiency of industrial growth, and (ii) the rate of industrial technological accumulation in industry. In the next two sub-sections we sketch the broad outlines of these differences. As we proceed, our descriptive generalisations will take the form of increasingly tentative hypotheses based on decreasingly adequate evidence; in particular, our argument that these two types of variation are causally linked should be taken as a hypothesis rather than a well-established proposition. In the final sub-section we explore some of the reasons for the wide inter-country differences in the intensity and structure of technological accumulation. We take a historical perspective in advancing hypotheses that relate more to Gerschenkron-type discussions about the characteristics of late industrialisation than to discussions of the details of government policy – although differences in broad approaches to policy are part of the argument.

The dynamic efficiency of industrial growth

A growing body of evidence shows considerable variation among developing countries in the efficiency of their expansion of industrial production capacity over the last three decades. Low levels of 'static' efficiency in a wide range of industries are evident in numerous sectoral studies of domestic resource costs and effective rates of protection, and also in more detailed micro-level studies of efficiency in using apparently 'given' technologies –

for example, Pack's (1987) examination of firms in the textile industry in Kenya and the Philippines. Here, however, we are more concerned with the dynamic efficiency of recent industrialisation.

Studies of industrial productivity growth rates in developing countries show that the earlier optimistic expectations of the 1950s and 1960s have been realised in only a very few cases – for example in South Korea where annual rates of growth of labour productivity in manufacturing have typically exceeded 10 per cent since the 1960s, and where growth rates of total factor productivity in manufacturing have been substantially higher than those in the advanced industrial countries (Dollar and Sokoloff, 1990). In very many other developing countries, however, rates of growth of total factor productivity in industry (or more narrowly in manufacturing) have not only been a fraction of those achieved in Korea, but also lower than in most of the advanced industrial countries, and quite frequently negative for long periods (see Nishimizu and Page, 1989, and Pack, 1988, 1992 for reviews of the available evidence). Even labour productivity alone seems to have grown more slowly in manufacturing in most of the developing world than in the advanced industrial countries (UNIDO, 1992).

Alongside such studies of productivity growth, a large body of firm-level case-studies has shown considerable variation in the intensity with which firms have adapted, improved and further developed the technologies they use. For example, in Latin America some firms have demonstrated significant innovation and technical change – see, for example, Dahlman and Cortes (1984), Dahlman and Fonseca (1987) and Sercovich (1984). More generally, however, the intensity of technical change in plants and industries in Latin America appears to have been relatively low during the 1960s and 1970s, as well as being focused more on adapting technology to (distorted) local market conditions than on further developing and improving it (Teitel, 1981, 1984, and the wealth of research summarised in Katz, 1984). Lall (1987) suggests that a similar pattern was also widespread in Indian industry. More recent studies in Latin America suggest this pattern has continued – see, for example, Coutinho and Suzigan (1991) on Brazil, or Azpiazu et al. (1988) and Katz and Bercovich (1993) on Argentina. In particular, in several industries there have been only limited efforts to exploit the potential of information-automation technologies and organisational innovation (e.g. Meyer-Stamer et al., 1991; Carvalho 1992). In contrast, Korean firms in a succession of new industries have moved rapidly on to continuous paths of change to both products and processes after the initial start-up of new plants (e.g. Westphal et al., 1985; Enos and Park, 1988); and Hobday (1994) shows similar patterns for firms in the electronics industry in Singapore.

More fragmentary studies in other countries have suggested that technical change in industrial firms has often been even more limited than in

Latin America and India. For example, despite many years of 'doing' production and of 'using' locally produced capital goods, technical change was totally absent in the steel-finishing industry in Thailand during the 1960s and early 1970s (Bell *et al.*, 1984); and many firms in the larger-scale sector of African industry have been unable even to achieve or maintain initial design-level standards of efficiency – see, for example, the summaries of evidence included in Mytelka (1992), Ohiorhenuan and Poloamina (1992) and Wangwe (1992).

Countries have also differed widely in their effectiveness in creating new bases of comparative advantage in increasingly technology-intensive industries. Particularly striking has been the limited development of such industries in several countries which began significant industrial growth in the earlier decades of this century, or even before. Already in the early 1980s, for example, Poznanski (1984) pointed to the poor performance of the (then) centrally planned economies in products in scale-intensive and specialised supplier technologies, when compared to some of the so-called newly industrialised countries (NICs) – a difference confirmed in the more recent comparisons by Ray (1991). Within the NICs, Latin American countries have performed less well than others. This has been particularly evident in recent years in connection with the development of electronics production (Riedel, 1988; Freeman, 1991), but constrained structural change in Latin American industry has a longer history that stretches back well into the nineteenth century – for example, to the absence of significant 'backward linkages' from the rapid expansion of railways during several decades from the 1870s (Felix, 1979). Later, although Brazil had already developed a substantial capital goods industry by the 1950s, neither that nor the subsequent development of scale-intensive sectors was followed by the emergence of substantial and internationally competitive production of more complex and specialised machinery and instrumentation, nor was this the case in science-intensive sectors. With some exceptions, a more common pattern involved *entry into* machinery production for larger user industries – especially into production of the less complex equipment used by particular industries (see, for example, Scott-Kemmis, 1988) – followed by very limited evolution from there into the production of more complex machinery and even difficulty in maintaining competitiveness in the face of technical change in the rest of the world. Similarly, the scale-intensive motor industry grew rapidly in Argentina during the 1950s and 1960s, and a nascent structure of specialised supplier industries emerged, but that has barely survived into the 1990s (Katz and Bercovich, 1993).

In contrast, some of the Asian NICs have rapidly, though in different ways, changed their structures of industrial production. South Korea, for example, moved rapidly from labour-intensive (supplier-dominated) sectors to develop a range of scale-intensive sectors (cars, steel, consumer durables, chemicals) and, with more difficulty, specialised equipment supplying industries. Overlapping with that diversification, firms in the electronics industry (or at least the larger ones) have been shifting from labour-intensive assembly production towards much greater technology-intensity, although they still remain a considerable distance from the science-based technological frontier. Singapore on the other hand has bypassed substantial development of the 'heavy', scale-intensive industries, moving instead from labour-intensive sectors towards engineering-intensive segments of the electronics industry and information-intensive service industries. Other countries in South-east Asia (e.g. Thailand, Malaysia and Indonesia) seem to be poised somewhere between the Latin American and East Asian patterns. It remains to be seen whether they will (i) shift rapidly into trajectories of structural change that lead towards competitiveness in the more knowledge-based sectors, or (ii) remain substantially locked into sectors where competitiveness rests primarily on relatively low wage rates and (temporarily?) abundant natural resources.

Obviously many factors must be considered in any explanation of the differences in the dynamic performance of firms and countries outlined above. It is striking, however, that they appear to be associated with considerable differences in the underlying patterns of technological accumulation.

Uneven technological accumulation

Three aspects of the inter-country variability in technological accumulation are outlined here: (i) the depth and intensity of accumulation within industrial firms; (ii) the structure of accumulation in terms of intra-firm and infrastructural capabilities, and the interaction between the two; and (iii) the complementarity between technology imports and local technological accumulation.

Intra-firm accumulation

The depth of technological capabilities accumulated within firms has been very substantial in a few countries which have to a large extent followed patterns of accumulation similar to those of earlier successful industrialisers. In particular, across a wide range of sectors in Korea and Taiwan, firms have developed strong capabilities for generating continuous incremental change in technologies initially acquired from industrialised countries, for synthesising diverse elements of increasingly complex imported technology into new plants and products, for independently 'replicating' technologies already developed elsewhere, and now for developing more original innovations. These accomplishments initially depended heavily on the accumulation of various kinds of engineering capability (Westphal *et al.*, 1985; Enos and Park, 1988; Amsden, 1989). More recently, especially in the electronics industry (but not only there), they have drawn on the rapid growth of business-financed R&D, which – as in the experience of earlier industrialisers – has included an evolving mix of imitative and innovative technological activities (Bloom, 1992; Ernst and O'Connor, 1992)

Substantial inter-firm migration of skilled personnel has played an important role in these patterns of technological accumulation; and that appears to have been especially important in contributing to change in the structure of industrial production. In part, this involved people returning to Korea with experience acquired from employment abroad. For example, data that are often cited to show the importance of customers in export markets as sources of product design information for exporting firms in the 1970s also show that 'experience acquired by personnel through previous overseas employment' was nearly three times as important as export customers as a source of basic process and production technology (Westphal *et al.*, 1981). Movement of people between firms *within* South Korea was also important. For example, the data referred to above show that 'experience acquired by personnel through previous domestic employment' was the second most important source of production technology for firms entering export markets. These flows of people-embodied technology were often especially important in providing key nuclei of competence that laid the basis for effective accumulation in new areas of technology. For example, the effectiveness with which foreign technology was acquired by one firm leading the country's entry into the petrochemical industry was greatly enhanced by drawing on engineering capabilities previously accumulated by another firm in the refinery industry (Enos and Park, 1988). Similarly, engineering and project management capabilities accumulated by the Korean Electric Power utility (KEPCO) subsequently diffused to enhance the efficiency of firms entering the power engineering and equipment industries (UNCTAD, 1985).

In other developing countries (e.g. in Latin America, India and China), the accumulation of these kinds of technological capability within industrial firms has been much more limited, or narrowly focused in particular sectors (e.g. in the aircraft industry and selected informatics product groups in Brazil, or in defence and space industries in India). In other countries (e.g. in Africa), the intra-firm accumulation of such capabilities has been virtually absent.

Infrastructural institutions
Although all the developing countries have given considerable attention to strengthening their education and training institutions, the

scale and orientation of these efforts have varied widely. For example, South Korea and Taiwan have achieved school enrolment rates at primary and secondary level that are much higher than in most other developing countries, and in higher education they have given much greater emphasis to engineering than have most others. Most developing countries have also established some form of institutional infrastructure to undertake R&D for industry. In Taiwan and especially Korea, the scale of this effort was perhaps greater than in most other countries during the 1970s, but at that time this component of the institutional infrastructure was similar in two important ways to that in most other developing countries: (i) it accounted for the major proportion of total industrial R&D – around 80 per cent compared with only about 20 per cent undertaken by firms themselves; and (ii) its innovative activities made only a limited contribution to technical change in industry. However, in three more detailed dimensions, the roles of these infrastructural institutions in the East Asian NICs, and their importance relative to the accumulation activities of firms themselves, have been similar to patterns in the earlier experience of the currently developed countries, but very different from the most common patterns in other developing countries.

First, especially since the 1970s, many of the R&D institutes in the East Asian NICs have emphasised the 'two faces' of R&D – both the innovation face and the learning (or technology absorption) face (Cohen and Levinthal, 1989). By emphasising their learning role in relation to existing technology, rather than concentrating solely on the generation of technological innovations, they have undertaken activities that differ from those typically emphasised in other countries. This has been especially evident in the institutes set up to support the development of the electronics industry. In Taiwan, for instance, the Electronic Research and Service Organisation (ERSO) under the Industrial Technology Research Institute (ITRI) has acted less as a generator of new technology and 'innovations' for industry, and more as a nodal point for acquiring existing foreign technology, for assimilating it, for training people in it, and then for diffusing both the technology and the people to firms. Naturally, it has also undertaken its own more independent research or development, but much of that 'duplicates' similar R&D in the developed countries in order to 'keep up' with the international evolution of technology (e.g. in high-definition television). A similar emphasis on acquisition, absorption, training and diffusion roles (and not just on the innovation-generating role) has characterised the activities of electronics-oriented R&D institutions established in Korea in the early and mid-1980s, and more recently in Singapore.

Second, although the education and training infrastructure has played an extremely important role in the East Asian NICs, it has nevertheless accounted for only part of the total education and training effort that has contributed to technological accumulation in industry. A very large part has also been played by firms themselves. There is little information about the importance of this role during the phase of rapid growth of labour-intensive (supplier-dominated) industries; and at that stage 'doing' may have been more important than more formally organised education and training within firms. But the latter appears to have become increasingly important in Korea and Taiwan as those countries diversified into more scale-intensive (and knowledge-intensive) industries. This was not very visible in conventional surveys and to the casual academic observer, but those who have looked more closely have highlighted how (often under government influence) firms built very significant training activities into their own operations. Particularly significant has been the emphasis given to training and explicitly managed experience accumulation in product and process engineering and in project management – not only in basic operations and maintenance (Enos and Park, 1988; Amsden, 1989). In these ways, as in the industrialised countries, firms were becoming increasingly significant as creators, and not just employers, of skilled human capital.

More recently, the training role of firms has become more visible: the largest electronics company in Taiwan (Tatung) has set up its own university – the Tatung Institute of Technology; in Korea the Samsung Advanced Institute of Science and Technology has been established; and the government of Singapore has been particularly skilful not only in mobilising the financial resources of multinational corporations to establish education and training institutes, but also in harnessing these corporations' own human resources to the implementation of a range of education and training programmes in technology and management.

There is surprisingly little information about the role of firms in other developing countries in training, and not just using, change-generating human resources. The available fragments suggest, however, that this kind of complementarity between the public infrastructure and intra-firm training efforts has been much less significant. It has been present, but limited or exceptional, in Latin America and India. It seems to have been highly variable among firms in other South-east Asian countries: in Indonesia, for instance, it has been significant in just one or two public-sector enterprises; and in Thailand, even in companies at the heart of pervasive information technologies, intra-firm human resource development has been significant in some cases and absent in others (Hobday and Baba, 1990). In Africa it has been virtually absent altogether (Mlawa, 1983; Mytelka, 1992; Ohiorhenuan and Poloamina, 1992; and Wangwe, 1992)

Third, the apparent distribution of R&D between infrastructural institutions and firms in the East Asian NICs in the 1970s is misleading in two ways. In the first instance, conventional surveys take little or no account of the (non-R&D) engineering and related resources that play a major role in generating and managing technical change in industry. However, as already outlined above, the intra-firm accumulation of these resources played a major role in the dynamics of industrialisation in these countries during the 1960s and 1970s. If they were included in the picture, the balance between infrastructural and intra-firm technological capabilities would be tipped substantially towards the latter – the typical pattern shown by R&D data for the advanced industrial economies.

In any case, even for R&D alone, the balance changed considerably during the 1980s. This was most striking in Korea where, within a rapidly growing total, the 20/80 per cent distribution in R&D activity between intra-firm and infrastructural institutions in the 1970s had been reversed to 80/20 per cent by the early 1990s.

Most other developing countries have continued to have a large proportion (80 per cent or more) of their R&D capabilities in infrastructural institutions – even those like Brazil or Argentina where substantial industrial expansion began in the early decades of the century. However, more important for many countries is the limited intra-firm accumulation of a much wider range of engineering and other change-generating capabilities. Even if one was to take account of these, the distribution of overall technological capabilities between infrastructural institutions and firms would frequently remain heavily 'imbalanced' – if one takes as a norm the historical experience of the industrialised countries or the contemporary experience of the East Asian NICs.

Complementarity between technology imports and local technology accumulation

As firms in the East Asian NICs enter new industries, they have commonly done so in much the same way as firms in other developing countries – by drawing very heavily on imported inputs of core technology, engineering services, equipment and know-how. But, as industries expanded, successive projects drew increasingly – though very seldom totally – on local sources for those technological inputs. Thus, the East Asian NICs have been massive importers of industrial technology through direct foreign investment (largely as joint ventures in some countries), through sub-contracting and original equipment manufacturing agreements with export customers, and via licensing and other contracts with unrelated suppliers of know-how, designs, equipment and services. But these inflows of technology have been complemented by very substantial elements of locally sourced technology within the overall packages needed for investment in new plants and for the introduction of new products.

This type of complementarity between technology imports and local capabilities in implementing technical change was matched by the intensive efforts to improve and develop what was initially acquired. In other words, firms did not choose between imported and local technology as sources of technical change. They chose both! This reflected, and stemmed in large part from, a deeper underlying form of complementarity: the contribution made by international technology transfer to the *development* of local capabilities. This has taken several forms.

First, the training and learning components of technology transfer agreement with foreign companies frequently covered much more than the acquisition of competences for operating and maintaining new facilities. They explicitly focused also on acquiring various combinations of design, engineering and project management skills (see especially Enos and Park, 1988).

Second, the experience of these countries also shows the importance of postgraduate education in the advanced countries for engineers and managers. Especially when this has been combined with subsequent work experience abroad, it has provided not only training in technological problem-solving, but also access to the informal international networks that are so important in science-based technologies.

Third, going beyond the activities of individuals in acquiring foreign technology through education and work experience abroad, some firms in the more knowledge-intensive segments of the electronics industry (especially Korean firms) have set up their own knowledge-acquiring operations in the industrialised countries: establishing R&D centres (concentrating heavily on technological learning in advance of the acquisition of existing technology), or acquiring established firms in those countries to gain access to particular skills, experience and knowledge.

In these and other ways, firms in the East Asian NICs have used international transfer as a channel for actively investing in learning – though not necessarily by doing. But having learned (often with pressure and/or support from government), they ensured that future doing was localised in order to strengthen and further develop the initially acquired stock of capabilities.

In other developing countries, technology transfer has been much less intensively linked into the process of domestic technological accumulation. It has played a major role in the expansion of production capacity, but a minor role in building technological capabilities. Commercial technology transfer arrangements quite evidently *have* been used in several firms and industries in the larger Latin American countries to augment technological capabilities as well as production capacity – for example, in the Brazilian steel industry (Dahlman and Fonseca, 1987) and petrochemical industry (Sercovich, 1980). However, such cases appear to have been relatively infrequent. In other countries, that type of complementarity has been rare (e.g. Girvan and Marcelle, 1990) or virtually absent – for example, see Mytelka (1978) and Vianna (1985) on some of the smaller Latin American countries; Farrell (1979) on Trinidad; Quazi (1983) on Bangladesh; Scott-Kemmis and Bell (1988) on India; Ng *et al.* (1986) on the non-NIC Southeast Asian countries; and Mlawa (1983), Mytelka (1992), Ohiorhenuan and Poloamina (1992) and Wangwe (1992) on a range of African countries.

It is not our intention to suggest that, apart from the East Asian NICs, the rest of the industrialising countries of the late twentieth century constitute some kind of enormous 'technological desert', in which the growth of industrial production capacity has been accompanied by no significant technological accumulation. Bearing in mind that technical progress in most of the industrialised countries continues to move ahead of the industrialising countries, what we have tried to suggest is the following.

- Many firms in most of a rapidly changing structure of industries in the East Asian NICs have increased production efficiency and product quality/performance at rates which imply some significant degree of 'catching up' (as reflected partially in the available productivity growth rates).
- A few firms in a few industries within less rapidly changing industrial structures in other developing countries (mainly in the larger countries with experience of industrialisation stretching back to the early years of the century) have demonstrated similar trajectories of change.
- Many firms in most industries in these and other countries have been generating increases in process and product performance at rates that are positive, but not as high as in the two previous groups, or not even high enough to allow any significant 'catching up'. Indeed, the achieved rates of change have often been below those in the industrialised countries, implying a widening, not narrowing, gap.
- Often for substantial periods of time, many firms in many industries in a large number of countries have not generated any significant improvement in production efficiency or product quality/performance, and consequently have been rapidly 'falling behind' as advances have been made elsewhere. In Africa in particular, performance has frequently declined over time – implying that industry has been falling behind even more rapidly.

Underlying these differences have been corresponding differences in the intensity and structure of technological accumulation – with some, but only very limited, accumulation of intra-firm capabilities in all except the first two groups of countries which may account for less than about 15 per cent of total industrial output in the World Bank's categories of 'low-income' and 'middle-income' countries.

Constraints on technological accumulation

One can obviously draw up a long list of plausible causes of the limited technology accumulation in such a large proportion of industry in developing countries over recent decades. Within such a list, some analysts might emphasise the importance of differences in trade policy, suggesting perhaps that we have simply drawn yet another contrast between countries with liberal, outward-looking policy regimes and considerable economic success, and those with protectionist and inward-looking regimes with much less success. However, as is increasingly well recognised, the industrialisation experience of the East Asian NICs encompasses a wide range of different trade policy regimes – for example, see Pack and Westphal (1986) on Korea and Wade (1990) on Taiwan. The experience of other developing countries also encompasses a wide range; and, over earlier periods, rapid technological accumulation in Japan was associated with highly protectionist and (initially) inward-looking regimes.

Thus, while it is very evident that incentives play a major role in stimulating technological accumulation by firms (Lall, 1992; Pack, 1992), it is much less evident that any particular form of trade policy will itself provide the most appropriate incentive system for all industries at all stages of their development in all industrialising countries. It is therefore not surprising that Pack (1988) suggests there has been no clear relationship between trade policy and total factor productivity growth in industry in recent years. It is necessary to take a longer-term perspective before focusing more narrowly on the details of government policy that may stimulate or constrain technological accumulation in particular circumstances.

One such perspective links success in assimilating transferred technology to different stages in the life-cycles of particular products or technologies. Nakaoka (1987), for example, notes the greater success of Korea than Japan in absorbing automobile technology in the early stages of industrial development, and attributes this in part to the technical immaturity and consequent difficulty of importing high-volume automobile technology at the time of Japan's attempt to do so in the 1920s. By the 1960s, Korea was able to import technically mature and reliable turnkey plant. But, Nakaoka suggests, Korea consequently accumulated less technological capability in related capital goods because of the more limited opportunities to learn from designing and making production equipment – a constraint on technological learning which may act as a general disadvantage to latecomers in many industries.

Despite the importance of the trade-off discussed by Nakaoka, such an argument does not help us explain the main differences outlined above. First, important as it is for technological accumulation, 'doing' (even the doing of design engineering and equipment production) is not the only basis for learning; and more explicit investments in learning may be able to overcome any handicap from technological maturity. Second, the Korean automobile industry seems in any case to be developing significant technological competence in product and equipment engineering. Third, the existence of a handicap from technological maturity does not explain the differences we have noted above between countries entering similarly mature industries during recent decades.

A related perspective focuses more on the sectoral differences we outlined in the previous section. A feature distinguishing the generation of technology today is that most of the fast-moving fields are located in large firms in science-based and scale-intensive sectors, with highly professionalised and specialised technological activities in R&D laboratories and similar institutions. This has made the process of technology accumulation by today's industrialising countries in these high-growth sectors more difficult and demanding. Also, the large firms that dominate in these sectors develop and control significant proportions of both their product and process technologies, and are reluctant to give other firms easy access to this major source of their competitive advantage. They perform most of their technological activities at home or in other developed countries, and prefer direct investment to licensing when producing abroad (Contractor, 1985; Patel and Pavitt, 1991a). On the other hand, the production of world-frontier capital goods technologies (machines, processes, instruments) for supplier-dominated sectors is relatively dispersed, with multiple sources of supply (Patel and Pavitt, 1991a); and firms developing them have every incentive to sell them embodied in capital goods to customer firms in developing countries (Cooper, 1991). However, access to the underlying, disembodied technology may often be more restricted, and hence acquisition of technologies for all but the more simple equipment produced in specialised supplier sectors remains difficult for late industrialisers.

Other perspectives have emphasised longer-term secular factors that make technological accumulation progressively more difficult for late-industrialising countries. For example, Nakaoka (1987) and Kim (1984, 1985) argue that developing countries today face difficulties in absorbing fast-moving technologies that are much more complex than those which were involved in the rapid industrialisation of Japan. That may be important in explaining what seem to be rather small differences between Japan and the East Asian NICs, but it does not help in explaining the much greater differences outlined above between the latter and most of the rest of the developing countries during the same late decades of the twentieth century. In any case, it is equally arguable that increased access to international higher education and advanced training in today's complex and sophisticated technologies offsets any inherently greater difficulty there may be in absorbing them.

We suggest that two other secular trends may be important. First, increased specialisation and differentiation has drawn an ever sharper distinction between production capacity and technological capabilities, making it increasingly possible to accumulate the former without necessarily accumulating the latter. Second, the steadily rising scale of industrial production has progressively reduced both the opportunities and incentives for technological learning associated with given increments of industrial production.

Increased specialisation and differentiation

The central feature of the cumulative technological trajectories in the early development of today's developed countries was the parallel and interacting accumulation of production capacity and technological capabilities. This was considerably facilitated by the substantial overlap in the knowledge-base and institutional location of both. In the late eighteenth and early nineteenth centuries, for example, the kinds of knowledge required to improve, design and produce textile machinery were not incomprehensible and inaccessible to many of the people who used and operated it. Consequently, 'doing' the latter provided a basis for learning about the former. This was facilitated by the fact that both types of competence typically existed in the same organisational location – not just in the same firms, but often within the same parts of firms (e.g. the machine shops of textile mills).

However, across a range of industries and technologies, increasing specialisation has widened the gap between the kinds of knowledge and skill required to use and operate given technologies, and those required to create and change technology. At the same time, the organisational locations of those two kinds of competence have become increasingly separated. Some of this organisational differentiation has involved the emergence of distinct engineering departments, design units and R&D centres *within* firms. In part, it has also involved the emergence of separate firms and industries. This has perhaps been most evident in the industries where technical change is now supplier-dominated. For example, Lowell textile mills in the nineteenth-century United States developed and produced much of their own machinery, but growing specialisation and vertical disintegration created the separate textile machinery industry (e.g. Gibb, 1950; Navin, 1950), and the textile industry itself has become increasingly supplier-dominated.

One implication of this long-term trend is that, with successively later entry into industrialisation, the accumulation of technological capability is less and less automatically linked to the accumulation of production capacity. And, as the 'doing' of ongoing production yields a progressively smaller by-product of learning about creating and changing technology, explicit investment in learning has become increasingly important as the basis for accumulating that kind of capability.

A further implication is that the trajectories of diversification and structural change in industry have become increasingly stunted for later industrialisers Thus, as we suggested in the previous section, the trajectories of diversification in earlier industrialisation often depended heavily on prior experience that encompassed both creating technology as well as using it. As a consequence, large parts of the basis for new areas of competitiveness were present in, and emerged out of, old areas of competitiveness – as in the case of the US textile machinery industry noted above.

However, with growing specialisation and vertical disintegration in these increasingly supplier-dominated industries, opportunities to pursue such trajectories of development have narrowed. This appears to have been the case even in the Korean textile industries. Despite their rapid growth over a long period with significant accumulation of technological capabilities, cotton spinning and weaving had limited importance as the foundation of more complex industrial activities (Amsden, 1989). Such structural discontinuities may present increasing obstacles to the evolution of comparative advantage from starting points in these types of increasingly supplier-dominated industry. Scale-intensive or knowledge-intensive sectors (e.g. automobiles and telecommunications) may have replaced textiles and other labour-intensive and supplier-dominated sectors as the initial sources of technological accumulation for the development of mechanical or electronic capital goods production – for example, see Hobday (1990) on the experience of Brazil in telecommunications.

Increasing scale of production

As is well known, the steady increase in minimum efficient scales of production since at least the early decades of this century has made it increasingly difficult for industrialising countries to enter new industries efficiently solely on the basis of their domestic markets. However, increasing scale has almost certainly also had a major effect on the process of technological accumulation in late-industrialising countries. As the minimum efficient scale of new units of plant and equipment has risen, the frequency of investment projects per unit of industrial expansion has fallen. With that have fallen both the incentives and opportunities for investment in technological learning. As the frequency of investment projects expected for given increases in output in particular industries has fallen, so also have the returns that firms and individuals would expect from investing in the kinds of engineering and managerial knowledge and skill required for implementing such projects – similar kinds of knowledge and skill that would also contribute to ongoing technical change in existing production facilities. Also, it is at the time of major investment projects that opportunities for significant technological learning are usually greatest – access to training and opportunities for experience acquisition with suppliers of equipment and engineering services is much more open at that investment stage than during the subsequent operational lifetime of projects. Thus, with a secular decline in the frequency of investment projects per unit of industry expansion, there is also a secular decline in the frequency of opportunities for the kinds of learning that contribute especially effectively to the accumulation of technological capabilities.

To conclude, the long-term trends of increasing specialisation and increasing production scale have resulted in technological accumulation becoming less and less 'built-in' to the process of industrialisation. It has required increasingly explicit investment in its own right. But, on top of the age-old problem about the limited appropriability of returns to investment in knowledge, these trends have made the returns increasingly distant and uncertain, while also decreasing the frequency of opportunities for making such investments.

It is in this historical context, that one should view the inter-country differences in technological accumulation outlined earlier. The experience of the East Asian NICs has involved several special features that have assisted the process of technological accumulation; but it has also involved particular approaches to policy that have offset to some extent the secular trends outlined above. Trade policy *has* been important. Export orientation has not only generated competitive pressures and other incentives for technological accumulation, it has also raised the frequency of investment projects in particular industries (hence increasing incentives and opportunities for learning), and it has opened other forms of access to learning opportunities. However, at least in Taiwan and Korea, inward-looking periods of import substitution also were important in providing initial opportunities for technological accumulation.

Nevertheless, while particular *sequences* of trade policy (Pack and Westphal, 1986) were clearly important, so too were other aspects of policy which acted more directly to stimulate firms' investments in technological capabilities. In ways that are poorly understood, these seem to have offset uncertainties and the limited appropriability of returns to such investments.

In other countries, trade policy often failed to provide the incentives and opportunities for rapid technological learning – with persisting protection and limited competitive pressures often permitting the accumulation of production capacity over long periods with little or no accumulation of technological capabilities. But so also did many other aspects of policy – in particular:

- policies which focused on accumulating technological capabilities in infrastructural institutions, while providing no direct incentives for their accumulation in firms;
- policies for the growth of particular industries which fragmented scale-intensive activities among firms so that, besides the common failure to realise efficient scales of production capacity, firms were often too small to accumulate the technological capabilities required for efficient dynamic performance over the longer term;
- policies for the development of new industries which stimulated short bursts of investment in numerous plants, thus precluding the managed sequences of cumulative learning opportunities that had characterised substantial parts of earlier Japanese industrialisation (Ozawa, 1980; Nakaoka, 1987).

Conclusions

Given its rudimentary empirical and conceptual basis, this chapter on technological accumulation in developed, developing and formerly centrally planned economies is bound to have numerous loose ends, and we shall not attempt to tie them all up here. Instead, we shall draw, briefly and sharply, the main conclusions that emerge from the above analysis.

The first is that a model of technical change based simply on the adoption of new vintages of machinery, accompanied by blueprints and operating instructions, and followed by productivity improvements resulting automatically from experience in production is inadequate. Apart from failing to explain how new vintages of machinery emerge in the first place, it does not even square with the empirical evidence about 'technology-borrowing' late-industrialising countries: it completely ignores the investment in intangible capital that is necessary not just to operate machines, but to 'choose' them in the first place, to improve their performance once acquired, to replicate them and further develop both them and the products they produce, and to lay the basis for related and higher value-added activities in future. In other words, such a model ignores the central importance of the stock of resources for generating and managing change that we have described as 'technological capabilities', and it ignores the conscious and deliberate learning required to accumulate those resources.

The second is that these change-generating resources have become increasingly complex and specialised. As a whole they have become increasingly differentiated from the resources required to use given technologies (described here as 'production capacity'), and they have themselves become increasingly differentiated, e.g. into resources for design, production engineering, quality control, R&D, and even – in certain fields – basic research. In an increasingly dynamic and competitive world they also involve knowledge and skills throughout the operating work-force that are additional to what is needed for the routine use of unchanging technologies.

The third is that the learning processes by which those resources are accumulated are also complex and specialised. In particular, although formal education and training in institutions outside industry provide essential bases of skill, this has to be augmented by learning within firms. However, important as it is, learning by doing provides only part of what is needed: in addition, and often in large part ahead of doing, accumulating a particular area of competence will require learning by explicit intra-firm training, managed experience accumulation and other means. Also learning by whatever means in one specialised area of competence (e.g. routine production or maintenance) will make only a limited contribution to learning in others (e.g. process engineering).

The fourth is that the experience of today's developed and developing countries shows that the differentiated and path-dependent processes of learning are the basis for changing patterns of comparative advantage as they develop. Both historical and contemporary analysis needs to be undertaken in order to understand the dynamics of these processes more fully. In the meantime, we can safely conclude that the conditions for effective learning in today's late-industrialising countries are different to those of earlier periods. In particular, the accumulation of technological capabilities has become increasingly uncoupled from the accumulation of production capacity as (i) its knowledge and institutional bases have become increasingly differentiated from those involved in routine production, and (ii) increasing production scale has reduced the learning incentives and opportunities associated with given increases in industrial output.

Finally, this means that the recurrent debate about the implications of alternative trade policies misses at least half the point about the longer-term dynamics of industrial growth. Policies for protection (plus the development of education and training institutes) may have been a sufficient basis for the accumulation of technological capabilities in late-industrialising countries in the nineteenth century – for example in Friedrich List's Germany. At that time, the locus of technological learning was close to production and, with optimum scale relatively small, significant learning incentives and opportunities were associated with relatively small increments in output. However, protection will not be a sufficient basis in the late twentieth century, when optimum scale is much bigger, and change-generating activities are increasingly separate from production. At the same time, while export-oriented policies are likely to enhance the pressures, incentives and opportunities for technological accumulation, they are unlikely to generate the optimum rate of investment in learning, given the complexities involved and the partial appropriability of the returns. At the end of the twentieth century, we need to move on from what is so often not a lot more than the old debate between List and Adam Smith.

For this reason, we conclude that learning activities – their nature, determinants and dynamic economic effects – should themselves become the focus of analytical and policy attention in future.

References

Abernathy, W. and Hayes, R. 1980. Managing our way to economic decline, *Harvard Business Review*, July/August: 67–77.

Abramovitz, M. 1986. Catching up, forging ahead and falling behind, *Journal of Economic History*, 46(2): 385–406.

Amsalem, M. A. 1983. *Technology Choice in Developing Countries: The Textile and Pulp and Paper Industries*, Cambridge, Mass., MIT Press.

Amsden, A. 1989. *Asia's Next Giant: South Korea and Late Industrialization*, Oxford, Oxford University Press.

Arora, A. and Gambardella, A. 1990. Complementarity and external linkages: the strategies of the large firms in biotechnology, *Journal of Industrial Economics*, 38: 361–79.

Arrow, K. 1962. The economic implications of learning by doing, *Review of Economic Studies*, 29: 155–73.

Azpiazu, D., Basualdo, E. and Nochteff, H. 1988. *La Revolución Tecnológica y las Políticas Hegemónicas: El Complejo Electrónico en la Argentina*, Buenos Aires, Legasa.

Barras, R. 1990. Interactive innovation in financial and business services: the vanguard of the service revolution, *Research Policy*, 19: 215–38.

Baumol, W. J. 1986. Productivity growth, convergence, and welfare: what the long-run data show, *American Economic Review*, 76: 1072–85.

Bell, M. 1984. Learning and the accumulation of technological capacity in developing countries, in M. Fransman and K. King (eds.), *Technological Capability in the Third World*, London, Macmillan.

Bell, M. and Oldham, G. 1988. Oil companies and the implementation of technical change in offshore operations: experience in development drilling and the design and operation of production facilities in the North Sea, mimeo report, Science Policy Research Unit, University of Sussex, Brighton.

Bell, M., Ross-Larsen, B. and Westphal, L. 1984. Assessing the performance of infant industries, *Journal of Development Economics*, 16: 101–28.

Bell, M. and Scott-Kemmis, D. 1997. The mythology of learning-by-doing in world war II airframe and ship production, *Industrial and Corporate Change* (forthcoming).

Bell, M., Scott-Kemmis, D. and Satyarakwit,W. 1982. Limited learning in infant industry: a case study, in F. Stewart and J. James (eds.), *The Economics of New Technology in Developing Countries*, London, Pinter.

Bloom, M. 1992. *Technological Change in the Korean Electronics Industry*, Paris, OECD Development Centre.

Bruland, K. 1989. *British Technology and European Industrialisation: The Norwegian Textile Industry in the Mid-Nineteenth Century*, Cambridge, Cambridge University Press.

Cainarca, G. C., Colombo, M.G. and Mariotti, S. 1992. Agreements between firms and the technological life cycle model: evidence from information technologies, *Research Policy*, 21: 45–62.

Cantwell, J. 1989. *Technological Innovation and Multinational Corporations*, Oxford, Blackwell.

Carlsson, B. and Henriksson, R. 1991. *Development Blocks and Industrial Transformation: The Dahmenian Approach to Economic Development*, Stockholm, Industrial Institute for Economic and Social Research (IUI).

Carvalho, R. de Q. 1992. Why the market reserve is not enough: the diffusion of industrial automation technology in Brazilian process industries, in H. Schmitz and J. Cassiolato, *Hi-tech for Industrial Development: Lessons from the Brazilian Experience in Electronics and Automation*, London, Routledge.

Chandler, A. 1989. *Scale and Scope*, Cambridge, Mass., Harvard University Press.

Chesnais, F. 1988. Technical co-operation agreements between firms, *Science Technology Industry Review*, no. 4 pp. 57–119.

Cohen, W. and Levinthal, D. 1989. Innovation and learning: the two faces of R&D, *Economic Journal*, 99: 569–96.

Contractor, F. 1985. Licensing versus foreign direct investment in U.S. corporate Strategy, in Rosenberg and Frischtak (eds.).

Cooper, C. 1991. Are innovation studies on industrialized economies relevant to technology policy for developing countries? mimeo, UNU/INTECH, Maastricht, Netherlands.

Corbett, J. and Mayer, C. 1991. *Financial Reform in Eastern Europe*, Discussion Paper no. 603, London, Centre for Economic Policy Research.

Coutinho, L. and Suzigan, W. 1991. Desenvolvimento tecnologico da industria e a costituição de um sistema nacional de innovação no Brasil, Instituto de Economia, Universidade Estadul de Campinas.

Dahlman, C. and Cortes, M. 1984. Mexico, *World Development*, 12: 601–24.

Dahlman, C. and Fonseca, F. 1987. From technological dependence to technological development: the case of the USIMINAS steel plant in Brazil, in Katz (ed.).

Dahlman, C., Ross-Larsen, B. and Westphal, L. 1987. Managing technological development: lessons from newly industrializing countries, *World Development*, 15: 759–75.

David, P. 1975. *Technical Choice, Innovation and Economic Growth*, Cambridge, Cambridge University Press.

De Long, B. 1988. Productivity growth, convergence, and welfare: comment, *American Economic Review*, 78: 1138–54.

De Melto, D., McMullen, K. and Wills, R. 1980. *Innovation and Technological*

Change in Five Canadian Industries, Discussion Paper, no. 176, Ottawa, Economic Council of Canada.

Deiaco, E. 1992. New views on innovative activity and technological performance: the Swedish innovation survey, *Science Technology Industry Review*, no. 11.

Desai, A. 1980. The origin and direction of industrial R&D in India, *Research Policy*, 9: 74–96.

Dollar, D. and Sokoloff, K. 1990. Patterns of productivity growth in South Korean manufacturing industries, 1963–1979, *Journal of Development Economics*, 33: 309–27.

Dosi, G. 1988. Sources, procedures, and microeconomic effects of innovation, *Journal of Economic Literature*, 36: 1120–71.

Dosi, G., Freeman, C., Nelson, R., Silverberg, G. and Soete, L. (eds.) 1988. *Technical Change and Economic Theory*, London, Pinter.

Dosi, G., Pavitt, K. and Soete, L. 1990. *The Economics of Technical Change and International Trade*, London, Harvester Wheatsheaf.

Dowrick, S. and Gemmell, N. 1991. Industrialisation, catching up and economic growth: a comparative study across the world's capitalist economies, *Economic Journal*, 101: 263–75.

Eads, G. and Nelson, R. 1971. Government support for advanced civilian technology, *Public Policy*, 19: 405–27.

Enos, J. 1991. *The Creation of Technological Capability in Developing Countries*, London: Pinter.

Enos, J. and Park, W.-H. 1988. *The Adoption and Diffusion of Imported Technology: The Case of Korea*, London, Croom Helm.

Ernst, D. and O'Connor, D. 1992. *Competing in the Electronics Industry: The Experience of Newly Industrialising Economies*, Paris, OECD Development Centre.

Eurich, N. and Boyer, E. 1985. *Corporate Classrooms: The Learning Business*. Princeton, Princeton University Press.

Fagerberg, J. 1987. A technology gap approach to why growth rates differ, *Research Policy*, 16: 87–99.

  1988. International competitiveness, *Economic Journal*, 98: 355–74.

Farrell, T. M. A. 1979. A Tale of Two Issues: nationalisation, the transfer of technology and the petroleum multinationals in Trinidad and Tobago, *Social and Economic Studies*, 28: 234–81.

Felix, D. 1979. On the diffusion of technology in Latin America, in J. H. Street and D. D. James (eds.), *Technological Progress in Latin America: The Prospects for Overcoming Dependency*, Boulder, Colo., Westview Press.

Freeman, C. 1982. *The Economics of Industrial Innovation*, London, Pinter.

  Technology and Economic Performance: Lessons from Japan, London, Pinter.

  1991. Catching up in world growth and world trade, in M. Nissanke (ed.), *Economic Crisis in Developing Countries: Policies for Recovery and Development*, London, Pinter.

Fukasaku, Y. 1986. Technology imports and R&D at Mitsubishi Nagasaki shipyard in the pre-war period, *Bonner Zeitschrift für Japanologie*, 8: 77–90.

Gibb, G. S. 1950. *The Saco-Lowell Shops: Textile Machinery Building in New England, 1813–1849*, Cambridge, Mass., Harvard University Press.

Gibbons, M. and Johnston, R. 1974. The roles of science in technological innovation, *Research Policy*, 3: 220–42.

Girvan, N. and Marcelle, G. 1990. Overcoming technological dependency: the case of Electric Arc (Jamaica) Ltd, a small firm in a small developing country, *World Development*, 18: 91–107.

Grossman, G. and Helpman, E. 1990. Trade, innovation and growth, *American Economic Review, Papers and Proceedings*, 80: 796–815.

Guerrieri, P. 1991. Technology and international trade performance of the most advanced countries, BRIE Working Paper, University of California, Berkeley.

Hagedoorn, J. and Schakenraad, J. 1992. Leading companies and networks of strategic alliances in information technologies, *Research Policy*, 21: 163–90.

Hanson, P. and Pavitt, K. 1987. *The Comparative Economics of Research, Development and Innovation in East and West: A Survey*, Chur, Harwood Academic Publishers.

Harris, R. and Mowery, D. 1990. Strategies for innovation: an overview, *California Management Review*, 32: 7–16.

Henderson, R. M. and Clark, K.B. 1990. Architectural innovation: the reconfiguration of existing product technologies and the failure of established firms, *Administrative Science Quarterly*, 35: 9–30.

Henderson, W. O. 1965. *Britain and Industrial Europe 1750–1870: Studies in British Influence on the Industrial Revolution in Western Europe*, Leicester, Leicester University Press.

Hobday, M. 1990. *Telecommunications in Developing Countries: The Challenge from Brazil*, London, Routledge.

  1994. Technological learning in Singapore: A test case of leapfrogging, *Journal of Development Studies*, 30: 831–58.

Hobday, M. and Baba, Y. 1990. ISDN in Thailand: developing country stategies in digital telecommunications, *Information Technology for Development*, 5: 1–21.

Hoffman, K. 1989. *Technological Advance and Organizational Innovation in the Engineering Industries*, Industry Series Paper no. 4, Industry and Energy Department, World Bank, Washington, D.C.

Hollander, S. 1965. *The Sources of Increased Efficiency: A Study of Du Pont Rayon Plants*, Cambridge, Mass., MIT Press.

Imai, M. 1986. *Kaizen: The Key to Japan's Competitive Success*, New York, McGraw-Hill.

Independent. 1992. World's best leave British children trailing in science, 13 March, p.3.

Jeremy, D. J. 1981. *Transatlantic Industrial Revolution: The Diffusion of Textile Technologies Between Britain and America, 1790–1830s*, Oxford, Blackwell.

Justman, M. and Teubal, M. 1991. A structuralist perspective on the role of technology in economic growth and development, *World Development*, 19: 1167–83.

Katz, J. 1984. Domestic technological innovation and dynamic comparative advantage, *Journal of Development Economics*, 16: 13–37.

1991. Industrial restructuring, public expenditure and social equity: the experience of Argentina, *Science and Public Policy*, 18: 375–8.

Katz, J. (ed.) 1987. *Technology Generation in Latin American Manufacturing Industries*, London, Macmillan.

Katz, J. and Bercovich, N. 1993. National systems of innovation supporting technical change in industry: the case of Argentina, in Nelson (ed.).

Kim, L. 1980. Stages of development of industrial technology in a developing country: a model, *Research Policy*, 9: 254–77.

Kim, Y.-H. 1984. Kankoku no Yushutsushiko-gata Kogyoka no Junkanmakanizumu (The mechanism of business cycles in Korea's export-oriented economy), *Kikan Keizai-kenkyu*, 7: 86–122.

1985. Shuhenbu no Gijutsu-nijugyappa to Gijutsu-tsuisekikeiro (The double technological gap and the process of technological catching-up in the periphery), *Kikan Keizai-kenkyu*, 8: 44–66.

Kleinknecht, A. and Reijnen, J. 1992. Why do firms cooperate on R&D? An empirical study, *Research Policy*, 21: 347–60.

Kodama, F. 1991. *Analyzing Japanese High Technologies*, London, Pinter.

Krugman, P. 1986. *Strategic Trade Policy and the New International Economics*, Cambridge, Mass., MIT Press.

Lall, S. 1980. Developing countries as exporters of industrial technology, *Research Policy*, 9: 24–51.

1985. Trade in technology by a slowly industrializing country, in Rosenberg and Frischtak (eds.).

1987. *Learning to Industrialize: The Acquisition of Technological Capability by India*, London, Macmillan.

1990. *Building Industrial Competitiveness in Developing Countries*. Paris, OECD Development Centre.

1992. Technological capabilities and industrialisation, *World Development*, 20: 165–86.

Landes, D. S. 1969. *The Unbound Prometheus: Technological Change and Industrial Development in Western Europe from 1750 to the Present*, Cambridge, Cambridge University Press.

Lawrence, P. 1980. *Managers and Management in West Germany*, London, Croom Helm.

Levin, R., Cohen, W. and Mowery, D. 1985 R&D, appropriability, opportunity and market structure: new evidence on the Schumpeterian hypothesis, *American Economic Review*, 75: 20–4.

Levin, R., Klevorick, A., Nelson, R. and Winter, S. 1987. Appropriating the returns from industrial research and development, *Brookings Papers on Economic Activity*, 3: 783–820.

Lucas, R. E. 1988. On the mechanics of economic development, *Journal of Monetary Economics*, 22: 248–57.

Lundvall, B.-Å. 1988. Innovation as an interactive process: from user-producer interaction to the national system of innovation, in Dosi *et al.* (eds.).

(ed.) 1992. *National Systems of Innovation*, London, Pinter.

Malerba, F. 1992. Learning by firms and incremental technical change, *Economic Journal*, 102: 845–59.

Mansfield, E., Schwartz, M. and Wagner, S. 1981. Imitation costs and patents: an empirical study, *Economic Journal*, 91: 907–18.

Metcalfe, S. 1988. The diffusion of innovations: an interpretative survey, in Dosi *et al.* (eds.).

Meyer-Stamer, J., Rauh, C., Riad, H., Schmitt, S. and Welte, T. 1991. *Comprehensive Modernization on the Shop Floor: A Case Study on the Brazilian Machinery Industry*, Berlin, German Development Institute.

Mitchell, G. and Hamilton, W. 1988. Managing R&D as a strategic option, *Research-Technology Management*, 31: 15–22.

Mlawa, H. M. 1983. The acquisition of technology, technological capability and technical change: a study of the textile industry in Tanzania, D.Phil. dissertation, University of Sussex, Brighton.

Mody, A., Suri, R. and Sanders, J. 1992. Keeping pace with change: organisational and technological imperatives, *World Development*, 20: 1797–816.

Morita, A. 1992. S Does Not Equal T, and T Does Not Equal I, Innovation Lecture, Royal Society, London, 6 February.

Mowery, D. 1983. The relationship between intrafirm and contractual forms of industrial research in American manufacturing, 1900–1940, *Explorations in Economic History*, 20: 351–74.

Mowery, D. and Rosenberg, N. 1989. *Technology and the Pursuit of Economic Growth*, Cambridge, Cambridge University Press.

Myers, S. 1984. Finance theory and finance strategy, *Interfaces*, 14: 126–37.

Mytelka, L. 1978. Licensing and technological dependence in the Andean Group, *World Development*, 6: 447–59.

1985. Stimulating effective technology transfer: the case of textiles in Africa, in Rosenberg, and Frischtak (eds.).

1992. Ivoirian industry at the crossroads, in Stewart *et al.* (eds.).

Nakaoka, T. 1987. On technological leaps of Japan as a developing country, *Osaka City University Economic Review*, 22: 1–25.

Navin, T. R. 1950. *The Whitin Machine Works since 1831*, Cambridge, Mass., Harvard University Press.

Nelson, R. (ed.) 1993. *National Innovation Systems*, New York, Oxford University Press.

Nelson, R. and Levin, R. 1986. The influence of science, university research and technical societies on industrial R&D and technical advance, Policy Discussion Paper Series No. 3, Research Programme on Technology Change, Yale University.

Nelson, R. and Winter, S. 1982. *An Evolutionary Theory of Economic Change*, Cambridge, Mass., Bellknap Press.

Ng C. Y., Hirono, R. and Siy, R. Y. 1986. *Effective Mechanisms for the Enhancement of Technology and Skills in ASEAN – An Overview*, Singapore, Institute of Southeast Asian Studies.

Nishimizu, M. and Page, J. M. Jr 1989. Productivity change and growth in industry and agriculture: an international comparison, in J. G. Williamson and V. R. Panchamukhi (eds.), *The Balance between Industry and Agriculture in Economic Development*, London, Macmillan.

Odagiri, H. and Goto, A. 1992. Technology and industrial development in Japan, mimeo, Tskuba University, Japan.

Ohiorhenuan, J. F. E. and Poloamina, I. D. 1992. Building indigenous technological capacity in African industry: the Nigerian case, in Stewart *et al.* (eds.).

Oshima, K. 1984. Technological innovation and industrial research in Japan, *Research Policy*, 13: 285–301.

Ozawa, T. 1974. *Japan's Technological Challenge to the West, 1950–1974: Motivation and Accomplishment*, Cambridge, Mass., MIT Press.

1980. Government control over technology acquisition and firms' entry into new sectors: the experience of Japan's synthetic-fibre industry, *Cambridge Journal of Economics*, 4: 133–46.

1985. Macroeconomic factors affecting Japan's technology inflows and outflows: the postwar experience, in Rosenberg and Frischtak (eds.).

Pack, H. 1987. *Productivity, Technology and Industrial Development: A Case Study in Textiles*, Oxford, Oxford University Press.

1988. Industrialisation and trade, in H. B. Chenery and T. N. Srinivasan (eds.), *Handbook of Development Economics*, Amsterdam, North Holland.

1992. Technology gaps between developed and developing countries: are there dividends for latecomers?, paper presented at the World Bank Annual Conference on Development Economics, Washington, D.C., 30 April and 1 May.

Pack, H. and Westphal, L. E. 1986. Industrial strategy and technological change: theory versus reality, *Journal of Development Economics*, 22: 87–128.

Patel, P. and Pavitt, K. 1991a. Large firms in the production of the world's technology: an important case of 'Non-globalization', *Journal of International Business Studies*, 22: 1–21.

1991b. The limited importance of large firms in Canadian technological activities, in D. G. McFetridge (ed.), *Foreign Investment, Technology and Economic Growth*, Calgary, University of Calgary Press.

1991c. Europe's technological performance, in C. Freeman, M. Sharp and W. Walker (eds.), *Technology and the Future of Europe: Global Competition and the Environment in the 1990s*, London, Pinter.

1992. The innovative performance of the world's largest firms: some new evidence, *Economics of Innovation and New Technology*, 2: 91–102.

Pavitt, K. 1984. Sectoral patterns of technical change: towards a taxonomy and a theory, *Research Policy*, 13: 343–73.

1988. International patterns of technological accumulation, in N. Hood and J.-E. Vahlne (eds.), *Strategies for Global Competition*, London, Croom Helm.

1991. What makes basic research economically useful?, *Research Policy*, 20: 109–19.

Pavitt, K. and Patel, P. 1988. The international distribution and determinants of technological activities, *Oxford Review of Economic Policy*, 4: 35–55.

Pavitt, K., Robson, M. and Townsend, J. 1987. The size distribution of innovating firms in the UK: 1945–1983, *Journal of Industrial Economics*, 35: 297–316.

Porter, M. 1990. *The Competitive Advantage of Nations*, London, Macmillan.

Poznanski, K. 1984. *Competition Between Eastern Europe and Developing Countries in the Western Market for Manufactured Goods*, evidence prepared for the Joint Economic Committee of the US Congress, Washington, D.C.

Prais, S. 1981. Vocational qualifications of the labor force in Britain and Germany, *National Institute Economic Review*, 98: 47–59.

Quazi, H. A. 1983. Technological capacity and production performance in the fertiliser and paper industries in Bangladesh, D.Phil. dissertation, University of Sussex, Brighton.

Ray, G. 1991. *Innovation and Technical Change in Eastern Europe*, London, National Institute for Economic and Social Research.

Riedel, J. 1988. Economic development in East Asia: doing what comes naturally?, in H. Hughes (ed.), *Achieving Industrialization in East Asia*, Cambridge, Cambridge University Press.

Romer, P. M. 1986. Increasing returns and long-run growth, *Journal of Political Economy*, 94: 1002–37.

1990. Endogenous technological change, *Journal of Political Economy*, 98: 71–102.

Rosenberg, N. 1972. Factors affecting the diffusion of technology, *Explorations in Economic History*, 10: 3–33.

1976. *Perspectives on Technology*, Cambridge, Cambridge University Press.

Rosenberg, N. and Frischtak, C. (eds.) 1985. *International Technology Transfer*, New York, Praeger.

Rosenberg, N. and Nelson, R. 1992. American universities and technical advance in industry, Center for Economic Policy Research, Stanford University.

Rothwell, R. 1977. The characteristics of successful innovators and technically progressive firms, *R&D Management*, 7: 191–206.

Schmookler, J. 1966. *Invention and Economic Growth*, Cambridge, Mass., Harvard University Press.

Schumpeter, J. 1943. *Capitalism, Socialism and Democracy*, New York, Harper and Row.

Scientometrics. 1992. International Conference on Science Indicators for Developing Countries, 23, no.1.

Scott-Kemmis, D. 1988. Learning and the accumulation of technological capacity in Brazilian pulp and paper firms, working paper, Employment Programme Research, International Labour Organisation, Geneva.

Scott-Kemmis, D. and Bell, M. 1988. Technological dynamism and the technological content of collaboration: are Indian firms missing opportunities?, in A. Desai (ed.), *Technology Absorption in Indian Industry*, New Delhi, Wiley Eastern.

Senker, J. 1992. The contribution of tacit knowledge to innovation, mimeo, Science Policy Research Unit, University of Sussex, Brighton.

Senker, J. and Faulkner, W. 1992. Industrial use of public sector research in advanced technologies, *R&D Management*, 22: 157–75.

Sercovich, F. 1980. State-owned enterprises and dynamic comparative advantage in the world petrochemical industry: the case of commodity olefins in Brazil,

Development Discussion Paper No. 96. Institute for International Development, Harvard University.

1984. Brazil, *World Development*, 12: 575–99.

Smith, K. and Vidvei, T. 1992. Innovation activity and innovation outputs in Norwegian industry, *Science Technology Industry Review*, no. 11.

Soete, L. 1981. A general test of technological gap trade theory, *Weltwirtschaftliches Archiv*, 117: 638–66.

Stewart, F., Lall, S. and Wangwe, S. (eds.), 1992. *Alternative Development Strategies in Sub-Saharan Africa*, London, Macmillan.

Stigler, G. 1956. Industrial organisation and economic progress, in L. White (ed.), *The State of the Social Sciences*, Chicago, University of Chicago Press.

Stiglitz, J. 1987. Learning to learn, localized learning and technological progress, in P. Dasgupta and P. Stoneman (eds.), *Economic Policy and Technological Performance*, Cambridge, Cambridge University Press.

Tanaka, M. 1978. Industrialization on the basis of imported technology: a case study of the Japanese heavy chemical industry 1870–1930, M.Phil. dissertation, University of Sussex, Brighton.

1992. Technology transfer in the petrochemical industry, MIT Japan Program, MITJP 92–06, Massachusetts Institute of Technology, Cambridge, Mass.

Teitel, S. 1981. Towards an understanding of technical change in semi-industrialized countries, *Research Policy*, 10: 127–47.

1982. Skills and information requirements of industrial technologies: on the use of engineers as a proxy, in M. Syrquin and S. Teitel (eds.), *Trade, Stability, Technology and Equity in Latin America*, New York: Academic Press.

1984. Technology creation in semi-industrialized economies, *Journal of Development Economics*, 16: 39–61.

Tushman, M. L. and Anderson, P. 1986. Technological discontinuities and organizational environments, *Administrative Science Quarterly*, 31: 439–65.

UNCTAD 1985. *Technology Issues in the Energy Sector of Developing Countries: Technological Impact of the Public Procurement Policy – the Experience of the Power Plant Sector in the Republic of Korea*, United Nations Conference on Trade and Development, TT/60, United Nations, Geneva.

UNIDO 1992. *Industry and Development: Global Report 1992/93*, United Nations Industrial Development Organization, Vienna.

Vernon, R. 1987. Key factors in the application of industrial technology in developing countries, mimeo, Harvard University, Cambridge, Mass.

Vianna, H. A. 1985. International technology transfer, technological learning and the assimilation of imported technology in state-owned enterprises: the case of SODOR steel plant in Venezuela, D.Phil. dissertation, University of Sussex, Brighton.

Voss, C. A. 1988. Implementation: a key issue in manufacturing technology: the need for a field of study, *Research Policy*, 17: 55–63.

Wade, R. 1990. *Governing the Market: Economic Theory and the Role of Government in East Asian Industrialization*. Princeton, Princeton University Press.

Wangwe, S. 1992. Building indigenous technological capacity: a study of selected industries in Tanzania, in Stewart *et al.* (eds.).

Westphal, L., Kim, L. and Dahlman, C. 1985. Reflections on the Republic of Korea's acquisition of technological capability, in Rosenberg and Frischtak, (eds.).

Westphal, L. E., Rhee, Y.W. and Pursell, G. 1981. Korean industrial competence: where it came from, Staff Working Paper no. 469, World Bank, Washington D.C.

Wiggenhorn, W. 1990. Motorola U: when training becomes an education, *Harvard Business Review* (July/August), pp. 71–83.

Zahlan, A. 1991. *Acquiring Technological Capacity: A Study of Arab Consulting and Contracting Firms*, London, Macmillan.

5 Inward technology transfer and competitiveness: the role of national innovation systems

DAVID C. MOWERY AND JOANNE OXLEY[1]

Introduction

A central theme of global economic change during the post-war period has been the application in less developed countries of technologies developed within economically advanced regions. This phenomenon underpinned the post-1945 transformation of Japan and other East Asian economies, and influenced the reconstruction of Western European economies after the Second World War. The application of externally developed technologies within 'latecomer' economies is hardly unique to the post-war period, however. Samuel Slater's introduction of British textile manufacturing is but one example of inward technology transfer in the nineteenth-century US economy, and David (1992) traces the origins of patent monopolies to efforts by medieval European city-states and nations to attract experts in industrial arts to practise their craft within these jurisdictions. Both international technology flows and government efforts to influence them for national competitive advantage thus have ample historical precedent.

Several characteristics nevertheless distinguish the post-1945 era from earlier periods. The influence of international technology transfer on national economic development has increased, as the post-war development of such economies as Taiwan and South Korea has relied much less on natural resource endowments than nineteenth-century 'success stories' like the United States (Nelson and Wright, 1992). In addition, the post-war period has witnessed convergence of the growth rates in per capita income of developed economies and considerable catching up by Japan and such late industrialisers as South Korea and Taiwan (World Bank, 1991).[2] The 'technology gaps' among the industrial economies that typified the early post-war period have been reduced by more rapid international technology transfer (Nelson, 1990). The OECD has suggested that a growing disconnection between international flows of technology and international flows of goods embodying these technologies has created new opportunities for entry by firms from newly industrialising economies (NIEs) into the manufacture of sophisticated products (OECD, 1988).

The Japanese and East Asian experiences have drawn attention to the role of 'national innovation systems' in supporting the inward transfer and exploitation of technologies from external sources. The concept of a national innovation system (NIS) was developed by Freeman to analyse post-war Japanese economic policy and growth (Freeman, 1987), and has been applied to a broader cross-section of economies in more recent work (Lundvall, 1992; Nelson, 1993). A country's NIS comprises the network of public and private institutions that fund and perform R&D, translate the results of R&D into commercial innovations and effect the diffusion of new technologies. This chapter examines the role of national innovation systems in the inward transfer of technology, primarily in Japan and the 'late industrialisers' of the post-war period, but also in the industrialised Western economies.

The chapter is organised as follows: the next section examines the primary channels for international technology transfer in the post-war global economy – direct foreign investment, international strategic alliances, licensing and 'embodied' transfers through the import of technology-intensive goods. The subsequent section defines and discusses the concept of national innovation systems, and examines the characteristics of national innovation systems and broader government policies that have supported successful inward transfer and exploitation of technology, contributing to economic development and competitiveness.

The chapter's general conclusions may be easily summarised. There is considerable variation among the national innovation systems of economies that have successfully exploited foreign technologies, but the details of these differences appear to be less important than a few broad similarities. The economies that have benefited most from inward technology transfer have national systems of innovation that include public policies strengthening their 'national absorptive capacity' (Dahlman and Brimble, 1990). This capacity relies on investments in the scientific and production labour force, along with trade and economic policies that enforce competition among domestic firms and do not discriminate against exports of finished goods or against imports of capital goods. The particular channels for inward technology transfer, the specific identity of any 'strategic industries' targeted for public intervention, and the extent to which a nation's trade regime can be described as 'liberal' or 'restrictive' all appear to be of secondary importance. In drawing lessons from the experiences of these economies, however, it is important to recognise that the future environment may not resemble the past, and we discuss this issue in the concluding section.

Channels of inward technology transfer

Successful international technology transfer rarely resembles trade in conventional goods. The neoclassical view of technology, which is now fading into merciful oblivion, has too often treated technology as a 'book of blueprints', subject to modest or non-existent costs of transfer. But technologies can rarely be embodied in a 'book of blueprints', and even more rarely transferred as such. International technology transfer, like domestic technology transfer, is a costly, time-intensive and knowledge-intensive process.

The intangible nature of much of the process and content of international technology transfer means that measuring the level or results of this activity is very difficult. Licensing fees and royalties measure activity within one channel of international technology transfer, but this channel accounts for only a modest share of total international transfer (see below). Moreover, even technology transferred through a licensing agreement often requires considerable modification by the recipient. Measurements that focus solely on licensing transactions therefore capture only a small portion of the overall activities involved in absorbing and applying technology. Other measures of domestic technological activity and outputs, such as patents or R&D investment, do not distinguish clearly between technologies of domestic, as opposed to international, origin.

One indicator of the contribution of innovative and technology-related activities to economic growth is the contribution to output growth of total factor productivity (TFP), listed in table 5.1 for nine Asian economies for all or part of the 1955–80 period. Inasmuch as most of these economies were importers of technology throughout this period, higher shares of TFP in total output growth can be taken to indicate greater success in obtaining technology from international sources and applying it in the domestic economy. The data in table 5.1 suggest that the economies that were most successful in inward technology transfer from the mid-1950s to the early or mid-1970s were South Korea, Singapore and Taiwan, followed closely by Hong Kong, and more distantly by India. Although the contribution of total factor productivity to output growth declined during the 1970s in most of these economies (as it did in the industrial economies) the contribution of TFP growth remained high in both Taiwan and South Korea. In India, on the other hand, the contribution of TFP growth to output growth approached zero during the 1970s. This period's slow TFP growth in India appears to be consistent with abundant evidence of the economy's low reliance on inward technology transfer (Lall, 1985; Jacobsson, 1991).

A number of the findings from the extensive literature on domestic technology transfer are relevant to international technology transfer. For example, the exploitation of external technology requires the creation

Table 5.1. *Growth in output and total factor productivity in nine Asian economies, 1955–80*

	Period	Annual rate of output growth (per cent)	Contribution of total factor productivity (per cent)
Hong Kong	1955–1970	9.3	46.5
	1970–1980	9.6	21.3
India	1950–1980	3.5	39.1
	1970–1980	3.0	0.2
Indonesia	1970–1980	7.7	31.5
South Korea	1955–1970	8.8	56.4
	1970–1980	8.5	41.2
Malaysia	1970–1980	7.8	21.7
Philippines	1957–1962	4.9	0.0
	1963–1969	5.2	15.4
	1970–1980	6.2	20.6
Singapore	1957–1970	6.6	55.2
	1966–1972	12.5	4.8
	1970–1980	9.1	19.7
Taiwan	1955–1977	8.0	53.6
	1970–1980	8.5	50.0
Thailand	1970–1980	6.9	19.7

Source: United Nations (1992) based on published data of Ikemoto.

within the firm of some 'absorptive capacity' (Cohen and Levinthal, 1989, 1990), an ability to understand an externally sourced technology and apply it internally. Caves and Uekusa (1976, p. 126) argue that post-war Japanese firms invested heavily in R&D in order to support the inward transfer of licensed technologies: 'Firms must maintain some research capacity in order to know what technology is available for purchase or copy and they must generally modify and adapt foreign technology in putting it to use.' Similarly, research on the growth of US industrial research during the 1900–46 period (Mowery, 1983) reported that in-house R&D operations tend to complement the use of contract research organisations.

The demands placed on absorptive capacity are also likely to vary with the age of the technology. In the case of contract research organisations, more complex research projects exhibit higher levels of complementarity with in-house R&D (Mowery, 1983; see also Cohen and Levinthal, 1989). Furthermore, different 'modes' of technology transfer (such as licensing,

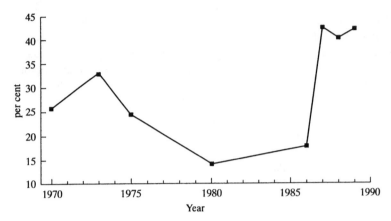

Figure 5.1. Share of inward DFI in long-term finance of trade deficit, all non-oil-exporting LDCs, 1970–89. (*Source:* United Nations, Conference on Trade and Development, 1991.)

joint venture or direct transfer to a wholly owned subsidiary) place different demands on the absorptive capacity of the recipient firm.

Most technologies consist of 'codified' and 'tacit' components, and the international (or domestic) transfer of a technology requires access to the tacit components as well as those codified in a blueprint, licence agreement or data package. The importance of this tacit component means that successful technology transfer often requires the transfer of people, as well as technology specifications and blueprints (Teece, 1977). Exploiting a technology's commercial possibilities, as Teece (1986) has pointed out, also demands skills that extend beyond R&D. Appropriating the economic returns to many technologies (whether created within a firm or obtained from external sources) requires the innovator, or licensee, to develop competence in the downstream activities of production, distribution and marketing.

Channels of international technology transfer: aggregate trends

The primary channels for international technology transfer during the post-war period have been direct foreign investment, joint-ventures and strategic alliances, licensing and trade in capital goods. The importance of these four channels has differed between the economies discussed in this chapter, and we therefore examine trends in international technology transfer within each channel, as well as the regional distribution of technology flows through each.[3]

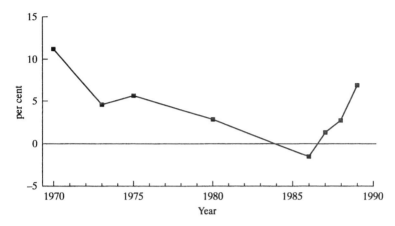

Figure 5.2. Share of inward DFI in long-term finance of trade deficit, least developed countries, 1970–89. (*Source:* United Nations, Conference on Trade and Development, 1991.)

Direct foreign investment

Following a substantial decline after 1973, direct foreign investment (DFI) has increased since the mid-1980s as a proportion of inward capital flows for developing economies. DFI surpassed all other forms of lending as a source of private foreign capital for developing economies in 1988, and its dominance has continued since that time. Figure 5.1 portrays recent trends for non-oil-exporting developing economies. *The Economist* (1993b), citing data from the World Bank, concluded that total flows of long-term capital to developing economies grew from $159 billion in 1981 to $205 billion in 1991; the share of this flow accounted for by commercial bank lending declined from 46% in 1981 to 17% in 1991, while the DFI share grew from 8.3% to 16.5%.

Reflecting the divergent trends in performance among developing economies, however, the share of DFI within the world's least developed economies has rebounded less dramatically, moving from net disinvestment in 1986 to roughly 7% of long term financing of current account deficits in 1989. This compares unfavourably with its 1970 share of more than 10% (figure 5.2).[4]

Figures 5.3 to 5.5 provide detail on the destination of direct investment outflows from two leading sources of DFI, Japan and the United States. Figure 5.3 indicates that the share of US non-petroleum DFI flows going to developing economies in the period 1975–92 fluctuated significantly.[5] From a share that exceeded that of Western Europe in 1975, the developing

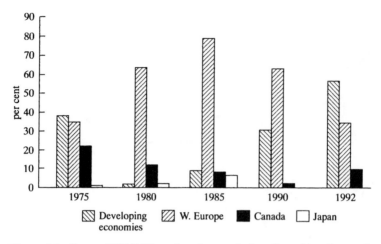

Figure 5.3. Share of US DFI outflow (net capital outflow plus reinvested earnings (excluding petroleum)) going to each region, 1975–92. (*Source:* United States Department of Commerce, *Survey of Current Business*, 1975–92.)

economies plummeted in the early 1980s to less than 5% of total outward US DFI. Western Europe dominated US non-petroleum DFI throughout the 1980s. By 1990, however, the developing economies' share of US outward DFI had rebounded to roughly 30%, and by 1992, developing economies once again constituted the leading destination for US non-petroleum DFI. Much of this resurgence reflects increases in the shares of US DFI accounted for by Latin America and Asia. Although the Asian economies accounted for a small and relatively stable share (slightly below 5%) in the period 1975–90, this grew sharply between 1990 and 1992, off-setting a decline in the Latin American share (figure 5.4).

The data in figure 5.5 show that developed-economy destinations dominated Japanese direct foreign investment during the late 1980s. Asian economies' share of Japanese DFI increased somewhat from 1986 (10.4%) to 1991 (14.3%), reflecting Japanese firms' search for lower-cost offshore production sites and their growing interest in penetration of the rapidly expanding consumer markets of South-east Asia. According to *The Economist* (1994), Asian economies' share of Japanese outward DFI has risen further since 1990, to nearly 20% of the total, with much of the most recent wave of investment concentrated on manufacture of consumer goods for regional markets. The share of Japanese DFI destined for the United States has declined from 48.2% in 1990 to 43.3% in 1992 (*Economist*, 1993a). Latin America's share of Japanese DFI has also declined, from more than 20% in 1986 to 8% in 1991.

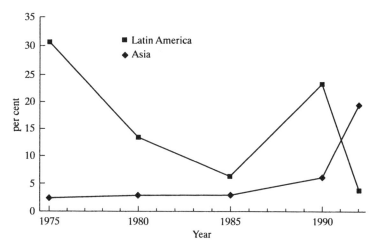

Figure 5.4. Shares of US DFI outflow (net capital outflow plus reinvested earnings (excluding petroleum)) going to Latin America and Asia, 1975–92. (*Source:* United States Department of Commerce, *Survey of Current Business*, 1975–92.)

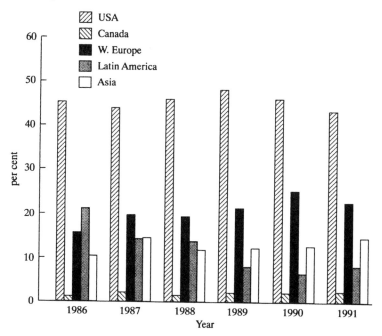

Figure 5.5. Share of Japanese DFI going to each region, 1986–91. (*Source:* OECD, 1990, 1992, 1993.)

146   David C. Mowery and Joanne Oxley

Table 5.2. *Asian inward DFI originating in Asian NIEs, 1983–6 and 1987–90 (percentage of average annual inflow for each economy)*

	1983–6	1987–90
India	1	3
Indonesia	11	19
Malaysia	19	41
Philippines	6	18
Thailand	13	31
South Korea	3	5
Taiwan	10	14
China	55	66

Source: United Nations (1992, p.25).

Another significant development in DFI patterns during the 1980s was the growth of direct foreign investment outflows from the NIEs, primarily South Korea, Taiwan, and the People's Republic of China (PRC). Total Asian NIE outflows amounted to roughly $8 billion in 1989 and 1990, having grown by 75% during 1986–90. Direct investment outflows from Taiwan exceeded inflows during 1987–90, and South Korea registered a similar net outflow during 1990. Outward DFI flows from the PRC have grown at an average rate of 17% per year since 1986. According to the United Nations (1992), most of these outflows are directed towards North America and Western Europe, which accounted for 64% of Taiwan's stock of DFI in 1990. NIEs are now also a significant source of direct foreign investment for countries within Asia, especially Indonesia, Malaysia, and Thailand (see table 5.2). NIE-sourced investments should provide a particularly effective channel for the transfer of manufacturing technologies into these countries, since the technologies will be tailored to regional conditions and factor prices.

Joint-ventures and strategic alliances
    Since 1980, there has been another significant development in the international operations of firms from the industrial economies: the growth of joint-ventures and 'strategic alliances' linking firms from two or more countries (Mowery, 1988, 1989). Many of these strategic alliances do not entail significant cross-border flows of capital, and therefore are not included in aggregate measures of DFI. In contrast to the joint-ventures of the 1950–70 period, which focused more on the development of natural

Table 5.3. *Pacific Rim joint-ventures in information technology, 1984–91*

	Japan	West Germany	France	UK	Taiwan	South Korea
US firms:						
Office automation	542	143	21	275	41	45
Computers, robotics, electronics	182	32	5	53	12	39
Media	115	27	18	126	1	5
Satellites, telecomms.	209	75	26	228	16	15
Video	232	27	8	64	6	13
Japanese firms:						
Office automation	542	39	8	69	11	13
Computers, robotics, electronics	182	15	4	22	9	8
Media	115	44	7	25	0	2
Satellites, telecomms.	209	13	4	39	4	1
Video	232	12	8	39	11	5

Source: Mowery (1992).

resources, many of the strategic alliances of the 1980s are concerned with the manufacture of goods for global markets and even joint development of new products. They are thus an important channel for international technology transfer (see, for example, Hagedoorn and Schakenraad, 1990).

Alliances between firms from industrial and industrialising economies are likely to expand in the future, but the limited available data indicate that, thus far, 'North–South' alliances are rare. Although there is no single authoritative database on these ventures, some indication of the distribution of 'North–North' and 'North–South' ventures involving US firms is contained in table 5.3, which covers international ventures in information technology involving Pacific Rim firms during 1984–91. These data indicate that collaborative ventures in this region primarily link US and Japanese firms. Alliances between US or Japanese firms with firms from other Pacific Rim economies mainly involve firms from South Korea and Taiwan, but these are far less important than ventures linking Japanese or US firms with firms from the largest economies in Western Europe. Similar findings were reported by Hagedoorn and Schakenraad (1990) and in a United Nations (1992) study, which concluded that no more than 2–3 per cent of the strategic alliances of the 1980s linked industrial-economy with

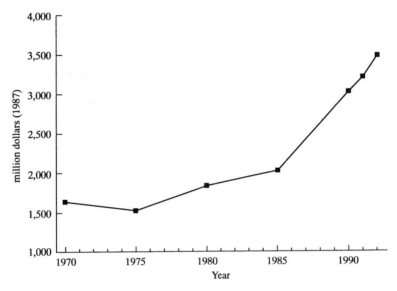

Figure 5.6. US royalty receipts, 1970–92. (*Source:* United States Department of Commerce, *Survey of Current Business.*)

developing-economy or NIE firms, and only 2 per cent linked firms from developing economies or NIEs with one another.

Asian NIEs do not yet appear to be forming international ventures with one another, in part because the domestic markets of many of them are so much smaller than those of the major Triad economies (the United States, Japan and Europe). Also, the technological and other assets of firms in the Asian NIEs may not complement one another as well as they do in ventures that link NIE firms with US, European or Japanese firms. These data also do not suggest the creation of a Japan-centred economic bloc based on international joint-ventures that exclude US or European firms. Instead, Pacific Rim joint-ventures appear to be linking the economies of the Triad more closely.

Technology licensing

Data on the growth and destination of technology licensing flows are much scarcer than those for foreign investment, but licensing appears to have been an important channel for technology transfer to such economies as South Korea, India, Japan, Brazil and Thailand during the post-war period. OECD members' licensing receipts grew by 6 per cent annually during the 1970s, exceeding the growth rate of DFI outflows

Table 5.4. *Machinery imports as a percentage of domestic expenditures on machinery (ISIC 38)*

India (1983/4)	0.18
South Korea (1983)	0.41
Sweden (1982)	0.56
Norway (1982)	0.57
Denmark (1982)	0.70
Netherlands (1980)	0.61

Source: Jacobsson (1991, p.51).

during that period (OECD, 1988). Figure 5.6, showing the growth rate of (constant-dollar) royalties and licensing fees received from 'unaffiliated foreigners' by US firms during 1970–92, indicates rapid growth in these flows during the 1980s (with receipts growing by more than 50 per cent during the 1985–90 period) followed by slower but still considerable growth, as US receipts grew by roughly 10 per cent during 1990–2.

A 1992 OECD report, identifying a startling example of this growth trend, states that South Korean spending on licences for imports of technology grew tenfold during the 1982–91 period (OECD, 1992, p.223). The regional sources of licensing and royalty payments received by US enterprises during 1970–90 were dominated by Western Europe, followed by Japan.[6]

Embodied technology transfer: capital goods imports and turnkey plants

A final important channel for inward technology transfer involves the embodied technology transfer that occurs through the import of advanced capital goods and, in some cases, turnkey industrial plants. The importance of both forms of embodied technology transfer for South Korean industrial development has been emphasised by Westphal *et al.* (1985) and Dahlman and Brimble (1990).

Table 5.4 displays data on imports of machinery and equipment for six economies at different stages of development. India, which has long pursued a policy of self-reliance in capital goods, relying on inward licensing of foreign technologies, displays a much smaller share of imports in domestic 'consumption' of these capital goods. Interestingly, despite the numerous references to the role of imported capital goods in its development, South Korea relies less heavily on machinery imports than the advanced European economies listed in table 5.4. This may be attributable to the continuing protection of certain Korean industries.[7]

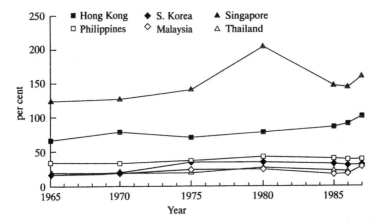

Figure 5.7. Capital goods imports as a proportion of GDP in selected countries, 1965–87. Because of re-exports, values may exceed 100 per cent. (*Source:* Dahlman and Brimble, 1990, p.17.)

Figure 5.7 shows the share of GDP accounted for by capital goods imports in a number of Asian developing economies during 1965–87. The economies that have the highest output growth (shown in table 5.1) since 1970, Hong Kong and Singapore, also have the highest levels of capital goods imports as a share of GDP.

Comparing technology transfer channels

The above discussion of aggregate trends emphasises the variation among countries in the importance of different channels of inward technology transfer. This raises an interesting question: to what extent are the various channels of inward technology transfer complements or substitutes? The data cited above on the regional distribution of US DFI outflows and royalty income suggest some complementarity between DFI and licensing in Western Europe, but the dominant relationship between these two channels of technology transfer elsewhere appears to be one of substitution, rather than complementarity. This hypothesis receives additional support in work by Contractor (1985), and is consistent with evidence from a number of post-war developing economies.

Table 5.5 shows the ranking of developing economies according to their reliance on inward technology licences in 1979. The economy with the most liberal policy towards inward direct foreign investment, Thailand, displays the lowest level of outward royalty and licensing fee payments. The other economies, all of which impose more stringent restrictions on inward foreign investment, rely more heavily on licensing.[8] Capital goods imports

Table 5.5. *Licensing fees as percentage of GDP, 1979*

Mexico	2.70
Brazil	1.90
South Korea	1.10
India	0.80
Thailand	0.13

Sources: All data from Lall (1985, p.53), except Thailand, from Dahlman and Brimble (1990, p.16).

on occasion have complemented technology transfer through licensing. During the high-growth era of the 1950s and 1960s, the Japanese government developed complementary policies for capital goods imports and inward technology licensing. Ozawa (1985, pp.229–30) argues that MITI acted to diffuse the embodied technology of imported capital goods internally, while protecting domestic producers against import competition. Imports of heavy electrical machinery, for example, were limited to one version of each type, and were bundled with a licence to produce copies of the equipment. Import substitution was accompanied by efforts to support entry by at least three domestic producers into the production of this equipment, so as to maintain competitive pressure on each firm.

Although they often complement one another, different channels for inward technology transfer convey different vintages of technology. DFI, for example, transfers more advanced technologies than alternative channels. According to Mansfield *et al.* (1982), the average age of technologies transferred to their developing-economy subsidiaries by US firms during the 1960–78 period was ten years, significantly younger than the average age of technologies transferred through licensing or joint ventures (thirteen years). And while there appear to be no similar studies comparing the age of licensed technologies with those transferred through capital goods imports, it is likely that imports of capital equipment embody technologies that lie somewhere between the age of those available through licensing and those transferred to wholly-owned subsidiaries. Technology that is transferred in an embodied form requires more modest technological capabilities than those needed to exploit licensed technologies of similar age and complexity.

There are several mechanisms through which a host country can reap the benefits of inward technology transfer. Technological benefits generally assume the form of spillovers, or external effects, that go beyond such direct sources of economic benefit as higher-productivity, higher-wage manufacturing jobs.[9] Important sources of spillovers are 'reverse engineering', which may result in the development of similar products for indigenous manufacture and export, and skills acquisition through 'learning by using'. The extent of these spillovers depends on several factors: the age of transferred technology, the channel of transfer and the level of indigenous technical capabilities. Potential spillovers are greatest for the most up-to-date technologies, but exploitation of these spillovers is limited by the controls imposed by the transferring firm, and by the level of indigenous technical capabilities.

Technology-related benefits to the host country from DFI operate though demonstration, observation, imitation and application of advanced technologies (defined here to include management methods as well as process and product technologies). Because of their high tacit component, demonstration of these technologies in local operating conditions is often essential for local firms to recognise their feasibility and to attempt to imitate them. Exploiting these spillovers also may require considerable mobility of labour and management personnel within the host economy, as well as sufficient competitive pressure on domestic firms to create incentives for them to adopt the advanced techniques.[10] Similar spillover benefits may be realised through linkages between foreign-owned firms and domestic suppliers – here too, competitive pressure and mobile human capital are essential prerequisites.

Since they transfer relatively mature technologies, licensing transactions have been particularly important in the early stages of the 'latecomer' pattern of industrialisation exemplified by Japan and South Korea, both of which undertook industrialisation and reconstruction with investments in mature industries (Kim and Dahlman, 1992). Subsequent efforts by Asian developing economies to enter more advanced industries that rely on 'younger' technologies have made DFI a more important mechanism for inward technology transfer. As the electronics industries of Taiwan and South Korea have expanded and increased their technological sophistication, for example, licensing of foreign technologies has become more difficult – there are fewer sources of supply and many of these firms are much more reluctant to license to firms that are strong competitors. In recognition of this fact, both Taiwan and South Korea liberalised their regulation of inward DFI during the 1980s (Westphal et al., 1985; Hou and San, 1993).

Outward DFI also has increased in importance with the emergence of new, technology-intensive industries in these economies. The efforts of Taiwanese and South Korean firms to invest in foreign markets reflects the need to establish operations in the industrial economies that dominate the supply of new industrial technologies, in order to better monitor competitive opportunities and threats and ease trade frictions.

Despite the significance of direct foreign investment as a channel for the transfer of advanced technologies, its importance within the development of various post-war economies differs significantly. Within East Asia, for example, Japan and South Korea both created internationally competitive electronics industries with relatively little reliance on DFI. On the other hand, the strong electronics industries of Singapore and Hong Kong have relied heavily on DFI, and Taiwan also has been more open to foreign investment than South Korea (Mowery and Steinmueller, 1991; Dahlman, 1992). Tight controls on DFI in Brazil's computer and information technology sectors have been associated with far less successful export or economic performance (Evans *et al.* 1992; Frischtak, 1992a) but low levels of DFI in the Brazilian aeronautics industry have not prevented the growth of an export-oriented industry (Frischtak, 1992b).

Differences in the effects of DFI on the creation of new industries in developing economies are paralleled by contrasts in the response of established industries in the industrial economies to foreign investment. Cantwell (1987) cites the UK motor industry as an example of a sector in which high levels of DFI have been associated with the decline of domestic firms. Heavy foreign investment in the UK pharmaceuticals industry, on the other hand, has been associated with a strong competitive response by domestic firms and growth in R&D spending and patenting (Burstall and Dunning, 1985).

Sharp contrasts in performance can also be found in countries with similar patterns in the inward licensing of technologies – in the case of Japan and South Korea, inward licensing of foreign technologies led to the growth of strong export industries in steel and electronics. Inward licensing of technology in India and Thailand, on the other hand, has not had comparable effects on industry growth or competitiveness.

Although the relative importance for any single economy of these channels of inward technology transfer appears to change over time, the contrasts suggest that the channel of technology transfer alone is far from sufficient to explain its dynamic effects on the host economy.[11] A number of enabling conditions must also be present. Some of these rely on the institutions associated with the national innovation system of an economy, including instruments of national economic policy. We consider this issue in the following section, where we define the concept of national innovation systems and discuss their contribution to inward technology transfer.

Contribution of national innovation systems to inward technology transfer and exploitation

Although a precise definition of a national innovation system is difficult, previous work on the Japanese and US national innovation systems

(Freeman, 1987; Nelson, 1990, 1992, 1993) have defined them as the network of public and private institutions within an economy that fund and perform R&D, translate the results of R&D into commercial innovations, and effect the diffusion of new technologies.[12] More concretely, a national innovation system includes the public agencies that support and/or perform R&D; a nation's universities, which may perform research and play an important role in the training of scientists and engineers; the firms within an economy that invest in R&D and in the application of new technologies; any public programmes intended to support technology adoption; and the array of laws and regulations that define intellectual property rights.

Table 5.6 contains descriptive information on an important structural feature of national innovation systems – direct government support for R&D – within seven industrial and two newly industrialising economies. The data in the table underline the international diversity in national patterns of R&D investment. The share of overall national R&D accounted for by government funds, the share of government R&D investment performed within intra-mural laboratories, and the share of R&D performed within industry that is funded by government all differ significantly among these economies. Many of the differences between developed economies reflect different levels of defence funding in central government R&D budgets. The government share of R&D investment in the two industrialising economies in table 5.6 also differs significantly, possibly because of the contrasting structure and financial resources of their domestic manufacturing firms.[13]

Our previous discussion of the technology transfer process emphasised that creation of a domestic 'absorptive capacity' is essential to an economy's exploitation of technologies transferred from abroad.[14] This capacity includes a broad array of skills, reflecting the need to deal with the tacit components of the transferred technology, as well as the frequent need to modify a foreign-sourced technology for domestic applications.

The stage of development of an economy affects the role of its national innovation system in technology transfer and absorption. Kim and Dahlman (1992) argue that many of the 'late-industrialisers' of the post-war period, such as South Korea, Taiwan and Hong Kong, initially exploited foreign sources of relatively mature technologies. Such technology could be transferred through channels that relied on arm's-length transactions, such as licensing, turnkey plants and capital goods imports. R&D investment and public policies aimed at increasing domestic R&D activity were less important during this phase, and domestic entrepreneurs demanded little by way of public R&D funding or other formal technology programmes.

The national innovation systems of these economies none the less con-

Table 5.6. *Patterns of finance of R&D, 1986*

	(1)	(2)	(3)	(4)
United States	2.7	48	35	12
W. Germany	2.7	21 (1989)	12	33
United Kingdom	2.4	38	27	16
France	2.3	53	38	27
Japan	2.8	20 (1987)	2	n.a.
S. Korea	1.9 (1987)	20	6*	32
Taiwan	1.04	60	n.a.	n.a.
Denmark	1.3 (1985)	46.5 (1985)	n.a.	n.a.
Sweden	2.8 (1985)	34 (1985)	n.a.	n.a.

Key:
(1) Total R&D/GDP (per cent).
(2) Central government share of national R&D (per cent).
(3) Central government share of R&D performed in industry (per cent).
(4) Share of central government-funded R&D performed in public labs (per cent).
Notes:
*Direct funding of industry R&D. As noted in the text, more than 94 per cent of S. Korean corporate R&D in 1987 was financed by low interest 'preferential loans', from state-controlled banks and public funds (Kim, 1991); n.a. = not available.
Sources: Keck (1993); Odagiri and Goto (1993); Walker (1993); Kim (1993); Edquist and Lundvall (1993).

tributed a critical input, in the form of scientists and engineers. In Taiwan, Korea and Singapore, and more recently in Hong Kong, government policy supported high levels of investment in a well-trained production work-force and in scientific and engineering manpower. Table 5.7 shows that South Korea, Singapore, Hong Kong and Taiwan are far ahead of other developing economies in the shares of the relevant populations enrolled in post-secondary educational programmes in scientific and engineering fields, and exceed Japan in many of these shares (Dahlman and Frischtak, 1993; Kuznets, 1988, presents similar evidence).[15] Although some of their recent expansion in higher education undoubtedly is an effect, rather than a cause, of rapid income growth, all of these economies had institutions and policies in place to support human capital formation well before their attainment of high-speed economic growth.[16]

Other government programmes for the support of technical training for employed workers have been expanded in recent years in Taiwan, in order to offset the effects of capital constraints within the relatively small firms that dominate the electronics industry (San, 1989). All four of these Asian

Table 5.7. *Indicators of investments in human capital*

	S. Korea	Taiwan	Hong Kong	Singapore	Brazil	Mexico	India	Indonesia	Japan
Percentage of age group enrolled in secondary education									
1965	35	38	29	45	16	17	27	12	82
1985	94	91	69	71	35	55	35	39	96
Percentage of age group enrolled in tertiary education									
1965	6	7	5	10	2	4	5	1	13
1985	32	13	13	12	11	16	9	7	30
Tertiary students in S&E[a] (as percentage of population)									
Total	1.39	1.06	0.67	0.89	0.40	0.70	0.21	0.14	0.58
Urban	2.02	1.36	0.72	0.89	0.58	1.02	0.97	0.53	0.77
Year	(1987)	(1984)	(1984)	(1983)	(1983)	(1986)	(1980)	(1985)	(1986)
Tertiary students in engineering (percentage of population)									
Total	0.54	0.68	0.41	0.61	0.13	0.35	0.06	0.07	0.34
Urban	0.78	0.85	0.42	0.61	0.17	0.50	0.27	0.27	0.45
Students in vocational training (percentage of working population)									
	3.06	3.24	0.86	0.54	1.83	2.00	0.10	1.14	1.71

Note:
[a] General science and engineering fields: natural science; mathematics and computer science; medicine; engineering; architecture; trade, craft; transport and communication; agriculture, forestry, fishery.
Source: Lall (1991).

economies have also benefited from their status as recipients of inflows of human capital, which, in the cases of Taiwan, Singapore and Hong Kong, included the emigration of Chinese entrepreneurs from the mainland after 1949. In South Korea, the return of scientists and engineers trained and employed abroad has also contributed to indigenous technological development. In addition, the Asian NIEs exploited the advanced higher education systems of the industrial economies, sponsoring foreign study for the 'best and brightest' among their citizens.

Despite these examples of the international scope of systems for the training of engineers and scientists, the fact remains that an economy's system for training workers at all levels is one of the most distinctively 'national' components of systems of innovation. Nelson (1992) points out that the national training and educational systems within the economies analysed by his research team display great contrasts, and thus far exhibit few signs of significant structural convergence. Moreover, international labour mobility remains sufficiently low, especially for production workers, that industrial and developing nations are both likely to capture a larger share of the returns to investments in training than is true of investments supporting the development by global firms of advanced industrial technologies. Individual economies will retain more autonomy in this area in the future than in either R&D or macroeconomic policy.

As an economy develops, the role of the formal R&D institutions within a national innovation system grows and public R&D investments play a more important role in the transfer and application of technologies from external sources. Expanded public R&D investments have, in most successful industrialising economies, complemented increases in private-sector R&D spending. The governments of both South Korea and Taiwan have expanded their investments in R&D to support research and advanced training of scientists and engineers for their domestic electronics industries. Two Taiwanese research institutes, and the affiliated Electronics Research Services Organisation (ERSO), have been an important source of new technology and trained manpower for the domestic electronic components industry. ERSO also provides a wide range of technical services to Taiwanese firms, and recently supported the indigenous development of an important advance in computer peripheral technology that proved to be unobtainable from foreign sources (Chaponniere and Fouquin, 1989, p.35).

In South Korea, the Korean Advanced Institute of Science and Technology (KAIST) and successor institutes were initially staffed by scientists and engineers trained in foreign universities, many of whom had little familiarity with the technological problems of Korean industry. As such, they were more interested in basic research than in the support of indigenous technological development and adoption of advanced foreign technologies. Over time, however, the focus of these institutes shifted from frontier scientific research to activities supporting the diffusion and adoption of technologies by Korean firms. The improved in-house technological capabilities of Korean firms also have made it easier for the publicly financed research institutes to establish fruitful links with these firms.[17] The research efforts of the public research institutes have been devoted in several instances to reverse engineering and 'localising' of products manufactured abroad (Bloom, 1989, p.21). As in Taiwan, government research institutes have recently contributed to the development of advanced technologies that could not be licensed from foreign sources.[18]

Efforts in developing economies to build up public-sector R&D programmes in the absence of demand from the private sector often fail to produce results. In South Korea, the efforts of the 1960s to strengthen public R&D institutions appear to have been somewhat premature (Kim and Dahlman, 1992). Nevertheless, even at the earliest stages of industrial development, publicly funded programmes of technology demonstration, extension and technical standards development can play an important role. Unfortunately, such programmes often are overlooked by developing-economy governments in favour of basic research facilities. In other cases, a lack of financial incentives isolates public research facilities from industrial concerns and priorities. Dahlman and Brimble (1990, p.33), for example, criticise the Thai government's public R&D infrastructure for insufficient links with private firms, and argue for greater reliance by these public laboratories on private sources of funding as a means of reorienting their agenda and activities. Katz and Bercovich (1993) present a similar diagnosis of the weaknesses of Argentina's public-sector R&D institutions.

Although important, the creation of domestic absorptive capacity and R&D activities, and even the successful inward transfer of technology, are not themselves sufficient to ensure economic growth. It is the returns to these investments of scarce resources and human capital, after all, that are critical to supporting economic development, and these returns are significantly affected by the broader economic policy environment. Protection of domestic industry against imports, for example, may tilt domestic engineering investments toward the adaptation of foreign-sourced process and product technologies to the needs of a small domestic market, rather than modifying these technologies for the production of exports (see Katz and Bercovich, 1993). Restrictions on capital goods imports mean that large investments in R&D and engineering are required to 'reinvent the wheel', recreating capital goods available from foreign sources at substantially less cost. Such investments may have important spillovers and dynamic effects, but the opportunity costs of misallocation of scarce technical talent are very high.[19]

Thus, empirical efforts to ascertain whether inward technology transfer complements or substitutes for indigenous R&D effort must be interpreted cautiously – the important issue is the return on the indigenous R&D investment (including dynamic and spillover effects), rather than just the size of this investment. Teubal (1993) observes that the extraordinary Israeli endowment of skilled technical manpower has not been sufficient to overcome the impediments imposed by economic policies that discourage effective exploitation of this endowment. (Similar points are also made by Deolalikar and Evenson, 1989; Arora, 1991; and Fikkert, 1992.)

Government performance requirements for DFI have long sought to strengthen spillover effects through mandates governing the transfer of technology or requirements that specific activities (e.g. production or R&D) be undertaken within the host nation. Brazil's local content requirements for foreign-owned motor companies, for example, are cited approvingly by Dahlman *et al.* (1987) as strengthening linkages between foreign-owned enterprises and local suppliers. During the period of high-speed growth in the 1950s and 1960s, Japan's Ministry of International Trade and Industry (MITI) demanded that IBM, Texas Instruments and other foreign firms license critical technologies to Japanese firms in exchange for the opportunity to invest in the large and rapidly growing Japanese market (Steinmueller, 1988). Restrictive policies towards foreign investment were also used by the South Korean and Taiwanese governments to increase inward technology transfer during the 1970s (Mowery and Steinmueller, 1991). The European Commission has creatively defined and aggressively enforced anti-dumping policies to induce foreign firms to locate more of their technology-intensive activities in Western Europe.[20] The EU policies focus on changing the location, rather than ownership, of key technological assets, but the underlying motives appear to resemble those of Japanese policy.

In many cases, especially in Latin America, such performance requirements have been applied to foreign-owned enterprises operating within a protected domestic market in which prices may not reflect scarcity values. Performance requirements in such an environment will support the development of linkages within a domestic economy, but the resulting spillovers may not improve international competitiveness.[21] Protection reduces the incentives faced by foreign enterprises to demand maximum performance from their suppliers, and may lead MNEs to transfer less advanced product and process technology to the host-economy subsidiary. Where they have been effective, in the East Asian NIEs and Japan, performance requirements have been applied in the presence of substantial public investments in secondary and post-secondary education for production workers and scientific and engineering personnel. They have been accompanied by policies that enforce strong domestic competition and/or force domestic firms to compete on global markets. Where these important enabling conditions are absent, performance requirements appear to have a weaker impact on inward technology transfer and competitiveness.

Although the resort to long-term import substitution policies appears to be detrimental to the domestic exploitation of inward technology transfer, regardless of its source, numerous scholars (e.g. Amsden, 1985; Westphal, 1990) have noted that the successful government trade policies identified with Japan and several leading East Asian NIEs cannot be accurately described as liberal.[22] Both South Korea and Taiwan pursued import substitution policies for much of the 1950s and 1960s, while other economies such as Singapore and Hong Kong did not, but still enjoyed solid long-term growth.

Assessing the contribution of import substitution policies to the performance of South Korea and Taiwan is complex. They contributed to the establishment of robust infant industries, but the eventual movement away from import substitution policies surely aided their maturation into healthy adults. More important is the fact that in Japan, as well as these Asian NIEs, protection did not attenuate the forces of domestic inter-firm competition. Indeed, South Korea and Taiwan both provided incentives for their manufacturing firms to export, thereby exposing domestic firms to international competition and forcing them to invest in learning and improvement of products and processes. As Krueger (1990) has noted, these governments' efforts to maintain close links between their firms and the global market also provided quick feedback to policy-makers on the success or failure and real resource costs of their promotional policies.

According to Nelson (1992), a critical ingredient in differentiating among the performance of national innovation systems is the exposure of domestic firms to competition. Where direct foreign investment or licensing intensifies such competition, inward flows of technology are more likely to lead to domestic absorption and exploitation. In some important cases, intervention by the government of a would-be licenser nation has led to the negotiation of licences on particularly favourable terms. In the case of Japanese acquisition of basic oxygen furnace technology for steel-making, MITI controlled the competition among Japanese firms for the licences, and used its monopsonist power to obtain relatively favourable terms (Lynn, 1982; Goto and Wakasugi, 1988). Critical to the success of this policy, however, was the diffusion by MITI of the foreign-sourced technologies to numerous Japanese firms in the electronics and steel industries. MITI used domestic licensing of foreign technologies to 'level the playing field' among domestic firms, which enforced intense domestic competition in the application of these technologies.

Nelson (1992) further argues that international competitiveness and innovative performance build on overall strength in training scientists and engineers, and in the adoption of technology, rather than reliance on concentrated investments in 'strategic' sectors. The experience of post-war developing economies and Japan suggests that the possibilities for 'targeting' of selected industries may be greater in these latecomer economies, if they exploit the ample opportunities to observe and learn from the experience of firms and economies at the technological and scientific frontier. With the exception of Hong Kong, all of the East Asian post-war success stories have engaged in some sectoral discrimination in their policies. Their targeting efforts were not always successful, however, and the success of these economies stems in part from the speed with which managers and policy-makers reacted to evidence of failure. Moreover, such targeting as did occur was undertaken within a framework of economic policies (such as high investments in education) that provided strong support for all sectors of the economy. The formulation, implementation and frequent revision of these nations' 'semi-liberal' policies also relied on public-sector administration competence and integrity that is scarce and not easily reproduced elsewhere.

The importance of a *national* innovation system in mediating the inward transfer of technology from *international* sources emphasises the interaction between national institutions and international trade and technology flows. Although some scholars contest this characterisation,[23] there is little doubt that the national innovation systems of most industrial economies are more open to international influences in the 1990s than they were in the 1950s and 1960s. These national innovation systems nevertheless retain great influence over the long-term consequences of the exploitation of the international pool of technologies. What appears to be most important is the ability of an array of policies to support the following environmental conditions: (i) strong competitive pressure on domestic firms, be it from other domestic firms, foreign-owned enterprises, or competition in export markets; (ii) high levels of domestic investment in human capital; and (iii) stable macroeconomic policy.[24] The creation of these sources of benefit relies as much on trade and economic policies as on the institutions typically identified with national innovation systems, especially in the earlier stages of economic development. Trade and economic policies, especially the avoidance of a long-term commitment to import substitution policies, provide an environment within which domestic firms and suppliers are likely to feel greater competitive pressure, and invest in improving their innovative, managerial and manufacturing capabilities. By placing pressure on private firms to undertake such investments, a more competitive domestic environment is also likely to increase the demands of such firms for the technical services, R&D funding and skilled workers (including scientists and engineers) that the public components of a national innovation system can provide.

Conclusion

This discussion of national systems of innovation and inward technology transfer during the post-war period supports three broad conclusions:
(i)   the mix of channels through which an economy obtains technology from foreign sources appears to be less important than the overall effort to exploit foreign sources of technology;
(ii) the contribution of national innovation systems to the inward transfer of technology in the early stages of this process operates mainly through the creation of a skilled production and technical labour force; and
(iii) the contribution of national innovation systems to inward technology transfer and competitiveness is critically affected by overall economic and trade policies, which are most successful when they enforce competitive pressure on domestic firms in a relatively stable macroeconomic environment.

There is little evidence from the post-war experience of the East Asian and other industrialising economies that the structure of an economy's innovation system needs to be tailored to accommodate specific channels of inward technology transfer from foreign sources. The critical contribution of national innovation systems is to supply the human capital needed to exploit opportunities created by links with foreign sources of technology. Public research organisations also can contribute expertise to the absorption of foreign technologies by providing 'extension services' to domestic firms, including assistance in the evaluation of new technologies and in technical standards issues. Effective performance in this sphere requires the creation or maintenance of close links, possibly including financial ones, between private firms and these public entities. But the innovation system's contribution is only a necessary, not a sufficient, condition for successful exploitation of inward technology transfer. Trade and economic policies that reduce distortion in the prices of domestic inputs and foreign exchange, that enforce domestic competition, and that create incentives or pressure on domestic firms to seek export markets, are indispensable complements.

   The processes of inward technology transfer and the contribution of an economy's innovation system also appear to change as economies develop. Although the importance of DFI in the early stages of economic development has varied among the East Asian NIEs, the high-technology sectors in all of these economies have relied increasingly on inward technology transfer through DFI as they move closer to the technological frontier. Leading firms from South Korea and Taiwan are also now engaging in some *outward* technology transfer, through direct foreign investment, and are likely to become more heavily involved in strategic alliances to maintain access to foreign markets and to obtain technology from foreign sources.

The formal R&D component of these nations' innovation systems has expanded along with the efforts of domestic firms to enter more R&D-intensive industries, and the contribution of public research institutes and jointly funded industry-government technology development programmes also appears to have grown. The optimal sequence for public R&D investment is to target initially technical schools and universities that emphasise teaching, rather than basic research. These investments can be combined with the creation of public entities to provide low-level technical support to the adoption by domestic firms of foreign-sourced technologies. Public investments in more fundamental research in public laboratories or institutes appear to hold promise for economic returns only at a later stage of economic development.

Are the historical circumstances that supported the export-led development of the NIEs and reconstruction of Japan and Western Europe still present? Will the future environment for trade, investment and technology transfer resemble that of the recent past, or are these 'lessons' of history irrelevant to contemporary developing economies? These lessons will lose much of their validity if international trade and investment flows reverse their rapid recent growth, or if international supplies of industrial technology become cartelised. Predicting future trends in the global economy is a speculative exercise at best, but current trends do not appear to support the pessimistic view. Direct foreign investment flows grew rapidly during the 1980s, and the developing-economy share of these flows has grown. Far from confining the benefits of technology transfer to the industrial economies, DFI appears likely to expand its role in the diffusion of advanced technologies to the developing world. This is particularly true of DFI outflows from the East Asian industrialising economies.

Much of the surge in DFI in the 1980s, especially that from the Asian economies, was a pre-emptive strategy to deal with actual or threatened protection of industrial-economy markets. The effects on developing-economy exports of a major reversal in liberalisation of global trade policy are likely to be negative, but protection may redirect, rather than eliminate, DFI. Increasing protection would force greater regional concentration of DFI flows from each of the three industrial regions of the world – Japan in East and South Asia, the United States in Latin America, and Western Europe in Eastern Europe and Russia. Inasmuch as each of these regional blocs contains significant areas of economic underdevelopment, even this 'second-best' DFI scenario would continue to transfer technology from advanced to developing areas of the global economy.

The number and diversity of sources of advanced industrial technologies for developing-economy firms also do not appear to be shrinking. The OECD's 1988 report on the newly industrialising economies argued that the supply of technology from industrial sources had expanded during the post-war period, as Western European and Japanese technological capabilities increased. Reductions in 'technology gaps' between the industrial economies imply increased competition among would-be suppliers of these technologies, and this should continue to work to the benefit of developing-economy firms. Indeed, firms from the NIEs now are themselves important suppliers of such high-technology products as DRAM chips and computer peripherals, further intensifying competition in these industries. Nor is there much evidence that strategic alliances among private firms have significantly increased concentration among the potential suppliers of advanced industrial technologies. In most cases, these alliances cover only a single product line or technology – allies in one area are likely to be competitors in another. Moreover, many of these alliances have in fact worked to transfer and diffuse technologies among participant firms, increasing the number of sources. Like the effects of increasing protection on DFI and technology transfer, however, the effects of strategic alliances on international supplies of industrial technology deserve further research.

The strengthening of the standards and enforcement of intellectual property rights in many developing economies, achieved in the Uruguay Round of trade negotiations, also should not restrict the availability of industrial technologies as much as is widely feared. Many of these technologies in mature industries have little or no formal patent protection. Even for new technologies (with the exception of pharmaceuticals), Levin et al. (1987) argue that formal instruments of protection are relatively ineffective in excluding competitors. The conclusions of the study by Levin and colleagues are based on survey responses from US R&D managers that are now more than a decade old, however, and the importance of these formal instruments for the protection of intellectual property may have grown in the wake of legislative changes in the United States and other industrial economies.

One element of the future that will not resemble the past is the extent to which national innovation systems will remain national. Current trends seem likely to erode the 'national sovereignty' of governments over their domestic innovation systems. The proliferation of international sources of advanced industrial technologies is only one indicator of this trend. The regional and national agglomeration externalities of the sort associated with California's Silicon Valley remain important, and will serve as important magnets for inward foreign investment. These regional concentrations are a distinctively and enduringly 'national' (in many cases, sub-national) element of national innovation systems. To the extent that these regional complexes attract foreign firms, of course, they contribute to international flows of technology. Furthermore, the proximity to a major research university, which underpins many such regional complexes in the United States, emphasises another 'national' element of the NIS – investment in human capital, which seems likely to remain a less mobile factor of production for the foreseeable future.

This discussion of future trends suggests that the prospects for the 'second tier' of economies in South Asia, East Asia and Latin America should not worsen dramatically; the lessons of the previous post-war period will apply to these regions, barring catastrophic political or economic developments in the industrial economies. However, there is little indication that the disturbing divergent trends among the larger group of developing economies will be reversed. The least developed economies of the world, many of which are located in Africa, still lack many of the basic foundations of economic development, such as stable political systems. A number of economies, and a great many people, are thus likely to remain 'marginalised' within the global economy, and will require more substantial, targeted forms of bilateral and multilateral aid.

Notes

1 A longer and different version of this chapter was presented at the UNU/Intech research conference, Maastricht, Netherlands, 21–23 June 1993. We are grateful to participants in the conference, and especially to Dr Carlos Correa and two anonymous referees for useful comments. Research for this chapter was supported in part by the Alfred P. Sloan Foundation, the Canadian Institute for Advanced Research, the US Air Force Office of Scientific Research and the Consortium on Competitiveness and Cooperation.

2 The World Bank (1991, p.13) also noted, however, that there were divergent trends within the developing economies as a group: 'Asia, the world's most populous region, has recently begun to catch up – in some cases, at a spectacular rate. But Sub-Saharan Africa has seen its per capita incomes fall in real terms since 1973 . . . Latin America has also slipped, especially since 1980.'

3 Below, we discuss the extent to which these channels are substitutes for or complements to one another.

4 The World Bank (1992, pp. 95–6) report also noted the divergent trends outlined in figures 5.1 and 5.2: 'In real terms, DFI increased 12 percent a year between 1970 and 1988 in Asia, compared with 3 per cent in Latin America and a decrease in Africa . . .'.

5 The US direct foreign investment data are taken from the US Commerce Department's *Survey of Current Business* for the relevant years, and are defined

as the sum of 'net capital outflows' and 'reinvested earnings' in the Commerce Department tables.

6 These royalty payments reflect the 'stock' of licensing agreements, rather than the flow of new technology licensing contracts and therefore are a lagging indicator of the regional allocation of new licences. Teece (1993) suggests that increased Japanese spending on imported technologies during 1989–91 (reversing a long-term decline) reflects the success of many US firms in establishing the validity of their patents in Japan, so forcing Japanese firms to pay higher royalties and licensing fees.

7 None the less, South Korean imports of capital goods are reported to have tripled during 1982–91 (OECD, 1992, p.223).

8 Conclusions about the link between restrictions on DFI and licensing drawn from these data, nevertheless must be qualified. Lall (1985) notes that India, for example, complemented DFI restrictions with restrictions on licensing agreements, making India a less attractive market for foreign licensers. Also, as Contractor (1985) and others note, inward licensing increases with higher levels of R&D investment and technical personnel within an economy, both of which were substantially lower in Thailand in 1979 than in the other economies in table 5.5.

9 Other 'direct' benefits include expansion of exports of products with higher income elasticities of demand and stronger growth prospects, increased demand for the products of domestic suppliers of components and assemblies, and the expansion of demand for skilled labour and technical personnel.

10 Kim (1980) emphasises the domestic mobility of skilled technical personnel in the diffusion of consumer electronics manufacturing technologies within South Korea. Also, Blomstrom (1991) cites several studies showing that firms facing foreign-owned domestic competition displayed higher productivity growth rates.

11 This is consistent with the findings of Enos and Park (1988) who caution against comparing technology absorption across industries or countries in a simplistic fashion because of the intrusion of outside factors; for example, scarcity of raw materials, deficiency of demand for outputs or differences in the ease of adoption inherent in the technologies chosen.

12 Like the Holy Roman Empire, which was not holy, Roman, or an empire, innovation systems may be international, rather than national, in scope and structure; they may influence diffusion as much as innovation; and they often are *ad hoc*, rather than strategically conceived, in origin.

13 Average firm size in the Taiwanese private sector is much smaller than in South Korea; see Mowery and Steinmueller (1991), Hou and San (1993) and Kim (1993). Both the Taiwanese and South Korean governments have financed large military establishments. The R&D component of their military budgets, however, is relatively low and may not be fully reported in the data in table 5.6.

14 This is consistent with the conclusion in Blomstrom *et al.* (1992, pp.16–17): 'The "least developed countries" may learn little from the multinationals,

because local firms are too far behind in their technological levels to be either imitators or suppliers to the multinationals.'

15 Among these four NIEs, the less directive role of government in Hong Kong may be inferred from the somewhat lower shares of the urban population enrolled in such courses of study. Even Hong Kong, however, is ahead of such developing economies as Brazil or Mexico in these indicators of human capital formation.

16 Kuznets (1988) points out that total educational expenditures in South Korea accounted for as much as one-third of total investment in physical capital during 1966–75. As the recent World Bank report (1993, p.43) points out, Hong Kong, South Korea and Singapore had all achieved universal primary education by 1965, well before other developing economies, and Indonesia had a primary education enrolment rate of more than 70 per cent in this year.

17 Indeed, Dahlman (1989) notes that a portion of the Korean Institute of Electronics and Technology's semiconductor research facilities was sold to one of the *chaebol* in 1985.

18 'As the stakes have risen in the chip game, the field of players has grown smaller worldwide, meaning that few, if any . . . can be counted on to sell state-of-the-art chip design technology to Korean chaebols. So, Koreans had to tackle the 4M DRAM design alone. To avoid duplicate research and investment, the government stepped in and designated the R&D of the 4M DRAM as a national project' (Kim, 1993, p.38).

19 Jacobsson (1991) discusses this phenomenon in India.

20 See *The Economist* (1989). This example illustrates the interdependence of trade and technology policies and goals. EU anti-dumping policy in this and other cases has been employed as an instrument of regional technology policy, with uncertain consequences for both trade and technology policies.

21 'In Côte d'Ivoire, selective protection and subsidies to multinational textile firms led to inefficient production. Another study found that more than a third of foreign investment projects earned negative returns for the host country because of import protection.' (World Bank, 1991, p.85).

22 In a survey of post-war growth in developing economies, Sachs (1989, pp.15–16) noted: 'Contrary to a common view, outward orientation . . . is not at all the same thing as a free-market trade policy . . . The outward-oriented countries in the study, South Korea, Indonesia (to some degree), and Turkey in the 1980s, all had successful export growth with continued import restrictions and heavy government involvement in managing trade.'

23 Patel and Pavitt (1991), for example, argue that MNEs' R&D operations in fact remain centred on their home economies, suggesting that the 'globalisation' of R&D operations is in its infancy.

24 One useful definition of stable macroeconomic policy is provided by the World Bank's (1993, p.105) approving summary of East Asian policies: '. . . inflation was kept under control, internal and external debt remained manageable, and macroeconomic crises that emerged were resolved quickly, usually within a year or two'.

References

Amsden, A. 1985. The state and Taiwan's economic development, in P.B. Evans, D. Rueschemeyer, and T. Skocpol (eds.), *Bringing the State Back In*, New York, Cambridge University Press.

Arora, A. 1991. Indigenous technological efforts and imports of technology: complements or substitutes?, unpublished manuscript, Carnegie-Mellon University.

Blomstrom, M. 1991. Host country benefits of foreign investment, in D. McFetridge (ed.), *Foreign Investment, Technology and Economic Growth*, Calgary, University of Calgary Press.

Blomstrom, M., Lipsey, R. E. and Zejan, M. 1992. What explains developing country growth?, NBER Working Paper, no. 4132.

Bloom, M. D. H. 1989. Technological change and the electronics sector: perspectives and policy options for the Republic of Korea, Working Paper, OECD Development Centre, Paris, May.

Burstall, M. and Dunning, J. H. 1985. International investment in innovation, in N. E. J. Wells (ed.), *Pharmaceuticals Among the Sunrise Industries*, London: Croom Helm.

Cantwell, J. 1987. The reorganisation of European industries after integration: selected evidence on the role of multinational enterprise activities, *Journal of Common Market Studies*, 26: 127–51.

Caves, R. E. and Uekusa, M. 1976. Industrial organization, in H. Patrick and H. Rosovsky (eds.), *Asia's New Giant*, Washington, D. C., Brookings Institution.

Chaponniere, J. R. and Fouquin, M. 1989. Technological change and the electronics sector: perspectives and policy options for Taiwan, Working Paper, OECD Development Centre, Paris, May.

Cohen, W. M. and Levinthal, D. A. 1989. Innovation and learning: the two faces of R&D, *Economic Journal*, 99: 569–96.

1990. Absorptive capacity: a new perspective on learning and innovation, *Administrative Sciences Quarterly*, 35: 128–52.

Contractor, F. J. 1985. Licensing versus foreign direct investment in U.S. corporate strategy: an analysis of aggregate U.S. data, in Rosenberg and Frischtak (eds.).

Dahlman, C. J. 1992. Information technology strategies: Brazil and the East Asian newly industrializing economies, in Evans *et al.* (eds.).

Dahlman, C. J. and Brimble, P. 1990. Technology strategy and policy for industrial competitiveness: a case study in Thailand, Industry Series Working Paper, no. 24, Industry and Energy Department, World Bank, Washington, D.C.

Dahlman, C. J. and Frischtak, C. 1993. National systems supporting technical advance in industry: the Brazilian experience, in Nelson (ed.).

Dahlman, C. J., Ross-Larsen B. and Westphal, L. E. 1987. Managing technological development: lessons from the newly industrializing countries, *World Development*, 15: 759–75.

David, P. A. 1992. Intellectual property institutions and the panda's thumb, CEPR Working Paper, no. 287, Stanford University.

Deolalikar, A. and Evenson, R. 1989. Technology production and technology purchase in Indian industry: an econometric analysis, *Review of Economics and Statistics*, 71: 687–92.

Economist 1989. A gun that needs to get knotted, 9 September, 82–5.

1993a. Japan ties up the Asia market, 24 April, 33–4.

1993b. Capital flows to the Third World: from bank to market, 24 April, 84–6.

1994. Japanese firms in South-east Asia: the second wave, 7 May, 75–6.

Edquist, C. and Lundvall, B.-Å. 1993. Comparing the Danish and Swedish systems of innovation, in Nelson (ed.).

Enos, J. L. and Park, W. H. 1988. *The Adoption and Diffusion of Imported Technology: The Case of Korea*, London, Croom Helm.

Evans, P. B., Frischtak, C. R. and Tigre, P. B. (eds.) 1992. *High Technology and Third World Industrialization: The Brazilian Computer Industry in Comparative Perspective*, Berkeley: University of California Institute for International Studies.

Fikkert, B. 1992. An open or closed technology policy? The effects of technology licensing, foreign direct investment, and technology spillovers on R&D in Indian industrial sector firms, unpublished manuscript, Yale University.

Freeman, C. 1987. *Technology Policy and Economic Performance: Lessons From Japan*, London, Pinter.

Frischtak, C. R. 1992a. The international market and the competitive potential of national producers of equipment and systems, in Evans *et al.* (eds.).

1992b. Learning, technical progress, and competitiveness in the commuter aircraft industry: an analysis of Embraer, World Bank, Washington, D.C.

Goto, A. and Wakasugi, R. 1988. Technology policy, in R. Komiya, M.Okuno and K. Suzumura (eds.), *Industrial Policy in Japan*, New York, Academic Press.

Hagedoorn, J. and Schakenraad, J. 1990. Inter-firm partnerships and co-operative strategies in core technologies, in C. Freeman and L. Soete (eds.), *New Explorations in the Economics of Technical Change*, London, Pinter.

Hou, C. and San, G. 1993. National systems supporting technical advance in industry – the case of Taiwan, in Nelson (ed.).

Jacobsson, S. 1991. Government policy and performance of the Indian engineering industry, *Research Policy*, 20: 45–56.

Katz, J. and Bercovich, N. 1993. National systems of innovation supporting technical change in industry: the case of Argentina, in Nelson (ed.).

Keck, O. 1993. The national system for innovation in Germany, in Nelson (ed.).

Kim, L. 1980. Stages of development of industrial technology in a developing country: a model, *Research Policy*, 9: 254–77.

1993. Korea's national system for industrial innovation, in Nelson (ed.).

Kim, L. and Dahlman, C. J. 1992. Technology policy for industrialization: an integrative framework and Korea's experience, *Research Policy*, 21: 437–52.

Krueger, A. O. 1990. Asian trade and growth lessons, *American Economic Review Papers and Proceedings*, 80: 108–12.

Kuznets, P. W. 1988. An East Asian model of development: Japan, Taiwan, and South Korea, *Economic Development and Cultural Change*, 36: S11–S43.

Lall, S. 1985. Trade in technology by a slowly industrializing country, in Rosenberg and Frischtak (eds.).

1991. Explaining industrial success in developing countries, in S. Lall and V. N. Balasubramanyam (eds.), *Current Issues in Development Economics*, London, Macmillan.

Levin, R. C., Klevorick, A. K., Nelson, R. R. and Winter, S. G. 1987. Appropriating the returns from industrial research and development, *Brookings Papers on Economic Activity*, pp. 783–820.

Lundvall, B.-Å. (ed.) 1992. *National Systems of Innovation*, London, Pinter.

Lynn, L. 1982. *How Japan Innovates*. Boulder, Colo., Westview Press.

Mansfield, E., Romeo, A., Schwartz, M., Teece, D., Wagner, S. and Brach, P. 1982. *Technology Transfer, Productivity, and Economic Policy*, New York, W.W. Norton.

Mowery, D. C. 1983. The relationship between intrafirm and contractual forms of industrial research in American manufacturing, 1900–1940, *Explorations in Economic History*, 20: 351–74.

   1989. Collaborative ventures between U.S. and foreign manufacturing firms, *Research Policy*, 18: 19–32.

   1992. Joint ventures between U.S. and Pacific Rim firms: problems and prospects, North Pacific Region Advanced Research Center conference, Sapporo, Japan, 3–7 August.

Mowery, D. C. (ed.) 1988. *International Collaborative Ventures in U.S. Manufacturing*, Cambridge, Mass., Ballinger.

Mowery, D. C. and Steinmueller, W. E. 1991. Prospects for entry by developing countries into the global integrated circuit industry: lessons from the U.S., Japan, and the NIEs, CCC Working Paper, no. 91–8, Center for Research in Management, University of California, Berkeley.

Nelson, R. R. 1990. U.S. technological leadership: where did it come from, and where did it go?, *Research Policy*, 19: 117–32.

   1992. National innovation systems: a retrospective on a study, *Industrial and Corporate Change*, 1: 347–74.

Nelson, R. R. (ed.) 1993. *National Innovation Systems*, New York, Oxford University Press.

Nelson, R. R. and Wright, G. 1992. The rise and fall of American technological leadership: the postwar era in historical perspective, *Journal of Economic Literature*, 30: 1931–64.

OECD 1988. *The Newly Industrialising Countries: Challenge and Opportunity for OECD Industries*, Paris, OECD.

   1990. *Industrial Policy in OECD Countries, 1990*, Paris, OECD.

   1992. *Industrial Policy in OECD Countries, 1992*, Paris, OECD.

   1993. *Industrial Policy in OECD Countries, 1993*, Paris, OECD.

Odagiri, H. and Goto, A. 1993. The Japanese system of innovation: past, present, and future, in Nelson (ed.).

Ozawa, T. 1985. Macroeconomic factors affecting Japan's technology inflows and outflows: the postwar experience, in Rosenberg and Frischtak (eds.).

Patel, P. and Pavitt, K. 1991. Large firms in the production of the world's technology: an important case of non-globalisation, *Journal of International Business Studies*, 22: 1–21.

Rosenberg, N. and Frischtak, C. (eds.) 1985. *International Technology Transfer: Concepts, Measures, and Comparisons*, New York, Praeger.

Sachs, J. 1989. *Developing Country Debt and the World Economy*, Chicago, University of Chicago Press for NBER.

San, G. 1989. The status and an evaluation of the electronics industry in Taiwan, OECD Development Centre conference, Paris, June.

Steinmueller, W. E. 1988. Industry structure and government policies in the U.S. and Japanese integrated-circuit industries, in J. B. Shoven (ed.), *Government Policy Towards Industry in the United States and Japan*, Cambridge, Cambridge University Press.

Teece, D. 1977. Technology transfer by multinational firms: the resource costs of transferring technological know-how, *Economic Journal*, 87: 242–61.

1986. Profiting from innovation, *Research Policy*, 15: 285–305.

1993. Technology transfer and the emerging shape of business organization in the United States and Japan, unpublished manuscript.

Teubal, M. 1993. The innovation system of Israel: description, performance, and outstanding issues, in Nelson (ed.).

United Nations, Conference on Trade and Development (UNCTAD) 1991. *Handbook of International Trade and Development Statistics, 1991*, New York, United Nations.

United Nations, Department of Economic and Social Development 1992. *World Investment Report, 1992: Transnational Corporations as Engines of Growth*, New York, United Nations.

US Department of Commerce, Bureau of Economic Analysis. *Survey of Current Business*, various issues.

Walker, W. 1993. National innovation systems: Britain, in Nelson (ed.).

Westphal, L. 1990. Industrial policy in an export propelled economy: lessons from South Korea's experience, *Journal of Economic Perspectives*, 4: 41–59.

Westphal, L. E., Kim, L. and Dahlman C. J. 1985. Reflections on the Republic of Korea's acquisition of technological capability, in Rosenberg and Frischtak (eds.).

World Bank 1991. *World Development Report, 1991*, New York, Oxford University Press.

1992. *World Development Report, 1992*, New York, Oxford University Press.

1993. *The East Asian Miracle: Economic Growth and Public Policy*, New York, Oxford University Press.

6 The globalisation of technology: a new taxonomy

DANIELE ARCHIBUGI AND JONATHAN MICHIE[1]

Introduction

This chapter critically re-examines the meaning of a term which has become increasingly fashionable: 'techno-globalism'. The term is used to describe the phenomenon of 'globalisation' experienced by the world of invention and innovation.[2] In its most modest use the term is shorthand for the fact that the generation, transmission and diffusion of technologies is increasingly international in scope. Although the term originated with the media, the academic world has been quick to adopt it. Several international conferences have been devoted to exploring its nature (for a review, see OECD, 1992a; Freeman and Hagedoorn, 1992) and a major research programme has been carried out by the European Community's FAST programme on technological and economic globalisation (see Petrella, 1989). Recent studies have demonstrated how firms have exploited the new opportunities and developed 'global research strategies' (Casson, 1991) and 'networks' (Howells, 1990a) to undertake their innovation programmes which largely by-pass their home country. Governments have promoted policies to foster collaboration across borders by both the business and academic communities.[3]

All this has several implications for our understanding of the role of nation-states. It is generally assumed that globalisation will reduce the role and scope of nations, and it is not uncommon, including among technology analysts, for the terms 'national' and 'global' to be seen as opposites. In this case, globalisation reduces the effectiveness of policies at the national level for promoting and organising technological advance.

The aim of this chapter is to analyse these issues in more detail by developing a taxonomy defining three distinct categories of technological globalisation: (i) the global *exploitation* of technology; (ii) global technological *collaboration*; and (iii) the global *generation* of technology. We critically reconsider the evidence in the light of this categorisation and suggest that the patterns of globalisation differ significantly between the three categories of technological activities. An attempt to quantify the evidence relevant for each of the three factors, from both static and dynamic perspectives, is made.

The chapter is organised as follows: the next section briefly sets out the key trends on invention and innovation internationally. Then follows a presentation of our taxonomy of globalisation and for each of the three categories which we define, the available empirical evidence is reported. The subsequent section relates this to the recent body of literature on national systems of innovation; we argue that the globalisation of technological activities has not led to a convergence either in the methods adopted by countries to innovate or in their profiles of sectoral specialisation. The final section explores the policy implications, in particular for the role of national governments.

Resources devoted to invention and innovation

Has technology become more important in advanced economies? If this were the case, globalisation of technology might simply reflect the increasing *national* efforts to innovate. Resources devoted to formal research and development (R&D) activities, which are one of the most important sources of knowledge, have indeed increased substantially over the last twenty years. Table 6.1 reports the average growth rates for the 1970s and for the 1980s of both total (columns 1 and 2) and industrial (columns 3 and 4) R&D for all OECD countries. For the vast majority of nations the growth rates in the 1980s were much higher than in the 1970s (the most notable exception being the UK). A comparison between total and industrial R&D also shows that, over the 1980s, industrial R&D increased in importance compared to other R&D.

Investment in R&D is sensitive to economic conditions, though, so the increase in R&D expenditure should be considered in the light of general economic growth. Figure 6.1 reports total R&D as a share of GDP and figure 6.2 reports business R&D as a share of industrial production, both for the major six countries. In spite of a long-term trend towards an increase in R&D intensity in advanced economies, the data also show that a slowdown occurred from the mid-1980s: both the USA and the UK reduced the share of their GDP devoted to R&D, and in Germany and France its growth slowed.

It would be natural to expect that the growth of industrial R&D would lead to an increasing number of patent applications since the majority of patents are taken out by firms. Columns 5 and 6 of table 6.1 report the growth rates of domestic patent applications in the OECD countries; but, contrary to expectations, the growth rates have been moderate and some-

Table 6.1. *Rates of growth of total R&D, industrial R&D and patenting in OECD countries*

| | Average annual rates of change (per cent) | | | | | | | | | | (External patents)* ÷ (Domestic patents) | | |
| | Total R&D expenditure | | Industrial R&D | | Domestic patents | | Foreign patents | | External patents | | | | |
	1970–80	1981–90	1970–80	1981–90	1970–80	1981–90	1970–80	1981–90	1970–80	1981–90	1971	1981	1990
United States	1.4	4.4	2.0	4.3	-2.0	4.2	5.0	5.3	-0.6	6.6	1.5	2.0	2.7
Japan	6.3	7.8	6.1	9.4	5.1	6.3	-0.8	4.9	5.5	9.9	0.3	0.3	0.4
Germany	4.0[a]	3.9	4.9[a]	4.2	-0.7	0.3	0.8	6.4	1.7	4.6	2.2	2.7	3.9
France	2.9	4.7	3.7	5.0	-2.4	1.6	0.2	7.0	3.0	6.8	1.8	2.8	4.4
United Kingdom	2.9[e]	2.0	3.0[e]	2.9	-2.4	-0.8	0.8	6.2	-1.7	7.3	1.3	1.6	3.0
Italy	2.8	7.0	3.6	7.4	n.a.	n.a.	n.a.	n.a.	1.8	7.4	1.5	n.a.	n.a.
The Netherlands	2.2	3.1	1.4	3.7	-2.1	2.8	1.5	9.0	0.1	6.6	4.9	6.1	7.8
Belgium	2.4[b]	3.3[l]	6.7[d]	4.1	-3.0	-0.1	-0.1	10.7	0.5	6.8	3.0	3.7	7.4
Denmark	3.1	7.0[h]	3.8	8.4[h]	1.7	1.9	-0.3	12.2	1.0	8.7	3.4	3.4	6.1
Spain	10.3	11.0	12.7	14.1	-4.5	3.1	0.2	20.2	1.3	8.1	0.5	1.0	1.8
Ireland	4.0[d]	6.0	5.2[d]	10.1	6.8	5.3	4.9	4.7	6.7	8.5	1.2	1.3	1.5
Portugal	2.9[c]	8.4[i]	4.6[c]	4.1[i]	-6.4	1.3	-0.5	7.5	-24.2	33.6	0.8	0.1	0.8
Greece	n.a.	12.7[h]	n.a.	12.6[h]	-0.8	-12.3	2.4	28.8	n.a.	8.5	n.a.	0.1	0.7
Switzerland	1.4[a]	5.0[h]	0.8[a]	5.1[h]	-3.1	-1.2	2.2	9.4	-1.3	2.9	4.3	4.9	7.3
Sweden	6.4[d]	5.1[h]	5.9[d]	5.2[h]	-0.5	-2.3	2.5	9.4	3.0	3.6	2.1	3.0	5.3
Austria	9.6[a]	4.6	9.8[a]	5.0[h]	0.3	-1.5	3.4	10.8	1.4	5.7	1.6	2.0	3.5
Norway	6.1	6.0[h]	7.3	6.9[h]	-2.7	2.6	-0.1	9.0	0.8	9.9	1.3	2.1	3.4
Finland	6.8[d]	8.7	6.8[d]	10.4	4.7	4.2	0.7	12.3	5.7	13.2	1.4	1.9	4.0

Australia	0.2^f	6.6^g	n.a.	13.1^h	5.2	0.1	-2.0	5.8	6.7	10.5	0.5	0.7	1.8
Canada	2.5^c	4.4	5.5	5.7	-1.1	3.0	-2.1	4.6	-0.5	4.1	2.5	2.9	2.4
OECD weighted average					1.3	4.1	0.9	7.2	0.9	5.9	1.2	1.3	1.5
OECD weighted average (excluding Japan)					-1.6	1.8	1.1	7.4	0.4	5.4	1.8	2.4	3.5

Notes:

* External patent appl. in year t divided by domestic patent appl. in year $t-1$.

n.a. = not available.

^{a} 1970–81 ^{d} 1971–81 ^{g} 1981–8 ^{l} 1983–90

^{b} 1971–9 ^{e} 1972–81 ^{h} 1981–9

^{c} 1971–80 ^{f} 1973–81 ^{i} 1982–8

Source: Calculated from OECD (1992b).

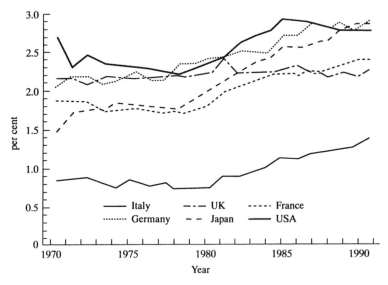

Figure 6.1. Total R&D as a proportion of GDP in selected countries, 1970–91.
(*Source:* Calculated from OECD, 1992b.)

times even negative. The only major country with a consistently high growth rate was Japan, at more than 5 per cent a year in the 1970s, and more than 6 per cent a year in the 1980s.[4]

These trends in domestic patenting and in R&D as a share of GDP suggest that the generation of knowledge has been relatively weak. One possible explanation might be that the international transmission of technology has become an effective alternative to the internal production of knowledge, allowing firms to avoid research duplication – the next section will explore this hypothesis looking at the channels of international technology transfer. The evidence presented in this section, though, suggests that any trend towards technological globalisation cannot be due to the growth of resources devoted to innovation at the national level *per se*.

Three meanings of 'techno-globalism'

As is often the case with neologisms, the term 'techno-globalism' may have different meanings in different contexts and for different authors (see Chesnais, 1992). One such meaning is that an increasing proportion of technological innovations are exploited in international markets: we term this the *global exploitation of technology*. Secondly, there is international collaboration between firms, sharing know-how with competitors from differ-

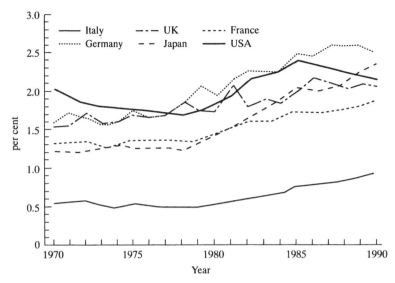

Figure 6.2. Business R&D as a proportion of GDP in selected countries, 1970–90. (*Source:* Calculated from OECD, 1992b.)

ent countries, along with a parallel process of international collaboration between governments and academic institutions: this we term *global technological collaboration*. A third meaning, dear especially to students of multinational corporations, is that firms are increasing the international integration of their R&D and technological activities: this we term the *global generation of technology*. These three meanings can be separated analytically.[5]

The global exploitation of technology

First we consider the case of companies exploiting their technology in international markets. This is certainly not a new phenomenon, but it has increased its importance in recent times. The attempt to profit from innovations in international markets is the technological equivalent of international export flows. If a larger share of firms' output is absorbed by foreign markets, it is natural that firms will also try to take advantage of their technological capabilities internationally.

Our hypothesis is therefore that the global exploitation of technology is the consequence rather than the cause of the increase in international trade. However, a few technology-specific factors should be stressed. First, technology-intensive products are more likely to be traded internationally;

Guerrieri and Milana (1991) found that high-tech exports rose from 12.2 per cent of world manufacturing exports in 1970 to 20.5 per cent in 1989. Moreover, tradable sectors, especially in manufacturing, are generally associated with high R&D and innovative performance (see Hughes, 1986). Secondly, several empirical studies have shown that countries' innovative capabilities are the main factor backing their export performance (see Soete, 1987; Fagerberg, 1988; Amendola *et al.*, 1994); in other words, a domestic technological capability is a necessary condition for a successful export performance. Thirdly, technology can be exploited in foreign markets even when disembodied from products, for example via the transfer of licences and know-how. These factors create important feedback effects leading to complex causal links: from domestic technological capabilities to export performance, and from export performance to the attempt to exploit technology internationally, either embodied or disembodied.

One way of measuring the international exploitation of innovations is to consider how firms protect them legally through patents in foreign markets. Firms undertake the cost and effort involved in extending a patent abroad if they expect to be compensated either by trading the invention disembodied or from exporting products which embody it. Firms also extend their patents into markets where they do not operate in order to block competitors and to prevent other firms from invading their own (or third) markets.[6]

From a static viewpoint, it should be stressed that a substantial share of the patent applications registered in advanced countries have a foreign origin (see table 6.2): 45 per cent of the total patent applications registered in 1990 in the United States came from abroad, while in countries with a lower volume of technological activities, such as Germany and France, they accounted for 67 per cent and 84 per cent respectively. The European Patent Office receives 45 per cent of its applications from non-member countries. In the other OECD countries the share of foreign patent applications is as high as 90 per cent. The only exception is Japan, where as many as 88 per cent of applications are from domestic inventors. Although this is partly due to the institutional differences of the Japanese patent system (which does not allow more than one priority claim per application), as well as to linguistic and cultural barriers, it nevertheless indicates that Western technological penetration of Japanese markets is still rather low.

Patent data can also supply information about the rate of increase in the exploitation of inventions internationally, i.e. on its *dynamic* dimension. There are two ways of looking at this: the first is from the viewpoint of the country 'invaded' by foreign patents, the second is from the viewpoint of the country 'invading' other countries. Columns 7 and 8 of table 6.1 report

Table 6.2. *Domestic/foreign breakdown of patents, 1990*

	Domestic patents (per cent)	Foreign patents (per cent)
USA	55.08	44.92
Japan	88.46	11.54
Germany	32.62	67.38
France	16.15	83.85
United Kingdom	21.46	78.54
Italy	n.a.	n.a.
The Netherlands	5.32	94.68
Belgium	2.09	97.91
Denmark	6.82	93.18
Spain	4.83	95.17
Ireland	15.50	84.50
Portugal	2.77	97.23
Greece	2.07	97.93
Switzerland	7.94	92.06
Sweden	6.92	93.08
Austria	5.13	94.87
Canada	6.76	93.24
Australia	24.63	75.37
OECD weighted average	43.17	56.83
OECD weighted average (excluding Japan)	22.17	77.83

Source: Calculated from OECD (1992b).

the rates of change in foreign patents (i.e. the patent applications presented by foreigners in a country) and columns 9 and 10 on external patents (i.e. the number of applications presented by inventors of one country in other countries).

All countries have been 'invaded' and 'invading' with much higher rates of growth during the 1980s than the 1970s, which were almost stagnant.[7] Thus the 1980s have been characterised by a dramatic growth in the exploitation of inventions in international markets. This compares with the stagnant or even declining growth rates of domestic patenting documented above. In other words, the data do not reflect an increase in the production of knowledge, but only an increase in its international exploitation. Some significant differences emerge across countries. Japan, for example, is 'invading' other countries at the highest rate among the G7 although it has been 'invaded' at a comparatively low rate. Countries which were on the periphery of technological competition are now both 'invading' and being 'invaded' at a substantial rate.

The final three columns of table 6.1 report an index of external patent applications per domestic application for the years 1971, 1981 and 1990 to identify cross-country differences.[8] Not surprisingly, the index is particularly high for technologically dynamic small- and medium-sized countries: The Netherlands ranks first, followed by Belgium, Switzerland, Denmark and Sweden. Firms based in small- and medium-sized countries do not find their internal market large enough to repay their investment in innovation so they would not be able to undertake many of their R&D projects if they were not able to exploit the results in international markets. Small countries with a low R&D intensity, including Greece, Ireland, Spain and Portugal, have a very low propensity to protect abroad their (already scarce) inventions. The value of the index is lower for larger countries than for smaller countries with a comparable R&D intensity. The value is very low for Japan (equal to only 0.4); although this result is due partly to the nature of the Japanese patent system (see above), it also suggests that, in spite of the fast growth of Japanese patents abroad over the last decade, Japan has a vast technological potential yet to be exploited internationally. In more general terms these data indicate that the contribution of small and technologically dynamic countries to the global exploitation of inventions is high. Although the same trend affects large countries, they are comparatively more oriented towards the national than the global market. Not all countries have the same propensity to exploit their inventions globally. But taken together, these data provide strong evidence for the first meaning of techno-globalism: firms' propensity to trade and exploit their inventions and innovations internationally has grown considerably.

Global technological collaboration

The second category we analyse is technological collaboration to develop know-how or innovations involving partners in more than one country, where each of the partners preserves its institutional identity and ownership. This can involve government research agencies and the academic community (the economic equivalent of non-profit cultural exchanges) as well as the business sector (the technological equivalent of international joint-ventures). International R&D joint-ventures have received much attention over the last few years. Governments, international organisations (most notably the EU), and business firms have been prone to collaborate and share know-how with foreign partners. This has led the academic community to create new databases to account for the phenomenon and to develop models to explain it (the empirical literature and the available databases are reviewed by Chesnais, 1988; and by Gugler and Dunning, 1992. The theoretical literature on R&D co-operation, although not necessarily at the international level, is reviewed in Katz and Ordover, 1990.)

Technological collaborations can be divided into those undertaken by non-profit institutions and those undertaken by the business sector. The two communities have different propensities to transfer know-how: non-profit institutions are generally more prone to collaborate and to disclose the results of their research and, in fact, the academic community has long been international in scope. In order to explore the dimension of cross-border collaboration, several studies have focused on internationally co-authored papers since they are one of the measurable outcomes. Frame and Narin (1988) found that the percentage of papers which are internationally co-authored (of the total number of co-authored papers) doubled between 1974 and 1984. As expected, authors from countries with a small scientific community have a higher propensity to co-author their papers with colleagues from other countries. While the proportion of co-authored scientific papers in 1984 having authors from more than one country was equal to 9.3 per cent in the USA, it was 16.1 per cent in Britain, 18.5 per cent in Germany, and 19.2 per cent in France. Japan produces a much lower proportion of internationally co-authored papers, at 6.8 per cent.

To what extent can a similar pattern be identified for the business community? Economists have traditionally viewed firms operating in competitive markets as unwilling to co-operate with their rivals, especially in a strategic area such as technical know-how. However, a closer look at the phenomenon has shown that firms are more willing than generally believed to share their technical know-how with their competitors (see Baumol, 1992).

To monitor technical agreements, Merit at the University of Limburg has developed a database of agreements made known to the press (Cati-Merit; see Hagedoorn and Schakenraad, 1990, 1993). Three new technology fields (biotechnology, new materials and, especially, information technologies) account for more than 70 per cent of all the agreements monitored. Moreover, in these areas there has been a dramatic increase in the number of agreements (see figure 6.3). To a large extent, therefore, the overall growth reflects the increasing importance of these fields, with agreements in other fields having increased at a much slower rate if at all (an exception being the chemical industry).

However, R&D joint-ventures may not be such a *new* trend as generally believed. During the 1960s and 1970s, there was less awareness of the willingness of firms to share their know-how. R&D joint-ventures may have gone unrecorded because of a lack of understanding as well as of interest. In the 1980s, the phenomenon became more visible and new surveys were

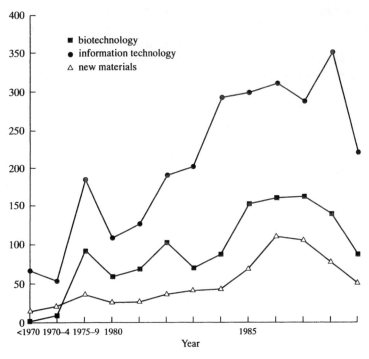

Figure 6.3. Growth of newly established technology co-operation agreements in biotechnology, information technology and new materials. (*Source:* Cati-Merit database, University of Limburg; see Hagerdoorn and Schakenraad, 1990, 1993.)

undertaken to account for it. We share the view that 'although technology cooperation between companies probably goes back many decades, it has experienced a major boost during the 1980s' (Hagedoorn and Soete, 1991, p.209), but we would also point out that this is confined to a very few, although crucial, fields. Two reasons why agreements are so popular in fast-growing technologies are, first, that these new technological paradigms are more knowledge-intensive than in the past, and successful innovative performance relies on the capability to acquire information on what is going on in the field; and, secondly, that for industries in their infant stage it is particularly necessary to acquire information, and therefore also to share it.[9]

Table 6.3 reports the international distribution of technology co-operation agreements in new technologies. Not all of them are international in scope.[10] The major agglomeration of joint-ventures is in the United States: as many as 63 per cent of the agreements recorded involve at least one US-based company and 28 per cent of the agreements occur within US-based

Table 6.3. *International distribution of technology co-operation agreements in biotechnology, information technologies and new materials, 1980–9 (number, with percentages given in parentheses)*

	Biotechnology	Information technologies	New materials	Total
Western Europe	233	509	118	860
	(18.4)	(18.7)	(17.2)	(18.6)
Western Europe–USA	245	599	133	977
	(20.2)	(22.0)	(19.3)	(21.2)
Western Europe–Japan	38	177	49	264
	(3.1)	(6.5)	(7.1)	(5.7)
USA	428	707	139	1274
	(35.3)	(26.0)	(20.2)	(27.6)
USA–Japan	155	406	94	655
	(12.8)	(14.9)	(13.7)	(14.2)
Japan	58	95	88	241
	(4.8)	(3.5)	(12.8)	(5.2)
Other	66	225	67	358
	(5.4)	(8.3)	(9.7)	(7.8)
Total	1223	2718	688	4629
	(100)	(100)	(100)	(100)

Source: Hagedoorn and Schakenraad (1990).

firms (the determinants of US firms' international collaborative ventures are discussed in Mowery, 1992). European firms collaborate more with American than with other European partners in all three fields: intra-European joint-ventures amount to 19 per cent of the total while European–US ones amount to 21 per cent. The Cati-Merit database divides the determinants of such international collaboration into 'market access' and 'technology access': in all three fields considered the technological determinant proves more relevant than does access to the market. This suggests that the reason for European firms co-operating more with US-based firms is because of the larger technological capabilities offered by American companies.[11]

Global generation of technology

We now turn to the third meaning of 'techno-globalism', i.e. the development of firm-based strategies in research and technology across different countries for generating inventions through the 'development of global research networks' (see Howells, 1990a, 1990b), made technically feasible by the new information networks (Antonelli, 1991). This third meaning is the technological equivalent of foreign direct investment.

While the first two uses of the term involve both national and multinational firms, the business and the public sectors, and innovations developed by organisations and by individuals, this third meaning applies to a single actor only: the multinational corporation. Governments and other public institutions, including universities, may collaborate internationally in R&D projects but it is unlikely that they will be in a position to generate inventions 'globally',[12] and, by definition, uninational firms base their production facilities, including their R&D laboratories, in their home country. This third meaning of techno-globalism is therefore more restricted than the former two.

Multinationals are key players in the technological race: according to the OECD, multinational firms account for 75 per cent of all industrial R&D in the OECD countries (OECD, 1992a).[13] The global generation of inventions has far-reaching implications for our understanding of the multinational corporation and not surprisingly it has received much attention from researchers of foreign direct investment (for a survey, see Dunning, 1992). For a long time, multinationals were viewed as organisations with headquarters centralising the most important assets: top management, strategic planning, and R&D laboratories. In other words, the multinational was seen as a sort of polyp with its brain in the home country and tentacles in the host countries. If a substantial proportion of inventions is now generated in host countries this would imply that a crucial part of the brain has been decentralised into the tentacles. In fact, researchers in the field of international production have argued that the implementation of foreign R&D laboratories by multinational companies is generally a consequence of their foreign direct investment (see Casson, 1991; Dunning, 1992).[14]

From the perspective of the individual nation-states, there are both pros and cons in having their firms locating R&D outside the borders of their country, and likewise for hosting the R&D of foreign firms. On the one hand, there are advantages in hosting the largest possible amount of skilled activities, although foreign firms are less controllable by national policies. On the other hand, having domestic firms based in foreign countries may weaken national technological capabilities in strategic areas; while this argument is generally understood for defence (governments rarely allow national military procurement to be heavily dependent on foreign-controlled firms), it is often overlooked for strategic civilian sectors.[15] A large share of R&D performed abroad by home-based firms may also indicate that the domestic infrastructure is inadequate.

A variety of approaches have been used to identify and measure the decentralisation of R&D and other inventive activities (for a survey, see Howells, 1990a). However, most of the research has focused on selected case-studies of specific multinationals. Although this evidence has provided some very useful insights at the microeconomic level, it is difficult to assess to what extent the cases of what are particularly internationalised firms can be generalised. Patel and Pavitt (1991a) analysed the global generation of inventions by considering the location of the inventions registered at the US patent office by the world's largest 686 firms for the period 1981–6.[16] Nearly all these firms have a substantial part of their production in host countries. Patents are a particularly appropriate measure to test the location of the inventions since they are attributed to the country of residence of the inventor rather than to that of the owner. Columns 1 and 2 of table 6.4 therefore report the share of patenting from nationally and foreign-controlled large firms as a percentage of total national patenting, and column 3 reports the share of patents granted to other firms, government agencies, universities and private inventors (these three columns are as a percentage of total national patenting in the United States).

The share of patenting controlled by foreign firms is 10 per cent or less in all the countries considered other than Belgium, the United Kingdom and Canada. The share of foreign-controlled patenting is very low for the two largest OECD countries, the United States and Japan, amounting to 3.1 per cent and 1.2 per cent respectively. European countries are more likely to host foreign R&D, although a substantial part of this is intra-European; the share of patenting in Europe controlled by non-European large companies is only slightly higher than for the United States and Japan, at 6.2 per cent: if Western Europe is seen as a 'single market', the amount of foreign-controlled inventions is not substantially higher than for the United States and Japan. This evidence indicates that the global generation of inventions is far from being with us.

However, the share of foreign-controlled patenting should be considered in relation to the sub-total of patents controlled by large firms since, as stated above, this third meaning of techno-globalism cannot be applied to the whole national economy but only to multinational corporations.[17] Column 4 of table 6.4 reports the share of patents controlled by foreign large firms as a share of the patents taken out by all (national and foreign) large firms. Foreign firms account for 82 per cent and 61 per cent of large firms' technological activities in, respectively, Belgium and Canada. They are also important in the UK (37 per cent) and Italy (32 per cent). Industrial and innovation policies towards large firms in these countries need therefore to take account of the fact that a substantial proportion of technological activities are undertaken by firms belonging to the 'foreign legion' which may prove more volatile than home-based large firms.

Table 6.4. *Large firms in national technological activities (patents granted by the US patent office)*

	National source of patenting (3 columns add up to 100%)			Patenting by foreign-controlled large firms as a % of total large firms' patenting from that country Cols. {2/(1+2)}×100	Patenting by large firms operating outside their home country (as a % of national total)	Patenting by large firms operating outside their home country (as a % of large firms' patents from outside and inside the country) Cols. {5/(1+5)}×100	Balance of patenting from foreign-controlled firms in the country and patenting abroad by nationally controlled firms Col. 2 − col. 5
	Large firms						
	Nationally controlled	Foreign-controlled	Other				
	1	2	3	4	5	6	7
Belgium	8.8	39.7	51.5	81.9	14.7	62.6	25.0
France	36.8	10.0	53.2	21.4	3.4	8.5	6.6
FR Germany	44.8	10.5	44.7	19.0	6.9	13.3	3.6
Italy	24.1	11.6	64.3	32.5	2.2	8.4	9.4
Netherlands	51.9	8.7	39.4	14.4	82.0	61.2	−73.3
Sweden	27.5	3.9	68.6	12.4	11.3	29.1	−7.4
Switzerland	40.1	6.0	53.9	13.0	28.0	41.1	−22.0
UK	32.0	19.1	49.0	37.4	16.7	34.3	2.4
W. Europe	44.1	6.2	49.7	12.3	8.1	15.5	−1.9
Canada	11.0	16.9	72.1	60.6	8.0	42.1	8.9
Japan	62.5	1.2	36.3	1.9	0.6	1.0	0.6
USA	42.8	3.1	54.1	6.8	3.2	7.0	−0.1

Note:
All columns refer to patents granted by the US patent office between 1981 and 1986. The first three columns are calculated as a percentage of total national patenting in the United States.

Source: Patel and Pavitt, 1991a, and calculations from the data.

Column 5 of table 6.4 reports the percentage of patents controlled by firms operating from outside the home country.[18] Not surprisingly, the countries ranking first are those traditionally associated with financial and international capital: The Netherlands (with a share as high as 82 per cent), Switzerland (28 per cent) and the UK (17 per cent).[19] This tendency to operate from host countries reflects a number of factors, such as in some cases a long tradition of foreign direct investment, but also, particularly in the case of smaller countries, the relative lack of technological expertise at home. German, French and Italian large firms have a much lower propensity to perform R&D in host countries. Both Japanese and US large firms carry out a negligible part of their technological activities in host countries: US and Japanese multinationals still operate along the lines of the well-known 'polyp' model and do not decentralise strategic activities, at least as far as R&D is concerned.

Column 7 of table 6.4 shows the balance between foreign-controlled patenting at home and patenting abroad of nationally controlled firms. For the majority of countries, the difference in the national technology level would not change much in the absence of multinational activity since the outward flows are balanced by the inward flows. The United States, Japan and Western Europe as a whole break even. The Netherlands and Switzerland have a net loss, while Belgium, Italy and Canada gain.

It has been argued that patenting in the United States is not a reliable indicator of the global generation of innovations (see Chesnais, 1992), and it is therefore important to compare the results based on patents with those found using other technological indicators such as R&D. Pearce and Singh (1992) considered the geographic distribution of R&D employees of a sample of multinational corporations and their results show an even smaller globalisation of multinationals' R&D activity than is indicated by the patent data. A detailed comparison is made by Patel (this volume, table 7.2) between overseas R&D and patenting for US multinationals, and this shows that the two distributions are rather similar, even at the industry level.

An additional step towards a dynamic analysis is made by Patel (this volume) providing evidence on the pace of internationalisation of large firms' patenting activity and finding that in a five-year period (1986–90) the patents of foreign-controlled firms increased, for all countries, by only 1 per cent. If we compare this rate of change to the rate of change in both foreign patent applications and patent applications extended abroad, we see that the global generation of technology is growing at a much slower pace than is its international exploitation. The available empirical results (Patel and Pavitt, 1991a; Cantwell and Hodson, 1991; Pearce and Singh, 1992; Patel, this volume) therefore suggest that a disproportionate importance has been given to the third meaning of techno-globalism. Large multinational firms do show a tendency towards a growing international integration of business. But, to repeat, however important large firms might be, they are not the only producers of innovations. In conclusion, we share Casson's (1991) view that 'the story of globalised R&D is the story of a fairly small number of very large firms carrying out research in a small number of leading industrialized countries' (p.272).

Finally, we compare how the generation of technology, on the one hand, and technological collaboration, on the other, vary across regions. The international generation of technology has to date been a peculiarly intra-European phenomenon. It is not only, as noted above, that the US and Japanese firms have not pursued the global generation of technology to any significant extent (table 6.4, columns 5 and 6), but also that European firms have tended to choose other European countries to locate their foreign R&D facilities, which tendency therefore has the character of European *regionalisation* rather than globalisation. This is even more significant when compared with the inter-firm technical agreements discussed above, which often involve partnerships between European and American firms. While European firms have a propensity to share their know-how with American competitors, they still prefer to locate foreign research within the European continent.

The impact of globalisation on national technological specialisation

The results obtained for each of the three categories above suggest that the role of national innovation policy is not necessarily becoming less important because of globalisation. The exploitation of innovations requires national governments to settle the regime according to which new technologies can be exploited within their borders. International collaborations rely on the nature of the national technological capabilities associated with the prospective partner. As for the generation of innovation, this is still largely organised within the boundaries of nation-states. These results – suggesting that the role of nations in the organisation of innovative activities remains crucial – are consistent with the new body of literature emphasising the role of national systems in organising and promoting innovation (see Porter, 1990; Lundvall, 1992; Nelson, 1993). More importantly, the categorisation proposed suggests that the dichotomy global/national is a false one.

The hypothesis of international technological accumulation (see Pavitt, 1988; Cantwell, 1991) stresses that capabilities are nation-specific, differentiated and cumulative. A large body of evidence has shown that nations have different sectoral strengths and weaknesses (see Soete, 1987; Patel and

Pavitt, 1991b; Archibugi and Pianta, 1992) which tend to persist over time (Cantwell, 1989). We therefore assume that one of the factors which influences firms in either co-operating with foreign firms or investing in a foreign country is the technical expertise that those firms or countries have to offer, and that firms will try to exploit these national advantages in their international innovation strategies. Thus American foreign investment in the German chemical industry is related to the traditional excellence of Germany in the field (see Cantwell, 1989). Similarly, a significant proportion of European companies' foreign direct investment in the United States is in biotechnology because of the higher technological competence of American firms.

The 'polyp' firm appears to use its tentacles to acquire from each country its excellence in research rather than to decentralise its brain. However, this is not always feasible since national technological capabilities may or may not be easily appropriated by foreign companies. Some of them will typically be associated with the technological advantages of national firms and are unlikely to be appropriable by foreign firms, as indicated by international business studies.[20] The Cati-Merit database indicates that technological complementarity is the key factor promoting joint R&D, while the technological competence of the partner is the main rationale for foreign direct investment in R&D (Hagedoorn and Schakenraad, 1990, tables 4 and 5). In other words, one of the key factors behind the internationalisation of R&D is the acquiring of knowledge. The choice between collaboration and foreign direct investment is influenced by the nature of ownership advantages: firms might decide on foreign direct investment when technology is easily appropriable, but on a partnership when it is not.

The effects of this strategy should also emerge at the sectoral level. We would expect: first, the sectors with a high presence of foreign firms to be those of national excellence of the host country; and second, that the difference between the sectoral strengths and weaknesses of countries tend to increase rather than to decrease over time. The first predicted outcome is confirmed by the empirical work of Patel and Pavitt (1991a) and Cantwell and Hodson (1991): the vector of the indices of national technological specialisation (as measured by patents) is positively associated with the vector of foreign-controlled patenting in the same nation for the majority of countries.[21] This evidence supports the hypothesis that multinational firms do not extend their R&D internationally to replicate research and innovations in the sectors where their home country is already strong, but rather to acquire the know-how which is lacking at home. The second outcome is confirmed by research showing that the differences in the degree of technological specialisation have increased for the majority of countries (Archibugi and Pianta, 1992).[22] Table 6.5 reports the degree of technological specialisation

Table 6.5. *The degree of technological specialisation. Chi-square values of the percentage distributions by sectors of patents and patent citations*

	Chi-squares by 41 SIC classes				Chi-squares by 31 IPC classes	
	Patents granted in the USA		Patent citations in the USA		Patent applications at the European Patent Office	
	1975–81	1982–8	1975–81	1982–8	1982–6	1987–91
United States	0.94	1.31	1.05	2.06	7.92	8.16
Japan	13.46	14.68	12.96	14.96	19.58	20.92
EEC	3.84	4.50	5.76	6.90	3.24	4.74
Germany	8.16	10.05	13.51	15.39	3.55	7.04
France	4.00	3.86	4.01	3.83	11.16	11.05
United Kingdom	5.91	6.85	10.43	17.91	5.97	4.35
Italy	21.85	24.53	25.55	25.21	34.92	32.81
The Netherlands	23.06	20.46	27.52	22.48	22.02	34.93
Belgium	30.72	38.84	56.02	110.56	39.01	49.64
Denmark	24.63	31.88	41.06	62.40	n.c.	n.c.
Spain	46.88	53.52	88.73	101.09	n.c.	n.c.
Ireland	77.99	22.42	84.78	50.58	n.c.	n.c.
Portugal	139.81	212.25	289.36	299.57	n.c.	n.c.
Greece	96.13	89.96	153.46	290.15	n.c.	n.c.
Canada	12.38	14.09	16.56	18.41	n.c.	n.c.
Switzerland	36.16	34.39	38.54	56.12	25.92	32.79
Sweden	24.72	24.74	23.70	23.15	44.24	49.97

Notes:
n.c. not calculated.
SIC Standard Industrial Classification.
IPC International Patent Classes.
(i) The chi-square values are used as measures of the distance between the percentage distributions of patents (by SIC or IPC classes) of the world and those of each country;
(ii) The EEC data by IPC classes include only six major countries: Germany, France, Italy, The Netherlands, Belgium, United Kingdom;
(iii) Residual classes (i.e. 'Other Industries' and 'Unclassified' for SIC classification and 'Others' for the IPC classification) have been excluded.
Source: Archibugi and Pianta, 1992 and calculations on data from the European Patent Office.

as measured by patents registered in the two main patent offices (the United States and the European Patent Office). It emerges that the majority of countries have increased their degree of specialisation.

The effects of techno-globalism on national technological specialisation does not seem therefore to be leading to any greater uniformity in patterns of strengths and weaknesses. Nations are becoming *increasingly* different and the international operations of large firms are exploiting and developing this diversity.

Conclusions

This chapter has brought empirical evidence to bear on the various hypotheses arising from the growing literature on the globalisation of technological activities. We have suggested that there is both reality and mythology behind the claims. We have introduced an analytical distinction between three different processes which were previously subsumed in the literature under the single term 'techno-globalism' (see table 6.6).

The strongest case for techno-globalism is the international exploitation of inventions developed within each nation. The majority of inventions are already exploited globally, and this process is continuing at a rapid pace. The willingness of firms to exploit their innovations in external markets does not necessarily imply that they will be successful. This depends on policies implemented by national governments, which can discourage the import of products which incorporate innovations or regulate in other ways the market for disembodied innovations. Significantly enough, one of the main new controversies in the GATT negotiations was the insistence by the USA on a higher degree of international protection for industrial and intellectual property rights.

The second aspect we have considered is that of global technological collaboration. Although it might be expected that firms would be more willing to share their know-how with other firms which do not compete in the same market, empirical results show that the main determinant is the competence of the partner rather than access to markets. This seems to be the reason why collaboration among European firms, in spite of all the policies designed to encourage it, has not taken place to a greater degree. A significant increase in technological co-operation has in fact taken place only in the fast-growing technological fields, and the growth in aggregate measures reflects the increasing importance of these technologies. The importance of technical partnership may be related to the slow-down in the growth of industry-financed R&D. Joint-ventures have become a source of know-how which is complementary to the financing of in-house R&D. They also effect national technological capabilities, since firms try to collaborate with firms

Table 6.6. *Three meanings of 'techno-globalism'*

	Actors	Economic equivalent	Measure(s)	Source	Results	
					Stock	Flow
(a) Global *exploitation* of technology	Profit-seeking organisations Uni- and multinational firms	International trade flows (as opposed to foreign direct investment)	Patents extended in foreign markets	Tables 6.1 and 6.2	Patents were on average extended in 3–4 foreign markets in 1990	6 per cent average annual growth rate for the OECD countries during the 1980s
(b) Global technological *collaboration*	Business sector	International joint-ventures	Inter-firm technical agreements	Hagedoorn and Schakenraad, 1990, 1993	Not available	6 per cent annual growth comparing 1985–9 to 1980–4
	Academic and public research communities	Non-profit cultural exchanges	Co-authored scientific papers	Frame and Narin 1988	10 per cent of co-authored papers in 1984	Doubled between 1973 and 1984
(c) Global *generation* of technology	Multinational corporations	Foreign direct investment (as opposed to trade flows)	Patents in the USA of firms from outside their home country	Table 6.4 and Patel and Pavitt, 1991a, and Patel, this volume	3.8 per cent of patents in 1981–86	1 per cent growth between 1981–5 and 1986–90

based in countries which have endowments lacking in the home country. We have suggested that this tendency is behind the measured increase in the diversity of national technological specialisation.

Thirdly, evidence of the globalisation of production of technology seems much weaker than for the above two concepts. The concept, and therefore the evidence, only relates to multinational corporations and, although these are major actors in technological innovation, they are not the only ones. Nevertheless, we have suggested that the technological activities of foreign firms compared to the total activities of large firms should be of concern for policy-makers in all European countries (and, to a lesser degree, in the United States).

These hypotheses are consistent with the theory of international technological accumulation, which indicates that countries have their own sectors and fields of competitive advantage. One reason why multinational firms do not globalise their technological facilities more is that they themselves are aware of the role of nations in providing infrastructure, facilities and other intangible assets for a successful location of their R&D and innovative capacity.

Notes

1 We wish to thank John Cantwell, Chris Freeman and Kirsty Hughes for detailed comments.
2 Globalisation is a term used by economists and sociologists alike. Giddens (1990), for example, has defined globalisation as 'the intensification of world-wide social relations which link distant localities in such a way that local happenings are shaped by events occurring many miles away and vice versa' (p.64).
3 The most notable example is provided by the European Union, which has launched a large variety of R&D and other programmes involving organisations based in more than one of its member-states.
4 Some authors (see, for example, Evenson, 1989) relate the slow-down in domestic applications to a decreasing productivity of scientific and technological research (this issue is also discussed by Griliches, 1990). However, the decrease in domestic patents may also be related to a greater realism regarding the opportunities offered by the patent system.
5 A firm might exploit its new products in international markets without necessarily integrating its R&D laboratories internationally, nor undertaking international research joint-ventures.
6 For an analysis of the foreign patenting policy of multinational companies see Wyatt *et al.* (1985). The use of patenting as a technology indicator is reviewed in Griliches (1990) and Archibugi (1992).
7 It is true that new institutional facilities have made it easier to extend a patent in more than one country, most notably the European Patent Office (EPO). However, countries which are not members of the EPO have also experienced

a comparable growth in the number of foreign patent applications received. Institutional developments seem to be more the consequence of the global exploitation of technology than its cause.

8 Since inventors are allowed one year to extend abroad the applications they have presented at home, the domestic patent applications considered here refer to the year $t-1$.

9 For a discussion of the necessity to disclose information in order to acquire it, see von Hippel (1987) and Carter (1989). Cainarca *et al.* (1992) have shown that inter-firm agreements are typical in the early phases of technological life-cycles.

10 The data at our disposal do not allow the separation of intra-European agreements into those which involve more than one European country and those within the same country. The Cati-Merit database is also likely to underestimate joint-ventures between Japanese firms because of linguistic barriers.

11 These issues are also addressed in Casson (1991) and Linne *et al.* (1991).

12 Universities and public research centres do not, as a rule, establish subsidiaries in foreign countries.

13 However, such figures for R&D (as well as patents, particularly patents extended abroad) are likely to overestimate the importance of large firms: see Archibugi *et al.* (1991). The role of large and small firms in technological change is the subject of continuing controversy in innovation studies (see, among a large literature, Acs and Audretsch, 1990; Malerba and Orsenigo, this volume).

14 Pearce and Singh (1992) show that the single most significant factor determining the development of subsidiary R&D units by multinationals is 'to help to develop new products for the local market'.

15 Tyson (1992) makes the additional point that 'foreign direct investment could threaten national security by transferring control over key military technologies to foreign firms or investors in concentrated industries' (p.146).

16 Patel and Pavitt (1991a) considered patents registered in one country only, i.e. a sub-set of the world patented inventions considered above. However, there is strong evidence to suggest that patents registered at the US patent office are a significant and representative sample of high-quality patented inventions (see Archibugi and Pianta, 1992).

17 This approach was applied to patenting in the United States by Cantwell and Hodson (1991) whose results proved very similar to those of Patel and Pavitt (1991a).

18 While column 2 of table 6.4 refers to the patents granted to inventors who reside in a given country and are employed by foreign firms, column 5 refers to inventors who are employed by national firms but reside in foreign countries.

19 The data of Patel and Pavitt (1991a) include ten Dutch-based firms, ten Swiss-based firms and sixty-four UK-based firms.

20 A review of this large literature is provided by Dunning (1992). See also Granstrand *et al.* (1992) and Kogut (1992).

21 The index of technological specialisation is defined as $I_{ij} = (p_{ij}/\Sigma_i p_{ij})/(\Sigma_j p_{ij}/\Sigma_{ij} p_{ij})$, where p_{ij} is the number of patents of country i in sector j. Both Patel and Pavitt

(1991a) and Cantwell and Hodson (1991) consider patents registered by all countries at the US patent office subdivided by country of residence of the inventor and home country of the owner firm.

22 By degree of specialisation is meant how a country concentrates or disperses its innovations across sectors. Chi-square values were calculated for each country on the vector containing the percentage distribution of its patents in the classes considered. The expected values with which the country shares have been compared are the values of the percentage distribution of the world total. The percentages of the vectors were multiplied by 100. The chi-square value of the country i is defined as $c = \Sigma_j \, (AS_{ij} - ES_j)^2/ES_j$, where AS_{ij} is the actual share of patents of country i in class j, and ES_j is the expected share, i.e. the share of the world total. If the sectoral distribution of a country is identical to the percentage distribution of the total for all countries, the value of the chi-square will be equal to 0 (see Archibugi and Pianta, 1992, p.104).

References

Acs, Z. and Audretsch, D. 1990. *Innovation and Small Firms*, Cambridge, Mass., MIT Press.

Amendola, G., Dosi, G. and Papagni, E. 1994. The dynamics of international competitiveness, *Weltwirtschaftliches Archiv*, 129: 451–71.

Amendola, G., Guerrieri, P. and Padoan, P.C. 1992. International patterns of technological accumulation and trade, *Journal of International and Comparative Economics*, 1: 173–97.

Antonelli, C. 1991. *The Diffusion of Advanced Telecommunications in Developing Countries*, Paris, OECD Development Centre.

Archibugi, D. 1992. Patenting as an indicator of technological innovation: a review, *Science and Public Policy*, 17: 357–68.

Archibugi, D., Cesaratto, S. and Sirilli, G. 1991. Sources of innovative activities and industrial organisation in Italy, *Research Policy*, 20: 299–313.

Archibugi, D. and Pianta, M. 1992. *The Technological Specialisation of Advanced Countries. A Report to the EC on International Science and Technology Activities*, Boston, Kluwer.

Audretsch, D., Sleuwaegen, L. and Yamawaki, H. (eds.) 1989. *The Convergence of International and Domestic Markets*, Amsterdam, North Holland.

Baumol, W.J. 1992. Horizontal collusion and innovation, *Economic Journal*, 102: 129–37.

Cainarca, G.C., Colombo, M. and Mariotti, S. 1992. Agreements between firms and the technological life cycle model: evidence from information technologies, *Research Policy*, 21: 45–62.

Cantwell, J. 1989. *Technological Innovation and the Multinational Corporation*, Oxford, Basil Blackwell.

1991. The technological competence theory of international production and its implications, in D.G. McFetridge (ed.), *Foreign Investment, Technology and Economic Growth*, Calgary, University of Calgary Press.

Cantwell, J. and Hodson, C. 1991. Global R&D and UK competitiveness, in Casson (ed.).

Carter, A. 1989. Knowhow trading as economic exchange, *Research Policy*, 18: 155–63.

Casson, M. (ed.) 1991. *Global Research Strategy and International Competitiveness*, Oxford, Basil Blackwell.

Chesnais, F. 1988. Technical co-operation agreements between firms, *Science Technology Industry Review*, no. 4, pp. 57–119.

1992. National systems of innovation, foreign direct investment and the operations of multinational enterprises, in Lundvall (ed.).

Dunning, J. 1992. *Multinational Enterprises and the Global Economy*, Wokingham, Addison-Wesley.

Evenson, R. 1989. Patent data: evidence for declining R&D potency, mimeo, OECD, Paris.

Fagerberg, J. 1988. International competitiveness, *Economic Journal*, 98: 355–74.

Frame, J.D. and Narin, F. 1988. The national self-preoccupation of American scientists: an empirical view, *Research Policy*, 17: 203–11.

Freeman, C. 1992. *The Economics of Hope*, London, Pinter.

Freeman, C. and Hagedoorn, J. 1992. *Globalisation of Technology*, Brussels, EC-FAST.

Freeman, C. and Soete, L. (eds.) 1990. *New Explorations in the Economics of Technical Change*, London, Pinter.

Giddens, A. 1990. *Consequences of Modernity*, Cambridge, Polity Press.

Granstrand, O., Håkanson, L. and Sjölander, S. (eds.) 1992. *Technology Management and International Business. Internationalization of R&D and Technology*. Chichester, Wiley.

Griliches, Z. 1990. Patent statistics as economic indicators: a survey, *Journal of Economic Literature*, 28: 1661–707.

Guerrieri, P. and Milana, C. 1991. Technological and trade competition in high-tech products, Working Paper no. 54, The Berkeley Roundtable on the International Economy, Berkeley, Calif., October.

Gugler, P. and Dunning, J.H. 1992. *Technology based cross-border alliances*, Discussion Paper in International Investment and Business Studies no. 163, University of Reading.

Hagedoorn, J. and Schakenraad, J. 1990. Inter-firm partnerships and co-operative strategies in core technologies, in Freeman and Soete (eds.).

1993. Strategic technology partnering and international corporate strategies, in Hughes (ed.).

Hagedoorn, J. and Soete, L. 1991. The internationalisation of science and technology policy: how do 'national' systems cope? in National Institute for Science and Technology Policy, *Science and Technology Policy Research*, Tokyo, Mita Press.

Howells, J. 1990a. The internationalisation of R&D and the development of global research networks, *Regional Studies*, 24: 495–512.

1990b. The location and organisation of research and development: new horizons, *Research Policy*, 19: 133–46.

Hughes, K. 1986. *Technology and Exports*, Cambridge, Cambridge University Press.

Hughes, K. (ed.) 1993. *European Competitiveness*, Cambridge, Cambridge University Press.

Katz, M.L. and Ordover, J.A. 1990. R&D cooperation and competition, *Brookings Papers on Economic Activity* (Microeconomics), pp. 137–203.

Kogut, B. (ed.) 1992. *Country Competitiveness: Technology and the Organizing of Work*, Oxford, Oxford University Press.

Linne, H., Magnaval, R. and Removille, J. 1991. *Key Factors for Industrial Partnership in the EC Programmes*, Brussels, Monitor/Spear, Commission of European Communities.

Lundvall, B.-Å. (ed.) 1992. *National Systems of Innovation*, London, Pinter.

Mowery, D. 1992. International collaborative ventures and US firms' technology strategy, in Granstrand *et al.* (eds.).

Mytelka, L.K. (ed.) 1991. *Strategic Partnership: States, Firms and International Competition*, London, Pinter.

Nelson, R. R. (ed.) 1993. *National Innovation Systems*, New York, Oxford University Press.

OECD 1992a. *Technology and the Economy. The Key Relationship*, Paris, OECD.

  1992b. Main science and technology indicators, diskette, Science, Technology, Industry Indicator Division, OECD, Paris, May.

Patel, P. and Pavitt, K. 1991a. Large firms in the production of world's technology: an important case of non-globalisation, *International Journal of Business Studies*, 22: 1–21.

  1991b. *Europe's Technological Performance*, in C. Freeman, M. Sharp, and W. Walker (eds.), *Technology and the Future of Europe*, London, Pinter.

Pavitt, K. 1988. International patterns of technological accumulation, in N. Hood, and J.E. Vahlne (eds.), *Strategies in Global Competition*, London, Croom Helm.

Pearce, R. and Singh, S. 1992. *Globalising Research and Development*, London, Macmillan.

Petrella, R. 1989. Globalisation of technological innovation, *Technology Analysis and Strategic Management*, 1: 393–407.

Porter, M. 1990. *The Competitive Advantage of Nations*, London, Macmillan.

Soete, L. 1987. The impact of technological innovation on international trade patterns: the evidence reconsidered, *Research Policy*, 16: 101–30.

Tyson, L.D. 1992. *Who's Bashing Whom? Trade Conflict in High-Technology Industries*, Washington, D.C., Institute for International Economics.

von Hippel, E. 1987. Cooperation between rivals: informal knowhow trading, *Research Policy*, 16: 291–302.

Wyatt, S., Bertin, G. and Pavitt, K. 1985. Patents and multinational corporations: results from questionnaires, *World Patent Information*, 7: 196–212.

7 Localised production of technology for global markets

PARI PATEL[1]

Introduction

Background

This chapter examines the volume and trends in the extent of internationalisation of technological activities of the world's largest firms based on data on their US patenting. There are two sets of reasons for addressing this issue.

The first is that debate continues about the implications of the globalisation of markets for the location of innovative activities. A number of recent analyses (Howells, 1990; Cantwell, 1992; Chesnais, 1992; Dunning, 1992; Granstrand and Sjölander, 1992; Håkanson, 1992;) have argued that large multinational firms, who are the main actors in the globalisation of markets, are now globalising their technological activities. The two main contentions of these studies are, firstly, that this process has accelerated since the 1980s, and secondly, that the reasons underlying firms' decisions to locate R&D outside their home countries have changed. In the earlier literature on the internationalisation of business the emphasis was on the role of home markets in determining firms' technological advantage. In particular Vernon (1966) argued that having established a new product or a new production process in the home market, firms would subsequently export and/or locate production facilities in overseas locations. This process would inevitably involve some overseas R&D activity mainly concerned with adapting the products (e.g. to account for differences in consumer tastes) and the production processes (e.g. to account for differences in the labour market) to suit the local market conditions. However, in his more recent work Vernon (1979) suggests that in some (high-technology) industries the product cycle has become highly compressed with firms engaged in programmes of almost simultaneous innovations in several major markets. In addition, in the most recent analyses (cited above) there is a strong emphasis on the role of 'supply-side' factors in the firms' decisions concerning the

198

location of R&D. Thus firms are now assumed to assess a wide range of different geographic locations purely in terms of the strength of their science and technology base and the availability of adequately qualified scientists and engineers. In such a scenario the home country of the firm is assessed on the same basis as all the other potential locations. Another element in such analyses is the role played by the latest advances in information and communications technology in solving the problems of co-ordination and control posed by having technological activities scattered in a number of different locations.

The second reason for addressing this subject is that there is still a debate concerning the available empirical evidence. In an earlier study (Patel and Pavitt, 1991) we argued, on the basis of US patenting data for the world's largest manufacturing firms, that the importance of the foreign technological activities of large firms had been exaggerated. We also showed, using correlation analysis, that home country conditions have a major impact on the levels and trends of the technological activities of nationally based large firms. This analysis has been criticised for three sets of reasons: (i) patenting is a particularly poor measure and different measures, e.g. those based on R&D expenditures, would have produced different results; (ii) the evidence from case-studies of individual firms or sectors cannot be reconciled with these results; and (iii) by only providing a static picture of the early 1980s, the widespread increases in the extent of globalisation in the late 1980s were neglected. Later we address each of these issues in turn, but before doing so we briefly summarise the main results of the most recent studies that have looked at the nature and extent of globalisation of technology.

Other recent studies

Archibugi and Michie (this volume, chapter 6) analyse quantitative evidence by making a distinction between three different (but complementary) meanings of globalisation of technology (or 'techno-globalism') as used in the literature. They are: (i) the global exploitation of technology; (ii) the global production of technology; and (iii) global technological collaboration. In relation to the first of these there is very little controversy, as there is strong evidence (quoted in their chapter) that firms are increasingly exploiting their innovations on a global scale. Most of the controversy surrounds the empirical evidence related to the other two meanings.

The studies concerned with analysing the global production of technology can be categorised into two groups. In the first group are those,[2] based on private surveys or case-studies in selected companies, industries, or countries, concerned with understanding the nature and the motivation of firms locating technological activities in foreign locations. The main results of these studies are: (i) most overseas R&D is still concerned with adapting existing products and processes to host country market conditions (Pearce and Singh, 1992); (ii) 'political' factors have been an important influence on firms in making decisions about locating their technological activities outside the home base (Håkanson, 1992); and (iii) most firms envisage an increase in the extent of activities undertaken abroad and also a change in the nature of these activities (Håkanson, 1992; and Pearce and Singh, 1992).[3]

The second group of studies consists of those concerned with a quantitative assessment of the extent of globalisation based on different measures of technological activities. Within this group are studies using data on the number of R&D personnel (Howells, 1990; Wortmann, 1990; Dorrenbacher and Wortmann, 1991); on R&D expenditures (US NSF Science Indicators reports); and on patenting activities (Etemad and Seguin Dulude, 1987); Patel and Pavitt, 1991; Cantwell, 1992). None of the results reported in these studies show that the foreign technological activities of the large firms are more important than those in their home base (most put the proportion of foreign activities between 10 and 30 per cent). Most of these studies also show that there has been an increase in the extent to which firms are locating technological activities outside the home country.

Quantitative studies based on the third definition of 'techno-globalism' analyse the trends and patterns in international collaborative agreements between firms involving a substantial technology element (Chesnais, 1988; Freeman and Hagedoorn, 1992). The main results of these studies[4] are: (i) over 90 per cent of all agreements in the 1980s were between firms based in the Triad countries[5]; and (ii) around 20 per cent were between firms in Europe and the USA, 14 per cent between those in Japan and the USA, and around 6 per cent between Japanese and European firms, with the remaining 60 per cent being inter-country agreements.

It is in the context of these studies that we address two sets of questions in the main section of this chapter. First, to what extent did firms, in the late 1980s, locate the production of their technology outside the home base, as shown by data on their US patenting activities, and were there changes from the early 1980s? Second, what were the main locations of large firms' technological activities in the second half of the 1980s and did these change from the early 1980s? Before turning to the results, we outline the main elements of the dataset used in looking at these questions.

Dataset

The dataset has been compiled from information, supplied by the US Patent Office, on the name of the company, the technical class, and the country of origin of the inventor, for each patent granted in the USA from 1969 to 1990. The main difficulty in using these data at the corporate level is that many patents are granted under the names of subsidiaries and divisions that are different from those of the parent companies, and are therefore listed separately. An additional difficulty is that the names of companies are not unified, in the sense that the same company may appear several times in the data, with a slightly different name in each case.

Consolidating patenting under the names of parent companies can only be done manually on the basis of publications like *Who Owns Whom*. In an earlier study (Patel and Pavitt, 1991) we unified the names and consolidated the data for 636 of the world's largest firms, in terms of sales, for the year 1984. Beginning with that sample, in the present study we have performed the same exercise on the basis of *Who Owns Whom* for 1988. After taking account of the firms that ceased trading and those that were taken over by other firms in the sample, we have 569 firms in our present sample. For each firm we also have information, from published sources (*Fortune, Disclosure*), on sales, employment, country of headquarters and principal product group.

In our earlier study (Patel and Pavitt, 1991) we described the main advantages and disadvantages of using patent statistics as a measure of technological activities. Briefly their main advantages over other indicators such as R&D expenditures are that they are available over a long period of time and can be broken down in great statistical detail according to geographic location and technical area. Their main disadvantage is that they do not satisfactorily measure two important areas of technology, namely, software and biotechnology.

The main added advantage of our current dataset is that, for the first time, it enables us to examine trends in the internationalisation of technological activities. Other analyses using similar data (our own previous work and that of Cantwell, 1992), have been based on a set of firms consolidated for one particular year, and hence have not been able to analyse changes. With the present dataset we can examine these changes by comparing the geographic distribution of the firms' patenting activities between the two sets of consolidations: 1984 and 1988. Such a comparison of the two cross-sections also enables us to look at the extent to which changes in internationalisation have been achieved through mergers and acquisitions or through organic growth.

Before describing the results, we list (table 7.1) the numbers of large firms in our database according to their home country[6] and principal product group. American firms accounted for 45 per cent of the sample, European firms 30 per cent and Japanese firms 25 per cent. Within Europe the largest contributor was the UK (54 firms), followed by Germany (42) and France

Table 7.1. *The distribution of the 569 large firms in the sample by nationality and principal product group*

Product group	Europe[a]	Japan	North America[b]	Total
Chemicals	18	25	28	71
Pharmaceuticals	7	4	14	25
Mining and petroleum	14	7	23	44
Textiles etc.	4	5	9	18
Rubber and plastics	3	2	5	10
Paper and wood	8	6	17	31
Food	11	11	19	41
Drink and tobacco	7	1	9	17
Building materials	10	6	10	26
Metals	24	13	19	56
Machinery	23	13	32	68
Electrical	13	17	28	58
Computers	4	2	11	17
Instruments	1	8	11	20
Motor vehicles	15	18	10	43
Aircraft	7	0	12	19
Other transport	2	1	2	5
Total	171	139	259	569

Notes:
[a] For the total number of firms from each European country, see table 7.5.
[b] 243 US firms and 16 Canadian firms.

(25). In terms of the industrial distribution, 21 per cent had machinery and metal goods as their principal product group, 16 per cent had chemicals and pharmaceuticals, and 13 per cent electrical (including electronics) and computing machinery.

International location of technological activities: results of the analysis

Comparison of US patenting and R&D expenditures

Apart from the data on US patenting, the only other systematic evidence of the extent of internationalisation of technological activities of firms is that on self-financed R&D expenditures of US firms and their overseas subsidiaries collected by the National Science Foundation in the United States. In Table 7.2 we compare, for the 1980s, the proportion of R&D spent by

Table 7.2. *A comparison of the overseas R&D and patenting activities of US firms[a]: percentage of the total undertaken outside the United States*

	R&D 1979–84	Patenting 1979–84	R&D 1985–9	Patenting 1985–90
Chemicals	6.9	6.9	9.3	8.7
Pharmaceuticals	10.4	11.0	12.7	12.5
Electrical	6.8	6.3	5.3	8.1
Machinery	8.4	8.5	9.3	9.1
Metals	5.3	3.6	6.1	3.1
Transport	9.9	5.0	11.0	6.6
Instruments	6.7	9.2	6.1	7.0
Total (of all product groups)	8.0	6.3	7.9	7.8

Note:
[a] The patent data are for the 243 US large firms in our database and the R&D data refer to all US firms covered by the National Science Foundation R&D Survey.
Source: National Science Foundation, *Science Indicators*, 1991 and Large Firms Database, Science Policy Research Unit, University of Sussex.

US firms outside the United States with the proportion of patenting activities undertaken outside the United States by the US-based firms in our database.[7] The two measures are almost identical at the aggregate level and for chemicals, pharmaceuticals, machinery and instruments.[8] For firms in transport and metals the proportion of R&D spent abroad is consistently higher than the proportion of their patenting abroad. Nevertheless, both these datasets clearly show that on average US firms undertook less than 10 per cent of their technological activities outside the United States in the 1980s. The similarity between them also allows us to place some confidence in the results reported below which are based on patenting activities alone.

Evidence at the firm level

One of the main advantages of our dataset is that it allows us to examine the patterns of internationalisation of technological activities at the level of the individual firm. In table 7.3 we present the cumulative distribution of firms according to the proportion of their US patenting undertaken outside the home country. Of the 569 firms in the sample, 43 located more than half their technological activities outside the home country. Any case-studies or anecdotal evidence based on these 43 firms would be seriously biased as

Table 7.3. *Distribution of firms according to their foreign technological activities, 1985–90*

Percentage of US patents from outside the home country ⩾	Cumulative distribution	
	No. of firms	Percentage
90	0	0.0
80	9	1.6
70	21	3.7
60	30	5.3
50	43	7.6
40	56	9.8
30	75	13.2
20	99	17.4
10	157	27.6
1	341	59.9
0	569	100.0

table 7.3 also shows that for more than 40 per cent of the sample (228 firms) the proportion executed abroad was less than 1 per cent, and for more than 70 per cent (412 firms) it was less than 10 per cent.

Table 7.4 contains the name, nationality,[9] and product group for each of the top fifty firms (amongst those with more than twenty patents granted in 1985–90) sorted according to the degree of internationalisation of their technological activities. The list contains the names of some firms, such as Ciba-Geigy, Philips and Shell, that have been used in the past as examples of 'global firms', but it also omits others, such as IBM which undertakes less than 15 per cent of its total patenting outside the United States.

In terms of nationality, by far the largest contributors to this list are firms from the UK (twenty-one out of fifty), followed by those from the smaller European countries (seventeen out of fifty). On the other hand, there is only a single firm from each of France, Germany and Japan, and only five from the United States. Thus any analysis that just concentrated on UK firms would produce results which would not be applicable to firms based elsewhere. The table also shows that for thirty-two of the fifty firms the United States is the most important foreign location of technological activities, and, within Europe, it shows the importance of Germany as a location (for ten out of the fifty firms).

The evidence presented in this section shows that US patenting data are a reasonable measure for analysing the extent of internationalisation of

Table 7.4. *Top fifty firms with largest share of US patenting outside the home base, 1985–90*

Company	Nationality	Product Group	% Abroad	Main foreign location	%
Hanson	UK	Building materials	88.8	USA	87.9
Molson	Canada	Drink and tobacco	87.0	USA	73.9
Grand Metropolitan	UK	Drink and tobacco	87.0	USA	87.0
Nova	Canada	Mining and petroleum	86.7	USA	83.3
Coats Viyella	UK	Textiles	82.9	France	54.3
Esselte	Sweden	Paper and wood	82.3	Germany	40.3
GKN Engineering	UK	Vehicles and parts	82.1	Germany	62.2
RTZ	UK	Mining and petroleum	79.2	USA	67.5
FKI Babcock	UK	Machinery	75.6	USA	51.2
Akzo	Netherlands	Chemicals	74.1	Germany	44.8
Imperial Metal Industries	UK	Machinery	72.7	USA	72.7
Unilever	UK	Food	72.6	USA	52.2
Shell	Netherlands	Mining and petroleum	71.6	USA	61.4
BOC	UK	Chemicals	70.8	USA	65.1
Inco	Canada	Metals	70.6	USA	67.0
SKF	Sweden	Machinery	70.2	Germany	45.6
Racal Electronics	UK	Electrical	69.9	USA	67.0
ITT	USA	Electrical	68.4	Germany	54.0
Labofina	Belgium	Mining and petroleum	67.3	USA	63.3
Wellcome	UK	Pharmaceuticals	67.3	USA	62.5
Nestlé	Switzerland	Food	66.7	USA	43.3
Solvay	Belgium	Chemicals	64.7	Germany	33.3
Pilkington	UK	Building materials	61.1	USA	47.3
Redland	UK	Building materials	60.7	USA	53.6
Gillette	USA	Machinery	60.1	Germany	40.4

Table 7.4. (cont.)

Company	Nationality	Product Group	% Abroad	Main foreign location	%
ABB	Switzerland	Electrical	59.3	Sweden	31.6
TI Group	UK	Machinery	59.2	USA	49.0
Electrolux	Sweden	Electrical	57.9	USA	37.9
Hoffman La Roche	Switzerland	Pharmaceuticals	55.0	USA	36.2
Philips	Netherlands	Electrical	53.8	USA	15.1
BAT	UK	Drink and tobacco	53.6	USA	40.4
Universal Match	Sweden	Paper and wood	50.9	UK	24.6
Sandoz	Switzerland	Pharmaceuticals	50.4	USA	30.2
Northern Engineering	UK	Machinery	50.0	Canada	30.0
ICI	UK	Chemicals	49.6	USA	38.7
Hawker Siddeley	UK	Machinery	48.5	USA	46.5
Alcan Aluminium	Canada	Metals	48.2	UK	29.4
BTR	UK	Machinery	47.5	USA	37.7
Reckitt & Colman	UK	Food	46.7	France	26.7
American Standard	USA	Building materials	45.3	Germany	36.5
BP	UK	Mining and petroleum	44.6	USA	25.9
Ciba-Geigy	Switzerland	Chemicals	42.3	USA	23.2
Elkem	Norway	Metals	41.9	USA	32.6
Metallurgie Hoboken-Overpelt	Belgium	Metals	41.4	USA	27.6
Hoechst	Germany	Chemicals	41.2	USA	31.9
Sara Lee	USA	Food	40.7	Netherlands	40.7
Black & Decker	USA	Machinery	39.9	Germany	15.7
Saint-Gobain	France	Building materials	39.8	Germany	26.7
Norsk Hydro	Norway	Chemicals	39.1	Sweden	21.9
Dainippon Ink & Chemical	Japan	Chemicals	38.2	USA	37.7

Table 7.5. *Geographic location of large firms' US patenting activities, according to nationality, 1985–90 (percentage shares)*

Firms' nationality	Home	Abroad	Of which			
			USA	Europe	Japan	Other
Japan (139)	99.0	1.0	0.8	0.2	—	0.0
USA (243)	92.2	7.8	—	6.0	0.5	1.3
Italy (7)	88.2	11.8	5.3	6.2	0.0	0.3
France (25)	85.7	14.3	4.8	8.7	0.3	0.6
Germany (42)	85.1	14.9	10.4	3.9	0.2	0.4
Finland (7)	82.0	18.0	1.6	11.5	0.0	4.9
Norway (3)	67.9	32.1	12.7	19.4	0.0	0.0
Canada (16)	67.0	33.0	24.9	7.3	0.3	0.5
Sweden (13)	60.8	39.2	12.6	25.6	0.2	0.8
UK (54)	57.9	42.1	31.9	7.1	0.2	3.0
Switzerland (8)	53.3	46.7	19.6	26.0	0.6	0.5
Netherlands (8)	42.2	57.8	26.1	30.6	0.5	0.6
Belgium (4)	37.2	62.8	22.2	39.9	0.0	0.6
All firms (569)	89.1	10.9	4.1	5.6	0.3	0.8

Note:
The parentheses contain the number of firms based in each country.

technological activities, and that such analysis needs to be based on systematic evidence, i.e. evidence covering a wide range of firms from different countries and product groups. It is to such an analysis that we now turn.

Recent trends in internationalisation

Aggregate level

Table 7.5 shows, for the 569 firms aggregated according to their nationality, the proportion of their total US patenting in 1985–90 that originated from different geographic locations, as identified by inventor addresses. According to this measure firms from Japan, the United States, Italy, France and Germany undertook 85 per cent or more of their technological activities from within their home country. Only Belgian and Dutch firms executed more of their technological activities outside their home country than within. In terms of locations, the table also shows that very few of these firms' activities were located outside the Triad countries, reinforcing

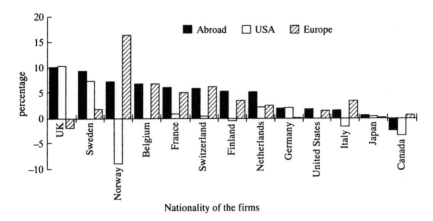

Figure 7.1. Changes in the location of US patenting activities of the world's largest firms, 1979–84 to 1985–90.

the view that what occurred in the late 1980s can, at best, only be described as 'Triadisation' and not 'globalisation'. Within the Triad countries, Japan was the least favourable foreign location for these large firms, and Europe was slightly more favourable than the United States. What our detailed data (not reported here) show is that within Europe, Germany was the most important foreign location for firms of all nationalities.

There is some evidence in table 7.5 to suggest that geographic proximity has an influence on location decisions: for firms from the smaller European countries (Belgium, Finland, The Netherlands, Norway, Sweden and Switzerland) Europe was more important than the United States, and the Canadian firms preferred the United States to Europe. The main exceptions to this were the UK large firms, who undertook around 32 per cent of their total technological activities in the United States and only around 7 per cent within Europe.

Trends

As mentioned in the section describing the dataset, one of its main advantages is that it allows us to examine changes in the importance of the various locations over the 1980s. In order to do this we compare the two geographic distributions of US patenting: (i) for firms as they were consolidated for 1984, and their total US patenting for the period 1979 to 1984; and (ii) for firms consolidated for 1988 and their total patenting for 1985 to 1990 (as reported in table 7.5).

Figure 7.1 shows changes in the proportion of firms' total activities (again aggregated according to their nationality) located outside their home countries, and the extent to which these changes were due to increases (or decreases) in the importance of Europe or the United States as locations. By way of illustration, the figure shows that UK large firms increased their technological activities abroad by around 10 per cent, comprising a 10 per cent increase in the importance of the United States, and a 2 per cent decrease in the importance of Europe, with all the other locations increasing by 2 per cent (not shown in the figure). All firms, except those from Canada, have increased the proportion executed outside the home country in the second half of the 1980s. Furthermore, the results of the trend analysis confirm and reinforce those reported above in terms of levels: Europe increased in importance as a location for firms based in Norway, Belgium, France, Switzerland, Finland and Italy; there was little change in the activities of the Japanese firms; and the UK large firms increased their activities in the USA.

Causes of increased internationalisation: acquisitions vs organic growth

The total change in the number of patents granted to a firm from one period to the next can be decomposed into that due to mergers and acquisitions and that due to a secular trend. The latter can be interpreted as being the result of organic growth, i.e. the change resulting from the firm's decision to increase technology production either from existing R&D facilities or by creating new facilities in a particular location. In terms of our data, the trend element is identified by taking the firm (or a set of firms) as consolidated for 1984 and looking at the change in its patenting from 1979–84 to 1985–90. The change due to mergers and acquisitions is identified by calculating, for the period 1985–90, the difference between the patenting of the firm as it was consolidated for 1984 and for 1988.

In figure 7.2 we have taken the total US patenting of firms executed from outside the home base and considered the proportion due to mergers and acquisitions and that due to a secular trend. By way of illustration, of the increase in the total number of patents granted to UK large firms from outside the UK, around 60 per cent can be attributed to acquisitions and around 40 per cent to increasing activities due to organic growth. A comparison of figures 7.1 and 7.2 shows that, in general, the firms with the largest increases in activities outside their home base did so more by a process of mergers and acquisitions than by organic growth. On the other hand, for firms based in the United States, The Netherlands, Canada, France and Japan, organic growth was a relatively more important means of increasing their foreign technological activities.

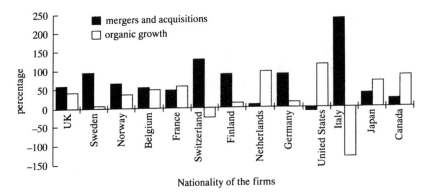

Figure 7.2. Decomposition of the total change in the number of US patents granted to large firms from outside the home country, 1979–84 to 1985–90.

Sectoral breakdown

Table 7.6 describes the main geographic locations of technological activities for the 569 firms aggregated according to their principal product group. It shows that the most internationalised firms (both in terms of levels and in terms of changes in the 1980s) are those with their principal activities in drink and tobacco, food, building materials, other transport, pharmaceuticals, and mining and petroleum, with between 15 and 30 per cent of their activities located outside the home base. What is of interest is that, with one exception (pharmaceuticals) these are not the 'high-tech' product groups or ones that are normally associated with having a 'world mandate' (cars and computers). In fact they are precisely the product groups where adaptive R&D for the purposes of serving local markets is important. Technological activities for such localised adaptation occur because of differences in consumer tastes (food, drink and tobacco), differences in government regulations (building materials and pharmaceuticals), and in order to exploit local natural resources (food, mining and petroleum). Indeed the evidence here suggests that firms involved in the product groups with higher than average R&D intensity – computers, aircraft, instruments and electrical equipment – are below average in terms of the internationalisation of their technological activities. One reason for this could be that in these 'high-tech' products, links between R&D and design, on the one hand, and production, on the other, are particularly important in the launching of major new products, and benefit from geographical proximity.

Table 7.6. *Geographic location of large firms' US patenting activities, according to product group, 1985–90 (percentage shares)*

Product group	Abroad (change[a])	Of which			
		USA	Europe	Japan	Other
Drink and tobacco (17)	30.7 (−6.6)	17.5	10.9	0.4	1.8
Food (41)	26.3 (6.1)	15.7	8.6	0.2	1.7
Building materials (26)	20.8 (9.4)	9.2	9.9	0.1	1.6
Other transport (5)	19.7 (9.5)	2.0	6.8	0.0	10.9
Pharmaceuticals (25)	16.7 (1.0)	5.5	8.3	1.1	1.7
Mining and petroleum (44)	14.7 (3.0)	9.1	3.5	0.1	1.6
Chemicals (71)	14.5 (3.1)	8.0	5.1	0.4	1.0
Machinery (68)	13.7 (1.2)	3.4	9.0	0.1	1.1
Paper and wood (31)	11.9 (3.9)	2.6	8.4	0.1	0.8
Metals (56)	11.4 (0.4)	5.1	5.9	0.1	0.3
Electrical (58)	10.2 (1.9)	2.6	6.9	0.3	0.4
Computers (17)	9.0 (0.7)	0.1	6.6	1.1	1.1
Rubber and plastics (10)	6.1 (2.4)	0.9	2.4	0.4	2.4
Textiles etc. (18)	4.7 (0.4)	1.5	1.8	0.8	0.6
Motor vehicles (43)	4.4 (−0.9)	0.9	3.3	0.1	0.2
Instruments (20)	4.3 (−0.8)	0.4	2.8	0.3	0.8
Aircraft (19)	2.9 (0.7)	0.3	1.8	0.1	0.7
All firms (569)	10.9 (1.1)	4.1	5.6	0.3	0.8

Note:
[a] See text for the definition of change.

Main findings and conclusions

The main conclusion of this chapter is that there is no systematic evidence (i.e. covering firms from different countries and product groups) to suggest that widespread globalisation of the production of technology occurred in the 1980s. The evidence presented above, based on the US patenting activities of 569 firms (based in thirteen countries, and in seventeen product groups), shows that for an overwhelming majority of them technological activities are located close to the home base. The analysis also shows the dangers of generalising on the basis of anecdotal evidence from a small sample of firms from a particular country or sector.

The main empirical findings of the study are:

• The only other systematic evidence available on the international technological activities of firms, based on data on their R&D expenditures abroad, is entirely consistent with the evidence on patenting activities abroad.

- There has been an increase in the proportion of activities undertaken by firms from overseas locations, with Europe becoming a relatively more important location for firms from most countries.
- The largest increases in internationalisation have occurred as a result of mergers and acquisitions and not by means of organic growth.
- UK large firms are the most internationalised in terms of their technological activities and the pattern they have followed is in general different from that followed by firms from other European countries: for UK firms the United States is the most important foreign location (and has become increasingly so), for other European firms Europe as a whole (and Germany in particular) is relatively more important.
- Japanese firms remain the least internationalised (with overseas activities accounting for around 1 per cent), and Japan remains unimportant as a location for firms from other countries.
- The most internationalised firms are not in the 'high-tech' product groups that are normally labelled as having a 'world mandate'. On the contrary they are in product groups where adaptation for serving local markets is important.

These results confirm the prediction in our earlier paper (Patel and Pavitt, 1991) that there would be increases in the amount of technological activities located outside the home base. The fact that Europe has become a relatively more important location is also consistent with some of the evidence from surveys reported in the first section, namely, that an important group of factors in the decision to locate technology outside the home country are labelled 'political'. In this case the most important influence, especially for the non-EEC European countries, has been the setting up of the European internal market. Our results also suggest that the process of internationalisation of technology is influenced more by the need to adapt products for market conditions in the host country than by supply-side reasons concerned with exploiting the science and technology base of the host country.

The evidence presented here is also consistent with the analyses of early Vernon (1966), Porter (1990) and the more recent literature on the 'national systems of innovation' (Lundvall, 1992; Nelson, 1993), in that, far from being irrelevant, what happens in home countries is still very important in the creation of global technological advantage for firms. Thus for policy analysis it becomes important to understand the nature of the country-specific factors that have an influence in creating national technological advantage, including the competitive climate, the financial system, and education, training and basic research institutions.

Finally, it also becomes important to improve our understanding of the reasons why firms involved in producing for a world market may keep most of their technology production close to the home base. Two key features related to the launching of major innovations may help explain the advantages of geographic concentration: the involvement of inputs of knowledge and information that are essentially 'person-embodied', and a high degree of uncertainty surrounding outputs. Both of these are best handled through intense and frequent personal communications and rapid decision-making, i.e. through geographic concentration. Thus it may be most efficient for firms to concentrate the core of their technological activities in the home base with international 'listening posts' and small foreign laboratories for adaptive R&D.

Notes

1 This chapter is based on research at the Centre for Science, Technology and Energy Policy established by the UK Economic and Social Research Council (ESRC) in the Science Policy Research Unit (SPRU) at the University of Sussex. It has benefited from comments from Keith Pavitt, Daniele Archibugi, Ove Granstrand and an anonymous referee of the Cambridge Journal of Economics.
2 See, for example, Håkanson (1992) and Pearce and Singh (1992).
3 For example Pearce and Singh (1992) report that for some firms an increasing proportion of the work of their foreign laboratories is concerned with development work and not just adaptation.
4 See Freeman and Hagedoorn (1992).
5 Europe, Japan and the United States.
6 There are sixteen Canadian firms that have been aggregated under the US total for convenience.
7 It should be noted that the two datasets involve different sets of firms: the NSF R&D survey almost certainly covered more firms than our large-firm patenting database (243). None the less, the basis for comparison between R&D and patenting is two strongly overlapping populations of large firms, defined according to their principal product group.
8 The correlation coefficient between the two measures (using a pooled sample of fourteen observations) is 0.59 which is significantly different from zero at the 5 per cent level.
9 There are three firms that may be described as having dual nationality and we have arbitrarily assigned their home country: ABB (Switzerland), Shell (The Netherlands) and Unilever (UK).

References

Cantwell, J. 1992. The internationalisation of technological activity and its implications for competitiveness, in Granstrand *et al.* (eds.).
Chesnais, F. 1988. Technical co-operation agreements between firms, *Science Technology Industry Review*, no. 4, pp. 57–119.

214   **Pari Patel**

1992. National systems of innovation, foreign direct investment and the operations of multinational enterprises, in Lundvall (ed.).

Dorrenbacher, C. and Wortmann, M. 1991. The internationalisation of corporate research and development, *Intereconomics*, 26: 139–44.

Dunning, J. 1992. Multinational enterprises and the globalisation of innovatory capacity, in Granstrand *et al.* (eds.).

Etemad, H. and Seguin Dulude, L. 1987. Patenting patterns in 25 multinational enterprises, *Technovation*, 7: 1–15.

Freeman, C. and Hagedoorn, J. 1992. Convergence and divergence in the internationalisation of technology, paper presented at the MERIT conference 'Convergence and divergence in economic growth and technical change', Maastricht, December 1992.

Granstrand, O., Håkanson, L. and Sjölander, S. (eds.) 1992. *Technology Management and International Business: Internationalisation of R&D and Technology*, Chichester, Wiley.

Granstrand, O., and Sjölander, S. 1992. Internationalisation and diversification of multi-technology corporations, in Granstrand *et al.* (eds.).

Håkanson, L. 1992. Locational determinants of foreign R&D in Swedish multinationals, in Granstrand *et al.* (eds.).

Howells, J. 1990. The internationalisation of R&D and the development of global research networks, *Regional Studies*, 24: 495–512.

Lundvall, B.-Å. (ed.) 1992. *National Systems of Innovation*, London, Pinter.

Nelson, R. (ed.) 1993. *National Innovation Systems*, New York, Oxford University Press.

Patel, P. and Pavitt, K. 1991. Large firms in the production of the world's technology: an important case of 'non-globalisation', *Journal of International Business Studies*, 22: 1–22.

Pearce, R. and Singh, S. 1992. *Globalising Research and Development*, London, Macmillan.

Porter, M. 1990. *The Competitive Advantage of Nations*, London, Macmillan.

Vernon, R. 1966. International investment and international trade in the product cycle, *Quarterly Journal of Economics*, 80: 190–207.

1979. The product-cycle hypothesis in a new international environment, *Oxford Bulletin of Economics and Statistics*, 41: 255–67.

Wortmann, M. 1990. Multinationals and the internationalisation of R&D: new developments in German companies, *Research Policy*, 19: 175–83.

8 The globalisation of technology: what remains of the product cycle model?

JOHN CANTWELL[1]

Introduction

This chapter re-examines two hypotheses associated with earlier versions of the product cycle model (Vernon, 1966), using new historical evidence on the international dispersion of corporate technological activity by large American and European industrial firms, based on patents granted to these companies at the US Patent Office since the turn of the century. The first hypothesis states that innovations are almost always located in the home country of the parent company, and usually close to the site of the corporate technological headquarters. The second hypothesis is that international investment is led by technology leaders, as a means by which they increase their share of world markets and world production. If the first hypothesis does not necessarily hold, then the second can be interpreted more specifically to state that the internationalisation of technological development is led by firms with the strongest records in innovation.

Contrary to the first hypothesis, a new literature on the recent internationalisation of industrial research (for example, Ronstadt, 1977; Lall, 1979; Pearce and Singh, 1992; Granstrand et al., 1992) has suggested that innovations may be geographically dispersed within multinational corporations (MNCs). US-owned MNCs have recently witnessed an increase in the degree of internationalisation of their research, from low levels in the 1960s. It is perhaps no accident that empirical support for the product cycle hypothesis and subsequent criticism of it was largely derived from data on US MNCs. The new trend towards the internationalisation of research and development (R&D) in US MNCs had become evident by the 1970s (see, for example, Mansfield et al., 1979).

Three kinds of theoretical justification were provided for the first product cycle hypothesis. First, there are economies of scale in the R&D function, and if they are strong enough R&D will be concentrated in a single centre. Second, there are locational economies of integration and agglomeration

215

in innovation. In new product development a close interaction is normally required between research and production facilities and users, while if several firms are engaged in the development of related new products (or processes) geographical proximity will encourage a greater volume of beneficial spillovers between them. Third, the original product cycle model viewed innovation as a demand-led process (see Schmookler, 1966, for another contemporary account), and thus for US MNCs innovation would be located in the more conducive environment of their home country, stimulated by the particular characteristics of the demand from high-income consumers and skill-intensive downstream production facilities.

However, more recent evidence has demonstrated that the internationalisation of technological activity in large MNCs is not simply the outcome of a new trend (Cantwell and Hodson, 1991; Patel and Pavitt, 1991). As early as the 1960s many European MNCs (especially those originating from the UK, The Netherlands, Belgium and Switzerland) had already been quite highly internationalised in their technological activity. In Europe, the largest French and German industrial MNCs come closest to the US pattern, recently increasing the extent of internationalisation of their R&D from comparatively low levels in the 1960s. By contrast, large Japanese firms owned few research facilities outside Japan in the 1960s. Although their international R&D has been expanding, research in Japan itself has been growing at least as quickly, so the degree of internationalisation of research in Japanese-owned MNCs has remained low.

Here, it is argued that the first product cycle hypothesis should be rejected, not so much as a result of recent trends, as on the basis of historical evidence. In particular, the leading US electrical equipment companies and European chemical firms enjoyed a significant international dispersal of their technological activity in the inter-war period. The source of evidence for this view is the US patenting of the largest US and European industrial companies over time, which identifies the location of technological activity at the corporate level, and thus provides a measure of the geographical dispersion of corporate invention. It is this same source of evidence that has been used often in other similar international comparisons that relate to the recent period, and which has helped to create the re-evaluation of trends in the international R&D of MNCs just described. What is new about the data in this study is the extension of records of corporate patenting back in time: here they are considered back to 1920.

The second early product cycle hypothesis states that international investment (and here, the international dispersion of technological activity) is led by technology leaders. The theoretical justification for this hypothesis is that the most technologically competent companies enjoy lower operating costs than their competitors and provide higher product quality, which generates higher profits and rising international market shares. In their turn, different degrees of technological competence across companies are a consequence of the firm-specific and path-dependent characteristics of technological change (Teece *et al.*, 1990; Cantwell, 1991b, 1994; Nelson, 1991, 1992; Dosi *et al.*, 1992; Pavitt, 1992). The greater capability of the most competent or technologically leading firms (or their greater capability to release able management resources and team expertise to plan for and organise growth, as argued by Penrose, 1959) enables them better to expand their activity in new fields or environments, and higher profits provide them with the financial wherewithal to offset the costs of doing so. An ancillary argument is especially important in the case of early internationalisation and is featured in the contemporary explanation of the product cycle hypothesis; that is, a technologically leading group of firms from a particular location may – past some point – find that the continued increase in its penetration of foreign markets is challenged by protectionist barriers, and by the gradual learning of local competitors in those markets. This raises the incentive to produce locally, and insofar as indigenous companies develop their own lines of related technological development there is also a greater incentive to internationalise innovation (in addition to the need to adapt products to the distinctive features of host country demand).

This hypothesis appears to be consistent with the historical evidence, except perhaps during phases of technological hegemony when innovative development is concentrated in the home country. However, the explanatory power of this hypothesis has been eroded by recent trends; the composition of firms involved in the internationalisation of technological activity has now been broadened, extending to cover a much wider range of companies. Therefore, an alternative version of the second hypothesis is proposed to fit the current situation. It is suggested that technology leaders are now ahead instead in the globalisation of technology – that is, in the development of international intra-firm networks to exploit the locationally differentiated potential of foreign centres of excellence. These networks are internal to the firm in order to build upon or extend its core technological competence through an internally co-ordinated learning process, but they are complementary to external inter-firm networks whose role is the exchange of knowledge and occasionally co-operation in learning through technology-based joint ventures (Cantwell, 1991b, 1994; Cantwell and Barrera, 1995).

The data employed are described further in the next section, while the two subsequent sections relate to the reassessment of the first and second product cycle hypotheses respectively. The first of these two examines the historical importance of the international dispersion of technological development in leading American and European firms. Particular attention is paid to firms in the chemical and electrical equipment industries broadly defined, as these are the industries which are most reliant on science-based technologies. Historically, US firms were strongest in the electrical equipment industry, while European (and especially German) firms were stronger in chemicals (Chandler, 1990; Cantwell and Barrera, 1993). Among leading companies such as these, technological activity is not always much more widely geographically dispersed today than it was in the inter-war or early post-war periods. However, the following section considers what has changed recently for these firms, and terms this a new trend towards the globalisation of technology – that is, the emergence of internationally integrated structures for technological development. It is suggested that globalisation in this sense is a modern characteristic of corporate technology leaders. Some conclusions are set out in a final section.

The data

Patenting is a measure of invention, and so corporate patenting is more a measure of wider technological activity (changes in production methods) in firms, not just R&D as such. For larger firms like those covered here, R&D is the most important source of new knowledge and skills, and so for them the internationalisation of technological activity revolves around the internationalisation of research. However, production engineering is often an important complementary source of new inventions that are incorporated into technology. It should also be noted that the location of basic R&D that feeds into the development of productive applications at some other site may not itself be picked up separately in the patent statistics. For these reasons the title of the chapter refers to the globalisation of technological activity (the development of new methods of production), and not to the internationalisation of R&D as such.

Two types of information have been collected manually from the *US Index of Patents* and the *US Patent Office Gazette*. First, all patents were recorded that were assigned to a selection of large US-owned and European-owned firms between 1890 and 1968. From 1969 onwards equivalent information has been computerised by the US Patent Office. The firms selected for the historical patent search were identified in one of three ways. The first group consisted of those firms which have accounted for the highest levels of US patenting after 1969; the second group comprised other US, German or British firms which were historically among the largest 200 industrial corporations in each of these countries (derived from lists in Chandler, 1990); and the third group was made up of other companies which featured prominently in the US patent records of earlier years (a method that proved most significant for a number of French firms that had not been identified from other sources).

In each case, patents were counted as belonging to a common corporate group where they were assigned to affiliates of a parent company. Affiliate names were normally taken from individual company histories. In all, the US patenting of 857 companies or affiliates was traced historically; together these comprise 284 corporate groups. Owing to historical changes in ownership, seventeen of the affiliates were allocated to more than one corporate group over the period as a whole. No significance has been attached to the location of the particular affiliate to which each patent is assigned, since this may be different from the location of the inventive activity that gave rise to the patent. However, the location of the parent company is an important dimension in the analysis, as this is treated as the home country or the country of origin of the corporate group. By consolidating patents attributable to international corporate groups, it is then feasible to examine the geographical distribution of technological activity within groups, and the possible formation of internal intra-group international networks (as opposed to external inter-firm networks, which are not the subject of this chapter). Each corporate group is also allocated to an industry on the basis of its primary field of production; occasionally, firms have moved between industries historically, sometimes associated with changes in ownership, and this has been allowed for.

The company to which a patent has been assigned (if any), and the name and location of residence of the inventor responsible for the underlying invention, are both recorded separately in the US Patent Office data, including the earliest data. Where patents have been assigned to firms, the inventor is normally an employee of the company or is directly associated with it in some other way, but occasionally independent individual inventors do choose to assign their patents to firms (Schmookler, 1966). Assignments by independent individuals were more common in the nineteenth century but, at least from the inter-war years onwards, the typical assignor was a prominent member of a corporate research laboratory, or some other similar in-house company facility. Although it is normally difficult to trace these named individuals in secondary sources on the firms concerned (as they are not usually also senior managers), the location of assignors can be checked against business history sources on the international location of activity in particular firms. Such checks on a selection of large firms have confirmed that whenever a location has been responsible for significant numbers of patents being assigned to a company, that firm did indeed have some in-house facility in the location in question at the relevant time. Companies checked in this fashion include various US firms active abroad and European companies in the USA (Stocking and Watkins,

1946; Beaton, 1957; Wilkins, 1974, 1989; Chandler, 1990), Courtaulds and British Celanese (Coleman, 1969), Du Pont and ICI (Hounshell and Smith, 1988), and General Electric and GEC (Reich, 1986; Jones and Marriot, 1971).

Second, using once again the *US Index of Patents* and the *US Patent Office Gazette*, for every patent granted in the years between 1890 and 1962 the country of residence of the inventor has been recorded. From 1963 this information has already been computerised by the US Patent Office. Where patents are assigned to companies, these data on the country of origin of invention indicate the location of the R&D facilities (or other sources of technological improvement) that gave rise to each patent. As this information on the location of invention relates to individually numbered patents, it can be combined with a sectoral classification of the technological activity with which the patent is associated. This employs the system of patent classes used by the Patent Office; fortunately, as these classes change the Office reclassifies all earlier patents accordingly, so the classification is historically consistent. Although patents may be assigned to several fields, the primary classification was used in all cases. Various broad categories of technological activity were derived by allocating classes or sub-classes to common groups of activity.

Two distinctions between different aspects of these classifications of the data are worth re-emphasising. First, the sectoral classification of patents, in terms of the type of technological activity with which each patent is associated, is distinguished from the main industrial output or markets of the companies to which patents may be assigned, both of which have been recorded separately. Most large companies have engaged in at least some development in most of the general spheres of technological activity (for instance, chemical firms develop many mechanical technologies, including chemical machinery and equipment), irrespective of the industry in which they operate.

Second, the country of location of the invention, which for large firms typically represents or is allied to the location of corporate R&D, is distinguished from the location of the firm to which a patent is assigned, and from the location of the parent company which owns this firm. While no significance is attached to the location of the assignee, the location of research and the location of ultimate ownership (the parent company) are critical. The extent to which these locations differ over the total patenting of each corporate group is the measure of the degree of internationalisation of that group's technological activity. These distinctions are crucial to understanding that the measurement of the degree of internationalisation of technological activity in what follows is not to be mistaken for a measure of the international spread of patents taken out by firms (the patents

Table 8.1. *Shares of US patenting of the largest nationally owned industrial firms due to research located abroad (per cent)*

	1920–39	1940–68	1969–90
USA	**6.81**	**3.57**	**6.82**
Europe	**12.03**	**26.65**	**27.13**
UK	27.71	41.95	43.17
Germany	4.03	8.68	13.72
Italy	29.03	24.76	14.24
France	3.35	8.19	9.55
Netherlands	15.57	29.51	52.97
Belgium	95.00	53.90	60.60
Switzerland	5.67	28.33	43.76
Sweden	31.04	13.18	25.51
Total	**7.91**	**8.08**	**14.52**

Source: US patent data compiled at the University of Reading, with assistance from the US Patent and Trademark Office, US Department of Commerce.

counted were all those (and only those) granted by the US Patent Office), nor should it be mistaken for a measure of the international dispersion of the legal departments or agents responsible for making patent applications on behalf of the group (the actual assignee is ignored once it has been linked to a parent company of a large group in the dataset). Instead, what is measured is the internationalisation of the underlying technological activity that gave rise to the knowledge which subsequently led to a patent being granted to the group.

The historical role of the internationalisation of technological activity

As just described, the degree of internationalisation of corporate technological activity is measured by the share of patenting that is attributable to research (or other sources of invention) located outside the home country of the corporate group or groups in question. The broad changes in the internationalisation of technological activity between 1920 and 1990 measured in this way are set out in table 8.1, organised by national groups of firms according to the location of ultimate ownership. The share of foreign research in the total corporate technological activity of the largest US and European industrial firms considered together averaged about 8 per cent in

1920–39 and 1940–68, before rising significantly to roughly 14.5 per cent in 1969–90. However, this recent average trend increase in the internationalisation of activity as measured by corporate patenting reflects primarily the rising share of US patenting accounted for by European firms (which are more internationalised) *vis-à-vis* their US counterparts.

There appear to be three categories of national groups of firms. In the first, German- and French-owned firms come closest to the standard view, in the sense that the degree of internationalisation of their technological activity was very low historically, but has been on a slowly rising trend, and has increased significantly recently. The second category comprises the historically more multinational British, Swiss and Dutch companies, whose technological activity became substantially internationalised after the Second World War, achieving an early increase in international scope that is reflected in the picture for large European firms as a whole. The third category is very different from the others. The technological activity of the largest US and Swedish firms was as highly internationalised historically as it is today; and, of course, for some individual companies (such as the American General Electric) the extent of internationalisation was much higher in the inter-war period than it has been recently. The largest American and Swedish firms retreated from their international research operations after the Second World War, and they have only recently regained the position they held before that time.

A more detailed periodisation of the records of each of these three groups of large firms can be gleaned from table 8.2. For French and German companies this shows that the upward trend in the internationalisation of technological activity is not as gradual as might have been supposed from table 8.1, but in fact is based on some discrete jumps. As for other European firms, there was an increase in internationalisation immediately after the Second World War, following the nationalist retreat of the late 1930s, and the expropriations of German-owned firms abroad in the 1940s. There was then a further rise in the early 1970s in German firms, and in the late 1980s for German companies again, but more especially for French firms (Cantwell and Kotecha, 1994). British and Swiss firms increased to much higher rates of internationalisation of technological activity after the war than did French or German companies. In the British case the origins of the process can be traced to a trend increase throughout the inter-war period, which was consolidated after the war, rising close to a peak by the late 1960s, before recovering again in the 1980s. The degree of internationalisation of Swiss firms reached a peak in the early 1970s, which has not quite been matched since.

For the largest US firms the internationalisation of technological activity peaked in the early 1930s (at a level they have only very recently

Table 8.2. *Shares of US patenting of the largest nationally owned industrial firms due to research located abroad, detailed periodisation (per cent)*

	USA	Europe	UK	Germany	France	Switzerland	Sweden	Total
1920–24	3.32	8.45	7.61	2.89	3.02	4.00	39.77	4.03
1925–29	6.61	8.19	14.26	5.42	2.67	3.73	29.88	6.87
1930–34	8.17	10.83	25.88	4.79	4.12	6.38	27.08	8.80
1935–39	6.94	15.11	34.63	2.83	3.33	6.04	30.23	8.86
1940–59	3.79	27.10	40.84	9.46	8.90	22.24	11.98	7.67
1960–64	2.85	24.22	39.52	8.26	7.46	27.28	13.24	7.62
1965–68	3.69	28.02	46.44	8.21	7.76	39.56	15.22	9.42
1969–72	5.22	28.21	42.66	12.65	7.71	45.86	18.14	12.21
1973–77	5.98	25.42	40.09	11.03	6.44	44.67	21.15	13.18
1978–82	6.65	24.60	39.17	12.14	6.66	43.68	27.25	13.82
1983–86	8.51	27.13	45.32	14.83	9.20	41.02	29.84	15.92
1987–90	8.95	30.86	50.55	17.76	18.26	42.74	31.49	18.56

Source: As for table 8.1.

equalled), while Swedish firms began in the early 1920s from a high point that they have not since recaptured. The internationalisation of research in both the US and Swedish groups fell sharply after the war, but picked up again from the late 1960s onwards. It is this latter trend that has been quite widely commented upon, perhaps not surprisingly, especially by American and Swedish scholars (such as Ronstadt, 1977; Mansfield *et al.*, 1979; or Granstrand *et al.*, 1992). However, this contrasts with the more general European experience. The internationalisation of technological activity in large European firms considered as a whole increased after the Second World War (as did all the constituent European national groups except the Swedish), and again from the mid-1980s (again this applies to all groups except, in this case, the Swiss).

Besides their national groups, firms may also be allocated to industrial groups. The broad industrial classification adopted here groups industries in accordance with the prevailing type of technological activity in the sector in question. Thus, firms in the chemical, pharmaceutical and coal and petroleum products industries all rely mainly on chemical and related technologies; firms in the electrical equipment and office equipment or computer industries base themselves principally on electrical technologies; and firms in the motor vehicle, aircraft and rubber and plastic products industries are concerned with the major transport technologies (engines and

Table 8.3. *Shares of US patenting of the largest nationally owned industrial firms due to research located abroad, grouped by industry (per cent)*

	USA	Europe	UK	Germany	France	Switzerland	Sweden	Total
				1920–39				
Chemical	2.75	12.42	41.48	4.88	4.64	5.02	4.44	6.88
Electrical	10.13	3.21	1.98	2.58	0.63	8.20	8.89	9.42
Mechanical	5.15	20.18	29.27	3.56	2.93	1.94	36.45	9.17
Transport	1.61	4.95	8.02	2.76	4.89	n.a.	0.00	2.01
Total	6.81	12.03	27.71	4.03	3.35	5.67	31.04	7.91
				1940–68				
Chemical	2.24	39.91	66.42	12.51	15.65	31.65	12.40	11.74
Electrical	6.03	14.15	8.81	6.01	5.16	14.31	8.40	7.26
Mechanical	3.27	23.54	37.94	4.15	12.72	17.12	15.70	7.85
Transport	1.41	4.26	5.52	2.36	2.22	n.a.	5.50	1.77
Total	3.57	26.65	41.95	8.68	8.19	28.33	13.18	8.08
				1969–90				
Chemical	5.65	32.65	55.33	18.08	9.03	46.84	14.52	17.91
Electrical	9.09	27.32	27.11	11.01	8.43	34.22	29.32	14.65
Mechanical	6.51	23.94	50.31	7.67	16.83	33.23	27.75	13.58
Transport	4.95	10.16	10.55	8.47	4.98	n.a.	12.36	6.53
Total	6.82	27.13	43.17	13.72	9.55	43.76	25.51	14.52

Note:
n.a. = not applicable
Source: As for table 8.1.

tyres). For ease of exposition these are each referred to collectively as the chemical, electrical equipment and transport industries. Firms in all other industries rely mainly on more traditional mechanical technologies, so the mechanical group is a much more heterogeneous mixture.

As shown in table 8.3, the US electrical equipment firms were much more internationalised in their research than were European firms in the equivalent industry in the inter-war period, despite the much higher overall rate of internationalisation of technological activity in the European group. In Britain, Germany and France, large chemical firms were more internationalised historically than those in the electrical equipment sector, although in Switzerland the electrical companies featured more strongly, and in Sweden it was mechanically based firms that were responsible for the very high overall internationalisation of research in the largest nationally owned firms at that time. The mechanical group were also highly internationalised in the UK (notably the textile companies British Celanese and Courtaulds), and British and French transport firms (particularly the tyre companies Dunlop and Michelin) appear more prominently than the other members of that group.

A similar discrepancy between the relative extent of internationalisation of research in chemical and electrical equipment firms in the USA and Europe still existed in recent years, but the difference is less marked than it was. Among European companies the stronger internationalisation of chemical than electrical firms also holds now for Switzerland, but not for Sweden. For Swedish firms the mechanical group does not dominate international research as it once did, but in the UK and France the mechanical group is relatively more prominent than it used to be. What this reflects in each case is a broadening of the range of firms engaged in the internationalisation of technological activity across a wider spectrum; for example, while the mechanical engineering firm Alfa-Laval accounted for the bulk of the foreign research of Swedish companies historically, its share has steadily declined as other firms have begun to engage in technological development abroad (Zander, 1994).

For US and European firms as a whole a more detailed periodisation for the major industrial groups can be found in tables 8.4 and 8.5. Table 8.4 shows that US-owned electrical equipment firms in the 1930s had a higher degree of internationalisation of technological activity than they have had at any time since, including the 1980s. About 12 per cent of their research was located abroad in the 1930s, compared to roughly 11 per cent in the 1980s. Two American-owned companies that contributed especially heavily to European-located research and production in the inter-war years were General Electric and RCA. The degree of internationalisation of technological activity in General Electric was 18.3 per cent in 1920–39 but only 2.4 per cent in 1968–90, while in RCA the equivalent proportions were 20.4 per cent and 5.4 per cent.

In contrast, the largest European firms sustained a sizeable increase in the extent of the internationalisation of their research between the early 1930s and the 1950s. This increase was led by companies in the science-based sectors, and especially those in chemicals. The share of foreign research in the leading European chemical firms rose from 8.2 per cent in 1930–34 to 42.6 per cent in 1940–59, while for electrical equipment companies it increased from 5.1 per cent to 11.0 per cent (see table 8.5). For the largest European chemical firms the immediate post-war rate of internationalisation proved to be a peak that has not since been surpassed (for them the foreign share stood at 34.8 per cent in 1987–90), but in the post-

Table 8.4. *Shares of US patenting of the largest US-owned industrial firms due to research located abroad, grouped by industry (per cent)*

	1920–24	1925–29	1930–34	1935–39	1940–59	1960–64	1965–68	1969–72	1973–77	1978–82	1983–86	1987–90
Chemical	0.96	1.90	4.03	2.36	1.87	2.12	3.08	4.37	5.21	5.33	6.36	7.71
Electrical	4.14	8.50	12.27	11.99	7.01	3.81	5.23	7.29	7.94	9.00	11.60	10.90
Mechanical	3.31	5.72	5.83	5.06	2.87	4.00	3.58	4.61	5.39	6.71	9.36	9.34
Transport	0.12	1.37	1.94	1.73	0.90	1.69	2.36	3.45	4.21	4.51	5.81	7.59
Total	3.32	6.61	8.17	6.94	3.79	2.85	3.69	5.22	5.98	6.65	8.51	8.95

Source: As for table 8.1.

Table 8.5. *Shares of US patenting of the largest European-owned industrial firms due to research located abroad, grouped by industry (per cent)*

	1920–24	1925–29	1930–34	1935–39	1940–59	1960–64	1965–68	1969–72	1973–77	1978–82	1983–86	1987–90
Chemical	7.07	7.52	8.15	18.22	42.55	37.17	38.46	35.40	31.25	30.51	32.30	34.77
Electrical	4.12	2.81	5.14	1.73	11.01	13.87	19.96	26.90	24.51	21.44	28.17	34.10
Mechanical	10.84	12.91	23.00	24.74	25.73	18.73	23.31	25.45	22.25	23.98	23.87	24.59
Transport	3.75	9.15	4.69	3.04	4.77	3.44	4.45	7.12	7.40	7.69	12.76	16.19
Total	8.45	8.19	10.83	15.11	27.10	24.22	28.02	28.21	25.42	24.60	27.13	30.86

Source: As for table 8.1.

war period the major European electrical equipment companies steadily increased their international research, to a point where the foreign share is now similar to that in chemicals.

The European story partly reflects the British experience, which is described in table 8.6. For UK-owned companies the increase in the internationalisation of technological activity between the early 1930s and the 1950s (from 25.9 per cent to 40.8 per cent) was also largely associated with a very strong internationalisation of research in the chemical industry (from 23.3 per cent to 66.7 per cent). The prominent contribution of the chemical companies is consistent with the view that, historically, internationalisation was linked to technological competence. European firms were technologically strongest in the chemical fields, in which areas they internationalised their research early; while American firms were relatively stronger in the development of electrical technologies, and in this field they led the early internationalisation of technological activity.

Thus, at least for technology leaders, the internationalisation of technological activity is not a new phenomenon. Of course, the first product cycle hypothesis might be rescued by a restatement to the effect that as a general rule the home country centre has been and remains the single most important site for the technological development of MNCs. Given that, as reported in tables 8.1 to 8.6, the foreign share of technological activity has rarely been greater than two-thirds and has usually been much less, MNCs are not 'stateless corporations' (Patel and Pavitt, 1991). The national origins of MNCs have been and continue to be critical in determining the geographical and sectoral composition of their technological activity, based on their path-dependent evolution from a nationally differentiated expertise (Kogut, 1987, 1990). While globalisation has been defined here as the international integration of MNC networks, some authors have used the term to mean the loss of national identity by companies, and when defined in this unhelpful way, globalisation has not taken place.

It is also clear that from the perspective of the MNC as a whole, or from that of its home country, the internationalisation of research is generally less than the internationalisation of production (Patel and Pavitt, 1991). One possible way of thinking about this is that most MNCs constitute an internal locational hierarchy of activity (Hymer, 1975). To simplify matters for the sake of exposition, suppose that the production of each firm is divided into the technologically sophisticated and the simple or assembly-type. Then, technologically sophisticated production tends to become geographically concentrated in certain locations, and assembly-type production tends to agglomerate in others (Cantwell, 1987). The home country operations of the MNC stand at the pinnacle of its hierarchy, as a base for technologically sophisticated production, as hinted at by both

Table 8.6. Shares of US patenting of the largest UK-owned industrial firms due to research located abroad, grouped by industry (per cent)

	1920–24	1925–29	1930–34	1935–39	1940–59	1960–64	1965–68	1969–72	1973–77	1978–82	1983–86	1987–90
Chemical	22.22	19.44	23.27	52.12	66.66	64.19	67.90	57.79	49.61	50.03	58.82	62.50
Electrical	7.14	4.67	0.55	0.67	5.61	6.94	17.37	27.09	33.56	24.85	19.53	26.53
Mechanical	6.55	16.34	36.51	32.13	35.57	38.53	44.70	50.06	48.10	45.47	51.14	59.88
Transport	5.45	14.46	8.13	5.68	5.75	4.37	6.03	7.75	7.65	7.77	13.29	20.31
Total	7.61	14.26	25.88	34.63	40.84	39.52	46.44	42.66	40.09	39.17	45.32	50.55

Source: As for table 8.1.

Vernon and Hymer. Since the siting of research facilities is normally linked to the local support of technologically sophisticated production while little or no research accompanies assembly-type production, it follows that production in total is more widely geographically dispersed than research. So, while the home country is the single most important site for innovation, it does not necessarily follow that production in the home centre is more research-intensive than in the other advanced centres in which the MNC establishes technologically sophisticated production.

This argument suggests that, of the original theoretical underpinnings of the first product cycle hypothesis, locational economies of integration and agglomeration play a greater role than do economies of scale in the R&D function. Previous criticisms of the first product cycle hypothesis had shown that, while there is a minimum efficient scale for R&D facilities, the effect of firm size on the degree of internationalisation of R&D is ambiguous (Mansfield *et al.*, 1979). By contrast, a good deal of evidence has been gathered in support of the importance of economies of agglomeration or local clustering in the location of production (Dahmen, 1970; Porter, 1990; Krugman, 1991; Sölvell, Zander and Porter, 1991), and especially in the geographical location of innovation (Jaffe, 1989; Cantwell, 1991a; Jaffe *et al.*, 1993; Feldman, 1993) and in the location of the technologically sophisticated production of MNCs (Cantwell, 1987). The lesson seems to be that economies of locational agglomeration are important, but that for MNCs they may occur in various centres and not exclusively in the home country, although the home base is the most significant single such centre.

The new globalisation of technology by corporate leaders

It has been shown that technological activity in some US MNCs was more widely dispersed internationally in the inter-war period than it is today, while many European MNCs were already geared up to technology creation abroad by the 1950s. The companies that achieved the greatest internationalisation of activity historically were generally technology leaders. This is what is suggested by the second product cycle hypothesis as formulated above, although there is a qualification to an acceptance of the hypothesis. This is, that where technology leaders are in a very strong or hegemonic position through rapid innovation at home, the home centre may exercise such a strong attraction for further research that the internationalisation of technological activity is weak – a situation that seems to have applied to US companies in the early post-war years, and to Japanese firms today. Yet despite the historical significance of the geographical dispersion of innovation by MNCs, it is only relatively recently that the literature on MNCs has devoted much attention to the international creation

Table 8.7. *The cross-firm coefficient of variation (expressed as a percentage) of the share of patenting due to research located abroad*

	USA	UK	Germany	France	Switzerland	Sweden
Chemical industry group						
1920–39	217.5	135.1	177.3	89.0	88.6	190.9
1969–90	121.1	84.6	47.4	90.4	25.1	21.1
Electrical equipment industry group						
1920–39	144.7	232.5	165.6	223.6	38.9	141.4
1969–90	148.5	31.7	95.9	74.7	86.1	73.5
Mechanical industry group						
1920–39	289.2	181.3	193.6	189.3	141.4	219.7
1969–90	106.0	63.3	119.8	118.3	36.1	115.3
Transport industry group						
1920–39	202.4	219.4	117.4	264.6	n.a.	n.a.
1969–90	101.0	157.1	126.2	207.1	n.a.	99.1

Note:
n.a. = not applicable.
Source: As for table 8.1.

of technology, as opposed to international technology transfer (Cantwell, 1994).

The more recent broadening of the internationalisation of technological development to a wider range of firms is partly responsible for finally drawing attention to this issue. The reduction in the industrial focus of internationalisation mentioned previously offers some indirect evidence consistent with the broadening of internationalisation across firms, but table 8.7 provides direct evidence of this process within industrial groups. This shows that the extent of variation across firms in the degree of inter-nationalisation of their technological activity has been generally on a downward trend. A wider range of companies has now engaged in foreign technological development, in what was once mainly the province of a smaller number of leading firms. However, there are occasional exceptions to this trend. In the US electrical equipment group, ITT has remained highly international, and Sperry (prior to the formation of Unisys) also became strongly committed to foreign research, leaving others in their wake. In the Swiss electrical equipment group it was Brown Boveri (prior to the formation of ABB) that pulled ahead of the pack in its foreign oper-ations, and in the German transport group the motor vehicle component producer Robert Bosch played this role, in each case sustaining the extent of cross-firm variation in the degree of internationalisation. Elsewhere, lower transport and communication costs contributed to a general expansion across large firms in the internationalisation of technological activity.

The other recent change which has often been discussed in other contexts is that formerly local market oriented affiliates have been increasingly integrated into international networks within their respective MNCs, such networks coming to resemble 'heterarchies' more than hierarchies (Hedlund, 1986; Doz, 1986; Porter, 1986; Bartlett and Ghoshal, 1989; Dunning, 1992). In technological activity, too, the location-specific capabilities of internationally dispersed MNC affiliates may have become more closely integrated than in the past, linked to a strategy for technology creation in the MNC as a whole, and not only with separate reference to each of the geographical parts of the company's business. This can be termed a new globalisation of technological innovation.

The theoretical rationale for the recent international integration of productive activity is that the economic benefits attributable to a more refined locational division of labour within the MNC have often come to outweigh the costs of being less nationally responsive in each market, costs associated with adverse political repercussions and the continued national differentiation of demand (Doz, 1986). In an integrated MNC network each affiliate specialises in accordance with the specific characteristics of local production conditions, technological capabilities and user requirements. The network benefits from economies of scale through the local concentration of particular lines of activity (increasing returns from local research in a specialised field as opposed to research in general), economies of locational agglomeration through an interchange with others operating in the same vicinity in technologically allied fields as suggested earlier, and economies of scope through the international intra-firm co-ordination of related but geographically separated activities. The experience acquired in a specialised activity in one location creates technological spillovers that can be passed on to other parts of the MNC network elsewhere. It has been shown that since the 1970s, in industries in which such net advantages to multinational integration were available, multinationality has been a source of competitive success and faster growth (Cantwell and Sanna-Randaccio, 1993).

The transformation of the MNC, from a mainly multi-domestic structure of separate affiliates each serving their local markets, to an integrated internal network structure, has relevance to other aspects of the product cycle model apart from the hypotheses mentioned earlier. The wider product cycle model extended beyond the two hypotheses discussed here, to various other hypotheses and assumptions, such as that foreign direct investment can be treated as essentially local market oriented, and that firms can be thought of as akin to single-product producers. It can be argued that this wider model broke down largely because of globalisation in the sense just described, entailing the international integration of MNC networks. A global scanning for (new sources of) innovation and greater international linkages between production facilities imply an interactive flow of products and technological knowledge between countries (Vernon, 1979). This contrasts strongly with the original product cycle perspective of innovation and technological knowledge essentially flowing outwards from a single major centre, namely the home country.

The new globalisation of the responsibilities of affiliates to the MNC as a whole can be illustrated with reference to the shift that has occurred in the pattern of technological specialisation of foreign-owned research facilities. To examine this issue the patent data were used to construct a measure of the distribution of technological specialisation across various types of activity, for different groups of firms within their industry. It is also possible to distinguish between the pattern of specialisation in domestic technological activity and in research abroad, with reference to a corporate group or groups. The index of technological specialisation across different fields of activity that has been calculated is often termed an index of revealed technological advantage (RTA). The RTA value of a selected group of firms in a particular sector of technological activity is given by its share of US patents in that sector granted to companies in the same industry, relative to that group's overall share of all US patents assigned to firms in the industry in question. Denoting as P_{ij} the number of US patents granted in the field of technological activity i (defined with reference to the patent class system, as described earlier) to the selected group of firms j in a particular industry, then the RTA index is defined as follows:

$$RTA_{ij} = (P_{ij}/\Sigma_j P_{ij})/(\Sigma_i P_{ij}/\Sigma_{ij} P_{ij}).$$

The index varies around unity, such that values greater than one suggest that a group of firms is comparatively specialised in the activity in question relative to other firms in the same industry, while values less than one are indicative of a lack of specialisation by the standards of the industry (see Cantwell, 1993, for a further discussion). For the purposes of historical comparison, attention is focused on the two groups of corporate technology leaders most prominent historically, each originating from major centres of innovation in their respective industries – that is, US-owned firms in the electrical equipment industry, and German-owned companies in the chemical industry. For each group the RTA index is separately calculated for activity located in its home research and its foreign research facilities, and for each of the two broad periods 1920–68 and 1969–90. In order to avoid the problems associated with low numbers of patents, the analysis is

Table 8.8. *The RTA values, in selected sectors of technological activity, of US-owned firms in the electrical equipment industry and German-owned firms in the chemicals industry*

	1920–68		1969–90	
	At home	Abroad	At home	Abroad
US-owned firms in the electrical equipment industry				
Lighting and wiring	0.96	1.30	0.94	0.77
General industrial equipment	1.07	0.67	0.97	1.96
German-owned firms in the chemicals industry				
Bleaching and dyeing processes	2.43	1.43	1.91	0.71
Organic chemicals (dyestuffs)	1.46	1.47	1.33	0.97
Pharmaceuticals	1.22	3.16	1.22	2.04

Source: As for table 8.1.

restricted to sectors of technological activity in which all large firms in the industry in question were granted 900 US patents or more in 1920–68. This involved nineteen sectors in the electrical equipment industry, and twenty in the case of chemicals. The values of the RTA index calculated for a few selected sectors are shown in table 8.8.

The European-located research of US-owned electrical equipment firms was not historically (1920–68) geared to local European strengths, but instead represented the local development of fields related to the core technologies that had been pioneered at home (in telecommunications and general electrical systems, including lighting). For these purposes, the pattern of technological specialisation of countries and broader regions such as Europe relative to one another was observed using an analogous RTA measure for countries rather than national groups of firms, grouping all patents (and not just those assigned to the largest firms) by the location of invention – indeed, it was in this country-specific (as opposed to firm-specific) form that the RTA index was originally proposed (Soete, 1987; Cantwell, 1989). In more recent years (1969–90), while the domestic activity of US-owned firms in this sector has continued to concentrate on general electrical equipment, the focus of their foreign research has shifted to specialised machinery and general industrial equipment, both of which are areas of European advantage. Thus, the technological activity of US-owned foreign affiliates (which is still mainly conducted in Europe) has shifted towards an attempt to exploit the technological potential of the location in which it is carried out.

Similarly, the largest German chemical firms were strongly specialised historically (between 1920 and 1968) in the same fields in developing technology both at home and abroad – namely, in bleaching and dyeing processes, in organic chemicals including dyestuffs, and to a lesser extent in pharmaceuticals. Thus, these large German companies quite directly exploited their major strengths abroad, further developing these new products and techniques for local industries and markets in other countries. In foreign research today (since 1969) these firms are no longer specialised in their corporate strengths of dyes and dyeing, but they retain a stronger focus on pharmaceuticals in which they are not quite so strong at home. Rather like the American electrical companies, the German chemical firms have shifted their international research strategies away from the pure exploitation of their own strengths adapted to the needs of each particular local market, and towards an attempt to tap into foreign centres of expertise, in their case mainly in the development of pharmaceuticals in the United States, Britain and Switzerland.

Other recent evidence also suggests that this type of internationally integrated or globalised strategy for innovation characterises corporate technology leaders today. The extent to which the affiliates of MNCs specialise within their industry across national boundaries in accordance with the comparative advantage of local expertise seems to depend upon the pattern of locational hierarchy that exists between alternative centres. In the European chemical industry Germany is the dominant centre, the UK is a second-order centre, and Italy is of the third order. In this sector, German MNCs (the leaders) are technologically specialised in the other European centres in line with host country strengths, and the same is true of British chemical MNCs in Italy (Cantwell and Sanna-Randaccio, 1992).

However, when operating in Germany, British chemical companies follow a pattern of technological specialisation that accords with their own comparative advantages in the industry and those of their home centre, the UK. They do not appear to be especially prone to try and tap into the areas in which Germany expertise is relatively greatest, but rather to treat Germany as a general reservoir of skills that can be used principally to extend those lines of operation on which they are already focused in their home base. Technology leaders originating from higher-order centres tend to establish a more extensive locationally specialised network of technological activity in support of an international innovation strategy than has been developed as yet by firms that originate from lower-order centres.

It is true that this result depends upon an analysis of cross-border technological specialisation conducted at a fairly broad level of aggregation – across twenty or thirty sectors of technological activity, as described earlier. It may well be that when companies from a lower-order centre locate research in a higher-order one to engage in the same broad lines of activity in which they are specialised at home, there is still some geographical specialisation at the more detailed level of particular products or processes, and at the more finely disaggregated patent class level (Zander, 1994). In this event, the distinction between corporate technology leaders and other firms would be more a matter of the degree of locational specialisation that they have managed to achieve in technological development, rather than the existence of such a strategy of specialisation across centres.

The globalisation of technological innovation in MNCs, in the sense here of an international integration of geographically dispersed and locally specialised activities, tends to reinforce and not to dismantle nationally distinctive patterns of development or national systems of innovation (Nelson, 1993). Contrary to what is sometimes alleged, globalisation and national specialisation are complementary parts of a common process, and not conflicting trends (see Archibugi and Michie, this volume, chapter 6). The incentive to organise affiliate specialisation is the desire to tap into the locally specific and differentiated stream of innovation in each centre, but by specialising in accordance with these local strengths the latter are reinforced. The creation of tacit capability is localised and embedded in social organisations (Nelson and Winter, 1982), and this organisational distinctiveness has a location-specific as well as a firm-specific dimension. The particular path of innovation followed in each country or region has historical origins (Rosenberg, 1976, 1982). In the period of globalisation since the late 1960s the general tendency has been for MNCs to become more technologically diversified as they establish newly integrated technological systems, while countries or locations have become more specialised in their technological activity (Cantwell, 1993).

Conclusions

One aspect of the product cycle model is now rather discredited, namely the idea that demand-led innovation (together with economies of scale in R&D) in the home country dictates the geographical restriction of corporate research and the most technologically sophisticated production to the site of the parent company. For one thing, the demand-led view of innovation that was prevalent in the 1960s is now more widely acknowledged to be one-sided and potentially misleading (Mowery and Rosenberg, 1979). Innovations generally rely on a firm-specific learning process that interacts with both the growth of demand and the creation of new scientific and technological knowledge. In a region or country that enjoys technological leadership, high incomes and demand are as much a consequence of that leadership (high technological capability and thus high productivity) as

they are a cause of it. For another thing, the peculiarities of foreign production conditions and demand have required leading MNCs historically
to develop innovations abroad, related to those that had been pioneered at
home.

For this latter reason, another aspect of the model can be extended to
provide a further historical application that remains relevant. That is, the
product cycle view that outward industrial investment is most widely associated with technology leaders, generally in conjunction with their holding
a strong export position; so, too, the earliest internationalisation of technological development was largely due to such leaders. Historically, some
highly competent US electrical equipment firms were considerably more
international in their technology creation then than they are now. In
Europe large chemical firms were relatively technologically stronger, and it
was they that led the historical internationalisation of corporate research
facilities.

In more recent times technology leaders have altered the nature of international technology creation by pioneering the international integration of
MNC facilities into regional or global networks. Globalisation in this sense
involves the establishment of new international structures for technology
creation. In the past, foreign technological activity exploited domestic
strengths abroad, it was located in response to local demand conditions, it
assisted in the growth of other high-income areas, and its role ranged from
the adaptation of products to suit local tastes through to the establishment
of new local industries. At that time the capacity to develop internationally
dispersed innovations derived from a position of technological strength in
the firm's home country base, and led to similar lines of technological development being established abroad. By contrast, today, for companies of the
leading centres, foreign technological activity now increasingly aims to tap
into local fields of expertise, and to provide a further source of new technology that can be utilised internationally in the other operations of the
MNC. In this respect, innovation in the leading MNCs is now more gen-
uinely international or, in the terminology used here, it has become 'globalised'.

There are two similarities between the theoretical rationale provided for
the product cycle model (which applied best to the United States and to US-
owned MNCs in the early post-war period) and that suggested for the
current globalisation of technological activity in MNCs. Both explanations
rely on the role of the economies of locational agglomeration, and on the
leadership exercised by the most technologically competent firms. The
essential difference is that in the product cycle model just one pre-eminent
centre for innovation was recognised, whereas in the globalisation story
there are multiple locations for innovation, and even lower-order or less

developed centres can still be sources of innovation. Hence, the theoretical concepts also used in the product cycle approach apply differently in the account of globalisation; locational agglomeration occurs in the clusters of distinctive innovations that occur in many centres and not only in one unique centre, while the greater capability of the most competent firms manifests itself not just in the wider geographical dispersion of their investments (a more important consideration historically), but in the broader degree of cross-border specialisation that they are able to manage.

The product cycle view of the MNC as a locational hierarchy also remains relevant, although this too needs extending. It is still true that the home country is generally the single most important site for corporate technological development. More interestingly, the form of locational hierarchy in the leading firms of the most advanced centres is now much more complex than it used to be, and more complex than is the equivalent hierarchy of other MNCs. The affiliates of the leading companies in other major centres may be thought of as constituting an interactive network. Cross-investments between the major centres in the most technologically dynamic industries (Dunning, 1988; Cantwell, 1989; Cantwell and Sanna-Randaccio, 1992) have probably helped to reinforce the existing pattern of geographical specialisation, and the importance of these centres as locations for innovation. Having been the first to establish an international spread of technological activity, MNCs from the leading centres in a given industry now exploit locational diversity in paths of innovation to a greater extent than do other firms.

Note

1 I am grateful to the UK Economic and Social Research Council (ESRC) for its support under research grant R000232250. I wish to thank also Pilar Barrera, who worked on related aspects of the project, Jane Myers and Jim Hirabayashi of the US Patent and Trademark Office for their invaluable assistance, and Cathy Jones and her many fellow students for their tremendous efforts during the data collection.

References

Bartlett, C. A. and Ghoshal, S. 1989. *Managing Across Borders: The Transnational Solution*, Boston, Mass., Harvard Business School Press.
Beaton, K. 1957. *Enterprise in Oil: A History of Shell in the United States*, New York, Appleton-Century-Crofts.
Cantwell, J. A. 1987. The reorganisation of European industries after integration, *Journal of Common Market Studies*, 26: 127–51.
    1989. *Technological Innovation and Multinational Corporations*, Oxford, Basil Blackwell.

1991a. The international agglomeration of R&D, in M.C. Casson (ed.), *Global Research Strategy and International Competitiveness*, Oxford, Basil Blackwell.

1991b. The theory of technological competence and its application to international production, in D.G. McFetridge (ed.), *Foreign Investment, Technology and Economic Growth*, Calgary, University of Calgary Press.

1993. Corporate technological specialisation in international industries, in M. C. Casson and J. Creedy (eds.), *Industrial Concentration and Economic Inequality*, Aldershot, Edward Elgar.

1994. Introduction, in J. A. Cantwell (ed.), *Transnational Corporations and Innovatory Activities*, London, Routledge.

Cantwell, J. A. and Barrera, M. P. 1993. The rise of corporate R&D and the technological performance of the largest European firms from the interwar years onwards, University of Reading Discussion Papers in Economics, no. 271, September.

1995. Inter-company agreements for technological development: lessons from international cartels, *International Studies in Management and Organisation*, 25: 75–95.

Cantwell, J. A. and Hodson, C. 1991. Global R&D and UK competitiveness, in Casson (ed.).

Cantwell, J. A. and Kotecha, U. 1994. L'internationalisation des activité technologiques: le cas français en perspective, in F. Sachwald. (ed.), *Les Defis de la Mondialisation: Innovation et Concurrence*, Paris, Masson.

Cantwell, J. A. and Sanna-Randaccio, F. 1992. Intra-industry direct investment in the European Community: oligopolistic rivalry and technological competition, in J. A. Cantwell (ed.), *Multinational Investment in Modern Europe*, Aldershot, Edward Elgar.

1993. Multinationality and firm growth, *Weltwirtschaftliches Archiv*, 129: 275–99.

Casson, M.C. (ed.) 1991. *Global Research Strategy and International Competitiveness*, Oxford, Basil Blackwell.

Chandler, A. D. 1990. *Scale and Scope: The Dynamics of Industrial Capitalism*, Cambridge, Mass., Harvard University Press.

Coleman, D. C. 1969. *Courtaulds: An Economic and Social History*, vol. II: Rayon, Oxford, Oxford University Press.

Dahmen, E. 1970. *Entrepreneurial Activity and the Development of Swedish Industry, 1919–1939*, Homewood, Ill., American Economic Association Translation Series.

Dosi, G., Giannetti, R. and Toninelli, P.A. (eds.) 1992. *Technology and Enterprise in a Historical Perspective*, Oxford, Oxford University Press.

Dosi, G., Teece, D. J. and Winter, S. G. 1992. Towards a theory of corporate coherence: preliminary remarks, in Dosi *et al.* (eds).

Doz, Y. 1986. *Strategic Management in Multinational Companies*, Oxford, Pergamon.

Dunning, J. H. 1988. *Multinationals, Technology and Competitiveness*, London, Unwin Hyman.

1992. *Multinational Enterprises and the Global Economy*, Wokingham, Addison-Wesley.

Feldman, M. P. 1993. An examination of the geography of innovation, *Industrial and Corporate Change*, 2: 451–70.

Granstrand, O., Håkanson, L. and Sjölander, S. (eds.) 1992. *Technology Management and International Business: Internationalisation of R&D and Technology*, Chichester, Wiley.

Hedlund, G. 1986. The hypermodern MNC: a heterarchy?, *Human Resource Management*, 25: 9–25.

Hounshell, D. A. and Smith, J. K. 1988. *Science and Corporate Strategy: Du Pont R&D, 1902–1980*, Cambridge, Cambridge University Press.

Hymer, S. 1975. The multinational corporation and the law of uneven development, in H. Radice (ed.), *International Firms and Modern Imperialism*, Harmondsworth, Penguin.

Jaffe, A. B. 1989. Real effects of academic research, *American Economic Review*, 79: 957–70.

Jaffe, A. B., Trajtenberg, M. and Henderson, R. 1993. Geographical localization of knowledge spillovers as evidenced by patent citations, *Quarterly Journal of Economics*, 108: 577–98.

Jones, R. and Marriot, O. 1971. *Anatomy of a Merger: A History of GEC, AEI and English Electric*, London, Cape.

Kogut, B. 1987. Country patterns in international competition: appropriability and oligopolistic agreement, in N. Hood and J. E. Vahlne (eds.), *Strategies in Global Competition*, London, Croom Helm.

1990. The permeability of borders and the speed of learning among countries, in J. H.Dunning, B. Kogut and M. Blomström (eds.), *Globalisation of Firms and the Competitiveness of Nations*, Lund, Lund University Press.

Krugman, P. R. 1991. *Geography and Trade*, Cambridge, Mass., MIT Press.

Lall, S. 1979. The international allocation of research activity by US multinationals, *Oxford Bulletin of Economics and Statistics*, 41: 313–31.

Mansfield, E., Teece, D. J. and Romeo, A. 1979. Overseas research and development by US based firms, *Economica*, 46: 187–96.

Mowery, D. C. and Rosenberg, N. 1979. The influence of market demand upon innovation: a critical review of some recent empirical studies, *Research Policy*, 8: 103–53.

Nelson, R. R. 1991. Why do firms differ and how does it matter?, *Strategic Management Journal*, 12: 61–74.

1992. The role of firms in technical advance, in Dosi *et al.* (eds.).

Nelson, R. R. (ed.) 1993. *National Innovation Systems*, New York, Oxford University Press.

Nelson, R. R. and Winter, S. G. 1982. *An Evolutionary Theory of Economic Change*, Cambridge, Mass., Bellknap Press.

Patel, P. and Pavitt, K. L. R. 1991. Large firms in the production of the world's technology: an important case of 'non-globalisation', *Journal of International Business Studies*, 22: 1–21.

Pavitt, K. L. R. 1992. Some foundations for a theory of the large innovating firm, in Dosi *et al.* (eds.).

Pearce, R. D. and Singh, S. 1992. *Globalising Research and Development*, London, Macmillan.

Penrose, E. T. 1959. *The Theory of the Growth of the Firm*, Oxford, Basil Blackwell.

Porter, M. E. 1986. Competition in global industries: a conceptual framework, in M. E. Porter (ed.), *Competition in Global Industries*, Boston, Mass., Harvard Business School Press.

　1990. *The Competitive Advantage of Nations*, New York, The Free Press.

Reich, L. S. 1986. *The Making of American Industrial Research: Science and Business at GE and Bell, 1876–1926*, Cambridge, Cambridge University Press.

Ronstadt, R. C. 1977. *Research and Development Abroad by US Multinationals*, New York, Praeger.

Rosenberg, N. 1976. *Perspectives on Technology*, Cambridge, Cambridge University Press.

　1982. *Inside the Black Box: Technology and Economics*, Cambridge, Cambridge University Press.

Schmookler, J. 1966. *Invention and Economic Growth*, Cambridge, Mass., Harvard University Press.

Soete, L. L. G. 1987. The impact of technological innovation on international trade patterns: the evidence reconsidered, *Research Policy*, 16: 101–30.

Stocking, G. W. and Watkins, M. W. 1946. *Cartels in Action*, New York, Twentieth Century Fund.

Sölvell, Ö., Zander, I. and Porter, M. E. 1991. *Advantage Sweden*, Stockholm, Norstedts.

Teece, D. J., Pisano, G. and Shuen, A. 1990. Firm capabilities, resources and the concept of strategy, Consortium on Competitiveness and Cooperation Working Papers, no. 90–8, University of California, Berkeley.

Vernon, R. 1966. International investment and international trade in the product cycle, *Quarterly Journal of Economics*, 80: 190–207.

　1979. The product cycle hypothesis in a new international environment, *Oxford Bulletin of Economics and Statistics*, 41: 255–67.

Wilkins, M. 1974. *The Maturing of Multinational Enterprise*, Cambridge, Mass., Harvard University Press.

　1989. *The History of Foreign Investment in the United States to 1914*, Cambridge, Mass., Harvard University Press.

Zander, I. 1994. *The Tortoise Evolution of the Multinational Corporation*, Stockholm, Institute of International Business, Stockholm School of Economics.

9 Schumpeterian patterns of innovation

FRANCO MALERBA AND LUIGI ORSENIGO[1]

Schumpeter Mark I or Schumpeter Mark II?

In the *Theory of Economic Development* and *Capitalism, Socialism and Democracy*, Schumpeter proposed two major patterns of innovative activities. The first one, labelled by Nelson and Winter (1982) and Kamien and Schwartz (1982) as Schumpeter Mark I, is proposed in the *Theory of Economic Development* (1934). In this work, Schumpeter examined the typical European industrial structure of the late nineteenth century characterised by many small firms. According to this view the pattern of innovative activity is characterised by technological ease of entry to an industry and by the major role played by new firms in innovative activities. New entrepreneurs enter an industry with new ideas, new products or new processes, launch new enterprises which challenge established firms and thus continuously disrupt the current way of production, organisation and distribution and eliminate the quasi-rents associated with previous innovations.

The second one, labelled Schumpeter Mark II, is proposed in *Capitalism, Socialism and Democracy* (1942). In this work, inspired by the features of American industry of the first half of the twentieth century, Schumpeter discussed the relevance of the industrial R&D laboratory for technological innovation and the key role of large firms. According to this view, the pattern of innovative activities is characterised by the prevalence of large established firms and by relevant barriers to entry for new innovators. Large firms have institutionalised the innovation process with the creation of R&D laboratories filled with researchers, technicians and engineers. With their accumulated stock of knowledge in specific technological areas, their advanced competence in large-scale R&D projects, production and distribution and their relevant financial resources they create barriers to entry by new entrepreneurs and small firms.

The Schumpeterian Mark I and Mark II patterns of innovation could also be labelled 'widening' and 'deepening', respectively. A widening pattern of innovative activities is related to an innovative base which is continuously enlarging through the entry of new innovators and the erosion of the competitive and technological advantages of the established firms in the industry. A deepening pattern of innovation, on the contrary, is related to the dominance of a few firms which are continuously innovative through the accumulation over time of technological and innovative capabilities. During the last forty years this characterisation of innovative activities by Schumpeter has encouraged different scholarly traditions aiming at the empirical verification of the two patterns.

The first, and older, tradition was mainly centred on the firm. It attempted to assess the role of firm size and of monopoly power in innovation (Kamien and Schwartz, 1982). Extensive empirical analyses were made in order to verify the innovativeness of small firms compared with large firms and of concentrated industries compared with atomistic industries. The inconclusive results obtained in these empirical analyses were due to the neglected role of opportunity and appropriability conditions in the various industries (Levin *et al.*, 1985) and of the endogenous relationship between firm size, concentration and technological change (Nelson and Winter, 1982).

A second, and more recent, tradition has inserted Schumpeter Mark I and II models according to the specific stage of an industry's life-cycle. According to the industry life-cycle view, early in the history of an industry, when technology is changing very rapidly, uncertainty is very high and barriers to entry very low, new firms are the major innovators and are the key element in industrial dynamics. However, when an industry develops and eventually matures and technological change follows well-defined trajectories, then economies of scale, learning curves, barriers to entry and financial resources become important in the competitive process and large firms with monopolistic power come to the forefront of the innovation process (Utterback and Abernathy 1975; Gort and Klepper 1982; Klepper, 1992).

Differently from the traditions centred on the firm and on the industry life-cycle, the present chapter discusses the widening and deepening Schumpeterian patterns of innovation across industries by focusing on the way innovative activities are organised and take place within an industry. The starting point of this chapter is that the Schumpeterian widening and the Schumpeterian deepening patterns of innovative activities are related to the key features of the technological regime which characterises an industry.

Inspired by Nelson and Winter (1982), Dosi (1988) and Cohen and Levin (1989), who have pointed out that the conditions of opportunity and appropriability may greatly affect the way innovative activities are carried out in an industry in terms of firm size and industrial concentration, we (Malerba and Orsenigo, 1990, 1993) have defined technological regimes in terms of opportunity, appropriability, cumulativeness and properties of the knowledge-base. We have examined the link between technological regimes and patterns of innovative activities at both the conceptual and the empirical levels. Opportunity conditions refer to the ease of innovation by would-be innovators, and are related to the potential for innovation of each technology. Appropriability conditions refer to the ability of innovators to protect their innovations from imitation, and therefore to reap results and profits from their innovations. Cumulativeness conditions refer to the fact that existing innovators may continue to be so also in the future with respect to non-innovators. Finally, knowledge-base conditions refer to the number and type of basic and applied sciences necessary to innovative activities, and to the tacit or codified, simple or complex, specialised or pervasive dimensions of knowledge underpinning innovation in an industry.

According to the above-mentioned analysis based on technological regimes, the widening and deepening Schumpeterian patterns of innovation may be seen as the results of well-defined regime conditions. Widening patterns are determined by high opportunity and low appropriability conditions, which favour the continuous entry of new innovators in the industry, and by low cumulativeness conditions, which do not allow the persistence of monopolistic advantages in the industry innovators. Deepening patterns are determined by high opportunity, appropriability and cumulativeness conditions, which allow innovators to accumulate technological knowledge and capabilities continuously and to build up innovative advantages over non-innovators and potential entrants (Malerba and Orsenigo, 1993).[2]

Of course, widening and deepening Schumpeterian patterns of innovative activities are two extreme cases that bound a large number of intermediate cases. These intermediate cases have been discussed at length in Malerba and Orsenigo (1990). Moreover, as previously mentioned, during their life-cycles industries may change patterns of innovative activity, passing from a Schumpeter Mark I to a Schumpeter Mark II type of model.

It must be noted that the claim that technological regimes affect the type of Schumpeterian patterns of innovative activities implies that these patterns of innovations ought to be relatively invariant across countries. This is so because the appropriability and cumulativeness conditions, the two dimensions of technological regimes that affect the widening and deepening patterns of innovation, are fairly similar across advanced industrialised countries (see Malerba and Orsenigo, 1990, and Heimler et al., 1993, for analyses of the Italian and American cases). Opportunity conditions among advanced countries are less similar, because these conditions are related to the level and range of university research, the presence and effectiveness of science–industry bridging mechanisms, vertical and horizontal links among local firms, user–producer interaction and the type and level of firms' innovative efforts (Nelson, 1993).

This chapter represents the first empirical analysis of the widening and deepening Schumpeterian patterns of innovation carried out at the firm level. It covers thirty-three technological classes and four countries: Germany (Federal Republic), France, the United Kingdom and Italy. The following section discusses the data used for the analysis. We then examine the individual indicators used to identify the two Schumpeterian patterns of innovation. Subsequently, we analyse the two Schumpeterian patterns while, in a final section, we discuss the relationships between the patterns of innovation and technological performance.

The data

Patent data have been used to investigate the two Schumpeterian patterns of innovation. Criticisms of the use of patent data are well known. Not all innovations are patented by firms. Patents cannot be distinguished in terms of relevance unless specific analyses on patent renewals or patent citations are made. Finally, different technologies are differently patentable and different types of firms may have different propensities to patent. However, patents represent a very homogeneous measure of technological novelty across countries and are available for long time-series. They also provide very detailed data at the firm and the technological class levels. As a consequence, they are an invaluable and unique source of data on innovative activity. As Griliches (1990) has pointed out, 'patents statistics remain a unique resource for the analysis of the process of technical change. Nothing else even comes close in the quality of available data, accessibility, and the potential industrial, organizational and technological detail.'

This chapter uses the OTAF-SPRU database which concerns patents granted in the United States to firms and institutions from all over the world.[3] The OTAF-SPRU database has been elaborated at the firm level for four European countries: Germany (Federal Republic), France, the United Kingdom and Italy. These countries represent a fairly heterogeneous dataset, with some countries at the technological frontier and others lagging behind. Extreme cases have not been taken into consideration: neither the United States, which may overrepresent small firms and whose firms may have a higher propensity to patent at the local United States Patent Office, nor Japan, which, given its high growth rate of patents during the period, may give distorted indications of the average pattern of innovative activities during a long period of time, is included.

The analysis was carried out for the period 1969–86. Given the length of this period, it is possible that a technological class may have moved over the period from a Schumpeter Mark I group to a Schumpeter Mark II group. Thirty-three technological classes are considered in the analysis (see the Appendix) including Class 33 'Other' (ammunition, road structures, plant and animal husbandry, and others). Economic data on firms patenting in the United States concern size in terms of number of employees in 1984. Therefore, a bias may be present in the analysis in favour of firms active during the 1980s. Firms which are part of business groups have been treated in the present analysis as individual companies. It must be noted that we also carried out an analysis[4] which considered industrial groups rather than individual firms: this confirmed the main results of this chapter.

Indicators of Schumpeterian patterns of innovative activities

Using patent data, the present analysis constructed a group of indicators of the Schumpeterian patterns of innovative activities. These indicators, examined individually in this section, will be used jointly in the subsequent section to identify those technological classes which belong either to a Schumpeterian widening pattern or to a Schumpeterian deepening pattern of innovative activity.

The indicators of patterns of innovative activities used in the present analysis can be grouped into four types. For each of the thirty-three technological classes, this chapter builds indicators of:

(A) Concentration of innovative activities (concentration ratio of the top four innovators) and asymmetries among innovators (Herfindahl index);
(B) Size of the innovating firms;
(C) Change over time in the hierarchy of innovators;
(D) Relevance of new innovators compared to established ones.

In addition, two further indicators, one of structure and the other of performance, have been used:

(E) Composition of innovative activities within each of the four countries;
(F) World technological performance of the four countries in a given technological class.

While indicators such as concentration (A) and firm size (B) have been generally used in traditional discussions of the Schumpeterian hypotheses, in this chapter two additional indicators, the change in the hierarchy of innovators (C) and the relevance of new innovators (D) are proposed. The two new indicators aim to shed light on the degree of 'stability' or 'dynamism' in the organisation of innovative activity at the industry level, in terms of degree of change in the hierarchy of the main innovators and relevance of firms that introduce innovations for the first time. These indicators are able to capture the degree of 'creative destruction' or the degree of 'creative accumulation' associated with innovative activities.

In the following sub-sections the meaning, the construction and the results of the various indicators of patterns of innovative activities are discussed briefly.

Concentration and asymmetries (C4 and HERFINDAHL)

A first indicator of patterns of innovative activities is the degree of concentration of innovations among leading innovators. In this analysis, the share of patents held by the four major innovators within each technological class is used (C4). In addition to this concentration ratio, a second indicator is used to identify the degree of asymmetries among all the innovators (large and small) in a technological class: this is the Herfindahl index (HERFINDAHL).

C4 has a high value on average in the four countries. It is consistently high in the chemical group and consistently low in the mechanical group. There is more variability in the electronic-electrical group, especially because the United Kingdom shows a much lower concentration than the other three countries (see table 9.1). This result indicates that oligopolistic structures dominate innovative activities in most technological classes.

HERFINDAHL on the contrary has low values on average. It is consistently high (indicating the presence of asymmetries) in the electronics group and in the chemical group; it is consistently low (indicating similarities among firms) in the mechanical group and in instrumentation; it has medium values, or variability in the values among countries, in automobiles and drugs (see table 9.1).

In addition the Pearson correlation coefficient (not reported here) shows a striking similarity in the level of C4 and HERFINDAHL for each technological class across countries and the Spearman rank correlation coefficient (not reported here) shows that there are similar hierarchies of technological classes in the four countries.

Size of the innovating firms (SIZE)

A second group of indicators, still in the Schumpeterian tradition, refers to the size of innovating firms. In this analysis, patenting firms with more than 500 employees are considered for each technological class for Germany, France, the United Kingdom and Italy. As expected, among the four countries Italy has on average the lowest share of patents held by large firms and Germany the largest, with France in the middle (see table 9.2). Among

Table 9.1. *Concentration ratio (C4) and Herfindahl index by technological class and country*

Code	C4						HERFINDAHL					
	Italy	FRG	France	UK	AVG[a]	STD[b]	Italy	FRG	France	UK	AVG[a]	STD[b]
1	72.3	45.9	52.3	36.8	51.8	13.0	0.18	0.06	0.09	0.06	0.10	0.05
2	48.9	71.3	48.3	47.6	54.0	10.0	0.09	0.18	0.07	0.13	0.12	0.04
3	90.0	87.1	70.6	75.9	80.9	7.9	0.40	0.25	0.16	0.21	0.26	0.09
4	34.1	36.2	26.3	28.7	31.3	4.0	0.04	0.04	0.03	0.04	0.04	0.01
5	74.4	46.0	76.5	73.0	67.5	12.5	0.25	0.08	0.38	0.20	0.23	0.11
6	47.4	77.7	78.3	69.0	68.1	12.5	0.08	0.19	0.34	0.22	0.21	0.09
7	38.4	59.6	43.9	44.3	46.5	7.9	0.06	0.14	0.07	0.07	0.09	0.03
8	48.2	36.0	54.6	50.5	47.3	6.9	0.08	0.05	0.16	0.09	0.09	0.04
9	24.0	29.5	23.7	33.1	27.6	3.9	0.03	0.03	0.02	0.04	0.03	0.01
10	53.6	47.9	37.2	42.0	45.2	6.1	0.13	0.14	0.05	0.07	0.09	0.04
11	27.9	22.4	19.9	18.4	22.2	3.6	0.03	0.02	0.02	0.01	0.02	0.01
12	24.4	14.8	17.8	16.6	18.4	3.6	0.02	0.01	0.01	0.01	0.02	0.00
13	25.2	24.6	29.8	29.6	27.3	2.4	0.04	0.03	0.03	0.03	0.03	0.00
14	30.3	43.5	28.9	22.6	31.4	7.6	0.03	0.07	0.03	0.02	0.04	0.02
15	18.1	10.5	14.8	16.0	14.8	2.8	0.01	0.01	0.01	0.01	0.01	0.00
16	23.0	18.7	21.8	12.9	19.1	3.9	0.02	0.01	0.02	0.01	0.02	0.01
17	27.9	17.3	17.6	17.5	20.1	4.5	0.03	0.01	0.02	0.01	0.02	0.01
18	85.0	81.3	93.2	86.8	86.6	4.3	0.34	0.20	0.47	0.40	0.35	0.10
19	49.1	42.5	45.2	68.2	51.3	10.1	0.09	0.06	0.10	0.20	0.11	0.05
20	49.0	70.4	44.1	41.8	51.3	11.3	0.09	0.23	0.07	0.08	0.12	0.06
21	22.7	32.6	24.4	16.7	24.1	5.7	0.03	0.05	0.03	0.01	0.03	0.01
22	83.3	73.9	50.7	60.6	67.1	12.5	0.22	0.24	0.09	0.10	0.16	0.07

Table 9.1. (cont.)

Code	C4						HERFINDAHL					
	Italy	FRG	France	UK	AVG[a]	STD[b]	Italy	FRG	France	UK	AVG[a]	STD[b]
23	54.0	55.6	48.5	32.4	47.6	9.2	0.10	0.14	0.08	0.05	0.09	0.03
24	65.0	66.5	52.1	32.4	54.0	13.7	0.15	0.31	0.10	0.04	0.15	0.10
25	69.2	90.3	76.3	45.9	70.4	16.1	0.19	0.61	0.22	0.09	0.28	0.20
26	29.5	57.2	39.4	28.2	38.6	11.6	0.04	0.22	0.07	0.03	0.09	0.08
27	80.6	58.1	55.1	26.7	55.1	19.1	0.36	0.17	0.11	0.03	0.17	0.12
28	43.8	65.2	56.6	27.3	48.2	14.3	0.07	0.13	0.16	0.04	0.10	0.05
29	81.1	80.5	48.4	47.9	64.5	16.3	0.22	0.36	0.09	0.07	0.19	0.12
30	28.7	34.9	33.2	13.5	27.6	8.4	0.03	0.06	0.04	0.01	0.03	0.02
31	12.9	11.3	20.3	8.2	13.2	4.4	0.01	0.01	0.02	0.01	0.01	0.00
32	39.5	35.3	41.4	14.1	32.6	10.9	0.06	0.05	0.06	0.01	0.04	0.02
33	33.3	45.5	39.2	29.2	36.8	6.1	0.04	0.07	0.06	0.04	0.05	0.01

Notes:
[a] Average.
[b] Standard deviation.

Table 9.2. *Innovative activities of medium-sized and large firms[a] (SIZE) by technological class and country*

Code	Italy	FRG	France	UK	AVG[b]	STD[c]
1	76.79	80.05	90.11	74.92	80.47	5.86
2	72.48	93.60	87.14	83.36	84.15	7.67
3	96.67	96.10	78.43	95.97	91.79	7.72
4	52.63	81.39	77.38	74.01	71.35	11.12
5	78.21	82.70	87.24	84.04	83.05	3.25
6	55.26	91.58	85.94	90.21	80.75	14.86
7	59.89	91.38	68.08	86.98	76.58	13.02
8	43.22	81.23	80.96	77.85	70.81	15.99
9	41.67	81.28	78.04	67.61	67.15	15.56
10	55.95	79.45	67.15	75.12	69.42	8.94
11	33.50	77.37	79.90	62.03	63.20	18.46
12	47.65	66.64	63.14	56.45	58.47	7.24
13	54.49	81.66	73.31	76.82	71.57	10.30
14	55.45	77.39	76.31	67.11	69.06	8.81
15	41.15	67.16	62.64	52.64	55.90	10.01
16	44.31	65.13	76.48	51.83	59.44	12.35
17	49.25	63.29	65.65	59.61	59.45	6.27
18	35.00	79.82	94.20	99.26	77.07	25.31
19	59.65	93.67	80.78	89.90	81.00	13.19
20	74.75	96.49	78.21	83.17	83.15	8.26
21	45.45	80.65	63.90	56.28	61.57	12.82
22	66.67	96.18	75.36	71.76	77.49	11.22
23	61.90	48.37	75.26	53.09	59.66	10.23
24	84.74	89.07	81.79	64.62	80.06	9.28
25	49.23	94.18	85.53	78.31	76.81	16.89
26	58.48	86.79	81.51	69.55	74.08	10.96
27	90.54	88.10	83.33	75.53	84.37	5.73
28	73.44	88.33	87.08	57.87	76.68	12.33
29	15.57	92.76	64.21	87.71	65.06	30.54
30	57.47	80.57	76.26	66.30	70.15	8.96
31	25.63	60.78	70.32	49.63	51.59	16.68
32	10.48	69.72	62.50	40.84	45.89	23.04
33	22.55	74.34	66.79	55.14	54.71	19.79

Notes:
[a] Percentage share of total patents held by firms with more than 500 employees.
[b] Average.
[c] Standard deviation.

technological classes, the mechanical and machinery groups and textiles show the greatest relevance of small firms in innovative activities.

Analysis of country differences based on Pearson and Spearman correlation coefficients (not reported here) shows again a striking similarity in the importance of large innovative firms in the thirty-three technological classes and very similar rankings of technological classes in the four countries.

Change in the hierarchy of innovators and entry to the core group of innovators (SPEA and NEWLEADERS)

A different set of indicators refers to the degree of change or stability in the hierarchy of firms which innovate in each of two periods (1969–77 and 1978–86) and of the leading innovators. These indicators aim to shed light on the degree of stability of technological advantage of the leading innovators and consequently on the degree of dynamism of the population of innovators.

In this respect, two indicators are used for each technological class. The first one is the Spearman rank correlation coefficient between the hierarchies of firms innovating in each period (1969–77 and 1978–86) (SPEA). The second is the share of patents held by the firms entering for the first time the group of the ten major innovators in the period 1978–86 compared to the period 1969–77 (NEWLEADERS).

As table 9.3 shows, there are differences among countries in terms of the degree of change in the hierarchy of innovators in each technological class (SPEA) and in the ranking of technology classes in terms of stability. France and the United Kingdom are very similar in the level and ranking of changes in the hierarchy within technological classes, while Germany and Italy are very different in level and ranking of technological classes.

In some technological classes, however, this indicator takes consistently high values in all countries (i.e. some classes of chemicals and electronics and road vehicles) or consistently low values (bleaching, dyeing and disinfecting, non-metallic minerals and other materials, some mechanical sectors, other transport, mining and well machinery, metal products and textiles).

On average the degree of stability over time in the hierarchy of innovators (SPEA) is high and similar for Germany, France and the United Kingdom (Italy has a lower value). The indicator of entry to the group of core innovators in each technological class (NEWLEADERS) shows that Germany has the lowest level of entry and Italy the highest (see table 9.3). However, there is a similarity in the ranking of technological classes in terms of share of patents held by the new innovators in the top ten leading innovators for Germany, Italy and the United Kingdom, but not for

Table 9.3. *Variability of the hierarchy: percentage share of total patents of the ten most innovative firms held by firms entering the top ten group (NEWLEADERS) in the period 1978–86 and Spearman rank correlation coefficient of firms which innovate continuously (SPEA), by technological class and country*

Code	NEWLEADERS						SPEA					
	Italy	FRG	France	UK	AVG[a]	STD[b]	Italy	FRG	France	UK	AVG[a]	STD[b]
1	33.3	12.0	36.8	16.9	24.7	10.5	0.69	0.35	0.50	0.68	0.56	0.14
2	2.2	2.0	16.1	3.4	5.9	5.9	0.47	0.61	0.57	0.51	0.54	0.06
3	16.7	6.0	63.6	5.9	23.0	23.8	0.00	0.64	1.00	0.88	0.63	0.39
4	5.3	3.8	0.0	7.2	4.1	2.7	0.57	0.54	0.56	0.69	0.59	0.06
5	65.2	13.0	14.2	24.7	29.3	21.3	0.00	0.49	0.71	0.67	0.46	0.28
6	62.5	12.0	7.3	18.9	25.2	21.9	-1.00	0.64	0.23	0.41	0.07	0.63
7	18.8	3.0	7.1	13.2	10.5	6.0	0.36	0.66	0.51	0.83	0.59	0.17
8	63.2	7.1	7.1	9.8	21.8	23.9	0.44	0.70	0.57	0.47	0.55	0.10
9	59.5	9.5	14.2	0.0	20.8	22.9	0.03	0.58	0.33	0.25	0.30	0.19
10	87.0	20.7	35.1	8.9	37.9	29.8	1.00	0.47	0.65	0.79	0.73	0.19
11	36.6	0.0	0.0	20.8	14.3	15.4	0.39	0.53	0.48	0.65	0.51	0.10
12	16.3	0.0	23.9	0.0	10.1	10.4	0.48	0.50	0.53	0.48	0.50	0.02
13	44.2	0.0	21.1	11.4	19.2	16.3	0.52	0.51	0.69	0.48	0.55	0.08
14	18.5	0.0	14.7	4.5	9.4	7.5	0.61	0.60	0.50	0.47	0.54	0.06
15	16.0	23.6	0.0	15.6	13.8	8.6	0.52	0.54	0.47	0.34	0.47	0.08
16	28.9	0.0	16.7	28.0	18.4	11.7	0.37	0.49	0.65	0.61	0.53	0.11
17	44.8	10.1	8.2	14.0	19.3	14.9	0.47	0.57	0.20	0.42	0.42	0.14
18	100.0	6.1	10.7	14.0	32.7	39.0	0.00	0.45	0.50	1.00	0.49	0.35
19	54.5	0.0	4.5	13.3	18.1	21.6	-0.18	0.72	0.67	0.79	0.50	0.40
20	43.8	0.0	11.2	20.5	18.9	16.1	0.66	0.77	0.74	0.39	0.64	0.15

Table 9.3. (*cont.*)

Code	NEWLEADERS						SPEA					
	Italy	FRG	France	UK	AVG[a]	STD[b]	Italy	FRG	France	UK	AVG[a]	STD[b]
21	58.3	5.7	37.3	37.3	34.7	18.8	0.41	0.64	0.41	0.25	0.43	0.14
22	100.0	21.6	10.2	61.7	48.4	35.4	0.00	0.52	0.48	0.80	0.45	0.29
23	47.4	9.9	41.1	12.7	27.8	16.7	0.90	0.29	0.74	0.42	0.59	0.24
24	24.8	3.0	5.0	6.3	9.8	8.8	0.47	0.53	0.77	0.67	0.61	0.12
25	29.0	6.4	3.8	15.2	13.6	9.9	0.00	0.84	0.56	0.53	0.48	0.30
26	29.3	3.9	5.0	4.6	10.7	10.8	0.32	0.42	0.63	0.58	0.49	0.13
27	6.2	5.6	0.0	10.4	5.6	3.7	0.86	0.56	0.79	0.63	0.71	0.12
28	66.7	1.4	5.7	16.0	22.5	26.1	-0.50	0.81	0.69	0.27	0.32	0.51
29	11.5	1.5	51.1	6.8	17.7	19.6	0.97	0.67	0.36	0.03	0.51	0.35
30	33.3	0.0	0.0	6.3	9.9	13.8	0.71	0.63	0.67	0.49	0.63	0.08
31	31.5	0.0	0.0	21.4	13.2	13.7	0.69	0.38	0.60	0.40	0.52	0.13
32	86.3	17.9	70.8	79.2	63.5	26.9	0.98	0.38	0.58	0.41	0.59	0.24
33	38.9	10.0	11.4	30.6	22.7	12.4	0.62	0.72	0.53	0.25	0.53	0.17

Notes:
[a] Average.
[b] Standard deviation.

France, as indicated by analysis based on the Pearson and Spearman correlation coefficients (not reported here).

New innovators (NATALITY)

The last set of measures concerns the importance of *new* innovators in each technological class. The indicator used is the share of patents granted to firms that patent for the first time in the period 1978–86 compared to the period 1969–77 (NATALITY). It should be noted that this index measures innovative birth and not entrepreneurial birth: a new innovator may already have been active in the industry for quite a long time. This measure may provide distorted information for those technological classes in which very few patents exist (such as agricultural chemicals, nuclear reactors and systems, power plants, aircraft), because the index of innovative birth may be quite high even with a very limited number of new innovators. The information provided by NATALITY, SPEA and NEWLEADERS sheds light on the degree of turbulence in each technological class: a high birth rate and low stability imply a high rate of turbulence, with new innovators emerging and a continuous change among innovators.

The four countries differ in terms of the importance of new innovators (table 9.4). The average value of NATALITY is highest in Italy (which is also the country with the lowest total number of patents) and is lowest in Germany (which is the country with the highest total number of patents). For this indicator, too, there is a striking similarity across countries (with the exception of the comparison between France and Italy) in the relevance of new innovators in each technological class and in the ranking of technological classes in terms of birth rates, as the Pearson and Spearman correlation coefficients (not reported here) show. The mechanical group and textiles have a relatively high rate of innovative birth in all the four countries, instruments a medium one, electronics and drugs a low rate, while the chemical group has different birth rates in the various classes (the majority of them, however, have low birth rates).

Schumpeterian patterns of innovation

The previous analysis has shown two further major general results. First, innovative activities are characterised by high degrees of both concentration and stability in the hierarchy of major innovators and by the importance of large firms in patenting activities. This result would seem to provide preliminary support to the Schumpeter Mark II model in the explanation of the patterns of innovation in contemporary advanced industrial economies.

Second, the various indicators of the patterns of innovative activities

Table 9.4. *Index of new innovators[a] by technological class and country (NATALITY)*

Code	Italy	FRG	France	UK	AVG[b]	STD[c]
1	0.39	0.24	0.44	0.31	0.34	0.08
2	0.25	0.05	0.26	0.17	0.18	0.09
3	0.17	0.08	0.64	0.12	0.25	0.22
4	0.46	0.16	0.29	0.32	0.31	0.11
5	0.69	0.30	0.17	0.34	0.37	0.19
6	0.65	0.18	0.12	0.34	0.32	0.20
7	0.38	0.09	0.20	0.19	0.21	0.11
8	0.74	0.36	0.34	0.42	0.47	0.16
9	0.77	0.32	0.48	0.42	0.50	0.17
10	0.89	0.36	0.54	0.32	0.53	0.23
11	0.65	0.31	0.37	0.49	0.45	0.13
12	0.59	0.26	0.48	0.45	0.44	0.12
13	0.60	0.21	0.31	0.36	0.37	0.15
14	0.55	0.17	0.29	0.35	0.34	0.14
15	0.55	0.32	0.41	0.47	0.44	0.08
16	0.62	0.26	0.49	0.55	0.48	0.14
17	0.71	0.33	0.43	0.52	0.50	0.14
18	1.00	0.10	0.11	0.14	0.34	0.38
19	0.57	0.15	0.22	0.26	0.30	0.16
20	0.56	0.09	0.36	0.34	0.34	0.17
21	0.78	0.27	0.46	0.57	0.52	0.18
22	1.00	0.23	0.21	0.64	0.52	0.33
23	0.50	0.25	0.50	0.35	0.40	0.11
24	0.39	0.20	0.16	0.31	0.26	0.09
25	0.29	0.10	0.07	0.31	0.19	0.11
26	0.44	0.21	0.18	0.31	0.29	0.10
27	0.21	0.21	0.14	0.39	0.24	0.09
28	0.72	0.17	0.18	0.32	0.35	0.22
29	0.16	0.04	0.54	0.22	0.24	0.18
30	0.56	0.18	0.23	0.37	0.34	0.15
31	0.76	0.34	0.45	0.52	0.52	0.15
32	0.88	0.42	0.75	0.81	0.72	0.18
33	0.63	0.26	0.43	0.56	0.47	0.14

Notes:
[a] Share of patents held by firms patenting for the first time in the period 1978–86.
[b] Average.
[c] Standard deviation.

differ consistently across technological classes. These differences, related to the characteristics of the relevant technological regime, may discriminate among different patterns of innovative activity, some of which are closer to Schumpeter Mark I and some to Schumpeter Mark II.

In order to explore these differences, it is necessary (i) to examine what kinds of relationship exist between the various indicators of the patterns of technological change supporting either of the two Schumpeterian models; and (ii) to identify groups of technological classes in which different but coherent relationships emerge between such variables. In particular, Schumpeter Mark II (deepening) technological classes should be characterised by a high degree of concentration of innovative activities, systematically associated with high degrees of stability in the hierarchy of innovators, a major role for large firms and a low share of new innovators. On the other hand, Schumpeter Mark I (widening) should be characterised by a lower degree of concentration of innovative activities, systematically associated with a lower degree of stability in the hierarchy of innovators, a greater role for small firms and a higher share of new innovators.

Widening and deepening patterns of innovative activities

In order to explore empirically the relationships between various indicators of the patterns of innovative activity, a principal components analysis for all the technological classes in each country was performed (not reported here). This exercise generated, in all four countries, one dominant factor which captured around 50 per cent of the variance and a second component which accounted for 20–25 per cent of the variance. These two factors clearly discriminate in all countries between the two groups of variables that characterise the two Schumpeterian patterns of innovative activities:

(i) indices of concentration and asymmetry, of the role of medium and large firms and of stability in the hierarchy of the persistent innovators
(ii) indices of new innovators and new leaders.

More broadly, the empirical analysis identified a more general dimension which could be labelled 'stability'. High stability is defined by:

(i) low ease of innovative entry (NATALITY and NEWLEADERS)
(ii) low change in the hierarchy of persistent innovators (SPEA).

Stability emerges as a very important feature of the patterns of innovative activities.

Patterns of innovative activities were analysed at two different levels: three macro technological *families* (mechanical, chemical and electronics) and thirty-three technological *classes*. At the macro technological level, major differences in the patterns of innovative activities can be found reflecting the widening and deepening models. Chemicals and electronics have the characteristics of the Schumpeter Mark II model, while mechanical industries show a Schumpeter Mark I model.

At the technological class level, it is indeed possible to define two groups of technological classes which can be labelled as Schumpeter Mark I and Schumpeter Mark II. In spite of the fact that some variability emerges in a between-country analysis, technological classes systematically characterised in all four countries by similar levels of concentration and stability, and by similar roles of large firms and new innovators, have been identified. Two major groups of technological classes emerge (see table 9.5). These groups have been confirmed by principal components analysis performed for each country (not reported here).

A first group broadly represents Schumpeter Mark I and the widening pattern of innovative activities: low concentration of innovative activities, symmetry among firms, instability in the ranking of innovators, high innovative natality and the importance of small innovative firms. It is composed of ten classes as listed in table 9.5 (a). Overall, this group includes the mechanical group and the 'traditional' industries.

A second group represents Schumpeter Mark II and the deepening pattern of innovative activities: high concentration and asymmetry among firms, stability in the hierarchy of innovators, low innovative natality and the importance of large and medium-sized innovative firms. This group is composed of fourteen classes as listed in table 9.5 (c). Thus, the Schumpeter Mark II model characterises most of the chemical and the electrical-electronic industries.

The remaining technological classes do not fit neatly into either of the first two groups. Two other small groups, however, are closer to Schumpeter Mark I classes than to Schumpeter Mark II ones. One has low concentration, high innovative birth rate, but relatively large firm size (table 9.5 (b)). It includes chemical processes and general industrial apparatus (electrical). The other also has low concentration, but low innovative birth rates and mainly medium and large firms (table 9.5 (d)). It includes electrical devices and systems, and instruments and controls.

The role of stability in international technological performance

One final question concerns the possible relationship between specific variables which define the pattern of innovative activities and technological performance. This has been a long-debated topic in the economics of technological change. Earlier results (Pavitt and Patel, 1991) have shown that no detectable relationship seems to exist between the 'traditional' Schumpeterian variables (such as concentration of the innovative activities and size of the innovative firms) and various measures of performance. Two

Table 9.5. *Taxonomy of patterns of innovative activity*

(a) Schumpeter I; low concentration, low stability, high birth rate, low firm size

    non-metallic minerals, glass and other materials
    metallurgical and other mineral processes
    apparatus for chemicals, food, glass etc.
    general industrial equipment (non-electrical)[a]
    non-electrical specialised and misc. industrial equipment
    metallurgical and metal-working equipment
    assembling and material-handling apparatus
    other transport equipment (excluded aircraft)
    miscellaneous metal products
    textile, clothing, leather, wood products

(b) Low concentration, high birth rate, high size[b]

    chemical processes
    general industrial apparatus (electrical)

(c) Schumpeter II; high concentration, high stability, low birth rate, high firm size

    inorganic chemicals
    organic chemicals
    agricultural chemicals
    hydrocarbons, mineral oils, fuel, igniting devices
    bleaching, dyeing and disinfecting
    drugs and bio-affecting agents
    plastics and rubber products
    nuclear reactors and systems
    power plants
    road vehicles and engines
    telecommunications
    semiconductors
    calculators, computers, other office equipment
    photography and photocopying

(d) Low concentration, low birth rate, high firm size

    electrical devices and systems
    instruments and control

(e) Other technological classes

    food and tobacco (processes and products)
    aircraft
    mining and well machinery and processes
    image and sound equipment
    other (ammunitions and weapons, road structure, bridges and animal husbandry)

Notes:
[a] The index of stability, SPEA, has a high value in two countries and the index of entry in the top ten innovators has a low value in three countries.
[b] The index of stability does not provide a uniform classification for all these classes, with the exception of aircraft and instruments.

reasons may explain this absence of a significant relationship. First, it may well be that such lack of correlation is due to the fact that the variables which may have an impact on international technological performance are not the 'traditional' Schumpeterian variables related to concentration or size. Second, the relationship may be different in the two groups of technological classes ('widening' and 'deepening').

In order to assess these relationships for all technological classes, principal components analysis for all technological classes was performed introducing a measure of international specialisation in innovative activities: revealed technological advantages with respect to total world patents (RTA) and to the total patents held by the four countries considered (RTA4). RTA (RTA4) is the world (four countries') share of a country in a technological class over the world (four countries') share of that country in all technological classes. RTA (RTA4) greater than one shows specialisation of a country in a technological class, while RTA (RTA4) less than one shows non-specialisation. The results from principal components analysis (not reported here) point to the important role played by the indicators of 'stability' in relation to performance, while the traditional variables such as concentration or size do not show any clear relationship with technological performance.

Exploratory regression analysis for all technological classes[5] with RTA4 as the dependent variable (see table 9.6) confirms the significant role played by SPEA in influencing RTA4.[6] In this regression, standardised values (HERFS, SPEAS, SIZES and NATS) were also used: they were calculated by dividing each variable by the average value of each country. Stability emerges from the regression analysis as the key factor affecting international technological specialisation and highlights the fact that 'creative accumulation' is a fundamental property of technological change: firms continuously active in a certain technological domain accumulate knowledge and expertise, and are able to master effectively and perform successfully in that technology.

Schumpeterian patterns of innovation and international technological specialisation

The second type of argument advanced previously (i.e. that the relationship between 'traditional' Schumpeterian variables and technological performance may be present but may be different between Schumpeter I and Schumpeter II types of sector) was explored by examining a restricted set of twenty-two Schumpeter I and II technological classes. Three key results emerged from regression analysis.

Table 9.6. *Factors affecting revealed technological advantages (RTA4) of four countries (FRG, France, UK, Italy): 31 technological classes[a]*

Dependent variable: RTA4

Independent variables	Specifications		
INTERCEP	0.826***	0.782***	0.786***
	[0.192]	[0.177]	[0.176]
HERF	−0.014	−0.118	
	[0.275]	[0.291]	
SPEA	0.389***	0.393***	
	[0.093]	[0.091]	
SIZE	−0.014		
	[0.193]		
NATALITY	−0.027		
	[0.166]		
HERFS			0.012
			[0.027]
SPEAS			0.174***
			[0.042]
SIZES		0.0583	0.039
		[0.124]	[0.126]
NATS		−0.027	−0.008
		[0.071]	[0.072]
No. of observations	124	124	124
d.o.f.	123	123	123
R^2	0.143	0.147	0.145
Adj. R^2	0.114	0.118	0.116
F value	4.968	5.111	5.025
Root MSE	0.257	0.257	0.257
Error mean square	0.066	0.066	0.066

Notes:
[a] Agricultural chemicals (class 3) and nuclear reactors and systems (class 18) have been eliminated from the original sample of 33 technological classes.
HERFS = standardised value of HERFINDAHL (per country).
SPEAS = standardised value of SPEA (per country).
SIZES = standardised value of SIZE (per country).
NATS = standardised value of NATALITY (per country).
Numbers in square brackets indicate standard errors.
  * Significant at the 10% level.
 ** Significant at the 5% level.
*** Significant at the 1% level.

Table 9.7. *Factors affecting revealed technological advantages (RTA4) of four countries (FRG, France, UK, Italy): 22 technological classes*

Dependent variable: RTA4

Independent variables	Specifications		
INTERCEP	0.477*	0.43*	0.431*
	[0.282]	[0.253]	[0.249]
HERF	0.334	−0.084	
	[0.354]	[0.363]	
SPEA	0.513***	0.381***	
	[0.134]	[0.119]	
SIZE	0.081		
	[0.277]		
NATALITY	0.587		
	[0.296]		
HERFS			0.009
			[0.035]
SPEAS			0.184
			[0.055]
SIZES		0.391**	0.356
		[0.178]	[0.178]
NATS		−0.04	−0.009
		[0.121]	[0.122]
DUMMY	0.892*	0.776	0.702
	[0.578]	[0.473]	[0.511]
DHERF	2.141	1.684	
	[3.3]	[3.118]	
DSPEA	−0.125	−0.015	
	[0.299]	[0.293]	
DSIZE	−0.710		
	[0.549]		
DNAT	−1.089**		
	[0.541]		
DHERFS			0.136
			[0.271]
DSPEAS			−0.037
			[0.14]
DSIZES		−0.779***	−0.674**
		[0.323]	[0.345]
DNATS		−0.036	−0.028
		[0.203]	[0.204]

Table 9.7. (*cont.*)

Dependent variable: RTA4			
Independent variables		Specifications	
No. of observations	88	88	88
d.o.f.	87	87	87
R^2	0.218	0.230	0.237
Adj. R^2	0.128	0.141	0.150
F value	2.417	2.586	2.701
Root MSE	0.253	0.251	0.250
Error mean square	0.064	0.063	0.063

Notes:
HERFS = standardised value of HERFINDAHL (per country).
SPEAS = standardised value of SPEA (per country).
SIZES = standardised value of SIZE (per country).
NATS = standardised value of NATALITY (per country).
Numbers in square brackets indicate standard errors.
 * Significant at the 10% level.
 ** Significant at the 5% level.
 *** Significant at the 1% level.

First, the introduction of a dummy variable D distinguishing Schumpeter Mark I from Schumpeter Mark II classes in regression analysis (see table 9.7) confirms that Schumpeter Mark I technological classes (with a dummy D) have specific and somewhat different effects on international technological performance (RTA4) compared to Schumpeter Mark II classes.

Second, exploratory regression analysis for Schumpeter Mark I and Schumpeter Mark II technological classes (see tables 9.8 and 9.9) confirms the significant role played by the 'stability' factor (in particular SPEA) in both the deepening and the widening groups of technological classes.

Third, SIZE is significant but has different coefficient signs in Schumpeter I (negative) and Schumpeter II (positive). This means that in widening patterns of innovative activities an industrial structure characterised by innovators of smaller size is more conducive to a satisfactory technological performance than a structure composed of larger-sized innovators. In deepening patterns of innovative activities an industrial structure characterised by innovators of larger size is more conducive to a satisfactory international technological performance than a structure composed of

Table 9.8. *Factors affecting revealed technological advantages (RTA4) of four countries (FRG, France, UK, Italy): 10 Schumpeter Mark I (widening) technological classes*

Dependent variable: RTA4			
Independent variables		Specifications	
INTERCEP	1.369***	1.206***	1.132***
	[0.384]	[0.304]	[0.346]
HERF	2.476	1.6	
	[2.5]	[2.36]	
SPEA	0.388**	0.365*	
	[0.204]	[0.204]	
SIZE	−0.629**		
	[0.36]		
NATALITY	−0.502		
	[0.346]		
HERFS			0.145
			[0.208]
SPEAS			0.147
			[0.1]
SIZES		−0.389	−0.318
		[0.205]	[0.23]
NATS		−0.076	−0.038
		[0.124]	[0.127]
No. of observations	40	40	40
d.o.f.	39	39	39
R^2	0.214	0.225	0.206
Adj. R^2	0.124	0.137	0.115
F value	2.385	2.545	2.272
Root MSE	0.193	0.192	0.194
Error mean square	0.037	0.037	0.038

Notes:
HERFS = standardised value of HERFINDAHL (per country).
SPEAS = standardised value of SPEA (per country).
SIZES = standardised value of SIZE (per country).
NATS = standardised value of NATALITY (per country).
Numbers in square brackets indicate standard errors.
  * Significant at the 10% level.
 ** Significant at the 5% level.
*** Significant at the 1% level.

Table 9.9. *Factors affecting revealed technological advantages (RTA4) of four countries (FRG, France, UK, Italy): 12 Schumpeter Mark II (deepening) technological classes*

Dependent variable: RTA4

Independent variables	Specifications		
INTERCEP	0.447	0.430	0.431
	[0.327]	[0.293]	[0.286]
HERF	0.334	−0.084	
	[0.41]	[0.42]	
SPEA	0.513***	0.381***	
	[0.156]	[0.138]	
SIZE	0.081		
	[0.321]		
NATALITY	0.587*		
	[0.343]		
HERFS			0.009
			[0.04]
SPEAS			0.184***
			[0.063]
SIZES		0.391*	0.356*
		[0.207]	[0.205]
NATS		−0.04	−0.009
		[0.14]	[0.14]
No. of observations	48	48	48
d.o.f.	47	47	47
R^2	0.215	0.227	0.245
Adj. R^2	0.142	0.155	0.174
F value	2.952	3.164	3.484
Root MSE	0.294	0.291	0.288
Error mean square	0.086	0.085	0.083

Notes:
HERFS = standardised value of HERFINDAHL (per country).
SPEAS = standardised value of SPEA (per country).
SIZES = standardised value of SIZE (per country).
NATS = standardised value of NATALITY (per country).
Numbers in square brackets indicate standard errors.
  * Significant at the 10% level.
 ** Significant at the 5% level.
*** Significant at the 1% level.

smaller firms. In a sense, the more a country has a structural feature that emphasises the 'right' dimension of the Schumpeterian pattern in terms of size, the better is its international technological performance.

Conclusions

This chapter has demonstrated the following:

(i) Patterns of innovative activities differ systematically across technological classes.

(ii) Remarkable similarities emerge across countries in the patterns of innovative activities for each technological class. This result strongly suggests that 'technological imperatives' and technology-specific factors (closely linked to technological regimes) play a major role in determining the patterns of innovative activities across countries.

(iii) It is possible to define two groups of technological classes in which innovative activities are organised according to either the Schumpeter Mark I or the Schumpeter Mark II model. The first represents a 'widening' pattern and the second a 'deepening' pattern of innovative activities. The former group comprises the mechanical industries and the 'traditional' sectors; the latter comprises chemicals and the electrical-electronic industries. Other technological classes show intermediate patterns, as a consequence of the specific features of the relevant technological regime.

(iv) Each of the two groups emphasises specific variables that affect international technological performance. In Schumpeter Mark I technological classes an industrial structure in which innovators are small is more conducive to technological performance than an industrial structure in which innovators are of a larger size. The opposite is true for Schumpeter Mark II technological classes.

(v) An additional dimension – 'stability' – emerges as an important feature of the patterns of innovative activity: technological performance is strongly associated with the emergence of a stable group of innovators, who innovate consistently and continuously over time, rather than with concentration or firm size. This result holds in both deepening and in widening technological classes.

This last result concerning the effect of stability on performance opens up several important theoretical questions and policy issues and calls for further research. From the theoretical point of view, it confirms the cumulative nature of technological change and vindicates the Schumpeterian insight that the patterns of innovative activities are to be analysed in an explicitly dynamic context. As far as policy is concerned, the implication is that a primary focus of government action should be on creating, strengthening and widening a core group of consistent and continuous innovators, as a necessary complement to actions directed towards the support to innovation in new, small firms.

Notes

1 Università L. Bocconi, Milan. F. Anzeloni, S. Breschi, F. Lissoni and M. Nannini provided skilful research assistance in the preparation and elaboration of the data. R. Helg provided useful advice. Research for this chapter was supported by the Italian CNR.
2 Malerba and Orsenigo (1993) provide a full discussion of these relationships and some examples taken from specific industries.
3 We wish to thank Keith Pavitt and Pari Patel of SPRU who allowed us to use this database.
4 Details may be obtained from the authors.
5 Agricultural chemicals and nuclear reactors and systems, which fall in the Schumpeter Mark II group, have not been included in regression analyses concerning revealed technological advantages, because they are too small in terms of the absolute number of patents and might therefore bias the results.
6 A spurious correlation exists between SIZE and RTA4 (the measure of international specialisation) since the same term, i.e. the number of patents of a given technological class, appears in the denominator of the first indicator and in the numerator of the second indicator. Similarly, in the relatioship between NATALITY and RTA4 the number of patents of a given technological class in the period 1978–86 appears in the denominator of the first indicator and is included in the numerator of the second term (total number of patents in the period 1969–86).

References

Cohen, W. and Levin, R. 1989. Empirical studies of innovation and market structure, in R. Schmalensee and R. Willig (eds.), *Handbook of Industrial Organization*, Amsterdam, North Holland.
Dosi, G. 1988. Sources, procedures and microeconomic effects of innovation, *Journal of Economic Literature*, 26: 1120–71.
Gort, M. and Klepper, S. 1982. Time paths in the diffusion of product innovations, *Economic Journal*, 92: 630–53.
Griliches, Z. 1990. Patent statistics as economic indicators: a survey, *Journal of Economic Literature*, 28: 1661– 707.
Heimler, A., Malerba, F. and Peretto, P. 1993. Sources, appropriability and directions of technological change: the cases of the United States and Italy, *BNL Quarterly Review*, no.185: 225–42.
Kamien, M. and Schwartz, N. 1982. *Market Structure and Innovation*, Cambridge, Cambridge University Press.
Klepper, S. 1992, Entry, exit and innovation over the product life cycle: the dynamics of first mover advantages, declining product innovation and market failure,

266 Franco Malerba and Luigi Orsenigo

paper presented at the conference of the International J. A. Schumpeter Society, Kyoto, August.

Levin, R., Cohen, W. and Mowery, D. 1985. R&D appropriability, opportunity and market structure: new evidence on some Schumpeterian hypotheses, *American Economic Review, Papers and Proceedings*, 75(2): 20–4.

Malerba, F. and Orsenigo, L. 1990. Technological regimes and patterns of innovation: a theoretical and empirical investigation of the Italian case, in A. Heertje, and M. Perlman (eds.), *Evolving Technology and Market Structure*, Ann Arbor, Michigan University Press.

1993. Technological regimes and firm behavior, *Industrial and Corporate Change*, 2: 45–71.

Nelson, R. (ed.) 1993. *National Innovation Systems*, New York, Oxford University Press.

Nelson, R. and Winter, S. 1982. *An Evolutionary Theory of Economic Change*, Cambridge, Mass., Bellknap Press.

Pavitt, K. and Patel, P. 1991. Europe's technological performance, in C. Freeman, M. Sharp, and W. Walker (eds.), *Technology and the Future of Europe*, London, Pinter.

1992. Contemporary patterns of technological change: the widespread (and neglected) importance of improvements in mechanical technologies, paper presented at the conference 'The Role of Technology in Economics: A Conference in Honour of N. Rosenberg', Stanford University, November.

Schumpeter, J.A. 1934. *The Theory of Economic Development*, Cambridge, Mass., Harvard University Press.

1942. *Capitalism, Socialism and Democracy*, New York, Harper.

Utterback, J.M. and Abernathy, W.J. 1975, A dynamic model of product and process innovation, *Omega*, 3(6): 639–56.

Appendix

List of the 33 technological classes
1 Inorganic chemicals
2 Organic chemicals
3 Agricultural chemicals
4 Chemical processes
5 Hydrocarbons, mineral oils, fuel, igniting devices
6 Bleaching, dyeing and disinfecting
7 Drugs and bio-affecting agents
8 Plastics and rubber products
9 Non-metallic minerals, glass and other materials
10 Food and tobacco (processes and products)
11 Metallurgical and other mineral processes
12 Apparatus for chemicals, food, glass, etc.
13 General industrial equipment (non-electrical)
14 General industrial apparatus (electrical)

15 Non-electrical specialised and misc. industrial equipment
16 Metallurgical and metal-working equipment
17 Assembling and material-handling apparatus
18 Nuclear reactors and systems
19 Power plants
20 Road vehicles and engines
21 Other transport equipment (excluding aircraft)
22 Aircraft
23 Mining and well machinery and processes
24 Telecommunications
25 Semiconductors
26 Electrical devices and systems
27 Calculators, computers, other office equipment
28 Image and sound equipment
29 Photography and photocopying
30 Instruments and controls
31 Miscellaneous metal products
32 Textile, clothing, leather and wood products
33 Other (ammunitions and weapons, road structures, bridges and plant and animal husbandry)

10 Technology systems and technology policy in an evolutionary framework

STAN METCALFE

In this chapter I propose to sketch some general aspects of an emerging evolutionary perspective on technology policy. This perspective has developed out of the wide range of literature on innovation summarised by Freeman (1994) and I do not propose to go over this ground again. Rather I shall draw out some of the themes which lead to the evolutionary perspective and to a concern with the institutional context of innovative activity. Details of policy I will not have space for and the reader is referred to the relevant literature (Tisdel, 1981; Rothwell, 1986; OECD, 1992; Nelson, 1992a; Tassey, 1992). Suffice it to say that policies and policy frameworks differ across countries and vary within countries over time. Indeed, the relation of policy frameworks to wider cultural and historical conditions remains a much under-investigated topic. The chapter falls into three sections. The first compares and contrasts market failure and evolutionary perspectives on innovation, leading to a distinction between the optimising and the adaptive policy-maker. The second section introduces recent themes in the accumulation of technological capability, of which the ideas surrounding technology paradigms and technology systems are of particular importance. The final section presents an application of these ideas to the concept of a national innovation system.

Old and new in the policy economics of innovation

Market failure

We cannot avoid from the outset some brief comments on the traditional welfare economic foundations of technology policy and the contrasting evaluation frameworks provided by the established equilibrium and recent evolutionary approaches to technological change. Left to itself will a market economy allocate the appropriate volume of resources to the generation and application of new technology? This is the traditional question.

In the equilibrium view the starting point is the proposition that states of perfectly competitive equilibrium are characterised by market prices which measure the marginal valuations of inputs and outputs attributable to individuals as consumers, producers and suppliers of production inputs. Such perfectly competitive states support Pareto-efficient allocations of resources in which the welfare of any one individual cannot be enhanced without diminishing the welfare of at least one other individual.

Much of the traditional economic theory of technology policy is concerned with the so-called 'market failures' which prevent the attainment of Pareto equilibria by violating one or other of the conditions for perfect competition (Hall, 1986; Wolf, 1986; Stoneman, 1987). The most important of these violations are related to missing or distorted markets. Put briefly, future markets for contingent claims in an uncertain world do not exist in any sense sufficiently for individuals to trade risks in an optimal fashion and establish prices which support the appropriate marginal conditions. Because the appropriate price structure is missing, distortions abound and the policy problem is to identify and correct those distortions. Missing markets imply constrained efficiency and constrained effects of policy intervention. Moreover, missing markets imply the need for agents to form expectations on the likely private values of their actions, expectations which policy can certainly influence. In such cases the question naturally arises of whether non-market processes – direct bargaining or political activity, for example – should be promoted to improve resource allocation (Newbery, 1990). Since the development of technology is uncertain and future-orientated it is certainly susceptible to these missing market distortions. The innovation process both generates and is influenced by uncertainty and this aspect of market failure is particularly damaging to the possibility of a Pareto-efficient allocation of resources to invention and innovation. The difficulty is deeply embedded in the nature of technical knowledge, the creation of which depends upon the establishment of information asymmetries (Dosi, 1988). In a quite fundamental sense, innovations and information asymmetries are one and the same phenomenon. Indeed such asymmetries can scarcely be termed market imperfections when they are necessary conditions for any technical change to occur in a market economy. As Stiglitz (1991) makes clear, the resulting unequal distribution of knowledge creates multiple problems of adverse selection and moral hazard which in turn deny the possibility of Pareto-optimal market processes. Notice that this involves much more than a trade-off between dynamic and static efficiency. Rather it is saying that innovation and information asymmetries are inseparable and thus innovation and Pareto optimality are fundamentally incompatible.

While problems of asymmetric information are at the heart of technology policy, other aspects of market failure are also relevant. Appropriation externalities have always been recognised as a major constraint on the incentives to innovate, as reflected in the fact that the patent system is one of the longest-established instruments of technology policy. Patents are the institutional device whereby market economies seek to cope with the peculiarities of knowledge production; limiting appropriability at the cost of creating temporary monopoly rights in exploitation. Similarly, the public good attributes of scientific and technological knowledge imply that market solutions to the allocation of resources to innovation will not be efficient. Finally, the indivisibilities inherent in the innovation process imply that there are increasing returns to the exploitation of technology and that it will be necessary for firms to retain some market power if they are to recover the costs of innovation. At best, an innovating industry can be monopolistically competitive, and from this different angle, Pareto efficiency and innovation are seen to be incompatible (Dasgupta and Stiglitz, 1980a; Dixit, 1988).

While the case for technology policy as a corrective to market failure is well established, one needs to recognise that government interventions can fail as well (Krueger, 1991). For a variety of reasons, imperfect information, the separation between those who benefit and those who pay, bureaucratic capture, pressure group activity, and political myopia, governments may undertake mistaken interventions (Eads and Nelson, 1971; Henderson, 1977; Wolf, 1987). It does not automatically follow that government policy will be welfare-improving. This is particularly so with respect to innovative activities, the formulation of which entails access to detailed microeconomic and social information. Indeed it has long been recognised that the strength of a market economy *vis-à-vis* a centrally planned economy is precisely the efficiency of and flexibility of the former in terms of the decentralised and distributed gathering, storing and communicating of detailed information (Nelson and Winter, 1982; Nelson, 1987).

The evolutionary perspective

At this point we turn to the evolutionary approach to technical change and the implications for policy. Firmly rooted in the behavioural theory of the firm its focus is upon decision rules, learning capabilities and adaptive behaviour and the interactions between these behaviours and various economic selection mechanisms (Nelson and Winter, 1982). The central policy issue that it prompts is the contrast between efficiency and the innovative creativity of firms. Creativity is intimately connected to uncertainty and the discovery processes by which firms find and exploit their own choice sets. Whether it is because of organisation, the individuals involved or historical happenstance, no two firms are expected to innovate in identical fashion and it is this emphasis on the decentralised emergence of technological diversity which is a defining characteristic of the evolutionary approach.

While there are a number of evolutionary approaches (Witt, 1991; Hodgson, 1993), they have in common a fundamental concern with processes of economic change. In assessing the contribution which they can make to technology policy, it is vital to understand the ways in which they jointly represent a change in perspective from the equilibrium viewpoint. For present purposes, evolutionary economics can be reduced to two central concerns, namely the processes which determine the range of available innovations, and the processes which alter the relative contributions which different innovations make to economic welfare. The fundamental issues are dynamic and intimately connected to a quite different view of competition from that deployed in equilibrium theory. Moreover, change is not to be interpreted as response to exogenous changes in data but rather change which occurs endogenously without reference to adjustment to some equilibrium state. This entails a shift from perceiving competition in terms of price to viewing competition in terms of those decisive cost and quality advantages which arise from innovative behaviour. It entails a shift from perceiving competition in terms of states of equilibrium characterised by different market structures, to competition as a process of change premised on the existence of the differential behaviour of firms and other economic agents (Downie, 1958; Nelson and Winter, 1982; Metcalfe and Gibbons, 1989). It is only with this process perspective that the role of entrepreneurial behaviour becomes intelligible, since an equilibrium theory cannot, as a matter of logic, determine the rewards to entrepreneurship which are necessarily transitional. It is only in the process perspective that many competitive behaviours of firms are explicable, behaviours which from an equilibrium perspective are typically interpreted as anticompetitive market imperfections. Indeed it is central to the evolutionary perspective that economic progress is only possible in what, from an equilibrium viewpoint, is an inefficient world. It is not in the least surprising therefore that scholars with a concern to understand historical patterns of technical change have begun to develop evolutionary theory (Mokyr, 1990, 1991). Equally, it is not surprising that together with concepts of individual equilibrium they have abandoned optimisation as the route to explaining individual behaviour and replaced it by adaptive learning and the creation of novelty. It is by this change in approach that attention is switched to the strategic, cognitive and organisational aspects of firms to explain why they behave differently.

A central purpose of policy now becomes that of stimulating the technological and innovative capabilities of the economic system: enhancing the learning processes in firms and other institutions to generate variety in behaviour. The focus of attention ceases to be market failure *per se* and instead becomes the enhancement of competitive performance and the promotion of structural change (Mowery and Rosenberg, 1989). Evolutionary policy is fundamentally tied up with the creativity of firms and supporting institutions, and, arguably, there is no more powerful source of differential behaviour than that provided by technological innovation. This granted, the problem in understanding reduces to the economic significance of diverse behaviour and here the distinctive feature of evolutionary theory is its intrinsic capacity to make sense of variety. Once this step is taken, one can immediately recognise that evolutionary economic processes are essentially open-ended and unpredictable. As Austrian and other subjectivist economists are fond of emphasising, there is an irreducible element of discovery in the working of the market process (Hayek, 1948; Buchanan and Vanberg, 1991). None the less, although the emergence of novelty is unpredictable, the processes which translate novelty into coherent patterns of change are not, and it is on this distinction that the role of technology policy hinges. There is nothing unscientific about this: science is much more than prediction, certainly for a historical science such as the economics of technological change (Gould, 1990). The temptation to view these developments as an illegal 'epistemological transfer' from biology to economics is easily dismissed: biology is simply one of many applications of that particular mode of thinking which defines evolutionary analysis. It has no claim to be the only evolutionary science. Whether biology or mechanics provides the appropriate background for economic thinking is not a question which it is fruitful to pursue here.

For present purposes, evolution means two things: the gradual unfolding of phenomena in a cumulative and thus path-dependent way; and, quite separately, a dynamics of system behaviour which creates change and emerging structure from variety in behaviour. From the technology policy viewpoint, change is to be interpreted in three different and interdependent ways: the emergence of genuine novelties in the form of new design configurations; the internal development of existing design configurations through sequences of innovations; and the comparative diffusion of competing alternatives in a market environment. Two of the immediate consequences of this are that it is natural to see innovation and diffusion as inseparable processes, and that technological change and structural economic change go hand in hand. There is nothing further from the evolutionary argument than the belief that technological progress can be understood as if it were an aggregate process of balanced growth. It follows that traditionally two questions have defined the scope of evolutionary analysis, the origin of variety and the nature of selection. In biology the answer to the first question is found in the concept of blind variation, that is variation which is independent of selective advantage (Campbell, 1987). In economics, this obviously is not the whole story: while no treatment of innovation can ignore a stochastic element, it is also true that innovation represents guided and intentional variation (Hodgson, 1991) purposely undertaken in the pursuit of competitive advantage. Economic agents learn from experience and anticipate future states of the selective environment in a way quite unknown in biological or ecological selection. Naturally, this greatly enriches the scope of the theory. Indeed, as Nelson has repeatedly stressed it is this guided element in innovation which explains the rapid and sustained rates of progress in capitalist market economies. The concept of a selective environment also requires careful handling. In the simplest cases, it can be equated to a market mechanism within which users and suppliers interact in traditional fashion. However, this represents only one level and mode of selection. Any framework in which agents interact in order to choose between competing patterns of behaviour has selective properties. In particular, organisations create their own internal selection environments to choose between competing alternative futures and their associated patterns of behaviour. As the discussion below of innovation systems indicates, the degree of matching between choices made at different levels of technological selection exerts a strong influence on patterns of technological change. Beyond the traditional two questions, a third must also be raised, that of the outcomes of selection processes feeding back onto the subsequent generation of variety – indeed this aspect is crucial to a full understanding of the evolutionary dynamic. All selection processes consume the available variety, and if evolutionary change is to continue, variety must be continually recreated by some other mechanism. Two issues are important here: the role of inertia and institutional limits in setting bounds to the generation of variety, and positive feedback mechanisms which link the generation of variety to the exploitation of increasing returns and endogenous innovation, that is link it back to the selection process. That one can have a theory of variety generation is too far fetched: it is not possible to treat novelty as if it were an analytical concept and it is certainly not possible to anticipate the emergence of novelty. However, one can make considerable progress in identifying important feedbacks which keep a balance between variety generation and variety dissemination.

At this point we sense that a clear framework for policy analysis is emerging which distinguishes polices which influence variety generation from policies which influence selection processes. As far as variety generation is concerned one of the major contributions of the evolutionary school has been its insistence that the pattern of technological innovation depends on much more than the behaviour of individual firms. This leads us directly to the idea of technology systems and national systems of innovation. Similarly, the treatment of selection processes leads us to the treatment of technological competition and the diffusion of innovations. In this chapter we focus attention on the first of these.

Optimising and adaptive policy-making

It is perhaps useful to approach the issue of technology policy with the help of three distinctions. First, we have a distinction familiar to all scholars in this field between the generation of technology and its application, akin to the equally familiar but treacherous distinction between innovation and the diffusion of innovation. Second, one can distinguish policies which assume that the innovative capabilities of firms are given from those which seek to enhance these innovative capabilities. Third, and more importantly, is a distinction between optimising and adaptive approaches to policy-making.

Equilibrium economic theory provides the leading example of the optimising approach. Here the problem of technology policy appears as the identification and adoption of superior economic equilibria, defined in terms of an appropriate economic surplus criterion. Left to itself, the market mechanism will generally fail to produce the best possible allocation of resources to the development and application of technology: the source of the inefficiency rests in inappropriate incentive mechanisms or in imperfect distribution of information across economic agents. Firms always do the best they can but, for whatever reasons, the constraints they face are the wrong ones. To change incentives becomes the central policy concern, a way of thinking best summarised as the theory of the optimising policy-maker. Such a policy-maker seeks to maximise social welfare in the context of individual agents who seek to maximise their personal welfare, where social and private welfare being out of step defines the arena of policy choice. The favourite metaphor here is of the policy-maker as a fully informed social planner who can identify and implement optima. While market failure virtually defines the equilibrium approach to policy-making, the very ubiquity of market failure in an innovative economy limits its practical insights and limits its role to providing a general policy rationale. Theory predicts that firms may spend too little or too much on innovation, generate those innovations too early or too late, and generate innovations which are too similar or too different. The nature of the policy advice therefore depends on the specifics of each case.

Evolutionary approaches are less developed but clear lines of differentiation from the equilibrium approach have already been established. The fundamental difference is the displacement of equilibrium and optimisation as the organising concepts. As outlined above, evolutionary theory is concerned with why the world changes endogenously, with the way in which technological competition is the driving force behind structural change and economic development. Process and change, not equilibrium and state, are its central concerns. Imperfect information is an integral part of this process; indeed, the development of privileged information is the mainspring of profit opportunity in a capitalist market system. To paraphrase G. B. Richardson (1960), knowledge which is available to everybody provides a profit opportunity to nobody. The central policy problem becomes that of increasing the probability and the profitability of experimental behaviour. Thus, the attention of the evolutionary policy-maker shifts away from efficiency towards creativity, and patterns of adaptation to market stimuli and technological opportunity (Smith, 1991). In fact the policy problem becomes one of confronting the evolutionary paradox that competitive selection consumes its own fuel, destroying the very variety which drives economic change. To maintain economic change, the conditions must be set in place to regenerate the requisite degree of variety: it is upon this that the continuation of economic progress depends (Beer, 1985). This is not likely to be best pursued in terms of a policy of 'picking national winners', an approach which smacks too much of the optimising policy-maker, when in practice technological challenges are rarely well defined enough to make rational calculation possible. In fact, the adaptive, evolutionary policy-maker is far more concerned to influence process than to impose predetermined outcomes, far more concerned to enhance the adaptive, learning capabilities of firms. Within this framework it is not individual innovations which are the focus of attention but rather the conditions which draw forth a sequence of innovations from a particular design configuration in a process which is strongly shaped by the related diffusion processes. Technology policy should focus on co-evolving technological and market environments, not upon individual innovations.

In short our claim is that the evolutionary policy-maker adapts rather than optimises, and his central concern is the innovation process, the operation of the set of institutions within which technological capabilities are accumulated. The canonical policy problem is defined in terms of the dynamics of innovation in a world characterised by immense micro-complexity (Allen, 1988). Moreover, just as individuals operate under the constraints of localised, imperfect and uncertain information so does the adaptive policy-maker. There can be no presumption that the policy-maker has a superior understanding of market circumstances or technological information; rather what he does enjoy is superior co-ordinating ability across a diverse range of institutions. Technology policies can fail just as easily as the technology strategies of firms and the issue is how well policy-makers learn and adapt in the light of experience. Options are politically

and administratively constrained, policy-makers have objectives other than
the general welfare, and one cannot expect the policies which emerge to be
independent of the processes by which they are formed. There is also the
question of policy delivery, how a policy is to interact with the agents it
seeks to influence. Many routes are often available to deliver a given policy
to its intended recipients but little is known as yet about their relative
advantages. For example, a framework which requires firms to compete
against each other for support will produce different outcomes from a
policy of support which is available to all who are willing to join the queue
for public support. Despite the differences between the equilibrium and
evolutionary viewpoints they work with the same salient features of the
economic system. These are three in number: the opportunities to innovate,
the incentives to innovate and the distribution of the resources to innovate.
With these three pillars of policy the evolutionary and equilibrium theorists
share common ground but draw different conclusions. In the following we
shall focus primarily on questions of opportunity.

The accumulation of technological capability

Any discussion of innovative capabilities is premised on the assumption of
a relationship between the amount of effort devoted to innovation and the
resulting innovative outputs. Indeed, without some regularity between
innovative input and output, an innovation possibility frontier, there is little
for the policy-maker or the company strategist to relate to. Not surprisingly, this is how most formal thinking on innovation proceeds (Machlup,
1962; Nordhaus, 1969; Dasgupta and Stiglitz, 1980a; Gort and Wall, 1986).
For any given state of knowledge it is expected that greater innovative effort
results in greater innovative output, and it is this expectation which moti-
vates the resources firms allocate to innovation and the way in which the
process is organised in R&D laboratories. Not surprisingly, such a formulation raises a number of difficult questions relating to the units in which
inputs and outputs can and should be measured, and with respect to the
inherent uncertainty surrounding the innovation process. A range of case-
studies from many different sectors have made it clear that technological
accumulation is not random; rather, technologies develop in a structured
fashion within frameworks which, at least with the benefit of hindsight,
appear well defined (Sahal, 1981; Dosi, 1982; Zuscovitch, 1986; Pavitt,
1987; Dosi and Orsenigo, 1988). Central to this perspective on technological change is an emphasis on learning processes. In an obvious sense all
knowledge acquisition involves learning but it is clear that many distinct
kinds of learning can be distinguished. As Malerba (1992) has emphasised,
learning phenomena have a number of attributes in relation to technologi-

cal change: learning is costly and occurs in different parts of the firm; it involves the interaction between internal and external sources of knowledge; it is cumulative; and it supports localised and primarily incremental innovation. Indeed, a crucial aspect of the innovation process lies in the exchanges of information which take place between the developers and the users of new technology. Malerba distinguishes six categories of learning activity which we may regroup into three broader categories: learning which is a joint product of activities producing and using artifacts – the famous categories of learning by doing (Arrow, 1962) and learning by using (Rosenberg, 1982); learning which involves the interaction with external sources of knowledge located in other institutions, whether other firms as suppliers or customers, or science and technology agencies; and internal, directed learning which is typically organised around a formal R&D programme. Malerba convincingly argues that the different kinds of learning activity are productive of different kinds of technological change so that firms with different learning structures will generate different patterns of innovation. This diversity in sources of innovation experiments is central to the evolutionary approach to technical change. Notice that not all learning activity is carried out through formal R&D programmes, even though policy is often focused on this dimension. Hence policy to support technology should address the diversity of learning mechanisms and the conditions which enhance the learning capabilities of firms, and should reflect the fact that successful innovation requires learning about markets and user needs as well as learning about technology.

At least four further attributes of the innovation process must be stressed (Dosi and Orsenigo, 1988). First, and more than is the case with a conventional input/output relationship, innovation possibilities are anticipated relationships in the minds of technologists and research managers, relating an investment in innovative effort to an expected technological improvement. Obviously, different individuals in different organisational contexts will anticipate the possibilities with different degrees of imagination and accuracy, and this is a major element in explaining the variety in innovative performance among firms. How such technological expectations are formed is a legitimate policy concern. Second, and following directly, the relations between input and output are subject to considerable uncertainty; indeed, the unforeseen and unintended consequences of innovation programmes are central to the history of technical progress. In many cases we have uncertainty proper where no probability calculus can be applied; the experiments are one-off, they change the conditions for the next experiment and it is never possible to enumerate completely the set of possible outcomes. However, in those cases where the potential range of innovative outcomes can be listed, it is possible to apply a probability calculus and interpret the innovation possibility frontier as some average of a stochastic process. Many approaches can be followed to introduce risk: making the probability of discovery an increasing function of innovative effort (Loury, 1979; Dasgupta and Stiglitz, 1980b; Reinganum, 1989); applying the theory of order statistics to define the expectation of improved performance as a function of innovative effort (Evenson and Kislev, 1975; Nelson, 1982); or, as in much recent evolutionary theory, using Markov theory to define the probabilities with which innovations take place and the probability distribution of improvements (Nelson and Winter, 1982; Winter, 1986; Dosi *et al.*, 1993). For the policy-maker uncertainty is a fundamental issue, for there can be no guarantee of the payoffs from any programme to improve technology: failures will be mixed with successes in a no doubt politically disconcerting fashion. Third, the relationships between input and output take as given the current state of the art. However, the consequence of devoting resources to innovation is to change the state of the art, and so redefine the innovation possibilities for the next period. New knowledge and enhanced skills are typically joint products with the improved artifacts which define innovative outputs. In this regard, Machlup (1962) has made a very useful distinction between those innovative activities which are agenda-enhancing and those which are agenda-reducing. The former increase the productivity of future innovative effort, by identifying new innovation possibilities, while the latter reduce future possibilities. Thus, over time, innovation possibilities systematically shift the very meaning of the cumulativeness of technical change, with a presumption that within any one technology the pattern of change is ultimately agenda-reducing as the long-term limits on improvement are reached (Kuznets, 1954; Gort and Wall, 1986).

Fourth, the innovative possibility frontiers are not only technology-specific, they are also firm-specific (Pavitt, 1990; Nelson, 1992b). The productivity of the innovative process is very much an organisational issue, depending on the individuals involved and the way in which their creative endeavours are organised and connected with the rest of the firm. Some firms are weak, some are strong at innovation, and those which are strong at one stage in their history may subsequently wane in creativity. What is at stake here is the capability of the firm as an innovating institution: the opportunities it perceives; the incentives to which it reacts; the resources it can marshal; and its ability to *integrate* and manage the R&D process in relation to other activities in the firm. On all these aspects there is a rich literature and it is clear that the field of innovation is one of the best areas to observe the inherent variety which surrounds any creative activity. Much depends on the management of research and development and, although this cannot be our concern here, we can note the significance of practices such as parallel R&D programmes in determining R&D productivity (Nelson, 1961; Arditti and Levy, 1980).

The notion that innovation possibilities are firm-specific and vary systematically over time is also at the core of the rich product cycle literature on technological change (Abernathy, 1978; Utterback, 1979; Majumdar, 1982). Product cycle analysis identifies typical stages in the development of design configurations – a fluid early stage with many competing alternatives leading finally to a stage of technological maturity – and an innovation pattern in which an initial focus on product innovation is replaced by an increasing focus on process innovation. While not all technologies fit this pattern (Pavitt and Rothwell, 1976), there are a substantial number of innovations where the regularities in innovation and patterns of industry development are remarkably consistent. Indeed, the technology cycle appears to be matched by an industry cycle of dynamic adjustments in output levels and growth rates with an initial increase in the number of firms followed by a sharp decline to a stable level (Klepper and Grady, 1990; Klepper, 1992). All this, of course, is strongly reminiscent of the retardation theories of industrial dynamics first presented in the 1930s (Burns, 1935; Kuznets, 1954).

Dimensions of technology

Any understanding of technology policy must obviously be premised on a clear understanding of the nature of technology, and, in particular, the important differences and interrelations between science and technology. It is usual to define technology as the ability to carry out productive transformations. It is an ability to act, a competence to perform, translating materials, energy and information in one set of states into another, more highly valued set of states. For present purposes it is vital to distinguish technology as three interdependent forms (Layton, 1974): as knowledge, as skills and as artifacts. In principle, policies can be designed to influence each of these aspects of technology independently, although in most circumstances all three elements are jointly produced. The artifacts dimension, products and their methods of production, 'technique' as it is often called, is the central concern of firms who develop new and improved artifacts in the search for competitive advantage. The skills and knowledge necessary to underpin technique are also the concern of firms but they are also produced by a much wider set of institutions. In fact the central fact about the modern process of innovation is that it is based on a division of labour, as Adam Smith clearly foresaw when he wrote about the role of philosophers and men of speculation. Division of labour produces efficiency gains from specialisation and professionalisation but it also requires a framework to connect together the component contributions of different agents. As far as knowledge and skills are concerned this aspect of connectivity, or technology transfer, cannot be effectively co-ordinated by conventional markets, for reasons explained above. As we shall see, the connectivity of technology-producing institutions should be a central concern of technology policy.

The technological division of labour is reflected in the many different kinds and branches of knowledge which are relevant to the innovation process. Technology is much more than science, and innovation involves much more than technology. These different types of knowledge are not only produced in specialised institutions they are also accumulated by different mechanisms. No satisfactory classification of knowledge for innovation has yet been produced, although several important distinctions are often made (Vincenti, 1990). Fundamental, basic or pure knowledge is distinguished from applied and engineering knowledge, as in the Frascati definitions, a distinction based on the nature of the knowledge. Fundamental knowledge is usually defined in terms of the 'laws' of natural phenomena and their empirical verification by replicable, experimental methods. Applied knowledge is more specifically focused on particular generic productive transformations and may or may not be capable of verification by scientific means. A further distinction which is made is between curiosity-based knowledge and mission-based knowledge, a distinction related to the motivations behind the process of knowledge accumulation. Since the communication of knowledge is such a central element in the innovation process a further classification in terms of the codifiability of knowledge is of considerable importance. All knowledge is transmitted in a codified form as Arrow (1969, 1974) has emphasised. However, the code may be more or less explicit and this is the basis for distinguishing codifiable from tacit knowledge. The fundamental point is that different kinds of knowledge are associated with different costs of writing and subsequently translating technological codes. These encoding and decoding costs are fixed outlays relative to the use of the information, and when average fixed costs are high it is not likely to prove economic to transfer knowledge in a codified form. It is not the case that knowledge once produced is freely available to all who demand access to it. There are significant reception costs as well as transmission costs: on this distinction rest many of the connectivity problems within national technology systems. Codified knowledge embedded in journals and books is the standard method of communication in science; coding is economic because widespread dissemination is intrinsic to science. However, even codified statements involve some tacit elements which are not readily expressible in language, as with the individual skills of a scientist which contribute to the detailed method of an experiment. At the other limit we have purely tacit information which cannot be transmitted at all, being inseparable from the individual in which it is embodied. This is what is often meant by pure skill or pure genius: it cannot readily be replicated by anyone else. Now much of the knowledge which defines a technology lies between the extremes of purely codifiable and purely tacit. In science the method of accumulation is through an experimental research programme, with the design of the experiment guided by established lawlike relationships. It is central to the notion of validity in science that the results of experiments be replicable by other scientists and for this they must be codifiable in considerable detail. By contrast, a research programme in engineering science may lack the benefit of a precise scientific understanding of the relevant laws. The process of knowledge accumulation is primarily empirical as trial after trial yields a gradual improvement in understanding (Vincenti, 1990). Even in strongly science-based industries such as pharmaceuticals, paints and pesticides, the primary mode of technology accumulation is by way of empirical development (Pavitt, 1987). In fact, a great many important technological transformations take place with only the vaguest scientific understanding of the details of why they work. From the humble automotive battery to the dynamics of combustion in an engine the contribution of scientific knowledge only provides a general background to understanding. As the tacit component of knowledge increases, the significance of learning by observation and induction also increases. Accumulation is more via experience and communication is increasingly verbal and through personal contact. In this way the accumulation of tacit knowledge is intrinsically connected to learning by doing and by using, that is, it is linked inextricably to specified activities carried out by specific organisations.

Paradigms and systems

Recent work on technological change has brought these various considerations together under the twin themes of technology paradigms and technology systems. Dosi (1982) was the first to articulate the concept of a technology paradigm. The point is not that the idea of a scientific paradigm can be carried over more or less exactly to the study of technology but rather that any paradigm provides shared cognitive frameworks for the individuals and institutions seeking to advance the technology. In this it provides a framework to identify opportunities and a set of constraints on the kinds of technical improvement which can be considered. In short, a technology paradigm is a device for dealing with the tyranny of combinatorial explosion. If we think of a technology as a set of design concepts integrated together to form a design configuration, the force of this point can be made immediately. With n possible design concepts there are $2^n-(n+1)$ possible integrated technologies, an impossibly large number for n as small as 100. What paradigms do is to abstract from this set of all possible concept combinations the much smaller sub-set which have been discovered and demonstrated to be workable. Once a workable design configuration has been established it provides a framework within which technologists can define problems and identify solutions: it becomes the framework for incremental artifact improvement within a stable broad knowledge and skill base. Rather than being random, technological development is guided in such a way as to reduce the rate of mutational error. From this it is a short step to characterising paths of advance as trajectories (Dosi, 1982) or as innovation avenues (Sahal, 1985) or as dominant designs (Abernathy, 1978; Utterback and Suarez, 1993). Each label captures the idea of canalised or creodic development, that is, change within constrained opportunities. An excellent account of these issues has been provided in a study of the engineering of the Britannia railway bridge by Rosenberg and Vincenti (1985). They summarise the emergence of the chosen design configuration for the bridge in these terms: 'In a broader and more general sense, the engineers learned something perhaps more important. By struggling with their problem and forming conceptual models, they learned to think synthetically about the design of an important class of wrought iron structures. This *intellectual framework* [emphasis added] enabled them to combine empirical data, theoretical understanding, and artful surmise – each limited and incomplete – to attain their practical goal' (pp.30–4). This is a splendid example of the exemplar properties of a technological paradigm and its role in guiding the development of technology. We would simply add here the further insight that in setting up learning mechanisms to exploit specific technological opportunities, organisations inevitably develop a degree of commitment to the required mode of learning and it is this commitment to a specific learning structure and associated competencies which helps explain their inability to adapt to the emergence of new design configurations based on different knowledge paradigms. Hence they have great difficulty in adapting to the change in the set of technological possibilities and in many cases are forced out of the industry (Cooper and Schendal, 1976; Starbuck, 1983; Abernathy and Clark, 1985; Zuscovitch, 1986).

The second modern theme is the systemic properties of a technology. This occurs most obviously at the artifact level but equally it applies to the underlying design principles and their interaction. Thus, Henderson and Clark (1990) have usefully distinguished between technical change in the components of a system and technical change in terms of the system architecture, the way these components interact. This leads them to a fourfold innovation taxonomy which fruitfully expands the usual distinction between incremental and radical change. For present purposes, however, the significance of a system perspective is its implications for the guided nature of technical change. Compatibility between components and balance in their performance capabilities provides a binding constraint on the development of the system as a whole. To make the most of improvements in one component or sub-system, it is necessary to improve complementary elements and in some cases engage in a thorough redesign of the system's architecture. Several authors have drawn attention to this phenomenon as a guide to learning effects: Rosenberg writes of imbalances and focusing devices, Sahal of technological guideposts, and Hughes of reverse salients. Each of these concepts is based on a systemic view of technology and the opportunities and pressures which shape innovative activity. We shall note here that the systems perspective provides a hierarchy of levels at which change can occur, as system divides into sub-systems and components in repeated fashion, such that radical change at one level can equally be interpreted as incremental change at higher levels. On the same grounds as systems shape opportunities to learn, they also place interrelatedness constraints on what might be achieved. An improvement in one sub-system can only be adopted if the costs of engineering compatibility with the rest of the system keep the overall portfolio of changes economically feasible.

The significance of all this for policy is that any programme of technical development draws on different kinds of knowledge created in different institutions and accumulated by different mechanisms. The integration of the relevant information and the variety in modes of acquisition is the crucial aspect. A scientific research programme is different from an engineering research programme and both differ from a process of technical development for a particular artifact. Timescales of 'experiments', methods of acquiring knowledge and the objectives of the process are simply different. Technology policies need to be sensitive to the different sources of knowledge and the different motivations and methods which underpin its acquisition.

However, it should not be overlooked that innovation involves much more than the accumulation of technological knowledge. Schumpeter (1934), it will be remembered, argued that innovation and invention are quite independent phenomena, that the creation of technology and the application of technology are different economic functions. Teece (1986) has drawn attention to how innovation in firms depends on their command of important complementary assets to translate new technology into innovation, the absence of which may thwart success. A wealth of research has established that a detailed knowledge of customer needs is crucial to the innovation process, a fact that partly explains the poor results of major government civilian technology programmes which failed to take this into account. Innovation studies have also made it abundantly clear how success depends on a particular creative competence, that of blending together information from different sources in a novel way. Innovation is neither technology push nor demand pull; rather, it is a subtle and varying blend of the two (Langrish *et al.*, 1972; Mowery and Rosenberg, 1979; Freeman, 1982; Georghiou *et al.*, 1986). It is this experimental capability of capitalism which is arguably more significant than its efficiency properties, and it is certainly this decentralised and localised creativity which marks the evolutionary nature of economic change (Antonelli, 1994). As Hayek (1948) emphasised, the process of market competition is essentially a creative process of discovery, and it is counter-productive to conceive of such a process in the context of perfect knowledge and perfect foresight. But, equally, policy-makers are part of the same discovery process and are subject to the same limitations as the individuals whom they seek to influence.

A policy dichotomy

Provided one accepts the idea of technology design configurations and their embodiment in firm-specific innovation possibility frontiers, one can immediately distinguish two broad categories of technology policy. On the one hand, policy can induce firms to shift around their given innovation possibility frontiers, that is, to apply more or less innovative effort. On the other hand, policy can seek to shift the innovation possibility frontiers in a productivity-enhancing fashion. However, to apply this dichotomy the policy-maker must identify the relevant design configurations and judge the current possibilities for innovation within any given design configuration. The scope for technological improvement, the likely productivity of innovative effort, the significance of developments in the underpinning knowledge-bases and their location in different institutions must be understood in some detail if policy is not to collapse into vague generalities. In short, a technology systems perspective is central to the effective pursuit of policy. Each technology is different in terms of the relevant institutions and dynamic processes of improvement, and it is on a comprehension of these differences that the formulation of technology policy depends. That the technology system which supports innovation in agriculture is quite different from that which supports innovation in aeronautics, for example, has long been recognised. Our conclusion is that this insight carries one to a much finer level of analysis, namely to individual design configurations which are the building blocks of technological advance. Carlsson (1992) makes this abundantly clear, as do the recent findings of Malerba and Orsenigo (this volume, chapter 9) which emphasise the systematic differences in the innovation process across different technology classes, differences which are reasonably similar across advanced countries.

With this policy dichotomy in mind we can now propose a simple classification of technology policy issues. We present this in terms of the general choices which policy-makers face:

- choices to support the development of or the application of technology;
- choices about the particular design configurations on which policy will focus;
- choices between knowledge, skills and artifacts as the primary targets of policy support;
- choices about the particular firms and supporting institutions which will be the channels to improve technology;
- choices to support formal R&D programmes or less tangible learning process; and
- choices to formulate policy in isolation or in joint action with other nations.

In short, technology policy can focus on technology, on the institutions developing technology and on different stages in the innovation process. No wonder that it is so complicated an area of policy-making.

Technology systems and national systems of innovation

At this point the question arises of how one might categorise technology policy in the light of the above observations. A useful place to begin is with Justmann and Teubal (1986) who have advocated a distinction between policies directed (strategically) at the infrastructure of elements in the economy which facilitate innovation, and those which are directed (tactically) at the development of specific technologies. More recently, the infrastructure aspects have been brought together with the concept of a national system of innovation (Freeman, 1987; Lundvall, 1988, 1992; McKelvey, 1991). A national system of innovation is that set of distinct institutions which jointly and individually contribute to the development and diffusion of new technologies and which provides the framework within which governments form and implement policies to influence the innovation process. As such it is a system of interconnected institutions to create, store and transfer the knowledge, skills and artifacts which define new technologies. The element of nationality follows not only from the domain of technology policy but also from elements of shared language and culture which bind the system together, and from the national focus of other policies, laws and regulations which condition the innovative environment. In the operation of national systems, governments play an important part in their support of science and technology generally and in their procurement of technologies to meet the needs of the executive. To define such a system empirically one must locate the boundaries, its component institutions and the ways in which they are linked together (OECD, 1992). Many institutions are involved: private firms working individually or in collaboration, universities and other educational bodies; professional societies and government laboratories; private consultancies and industrial research associations. Each national system reflects a strong division of labour, and owing to the economic peculiarities of information, a predominance of co-ordination by non-market means. When organised appropriately, national systems can be a powerful engine of progress. Poorly organised and connected they may seriously inhibit the process of innovation (Freeman, 1987).

Among modern industrial societies, private firms with an explicitly defined R&D function are key elements in any national system of innovation. Their motivation is to improve profitability through product and process innovation, by creating technology of an essentially proprietary nature. They are the primary institutions for designing and developing new technological artifacts and for applying them in the search for competitive advantage. In the process they also have a major impact on the skill and knowledge dimensions of technology, particularly the development of tacit knowledge. Some large firms also make considerable efforts in many applied and engineering sciences. The research budgets and facilities of some of these firms would be the envy of many a well-founded university department. By contrast, universities and other educational establishments are only minimally concerned with the development of artifacts, and make their major contributions in terms of knowledge and skills. Universities are composed of highly specialised groups of individuals, advancing knowledge and training students in the basic methods, findings and operating procedures of distinct disciplines. Unlike firms, universities and the science and engineering departments they contain are essentially open institutions committed to widespread dissemination of knowledge (Nelson, 1987). Some of the research is fundamental in nature but substantial proportions of university research effort are devoted to the applied or so-called transfer sciences (OECD, 1992), which act as a bridge between fundamental science and technology. Computer science, civil engineering, pharmacology, plant breeding science, medical science are typical transfer sciences, each one tied to identifiable technological activities while drawing on insights from a range of fundamental disciplines. Universities not only create new knowledge, they also act as repositories of the stock of established knowledge which may have important generic implications for a whole range of technologies including traditional ones. Indeed, the closeness of different industries to the science-base varies considerably, and within industries it can change markedly over time. Public research laboratories often play important roles either in transfer sciences or in underpinning the infratechnology of standards and metrology which is vital to the innovation system (Tassey, 1991). Private consultancies, professional societies and industrial research associations also play significant roles as bridging institutions between the worlds of industry and academic research.

That the division of labour in national systems is reflected in separate institutions for science and technology is of considerable significance for the connectivity on which their creativity depends. They reflect different cultures, responding to different research mechanisms and having different objectives. The boundary between them is almost certain to be fractured. As Dasgupta and David (1987, 1991) have emphasised, the science system is not profit-motivated and responds to a complex of motives, some arising from within disciplines and the search for priority in discovery, and others arising from the reward mechanisms for teaching and administration in universities. By contrast, the world of technology is profit-orientated, it works with relatively short-term horizons, and although priority in invention is important, priority is incompatible with unrestricted public disclosure. Moreover, peer review and market selection are quite different mechanisms for distributing rewards.

While it is therefore possible and sensible for some purposes to identify differences between science policy and technology policy, there remains from the national innovation system perspective a crucial interface around which policy must be integrated. This interface is concerned with more effectively drawing scientific and engineering knowledge into the design and development activities of firms. Management of this interface creates a number of difficult problems. Since science and technology compete for many of the same skills, how should policy influence the distribution of creative talent between the two worlds? What should be the appropriate balance between research and skill formation in higher education institutions? If science is to be directed more to supporting innovation, a number of questions need to be addressed. Is there to be more emphasis on the transfer sciences, or a greater use of extrinsic non-scientific criteria in the allocation of scientific funds (Weinberg, 1967)? Would closer links with technology together with research sponsorship from industry undermine the openness of science and thus its capacity to verify results and stimulate competitive development (Gibbons, 1987)? Is it best to design a policy to foster 'exploitable areas of science' through existing university institutions or through new bridging research institutions closely linked with industry? While these questions do not at all exhaust the domain of science policy proper they cover a highly significant proportion of the policy issues on which national innovation systems must depend.

To summarise, national innovation systems are to various degrees plu-
ralistic in nature. Strongly based on the division of labour their component
institutions make complementary contributions to the innovation process,
but they differ significantly with respect to motivation and with respect to
a commitment to dissemination of the knowledge they generate. Science is
not fully open, nor is technology fully closed; rather they lie towards different ends of the spectrum. They also differ in size and in the mechanisms
by which they accumulate knowledge. These differences are of considerable
significance in understanding how well the various components of a
national system interconnect. No institution can hope to be self-contained
in its technological activities. Firms, even large firms, have to rely on knowledge from other sources and access to external knowledge can be of the first
importance in raising the efficiency with which technologies are advanced
(Gibbons and Johnston, 1974). This is especially so in the early stages of
the development of a technology or whenever that technology has a rapidly
changing knowledge-base.

In practice, connectivity is achieved via a variety of mechanisms.
Mobility of scientists and technologists in the labour market and collaboration agreements to develop technology are important formal mechanisms
linking firms. Links between firms and universities are often instituted
through grants and contracts for research, especially in the transfer sciences. In recent years increased emphasis has been devoted to the various
informal networks which provide the connections within national systems.
In this regard, Lundvall (1988) and Anderson (1992) have emphasised links
between user firms and their suppliers, while von Hippel (1988) and
Schrader (1991) have drawn attention to the significance of informal but
'balanced' 'trading' of knowledge which takes place between engineers in
different firms in the same industry. Such informal networks are important
routes for technology transfer and for the transfer of more tacit knowledge.
They reflect the important fact that scientists and technologists are
members of common communities of practitioners with a common background in the methods of to problem-solving: to use de Solla Price's (1984)
phrase, they share common 'instrumentalities'. De Bresson and Amesse
(1991) have made the useful suggestion that we see networks as economic
clubs acting to internalise the problems of effective knowledge transmission. To this degree, networks are a substitute both for formal markets and
for organisational integration. They fall within the perimeter of non-
market devices by which firms seek to co-ordinate their activities with other
firms and with other knowledge-generating institutions (Richardson, 1972;
Langlois, 1992). However, much remains to be discovered about the operation of different kinds of networks – scientific, technological and industrial – and in particular the ways in which different networks may interact.

The costs and time taken to establish networks are also little understood at present, as is the role of networks in limiting the decision horizons of firms, locking them into conventional technological attitudes which become self-reinforcing (Torre, 1992). Moreover, as McDonald (1992) has emphasised, formal collaboration and informal network mechanisms may be in conflict as innovative support mechanisms.

It is clear that much is yet to be learnt about the structure and development of national innovation systems (Nelson, 1992a; Lundvall, 1992). None the less, some rich findings have already been obtained. In his study of the Japanese innovation system, Freeman (1987) has outlined the important role of MITI in promoting technological co-ordination between firms, and the network patterns of technology-sharing within areas in the *Keiritsu* system. Malerba (1993) has identified, in the context of the Italian national system, a sharp dichotomy between two independent sub-systems: one based on flexible networks of small and medium-sized firms, often co-located in distinct industrial districts; the other based on the universities, public research laboratories, and large firms performing R&D. He ventures to suggest that the former has been more effective than the latter in the post-1950 technological development of the Italian economy. Since national systems provide the context for technology policy, such a detailed understanding of these factors is clearly necessary. In particular, it is important to identify whether the appropriate boundaries are truly national (Carlsson and Stankiewitz, 1991). Science has always been international in its scope and it is increasingly the case that major R&D programmes are performed in multinational firms with laboratories in several countries. In his study of the British innovation system, Walker (1991) has drawn attention to the fact that the proportion of national R&D carried out by foreign multinationals increased threefold to 13 per cent of the total in the twenty or so years to 1988. Patent statistics also support the view of an increasing proportion of the UK's innovation activity being under the control of foreign firms (Patel and Pavitt, 1991). National firms in some industries are also observed to be developing detailed networks of international alliances to share knowledge and develop technology (Hagedoorn and Schakenraad, 1990). To the extent that national systems are so interconnected, technology policies in one country will spill over to affect other countries, and one could easily foresee the emergence of a beggar-thy-neighbour effect in which policy-makers in different countries compete to attract R&D-intensive companies. As Carlsson and Stankiewitz rightly point out, since science is intrinsically international in outlook, the growing 'scientification' of technology naturally opens up the nature of a technology system. On the other hand, the national unit may also be too broad to understand the complete dynamics of technological accumulation. Instead, one may have a

number of distinct technology-based systems each of which is geographically and institutionally localised within the nation but with links into the
supporting national and international systems. This is indeed the conclusion of an important Swedish study (Carlsson, 1992) which finds that the
institutional framework varies considerably according to the technological
area in question. Links with science, interaction between competent users
and suppliers, and the role of public research institutions each varies significantly in its contribution to the innovation process. All this lends strong
support to the view that integrated areas of technological activity form the
natural frame for policy intervention. Though how these areas are to be
defined and identified is not a trivial matter.

Although much remains to be clarified in this area, the concept of innovation systems is of crucial importance to the policy debate even though
they vary considerably across countries (Nelson, 1992b). They encourage
policy-makers to think in terms of institutions and their connectivity and
thus to address the mechanisms by which policy is translated into shifts in
the innovation possibility frontiers of firms. National boundaries clearly
define the domain for policy-making in the first instance, although increasingly policy-making can be interpreted in a multicountry context, as with
the European Framework programme (Eilon, 1992). The issue for policy-
making is to be aware of how different technologies are promoted by different accumulation systems, and the extent to which these systems are
connected internationally.

From the above account one conclusion is beyond contention: namely,
that while firms are the primary actors in the generation of technological
artifacts, their activities are supported by the accumulation of knowledge
and skills in a complex milieu of other research and training institutions.
Technology policy cannot be simply about the technological activities of
firms; it must necessarily encompass the wider context.

Conclusion

Downie (1956) has neatly summarised the conditions for a progressive evolutionary process as follows: efficient firms must be able to grow relative to
less efficient rivals; firms must have sufficient resources to experiment with
new technologies; and they must have sufficient incentives, that is, a sufficient degree of appropriability of innovation, to justify the risks of investment. From the evolutionary perspective two major policy questions
follow. Is the national innovation system an adequate experimental system
in that it generates an appropriate pattern of technological change consistent with policy objectives? If so, it is likely to be a pluralist system supporting many different sources of innovation with an emphasis on the
diversity of micro-level activity rather than a centrally driven conception of

the innovation process. In such a context the coupling together of institutions in the national system is of prominent importance. Enhancing the operation of the national system is the major route to increasing the creativity of firms. The second major issue is the openness of the competitive process: that every established market position can be challenged by some other innovating firm. Barriers to innovative entry and the efficiency of market selection processes are major concerns of the policy-maker here, and it is clear that they are inseparable from aspects of competitive policy more generally. In conclusion, one of the major contributions of the evolutionary school has been its insistence that the pattern of technological innovation depends on much more than the behaviour of individual firms. It is this that has lead us directly to the idea of technology systems and national systems of innovation, and it is around the operation of these systems that policy should be formed.

References

Abernathy, W.J. 1978. *The Productivity Dilemma*, Baltimore, Johns Hopkins University Press.

Abernathy, W.J. and Clark, K. 1985. Innovation: mapping the winds of creative destruction, *Research Policy*, 14: 3–22.

Allen, P. 1988. Evolution, innovation and economics, in Dosi *et al.* (eds.).

Andersen, E.S. 1992. Approaching national systems of innovation, in Lundvall (ed.).

Antonelli, C. 1994. *The Economics of Localized Technological Change and Industrial Dynamics*, Boston, Kluwer Academic.

Arditti, F.D. and Levy, H. 1980. A model of the parallel team strategy in product development, *American Economic Review*, 70: 1089–97.

Arrow, K. 1962. The economic implications of learning by doing, *Review of Economic Studies*, 29: 155–73.

1969. Classificatory notes on the production and distribution of technological knowledge, *American Economic Review*, 59: 29–35.

1974. *The Limits of Organization*, New York, Norton.

Beer, S. 1985. *Diagnosing the System for Organisations*, New York, Wiley.

Buchanan, J. and Vanberg, V. 1991. The market as a creative process, *Economics and Philosophy*, 7: 167–86.

Burns, A. 1935. *Production Trends in the United States Since 1870*, New York, National Bureau of Economic Research.

Campbell, D. 1987. Blind variation and selective retention, in creative thought as in other knowledge processes, in G. Radnitzky and W. Bartley (eds.), *Evolutionary Epistemology, Theory of Rationality and Sociology of Knowledge*, New York, Open Court.

Carlsson, B. 1992. Technological systems and economic development potential: four Swedish case studies, paper presented at the conference of the International Joseph A. Schumpeter Society, Kyoto, August.

292   **Stan Metcalfe**

Carlsson, B. and Stankiewitz, R. 1991. On the nature, function and composition of technological systems, *Journal of Evolutionary Economics*, 1: 93–118.

Cooper, A. and Schendel, D. 1976. Strategic responses to technological threats, *Business Horizons*, 19: 61–9.

Dasgupta, P. and David, P. 1987. Information disclosure and the economics of science and technology, in G. Feiwal (ed.), *Arrow and the Ascent of Modern Economic Theory*, New York, New York University Press.

1991. Resource allocation and the institutions of science, mimeo, CEPR, Stanford University.

Dasgupta, P. and Stiglitz, J. 1980a. Industrial structure and the nature of innovative activity, *Economic Journal*, 90: 266–93.

1980b. Uncertainty, industrial structure and the speed of R&D, *Bell Journal of Economics*, 11: 1–28.

de Bresson, C. and Amesse, F. 1991. Networks of innovators: a review and introduction to the issue, *Research Policy*, 20: 363–79.

de Solla Price, D. 1984. The science/technology relationship, the craft of experimental science and policy for the improvement of high technology innovation, *Research Policy*, 13: 3–20.

Dixit, A.K. 1988. A general model of R and D competition and policy, *Rand Journal of Economics*, 19: 317–26.

Dosi, G. 1982. Technological paradigms and technological trajectories: a suggested interpretation of the determinants and directives of technological change, *Research Policy*, 11: 147–62.

1988. Sources, procedures and microeconomic effects of innovation, *Journal of Economic Literature*, 36: 1126–71.

Dosi, G., Freeman, C., Nelson, R., Silverberg, G. and Soete, L. (eds.) 1988. *Technical Change and Economic Theory*, London, Pinter.

Dosi, G., Marsili, O., Orsenigo, L. and Salvatori, S. 1993. Learning, market selection and the evolution of industrial structures, mimeo, Centre for Management Research, University of California, Berkeley.

Dosi, G. and Orsenigo, L. 1988. Co-ordination and transformation: An overview of structures, behaviours and change in evolutionary environments, in Dosi *et al.* (eds.).

Downie, J. 1956. The control of monopoly II, *Economic Journal*, 56: 573–7.

1958. *The Competitive Process*, London, Duckworth.

Eads, G. and Nelson, R. 1971. Government support of advanced creative technology, *Public Policy*, 19: 405–27.

Eilon, S. 1992. R&D policy in the European Community, *International Journal of Technology Management*, 17: 113–28.

Evenson, R.E. and Kislev, Y. 1975. *Agricultural Research and Productivity*, New Haven, Yale University Press.

Freeman, C. 1982. *The Economics of Industrial Innovation*, London, Pinter.

1987. *Technology Policy and Economic Performance*, London, Pinter.

1988. Japan: a new national system of innovation, in Dosi *et al.* (eds.).

1994. The economics of technical change, *Cambridge Journal of Economics*, 18: 463–514.

Georghiou, L., Metcalfe, S., Gibbons, M. and Evans, J. 1986. *Post Innovation Performance*, London, Macmillan.

Gibbons, M. 1987. Contemporary transformation of science in M. Gibbons and B. Wittrock (eds.), *Science as a Commodity*, London, Longmans.

Gibbons, M. and Johnston, R. 1974. The role of science in technological innovation, *Research Policy*, 3: 220–42.

Gort, M. and Wall, R.A. 1986. The Evolution of technologies and investment in innovation, *Economic Journal*, 96: 741–57.

Gould, S.J. 1990. *Wonderful Life*, London, Hutchinson.

Hagedoorn, J. and Schakenraad, J. 1990. Inter-firm partnerships and co-operative strategies in core technologies, in C. Freeman and L. Soete (eds.), *New Explorations in the Economics of Technological Change*, London, Pinter.

Hall, P. (ed.) 1986. *Technology, Innovation and Public Policy*, Oxford, P. Allen.

Hayek, F. 1948. The meaning of competition, in F. Hayek (ed.), *Individualism and Economic Order*, Chicago, Chicago University Press.

Henderson, D. 1977. Two British errors and their probable consequences, *Oxford Economic Papers*, 29: 159–205.

Henderson, R. and Clark, K. 1990. Architectural innovation, *Administrative Science Quarterly*, 35: 9–30.

Hodgson, G. 1991. Evolution and intention in economic theory, in Saviotti, and Metcalfe (eds.).

1993. *Economics and Evolution*, London, Polity Press.

Hodgson, G. and Screpanti, E. (eds.) 1991. *Rethinking Economics – Markets, Technology and Economic Evolution*, Aldershot, Edward Elgar.

Hughes, T. 1983. *Networks of Power*, Baltimore, Johns Hopkins University Press.

Justmann, M. and Teubal, M. 1986. Innovation policy in an open economy: a normative framework for strategic and tactical issues, *Research Policy*, 15: 121–38.

Klepper, S. 1992. Entry, exit and innovation over the product life cycle: the dynamics of first mover advantages, declining product innovation and market failure, paper presented at the conference of the International Joseph A. Schumpeter Society, Kyoto, August.

Klepper, S. and Graddy, E. 1990. The evolution of new industries and the determinants of market structure, *Rand Journal of Economics*, 21: 27–44.

Krueger, A.O. 1991. Economists' changing perceptions of government, *Weltwirtschaftliches Archiv*, 127: 417–31.

Kuznets, S. 1954. *Economic Change*, London, Heinemann.

Langlois, R.N. 1991. Transaction cost economics in real time, *Industrial and Corporate Change*, 1: 99–127.

Langrish, J., Gibbons, M., Jevons, F. and Evans, B. 1972. *Wealth from Knowledge*, London, Macmillan.

Layton, E. 1974. Technology as knowledge, *Technology and Culture*, 15: 31–41.

Loury, G. 1979. Market structure and innovation, *Quarterly Journal of Economics*, 93: 395–410.

Lundvall, B.-Å 1988. Innovation as an interactive process: From user–producer interaction to the national system of innovation, in Dosi *et al.* (eds.).

(ed.) 1992. *National Systems of Innovation*, London, Pinter.

McDonald, S. 1992. Formal collaboration and informal information flow, *International Journal of Technology Management*, 7: 49–60.

Machlup, F. 1962. The supply of inventors and inventions, in R.R. Nelson (ed.) *The Rate and Direction of Inventive Activity: Economic and Social Factors*, New York, NBER.

McKelvey, M. 1991. How do national systems of innovation differ? in Hodgson and Screpanti (eds.).

Majumdar, B. 1982. *Innovations, Product Developments and Technology Transfers*, Washington, D.C., University Press of America.

Malerba, F. 1992. Learning by firms and incremental technical change, *Economic Journal*, 102: 845–59.

     1993. The national system of innovation: Italy, in R. Nelson (ed.), *National Innovation Systems*, New York, Oxford Universtiy Press.

Metcalfe, J.S. and Gibbons, M. 1989. Technology variety, and organisation: a systematic perspective on the competitive process, *Research on Technological Innovation, Management and Policy*, 4: 153–93.

Mokyr, J. 1990. *The Leaver of Riches*, Oxford, Oxford University Press.

     1991. Evolutionary biology, technical change and economic history, *Bulletin of Economic Research*, 43: 127–49.

Mowery, D. and Rosenberg, N. 1979. The influence of market demand upon innovation: a critical review of some recent empirical studies, *Research Policy*, 8: 103–53.

     1989. New developments in US technology policy: implications for competitiveness and international trade policy, *California Management Review*, 32:107–24.

Nelson, R.R. 1961. Uncertainty, learning and the economics of parallel research and development efforts, *Review of Economics and Statistics*, 43: 351–64.

     1982. The role of knowledge in R&D efficiency, *Quarterly Journal of Economics*, 97: 453–70.

     1987. *Understanding Technical Change as an Evolutionary Process*, Amsterdam, North Holland.

     1992a. National innovation systems: a retrospective on a study, *Industrial and Corporate Change*, 1: 347–74.

     1992b. The role of firms in technical advance: a perspective from evolutionary theory, in G. Dosi, R. Giannetti and P. Tonineli (eds.), *Technology and Enterprise in a Historical Perspective*, Oxford, Oxford University Press.

Nelson, R. and Winter, S. 1982. *An Evolutionary Theory of Economic Change*, Amsterdam, Holland Press.

Newbery, D.M. 1990. Missing markets: consequences and remedies, in F. Hahn (ed.), *The Economics of Missing Markets, Information and Games*, Oxford, Oxford University Press.

Nordhaus, W. 1969. *Invention, Growth and Welfare*, Cambridge, Mass., MIT Press.

OECD 1992. *Technology and the Economy: The Key Relationships*, Paris, OECD.

Patel, P. and Pavitt, K. 1991. The innovative performance of the world's largest firms, *Economics of Innovation and New Technology*, 1: 91–102.

Pavitt, K. 1987. The objectives of technology policy, *Science and Public Policy*, 14: 182–8.

1990. What do we know about the strategic management of technology?, *Californian Management Review*, 32: 17–26.

Pavitt, K. and Rothwell, R. 1976. A comment on 'A dynamic model of process and product innovation', *Omega*, 4: 375–7.

Reinganum, J. 1989. The timing of innovation: research, development and diffusion, in R. Schmalensee and R. Willing (eds.), *Handbook of Industrial Organization*, vol. I, Amsterdam, Elsevier.

Richardson, G.B. 1960. *Information and Investment*, Oxford, Oxford University Press.

1972. The organization of industry, *Economic Journal*, 82: 883–98.

Rosenberg, N. 1976. *Perspectives on Technology*, Cambridge, Cambridge University Press.

1982. *Inside the Black Box*, Cambridge, Cambridge University Press.

Rosenberg, N. and Vincenti, W. (1985), *The Britannia Bridge: The Generation and Diffusion of Technological Knowledge*, Cambridge, Mass., MIT Press.

Rothwell, R. 1986. Reindustrialization, innovation and public policy, in Hall, (ed.).

Sahal, D. 1981. *Patterns of Technological Innovation*, London, Sage.

1985. Technological guideposts and innovation avenues, *Research Policy*, 14: 61–82.

Saviotti, P. and Metcalfe, S. (eds.) 1991. *Evolutionary Theories of Economic and Technological Change*, London, Harwood.

Schrader, S. 1991. Informal transfer between firms: cooperation through information trading, *Research Policy*, 20: 153–70.

Schumpeter, J. 1934. *The Theory of Economic Development*, Oxford, Oxford University Press.

Silverberg, G., Dosi, G. and Orsenigo, L. 1988. Innovation, diversity and diffusion: a self organisation model, *Economic Journal*, 98: 1032–54.

Smith, K. 1991. Innovation policy in an evolutionary context in Saviotti and Metcalfe (eds.).

Starbuck, William H. 1983. Organisations as action generators, *American Sociological Review*, 48: 91–102.

Stiglitz, J.E. 1991. The invisible hand and modern welfare economics, in D. Vines, and A. Stevenson (eds.), *Information, Strategy and Public Policy*, Oxford, Blackwell.

Stoneman, P. 1987. *The Economic Analysis of Technology Policy*, Oxford, Oxford University Press.

Tassey, G. 1991. The functions of technology infrastructure in a competitive economy, *Research Policy*, 20: 345–61.

1992. *Technology Infrastructure and Competitive Position*, Dordrecht, Kluwer.

Teece, D.J. 1986. Profiting from technological innovation: implications for integration, collaboration licensing and public policy, *Research Policy*, 15: 285–305.

Tisdell, C. 1981. *Science and Technology Policy: Priorities of Governments*, London, Chapman and Hall.

Torre, A. 1992. Untraded and technological interdependencies: some new developments and conclusions, communication to the conference of the International Joseph A. Schumpeter Society, Kyoto, August.

Utterback, J. 1979. The dynamics of product and process innovation in industry, in C. Hill, and J. Utterback, (eds.), *Technological Innovation for a Dynamic Economy*, Oxford, Pergamon.

Utterback, J. and Suarez, F. 1993. Innovation, competition and industry structure, *Research Policy*, 22: 1–21.

Vincenti, W.G. 1990. *What Engineers Know and How They Know It*, Baltimore, Johns Hopkins University Press.

von Hippel, E. 1988. *The Sources of Innovation*, Oxford, Oxford University Press.

Walker, W. 1991. Britain's dwindling technological aspirations, Review Paper no. 1, Science Policy Research Unit, University of Sussex.

Weinberg, A.M. 1967. *Reflections on Big Science*, London, Pergamon.

Winter, S. 1986. Schumpeterian competition in alternative technological regime, in R. Day and G. Elliasson (eds.), *The Dynamics of Market Economics*, Amsterdam, North Holland.

Witt, U. 1991. Reflections on the present state of evolutionary economic theory, in Hodgson and Screpanti (eds.).

Wolf, C. 1986. Market and non-market failures: comparison and assessment, *Journal of Public Policy*, 7: 43–70.

Zuscovitch, E. 1986. The economic dynamics of technological development, *Research Policy*, 15: 175–86.

Index

Abernathy, W., 102, 242, 279, 282, 283
Abramovitz, M., 11, 43, 52, 53, 83
absorptive capacity, 141, 142, 150, 154
academic research, 31, 100, 106
Amsden, A., 103, 114, 116, 124, 160
Antonelli, C., 44, 184, 284, 288
Archibugi, D., 1, 9–11, 36, 172, 179, 235
Arora, A., 102, 159, 189
Arrow, K., 277, 280
assembly-type production, 227, 229

Baba, Y., 34, 117
barriers to entry, 12, 241, 242, 255, 291
Baumol, W., 83, 181
Bell, M., 10, 83, 87, 89, 92, 96, 97, 99, 102, 113, 120
Bercovich, N., 112, 113, 158
Bloom, M., 115, 158
bounded rationality, 37
Brazil, 35, 36, 87, 112, 113, 115, 118, 119, 124, 153, 159
Brimble, P., 139, 149, 158

Cambridge Journal of Economics, xvii
Cantwell, J., 14, 83, 153, 157, 187, 188, 189, 200, 201, 215–18, 222, 227, 229, 230–5, 237
capital accumulation, 42
capital flight, 45
capital flows, 13, 38, 187
capital markets, 45, 78
Carlsson, B., 31, 110, 284, 289, 290
catching-up, 7, 8, 11, 32, 43, 61, 83, 85, 116, 120
Casson, M., 172, 184, 188
Cati-Merit, 181, 189
centrally planned economies, 94, 113, 126, 270
chemical industry, 28, 224, 225, 232, 234, 236, 246, 255, 256, 264
  German, 28, 234

citizenship, 13
civilisation, 6
Chesnais, F., 5, 13, 44, 93, 176, 184, 187, 200
Clark, K., 53, 95, 282
Cohen, W., 96, 116, 141, 242
collaboration, 14, 71, 72, 76, 146, 200, 244, 288
commercialisation, 76
communications, 4, 17
competition, 52, 53, 84, 95, 160, 161, 212, 271, 275
  international, 8, 103
comparative advantage (*see also* competitive advantage), 7, 37, 91, 107, 108, 113, 122, 242
competencies (downstream/upstream), 75, 77
competitive advantage (*see also* comparative advantage), 5, 11, 37, 77, 85, 107, 108
competitiveness, 14, 62, 72, 73, 74, 75, 76, 92, 94, 98, 108, 124, 151, 152, 153, 159, 291
  national, 17
complementarity, 101
consumer tastes, 210
convergence, 52, 61, 74, 83, 107, 157, 173
core technologies, 95, 110, 233
creative accumulation, 246
creative destruction, 246
cross-border linkages, 14, 50, 146
culture, xv, 4, 6, 37, 39, 40, 41, 178
cumulativeness, 94, 108
customs unions, 8

Dahlman, C., 87, 89, 112, 119, 139, 149, 153, 154, 155, 156, 159, 229
Dasgupta, P., 270, 276, 279, 287
David, P., 1, 11, 99, 108, 138, 287
decentralisation, 15
demand-led, innovation as, 216, 235
differentiation, 40, 107, 123, 126